The Complete Guide to Securities Transactions

Enhancing Investment Performance and Controlling Costs

Edited by **Wayne H. Wagner**

WILEY
JOHN WILEY & SONS
New York · Chichester · Brisbane · Toronto · Singapore

Library of Congress Cataloging in Publication Data:

The Complete guide to securities transactions : enhancing investment per-
    formance and controlling costs / edited by Wayne H. Wagner.
        p.   cm.
    Includes bibliographies and index.
    ISBN 0-471-61013-5
    1. Securities.   I. Wagner, Wayne H.
HG4515.C65   1989
332.63'2—dc19   88-27616
                                                              CIP

ISBN: 0-471-61013-5

Printed in the United States of America

10 9 8 7 6 5 4 3 2 1

CONTENTS

Preface   *vii*

Contributors   *xi*

PART ONE   THE SECURITIES MARKETS OF TODAY   *1*

**1 How We Got Here: The Origins of Today's
Volatile Trading Environment**   **3**
Dexter D. Earle

*PART TWO   SECURITIES TRANSACTIONS AND INVESTMENT
PERFORMANCE*   *13*

2 A Sponsor Looks at Trading Costs   **15**
Robert E. Shultz

3 Liquidity and Trading Costs: A Modest Proposal   **27**
Charles D. Ellis

4 How Important Are Transaction Costs?   **31**
Stephen A. Berkowitz and *Dennis E. Logue*

PART THREE   HOW A TRADE WORKS   *43*

  5   Portfolio Manager to Trader   **45**
     Mark Edwards

  6   Trader to Broker   **63**
     Stanley S. Abel and *Eugene A. Noser, Jr.*

  7   Broker to Floor   **79**
     Wayne H. Wagner

  8   Transaction Settlement: The Final Step   **91**
     Vincent Walsh

PART FOUR   THE COSTS OF TRANSACTING   *109*

  9   A Taxonomy of Trading Techniques   **111**
     Wayne H. Wagner

  **10   Trading Costs: The Critical Link between
     Investment Information and Results**   **125**
     Thomas F. Loeb

  11   Evaluating Transaction Costs   **137**
     Gilbert Beebower

PART FIVE   CURRENT TRENDS IN TRADING   *151*

  **12   Upstairs, Downstairs: The Block Traders
     and the Specialists**   **153**
     Donald L. Luskin

  13   Electronic Trading on the Exchanges   **161**
     George M. Spehar

  14   Package Trading   **171**
     Patricia C. Dunn

15 **Passive Trading**   185
     Stephen P. Manus

16 **Electronic Crossing Markets**   197
     Edward C. Story

17 **Trading Illiquid Stocks**   211
     Jeanne Cairns Sinquefield and *Cem Severoglu*

18 **Sunshine Trading**   223
     Steven Bodurtha

19 **Electronic Trading: The Batterymarch Experience**   237
     Evan Shulman

20 **International Trading**   251
     Thomas Burnett

PART SIX   *FUTURE DIRECTIONS IN TRADING*   265

21 **Electronic Equity Trading: A Necessity
     for Efficient Markets**   267
     William A. Lupien

22 **The Single-Price Auction**   279
     Steven Wunsch

23 **Trading Tactics in an Inefficient Market**   291
     Bruce I. Jacobs and *Kenneth N. Levy*

24 **Intelligent Trading Systems**   309
     David Leinweber

25 **Bond Transactions and Bond Transaction Costs**   327
     Greta Marshall and *Wayne H. Wagner*

PART SEVEN MARKET STRUCTURES AND MARKET
EFFICIENCY   335

26   Ethical Issues in Trading   337
     John J. Morton

27   The Economics of the Dealer Function   345
     Jack L. Treynor

28   Buttonwood II: Considering Alternative
     Market Structures   359
     Wayne H. Wagner

     Index   373

PREFACE

The crash of October 1987 was a stunning demonstration that events of subtle meaning can profoundly affect securities markets with little forewarning. Even with the perspective of the months that followed, very few individuals have demonstrated a clear understanding of how those markets work and how they might be improved.

There are many books that suggest trading strategies oriented toward increasing one's wealth. This one has a different goal: to deepen the understanding of how markets work and how traders can best use them.

This book is aimed toward the professional securities trader who wants to deepen his understanding and sharpen his professional skills.[1] It is also written for anyone who interacts with that trader, anyone whose decisions and outcomes are affected by that trader, and anyone who is curious about the fascinating topic of today's markets and securities trading.

Trading is a learn-by-doing occupation. No one goes to trader school and comes out a certified trader. Traders learn on the job: As they learn more difficult and complicated tasks, they progress from apprentice to journeyman to master. Knowledge, skill, adaptivity, relationships, and trust are built up slowly over a period of years.

The trading process is guided by a code of ethics that permits multimillion-dollar transactions to be completed on the basis of a brief phone call. The catch phrase is "My word is my honor." Nothing works without this fundamental sense of honesty and fair dealing.

The basic job of the institutional trader revolves around a set of daily orders generated by a portfolio management process. In many institutions, the trader is only peripherally involved in those portfolio decisions. The job

---

[1] Note that for simplicity, but with no bias intended, *he* has been used throughout rather than *he/she* or *he or she*.

of the trader is to execute the desired trades expeditiously, without error, and at favorable prices. It sounds like a critical link in the investment process, and it assuredly is.

The institutions' trader spends most of his time in telephone contact with the securities broker. He is often referred to as the *street-side* trader or the *sell-side* trader, in contrast to the *buy-side* institutional trader. There is a strong tendency for sell-side traders to be more aggressive and much more highly compensated than buy-side traders.

While the sell-side trader gets starring roles in movies, the buy-side trader is almost invisible. Buy-side traders are seldom known outside their own organizations. Even there, many traders are considered the least critical link in the securities analyst to portfolio manager to trader decision sequence. In some organizations, the trader is little more than a clerk, relaying instructions without questioning and without discretion: ''Call the broker who provides us the research and give him a market order.'' The sell-side broker is left in charge of determining when, where, and how the orders are to be executed.

This limited view of the trader's contribution originates from one of the three common ways of thinking about trading and transaction costs, which is summed up as follows.

1. Trading is low cost and unimportant relative to the advantage to the portfolio from securities research.

This view was prevalent through the 1950s and 1960s and into the 1970s. These were the early days of institutional investment management, when managers were highly dependent on Wall Street firms for investment intelligence and ideas. The traditional way of rewarding the broker was to channel the resultant trading activity through him. It is no exaggeration to state that professional investment management grew out of seeds planted by the Wall Street firms.

Furthermore, the New York Stock Exchange in those days was truly the only game in town. Venerable traditions and well-tested procedures assured that all orders received equivalent execution. When most portfolios were run with a similar ''search for undiscovered value'' philosophy and trades were small relative to Exchange capacity, little more was required from a trader.

In the early to mid-1970s several important trends converged to change trading forever. As pension assets grew, trading costs became glaringly noticeable under the prevailing fixed commission schedule. Investment managers and pension sponsors pressured the brokers and the exchanges to bring commission charges more in line with the cost of providing the service.

In addition, aficionados of the efficient market hypothesis developed the first practical applications in the form of index funds. This theory postulates that all available information is already embedded in securities prices. Taking up that banner, index funds shunned security analysis and emphasized the merits of diversification by constructing portfolios holding hundreds of securities.

When index fund managers turned their attention to the trading process, they came into strong disagreement with traditional assumptions about trading, and developed a different view of the trading function. This second view also represented a limited view of the value of the trader.

2.   Since all stocks are fairly priced, trading is not worthwhile and trading costs are to be minimized as much as possible.

The professors who came up with the efficient marketplace, and their cohorts, followed the interests of the practitioners into trading costs and trading processes, and a new science was born. Now trading and markets could be analyzed: Costs could be measured, different market structures could be seen to lead to different trading attributes, and styles of trading could be attuned to the specific needs of the investment decision. In the 1980s, however, faith in the efficient market model became strained as further investigations discovered more and more regularly occurring discrepancies from the expectations suggested by the theory.

In addition, institutional investors—pension sponsors in particular—began to voice concerns that trading costs were too high and extracted too great a penalty for investment performance. Thus evolved the third, emerging view of transacting. At last, the trader was viewed as a critical component of the investment management process.

3.   Trading is expensive, and trading strategies need to be a carefully designed component of investment decision making.

Never before have traders had more paths open to them to accomplish the same investment result. As a result, the job of the securities trader has become much more complicated. Today's trader has at his command multiple alternative methods of accomplishing the same investment goals. A trader can go to the exchange, to the block houses, or to the "meet" markets such as the crossing networks. He can gain equity exposure through equities, through American Depository Receipts (ADRs), through convertible bonds, through warrants, through options or futures. He can insist on immediate liquidity and pay what is demanded or he can lay back and hope to draw interest from a more anxious trader at a favorable price. Finding which tactic is likely to work best for a given situation is the new challenge to the trader.

But despite the attention now paid to the trading process, there are still many elements that are not clearly understood. Many of these areas of uncertainty concern the core concepts of trading. For example:

- We cannot reconcile widely divergent estimates of the magnitude of trading costs.
- We believe that the current market mechanisms are efficient and effective, but we cannot agree on whether recommended changes to the process will be helpful or harmful.
- We place great value on market liquidity, but we cannot measure how much it costs to provide the liquidity, nor can we estimate what value is added by liquidity.

Clearly, more work needs to be done.

The events of October 1987 focused new attention on how the markets work. Yet little consensus has been reached on what changes—if any—are needed. We seem highly vulnerable to market events beyond our understanding and expectations. We have a pressing need for a better understanding of how markets operate and how best to perform the trading task.

The chapters in this book serve two purposes: The first goal is to widen the reader's understanding of what makes markets tick and how traders use them. The second goal is to offer some specific useful information that will increase the effectiveness of trading in today's security markets.

At the end of each chapter, the author is asked to respond to a question under the heading "The Editor Asks. . ." Think of this as a question asked of a speaker, submitted from the floor and edited by a moderator. The intent of these questions in twofold: (1) to extend the author's presentation concerning a critical point raised in the chapter, and (2) to attempt to contrast the varying attitudes, experiences, and opinions of the authors with respect to some of the common themes of this book.

The chapter authors who have graciously contributed their time and intellects were selected for the depth of their understanding and the challenge of their ideas. I am greatly in their debt.

Wayne H. Wagner

Santa Monica, California
February 1989

CONTRIBUTORS

WAYNE H. WAGNER, *Editor*   Mr. Wagner is partner and chief investment officer of Plexus Group, a Santa Monica–based investment advisor and provider of services to pension funds, investment managers, and traders. Mr. Wagner provides conceptual direction and strategic product development to the Plexus Group, and also serves as portfolio manager. He previously served as chief investment officer of Wilshire Associates' Asset Management Division, where he managed over $2.5 billion. He also created and operated the Trust Universe Comparison Service (TUCS), the Index Fund Management Service, and the Special Consulting Division at Wilshire. Mr. Wagner was a founder of Wilshire Associates.

Before joining Wilshire Associates, he designed quantitative investment systems at Wells Fargo Bank, where he participated in the design and operation of the first index funds. He has written and spoken frequently on many investment subjects, especially trading methods and trading costs. He has received two Graham and Dodd Awards from the *Financial Analysts Journal* for excellence in financial writing.

Mr. Wagner has a master's degree in statistics from Stanford University and a bachelor's degree in business administration from the University of Wisconsin.

STANLEY S. ABEL   Mr. Abel has served as chairman of the board of Abel/Noser since 1975. He began his Wall Street career in 1956, and had worked for such firms as Lehman Brothers, Hornblower & Weeks, and H. Hentz & Company. Mr. Abel is a director of Diversified Industries and the First City Federal Savings Bank. A graduate of Cornell University, he also served as an officer in the U.S. Army. He is a member of the New York Stock Exchange.

GILBERT BEEBOWER   Mr. Beebower is executive vice president in the research division of SEI Corporation. He has pioneered in the development of the measurement of equity trading costs. He has worked in the field of portfolio theory, performance measurement, and related topics since 1968. His work has been published in the *Financial Analysts Journal,* the *Journal of Portfolio Management,* and the *Chartered Financial Analysts Federation Handbook.* He is a frequent speaker at various seminars in finance.

Mr. Beebower served on the professional staff of the Presidential Task Force on Market Mechanisms (the Brady Commission) in November 1987. He is a graduate of California Technical Institute in Pasadena.

STEPHEN A. BERKOWITZ   Mr. Berkowitz is a principal in the Baltimore office of Mercer Meidinger Hansen and serves as asset planning practice leader for the Baltimore and Washington offices. Prior to joining Mercer Meidinger Hansen, he was president of Berkowitz, Logue & Associates.

Mr. Berkowitz has published numerous articles and is co-author of *Report Card on Private Pension Plans.* He received an M.B.A. at the Wharton School, University of Pennsylvania. He also holds an M.A. from New York University and a B.A. degree from the University of North Carolina.

STEPHEN BODURTHA   Mr. Bodurtha is in charge of trading-cost research for Kidder, Peabody & Company's financial futures department. As a member of Kidder's customer desk for equity index products and portfolio trading, he works with clients to understand and reduce their transaction costs. Prior to joining Kidder, Peabody, he was an associate fellow at Harvard Business School, where he developed course material and taught classes on equity trading. Mr. Bodurtha received his M.B.A. from Harvard Business School.

THOMAS BURNETT   Mr. Burnett is director of International Equity Trading, Merrill Lynch, and has been with the firm since 1986. He is responsible for managing non-U.S. equity investing and trading in London, Hong Kong, Tokyo, Toronto, and New York.

Prior to joining International Equity Trading, Mr. Burnett was department manager, risk arbitrage, of L. F. Rothschild & Company. He was also a financial analyst with the Securities and Exchange Commission in Washington, D.C. Mr. Burnett has taught classes in risk arbitrage and foreign stock markets. He has published articles in *Barrons, The Accounting*

Review, and *Mergers and Acquisitions.* Mr. Burnett received his B.A. from Williams College and his M.B.A. from Stanford University.

PATRICIA C. DUNN Ms. Dunn is president of Wells Fargo Investment Advisors. She has been with the firm since 1978 and has served in a variety of marketing, consulting, and investment management roles. She has been closely involved with the development and enhancement of the firm's passive trading techniques, and works extensively with clients to implement their objectives through the firm's investment and trading expertise. She received her B.A. in journalism and economics from the University of California at Berkeley.

DEXTER D. EARLE Mr. Earle is a vice president at Goldman, Sachs and Company, in the Trading and Arbitrage Division, and has been primarily responsible for portfolio restructurings since November 1981. Prior to joining Goldman, he was senior vice president, pension investment and administration, at Bankers Trust Company from 1964 to 1980, and president and chief operating officer at Morgan Stanley Asset Management in 1981. He holds a B.A. from Rutgers University.

MARK EDWARDS Mr. Edwards is the internal equity manager for the Minnesota State Board of Investments. He joined the organizaiton in 1979 as a financial analyst and subsequently learned trading and derivatives management as an adjunct to portfolio management. Currently, he runs the internal equity effort, focusing on quantitative methodologies. Mr. Edwards has spoken frequently on investment topics, especially trading.

CHARLES D. ELLIS Mr. Ellis is managing partner of Greenwich Associates, the business strategy research and consulting firm. The author of three books and four dozen articles on business, finance, and investment management, he has been a trustee and president of the Institute of Chartered Financial Analysts and, for twenty years, an associate editor of the *Financial Analysts Journal.*

Mr. Ellis earned his B.A. degree at Yale; his M.B.A. (with distinction) at Harvard Business School, where he has twice taught the second-year course in investment management; and his Ph.D. at New York University.

BRUCE I. JACOBS Dr. Jacobs is a principal of Jacobs Levy Equity Management. Formerly, he was vice president of the Prudential Insurance Company of America and senior managing director of a quantitative equity management affiliate. Earlier, he was managing director of Prudential's

Pension and Asset Management Group, specializing in asset allocation. Dr. Jacobs is a contributor to investment journals and a frequent conference speaker. He was formerly on the faculty of the Wharton School. He received a B.A. and an M.S. from Columbia University, an M.S.I.A. from Carnegie-Mellon University, and a Ph.D. in finance from Wharton.

DAVID LEINWEBER Dr. Leinweber is chief scientist at Integrated Analytics, a firm specializing in the development of embedded artificial intelligence applications for the financial service industry. Prior to joining Integrated Analytics, he was a senior scientist and manager of financial marketing at Inference Corporation, an early high-end expert system tool vendor, where he directed the design of expert systems to support securities trading and other financial applications. Dr. Leinweber holds bachelor of science degrees in electrical engineering and physics from the Massachusetts Institute of Technology, and doctoral degrees in applied mathematics and physics from Harvard University.

KENNETH N. LEVY Mr. Levy is a principal of Jacobs Levy Equity Management. Formerly, he was managing director of an affiliate of the Prudential Asset Management Company. Earlier, he was responsible for quantitative research in Prudential Equity Management Associates. Mr. Levy has written articles and has spoken at conferences on a variety of investment topics. He holds a B.A. from Cornell University and an M.B.A. and M.A. from the Wharton School at the University of Pennsylvania. He has completed all requirements short of dissertation for his Ph.D. in finance at Wharton.

THOMAS F. LOEB Mr. Loeb is co-founder, president, and chief executive officer of Mellon Capital Management Corporation, a five-year-old firm with 120 institutional clients and $20 billion under management. He is responsible for the firm's business and investment management activities.

He managed Wells Fargo's Index Fund and Core Investment Management activities during their initial 1973–1983 decade, and introduced "program" trading at Wells Fargo in 1975. Mr. Loeb received the Graham and Dodd Plaque for his article on trading costs, entitled "Trading Cost: The Critical Link between Investment Information and Results." Mr. Loeb holds a B.A. degree in economics from Fairleigh Dickinson University and an M.B.A. degree from the Wharton School at the University of Pennsylvania.

DENNIS E. LOGUE Dr. Logue is Nathaniel Leverone Professor of

Management at the Amos Tuck School of Business Administration, Dartmouth College. He has written extensively on markets, investments, and other issues in finance and management. He has been editor or associate editor of several academic journals. He received his Ph.D. from Cornell University and also holds an M.B.A. degree from Rutgers and an A.B. degree from Fordham University.

WILLIAM A. LUPIEN   Mr. Lupien is chairman of the board of Mitchum, Jones & Templeton, Inc., a Los Angeles–based broker/dealer. Prior to re-forming Mitchum, Jones & Templeton in 1988, he was chairman of the board of Instinet Corporation. He has been in the securities business since he joined the original Mitchum, Jones & Templeton, Inc., in 1965. He served the firm as a specialist on the floor of the Pacific Stock Exchange and in 1974 was elected president of the firm. Subsequently, he was managing general partner of Trading Company of the West.

Mr. Lupien has been a member of the board of the Pacific Stock Exchange for six years and served on the committee that designed the Intermarket Transaction System. He also served as chairman of the floor trading and nominating committees, as a member of the Pacific Clearing Corporation Board, as a member of the SEC's advisory committee for the development of a national market system, and on numerous private and public company boards.

DONALD L. LUSKIN   Mr. Luskin is senior vice president and manager of portfolio management and trading at Wells Fargo Investment Advisors, the world's largest institutional equities manager. Prior to joining Wells Fargo, he was senior vice president and director of Jeffries and Company, where he managed the Investment Technologies Group. He has been a market maker on the New York Stock Exchange, the Chicago Board Options Exchange, the Pacific Coast Stock Exchange, and the NASDAQ automated quotations network.

Mr. Luskin is author of *Index Options and Futures: The Complete Guide* and *Portfolio Insurance: A Guide to Dynamic Hedging,* both published by John Wiley & Sons, and of numerous papers and articles on modern investment strategy.

STEPHEN P. MANUS   Mr. Manus is a vice president of the American National Bank and Trust Company of Chicago, where he has worked since 1977. Since 1981 he has served as the director of Passive Equity Management. His responsibilities include overseeing the management and trading of the index funds managed at American National Bank, one of the leading index fund management organizations. Mr. Manus received his B.A. in economics from Union College and his M.B.A. from the University of Rochester.

GRETA MARSHALL Ms. Marshall is investment manager of the California Public Employees' Retirement System, the largest public pension plan in the country, with approximately $45 billion in assets. Prior to joining PERS, she was president, BayBanks Investment Management, where she created the investment management subsidiary of this Boston-based bank. Previously she ran the pension and foundation investment programs at Deere and Company.

Ms. Marshall is a frequent speaker on the many inventive investment programs she has implemented. She is a chartered financial analyst and holds B.A. and M.B.A. degrees from the University of Louisville.

JOHN J. MORTON Mr. Morton is managing director–trading of Dewey Square Investors. His past affiliations include membership on the NASDAQ Committee; the National Market Trading Systems Committee; the Boston Stock Exchange Board of Governors; and the Executive Committee of the National Organization of Investment Professionals. He is chairman of the Institutional Traders Advisory Committee to the Board of Governors of the New York Stock Exchange. He was a member of the Market Performance Committee of the New York Stock Exchange.

EUGENE A. NOSER, JR. Mr. Noser has served as president of Abel/Noser Corporation since its founding in 1975. He has twenty-seven years of experience in the securities industry and has been a portfolio manager for a pension fund. Prior to that, he was a director of investment planning for Delaware Investment Management. He is now a director of the First City National Bank & Trust Company of New York. Mr. Noser was graduated from the University of Houston, Houston, Texas.

EVAN SHULMAN Mr. Shulman is vice president and chief investment officer of Mitchum Jones & Templeton Advisors, Cambridge, Massachusetts. Previously, Mr. Shulman co-founded Batterymarch: Canada to provide specialized equity management in the Canadian, U.S., and international markets for Canadian institutional funds. Before that, he was senior vice president, Batterymarch Financial Management, after holding research assignments at Keystone Custodian Funds and the Royal Trust Company in Montreal.

Mr. Shulman has written numerous articles and has given speeches to the Financial Research Foundation, among others. He received his B.A. at the University of Toronto and passed the Ph.D. Core Exam in Economics at the University of Chicago.

CEM SEVEROGLU   Mr. Severoglu is a portfolio manager with Dimensional Fund Advisors in Santa Monica. Mr. Severoglu holds a master's degree in finance from the University of California–Los Angeles and a bachelor's degree in engineering from Harvey Mudd College.

ROBERT E. SHULTZ   Mr. Schultz is vice president, pension asset management, for RJR Nabisco, Inc. Mr. Shultz joined RJR Nabisco from IBM Corporation, where he has been director of U.S. retirement funds. Previously, he managed pension funds at Western Electric Company and New York Telephone Company. Mr. Shultz is president of the National Investment Sponsor Federation and a frequent speaker on retirement fund issues at professional conferences. He holds a B.S. degree in Business Administration from Norwich University in Northfield, Vermont.

JEANNE CAIRNS SINQUEFIELD   Ms. Sinquefield is executive vice president of Dimensional Fund Advisors, where she is in charge of trading operations. Previously, she was associated with the Chicago Board of Options Exchange. She is the author of a highly respected book on options and options trading. Ms. Sinquefield holds an M.B.A. and a Ph.D. from the University of Chicago. She also holds a bachelor's and a master's degree from the University of California–Santa Barbara.

GEORGE M. SPEHAR   Mr. Spehar is an associate director of Bear Stearns and Company, New York. His primary responsibility is transacting equity portfolios for the firm's institutional clients. Prior to joining Bear Starns in 1984, he was a member of the New York Futures Exchange. He is a graduate of Colorado College.

EDWARD C. STORY   Mr. Story is a founding partner of Plexus Group, a Santa Monica–based investment advisor and provider of services to pension funds, investment managers, and traders. Plexus serves as the marketing arm of Instinet Corporation in bringing The Crossing Network to the investment management communities. Mr. Story has played an integral part in the market development of The Crossing Network. Prior to the formation of Plexus Group, Mr. Story was director of marketing for Wilshire Asset Management. He holds an M.B.A. from Harvard University and a B.A. in international relations from Pomona College.

JACK L. TREYNOR   Mr. Treynor is visiting associate professor of finance at the University of Southern California. He also heads his own investment advisory firm. Previously, he was chief investment officer of Treynor-Arbit Associates and, before that, editor of the *Financial Analysts Journal*. Mr. Treynor has published extensively and broadly in the field of finance, and is often called on to share his unique insights at investment seminars. He was awarded the Graham and Dodd Plaque for the best paper published in the *Financial Analysts Journal* in 1981. He is one of the five investment professionals ever to receive the Nicholas Molodovsky Award for "contributions to the profession of financial analysis of such significance as to change the direction of the profession."

VINCENT WALSH   Mr. Walsh is senior vice president in charge of clearing operations for Instinet Corporation, a subsidiary of Reuters Holding Ltd. He has day-to-day responsibility for clearance and settlement of all Instinet securities transactions, and is a member of the credit committee. Prior to joining Instinet, Mr. Walsh was manager of finance and administration for Morgan Stanley Operations. Earlier, he worked for General Electric Credit Corporation, and at Citibank and American International Group. He is a member of the operations committee of the Securities Industry Association (IOA). Mr. Walsh has been chairman of the IOA Symposium Committee for the past four years, and organized programs on global investments and securities clearance in world markets. He has an M.B.A. from Columbia University and a B.B.A. from the University of Notre Dame.

STEVEN WUNSCH   Mr. Wunsch is a vice president of Kidder, Peabody's Financial Futures Department. He prepares a widely appreciated monthly commentary and has spoken at many conferences on topics related to the design and functioning of financial markets. Prior to joining Kidder Peabody, Mr. Wunch was a floor trader and broker at the New York Futures Exchange. He is a graduate of Princeton University.

PART ONE

The Securities Markets of Today

1

HOW WE GOT HERE: THE ORIGINS OF TODAY'S VOLATILE TRADING ENVIRONMENT

Dexter D. Earle

In order to discuss how we got here, it is important to define what we mean by *here*.

In the closing days of the tumultuous year of 1987, the worldwide equity markets had weathered the crash of 1987, the advent of global (24-hour) trading, and Big Bang in the United Kingdom.

In the United States, institutional investors continue to dominate the equity marketplace. The public investor primarily accesses the equity markets through pension plans, savings plans, mutual funds, individual retirement accounts (IRAs), and an assortment of other investment vehicles managed by professional money managers. There is more than $1.2 trillion invested by private and public pension plans in the United States. About 40% of these funds are invested in equities. In the global marketplace, all news, good or bad, travels around the world rapidly and is instantly translated into the prices of securities.

Beginning on Friday, October 16, and throughout the infamous week of October 19, we truly experienced the phenomenon of an efficient global marketplace, where information is rapidly transmitted, disseminated, and reflected in the securities markets of the Pacific Basin, the United Kingdom and Western Europe, and North America. We are in an extremely volatile marketplace, and all investors are trying to understand and quantify what this volatility will mean to the global investment process in the future.

To appreciate fully where we are today, one needs to go back to the post–World War II period and trace the changes that occurred in the securities industry from 1949 through the end of 1987. In 1949 pension funds in the United States were primarily invested in fixed-income issues. Bonds were purchased and carried at their original or book price until maturity. The investment return on a bond portfolio was the coupon interest received each year. Bonds were bought and held to maturity, and there were virtually no secondary market transactions on the part of the portfolio manager.

To the extent that equity investments took place, a similar buy and hold strategy was employed by the portfolio manager. Stocks that consistently paid dividends were in favor. The preferred trading strategy that portfolio managers used to buy stocks was to dollar average their stock purchases carefully over time until the total position had been purchased. Their stock purchases were subject to fixed commission charges, which were found in a book of commission tables prepared by the Association of Stock Exchange Firms covering all round lot and odd lot transactions on the New York Stock Exchange (NYSE) and the American Stock Exchange. These fixed commissions remained in force up to and including May 1, 1975, when all commission charges for stock transactions became fully negotiable.

BUILDING THE BASE

In 1950 a significant event occurred that would alter the future of how pension funds in the United States were managed. This event was the decision on the part of General Motors Corporation to set the asset allocation mix for the company's pension fund at a 50% equity and 50% fixed income level.

As a result of this decision, many other corporate pension plans began systematically to increase their equity exposure. Over the next decade, these corporate pension plans began to invest in equities for the first time.

The environment in the securities industry of the 1950s paralleled to some extent the mood of the country at that time. The 1950s in the stock market came to be viewed as a decade of base building in terms of the United States' equity capital markets. The U.S. economy reflected a country weary of two world wars and the Korean conflict. Corporate America was beginning to adjust to the postwar period. As economic conditions improved, so too did the prospects for the U.S. stock market. This was still a market that was self-regulated and charged high, nonnegotiable commissions to all investors. Volume on the New York

Stock Exchange was extremely low by today's standards (in 1949 the average daily trading volume was 1,023,000 shares[1]).

Probably the most significant event for the equity markets in the 1950s was the rejuvenation of the public interest in buying common stocks. Since the crash of 1929, the Depression, World War II, and the Korean conflict, individual investors in common stocks had been noticeably absent. By the 1950s this trend had started to reverse.

Perhaps the person who had the most influence in bringing the public into the equity market was G. Keith Funston (president of the New York Stock Exchange from 1951 to 1967). In 1954 he introduced a marketing campaign: "Own Your Share of American Business." This campaign was a well-orchestrated attempt on the part of the New York Stock Exchange to rebuild investor confidence in the stock market and rejuvenate public orders on the books of the New York Stock Exchange's specialists.

Many of the large retail brokerage firms, such as Merrill Lynch, introduced, through their retail sales force, the Monthly Investment Program as a way for individuals to invest portions of their savings in common stocks each month.

The combined effect of corporate pension plans slowly shifting their asset mix in the direction of equities and the return of the individual investor to the stock market laid the foundation for the explosive decade of the 1960s. It is important to remember that at the end of the 1950s, individual and institutional equity investors transacted at fixed commission rates in a low trading volume environment where agency orders and dollar averaging made up the trading strategy of this time. Most investors employed a buy and hold strategy, and there was very little trading in the secondary market by either individuals or institutions.

THE ACTIVISTS

In the decade of the 1960s, equity investing changed radically as a result of the introduction of block stock trading, major asset allocation shifts from bonds to stocks, the era of "growth" stocks, and the advent of investment performance consultants. The 1960s are referred to as the "go-go" years and included an eight-year economic cycle often called the "super" cycle (1961–1969). The whole pattern of equity investing changed dramatically during this decade. As Americans embraced the challenge of space exploration, they also began to look at equity investments in an aggressive and opportunistic way.

[1] New York Stock Exchange Fact Book, 1987.

In 1962, the average daily reported share volume on the New York Stock Exchange was 3.8 million shares.[2] During the decade the average daily volume grew by a multiple of four, as follows[3]:

1960	3,042,000
1965	6,176,000
1970	11,564,000

Part of the reason for this dramatic growth in share volume can be traced to the aggressive purchase of equities on the part of pension funds during this decade. A good illustration of this trend can be shown by the pattern of equity invested in the Bell System Pension Funds. In 1962, Southern New England Telephone Company became the first Bell System company to invest pension assets in equities. By 1964 the Bell System had about 40% of its $3 billion pension assets invested in equities. The limit for equity investments was increased to 50% in 1965, and by 1968 there was no limit for equity investing.

During this decade, institutional investors as well as individual investors began to invest heavily in companies that did not pay dividends, but instead reinvested earnings into the business of the company to further its growth potential. Growth stock investing became the focal point of all investors by the middle of the decade. Stocks like Disney, Polaroid, and Avon Products became the favorites of investors. Individual and institutional money poured into this select group of growth stocks with predictable upward movement in the price of each of the securities. This was the era of the "nifty fifty," in which about 50 growth stocks garnered the attention of the majority of investors as well as their cash flow.

Two developments helped expand the markets during the 1960s. First, institutional investors moved away from the buy and hold strategy of prior decades and began to trade their portfolios aggressively. The introduction of block stock trading by Goldman, Sachs & Company, Bear Stearns, and Salomon Brothers allowed institutions to trade into and out of large blocks of growth stock holdings.

The introduction of investment performance consultants was the second key development of the decade. For the first time, pension plan sponsors began to evaluate their money managers quarterly. Poor investment performance often resulted in the firing of the underperforming manager. Pension plans began to hire investment counselors with excellent investment

[2] New York Stock Exchange Fact Book, 1987.
[3] New York Stock Exchange Fact Book, 1987.

performance who were recommended by their consultants. They diversified their equity monies into a multiple money manager lineup that differed drastically from the concentrated, one-manager approach of prior decades.

Money managers were encouraged to trade their equity portfolios aggressively in order to achieve an incremental performance advantage over the old buy and hold strategy. As the volume on the New York Stock Exchange multiplied by a factor of four, the liquidity available to equity institutional investors grew proportionally. At the same time, so too did the willingness of the block trading firms to commit capital to provide liquidity to their institutional investor clients. As a result of the prolonged economic cycle during this decade and the insatiable demand for growth stocks, pension funds continued to move aggressively away from bonds and into the higher risk, higher reward equities. By the end of the decade, multiples on the "nifty fifty" had risen to unprecedented levels. Many growth stocks were trading at multiples of more than 35 times forecasted earnings. As the decade came to an end, the public began to participate in the equity market directly as many initial public offerings of the next generation of growth stocks were brought to market. By 1970, more than 63% of the $105.5 billion private pension fund market was invested in equities. At the beginning of this decade, it had been unusual to have 25% of the pension funds' assets invested in common stock.

Active equity portfolio managers began to trade their portfolios aggressively by buying and selling large blocks of stocks every day. Accordingly, in 1965 the NYSE began to collect data on trades of 10,000 shares or larger (blocks) in 1965. Large block transactions increased rapidly, from 2,171 in 1965 to 34,420 in 1975, to 539,039 in 1985.[4] Several major brokerage houses began to employ their own capital to facilitate the block stock trade demands of their institutional clients. Firms like Goldman Sachs, Bear Stearns, and Salomon Brothers typically traded numerous blocks of 50,000 to 100,000 shares every day. Since the commissions associated with these trades were fixed, it is important to understand the economics of block stock trading at the outset. For example, a $50 stock had a fixed commission of 28 cents per share charged for all shares after the first 1,000.[5] If a broker bought a 25,000-share block from a money manager at $50, the broker could sell out this position at $49.75 or higher with no economic risk. The commission spread of 28 cents per share or 0.56% was a reasonable cushion for the broker to risk his capital. On larger blocks of 100,000 shares or more, the broker often

[4] New York Stock Exchange Fact Book, 1987.
[5] New York Stock Exchange and American Stock Exchange Commission Tables, 1968.

required a price discount from the current market price as well as the fixed commission. Active equity money managers were able to trade their portfolios aggressively, in part because of the availability of the block trading firm's capital. The risks to both the money manager and the broker were significant. The broker often was unable to trade out of his position and spent more than his commission to close out the trade. The money manager paid a premium for liquidity and would suffer poor investment performance if his strategy did not work out.

THE INSTITUTIONALIZATION OF THE MARKET

As the decade of the 1970s began, equity investments in private pension plans had reached historic proportions. By 1972, according to A. G. Becker, the median equity investment exceeded 75% of total assets for private pension plans in their survey. This decade started favorably for equity investors, but radical changes occurred along the way. The stock market suffered back-to-back down years in 1973 and 1974. This marked the end of the growth stock era in the United States. From 1973 through the end of the decade, investors had to confront prolonged periods of inverted yield curves where short-term interest rates were higher than intermediate and long-term rates. This condition of hyperinflation was exacerbated by the 1974 oil embargo, which produced dramatically higher energy prices and added pressure to the already historically high interest rates. On May 30, 1975, another historic event occurred with the elimination of fixed equity commission rates in favor of fully negotiated commissions. For the first time, equity investors were able to negotiate and ultimately to dictate a substantially lower commission structure. For example, a $50 stock that used to trade with a fixed 28-cent commission quickly traded at rates of 10 cents (0.2%) or lower in the early days of fully negotiated rates. The impact of being able to transact at commission rates discounted between 50% and 75% can be seen in the dramatic increase of daily volume transacted on the New York Stock Exchange[6]:

1975	18,551,000
1978	28,591,000
1982	65,052,000

Equity managers who had typically traded their portfolios in the range of 15% to 30% annual turnover were by the early 1980s transacting at a turnover rate in excess of 100%.

[6] New York Stock Exchange Fact Book, 1987.

In September 1974, Congress passed the Employee Retirement Income Security Act (ERISA), which effectively restated the prudent man rule and required that specific investment guidelines be established for all private pension plans. This new legislation served as a check and balance against the excesses experienced during the "go-go" era of the 1960s. Pension plans were required to establish formal minimum and maximum guidelines for the various asset classes invested in their plans. New funding requirements required substantial infusions of new money into private pensions, most of which were in a sizable deficit condition as a result of the 1973–1974 drop in the equity markets. Typically, this new money was allocated to fixed income and other nonequity investments. By the end of the decade, the average private pension plan had a balanced asset allocation between stocks and bonds, in contrast to the 75% equity positions of 1972–1973.

The decade of the 1970s contained numerous historical events that shaped the style and approach of professional investors and laid the groundwork for investments. In the first part of the decade, investors experienced the sudden end of the growth stock era. Hyperinflation dominated the balance of the decade and helped bring about active bond management beginning in 1972. With the passage of ERISA, investment guidelines became an integral part of private pension fund investment policy. Finally, the introduction of fully negotiated equity commissions set the stage for the explosive equity trading volume that would come in the 1980s. After a decade in which stocks underperformed bonds, this unusual investing condition quickly reverted in the 1980s to a more typical risk–return profile in which common stocks proved to be the higher risk, higher return asset. In the 1980s common stock prices and trading volume soared to unprecedented heights. Volume on the New York Stock Exchange averaged 141 million shares in 1986 and, on December 19, 1986, set a record for one day at 244.3 million shares.[7] Average daily volume grew dramatically during the early part of the decade[8]:

1980	44,871,000
1982	65,052,000
1986	141,028,000

The Dow Jones Industrial Average rose to an all-time high of 2,720 on August 25, 1987, a peak soon followed by the crash of October 19, 1987,

[7] New York Stock Exchange Fact Book, 1987.
[8] New York Stock Exchange Fact Book, 1987.

in which the stock market experienced the biggest single-day percentage decline in its history. In the more than 40 years since the end of World War II, the equity marketplace has changed radically from a low-volume, fixed-cost, dollar-averaging arena to a global arena characterized by high volume, negotiated costs, and high turnover. Countless products have been introduced into this marketplace, including active, passive, and synthetic strategies applicable to equity markets throughout the world. It has been an interesting and challenging period, which has taxed the creative energy of the many investment professionals employed in managing the growing pool of public and private pension fund monies. Flexibility and a willingness to adapt to a changing marketplace have been the two key requirements for all those involved in managing money since World War II.

GLOBALIZATION: INTO THE FUTURE

As the decade of the 1980s draws to a close, investors have evolved from a domestic, local currency approach to a sophisticated and complex global investment strategy. The ability to transact quickly and cost-effectively has become one of the most crucial elements of the global investment process. Today's money managers aggressively and frequently change their asset allocation strategies during a market cycle. These changes often involve sizable trades in stocks, bonds, and cash equivalents, with multiple securities in each category. International asset allocations introduce currency strategies and transactions into the equation. The demands placed on the securities markets by today's global investors are truly awesome. So far, the world's marketplaces have adapted to the dramatic volume increases that have occurred over the last 40 years. The biggest challenge for global investors in the 1990s may be the inability of the world's securities markets to cope with investor demands.

The Editor Asks

Q   *The changes you have documented are striking, as is the massive change in thinking patterns that is both cause and effect of these changes. If you gaze into your crystal ball, what trends do you expect to dominate changes in securities trading over the next ten years?*

A As we enter the 1990s, investor demand has exceeded the local market's ability to process this order flow in all countries except the United States. Currently, the settlement procedures around the world vary widely from country to country. Several countries still require physical delivery of all securities. Early in the 1990s, the global marketplace will establish a Depository Trust Company (DTC) automated settlement system whereby all securities that trade will have common settlement rules. Physical settlements will be replaced by bookkeeping entries stored on the computers of the global depository system.

The effect of this long-overdue change will be similar to the experience of the United States in the mid-70s. Specifically, trading volume will increase around the world, and global investors will experience improved liquidity. Global money managers will maintain 24-hour investment operations and transact around the clock with their executing brokers. Each of the world's markets will have liquid, derivative instruments that will allow brokers to hedge their trading positions and afford investors greater liquidity. Trading strategies will focus on quantifying and minimizing total transaction costs as a means to enhance investment performance. I envision the next 10 years as challenging, demanding, and exciting ones for all those involved in the investment business.

If someone had explained to an investor in 1950 what the global marketplace would be like just prior to the crash on October 19, 1987, I am sure that this investor would have had difficulty believing that such dramatic events could really happen. My crystal ball shows a continuation of these dramatically changing events over the next 10 years. Fasten your seat belts, this could be quite a ride!

PART TWO

Securities Transactions and Investment Performance

2

A SPONSOR LOOKS AT TRADING COSTS

Robert E. Shultz

Plan sponsor interest in trading costs is a natural and logical progression in the evolution of the pension services industry in the United States and, in particular, in the professionalism of the plan sponsor.

The early focus on transaction costs can be traced to two primary trends that began to take shape in the mid-70s. First, the trend toward multiple specialty managers and away from balanced managers sowed the seeds for plan sponsor interest and involvement in the trading process. Coupled with the growth of the master trust industry, plan sponsors entered the early stages of exerting control over the destiny of their specific funds. The second major event that focused interest was the trend toward indexing; core/noncore was the earliest label, later to be renamed active–passive strategies.

The need to manage funds differently because of size and projected growth became the focal point for plan sponsors and was the dominant topic of industry seminars. Size and the projected growth in assets began to distinguish the plan sponsor's needs from those of other investors in the marketplace. With the shift in focus, the sponsor began to think more as a manager of managers and less as a portfolio manager of specific securities. Thus, the perspective became one of portfolio characteristics, tilts, biases, and an evolving view of securities as composite assets rather than individual stocks.

My personal introduction to trading came in 1974 when I was switching assets from balanced to specialty managers. I was quickly introduced to the notion of ''penny a share crosses,'' which were new and mysterious to those of us on the sponsor side. I was also in the unique position, when indexing was in its infancy, of buying an index fund from a fellow sponsor and introducing it into my portfolio for a penny a share. Incidentally, those of you in the business in that time will appreciate the source of my in-kind index fund purchase. The chairman of the company from whom I purchased the fund, when informed by the pension manager about the new and wonderful product, immediately declared the index fund un-American and made further comments about his company not being willing to accept mediocrity. He ordered the pension manager to ''get rid of it.'' Hence, my introduction to portfolio trading.

The point of mentioning this particular trade is to show that from early on an informal network existed among sponsors, and particularly among index fund managers. This represents early sponsor interest in reducing the transaction costs. What was missing in those days of the informal network was a central point at which to locate the other side of the trade. What was lacking was that one phone number to call down at the gas station where someone would write on the wall of the phone booth that sponsor or manager X wants to buy a diversified Standard & Poor's (S&P 500) portfolio and is looking for an opposite interest.

From these early days in the mid-70s until quite recently, there was no significant growth in sponsor interest in trading costs. Substantial progress was made, however, in the ''manager restructuring process.'' In-kind transfers between the new manager and the old manager, with the assistance of the master trustee, became increasingly commonplace. Today, manager changes very seldom involve full round-trip commissions with conversion of portfolios to cash and subsequent conversion to new portfolio securities.

Lest sponsors be accused of learning only from our good experiences, one seemingly incorrect direction can be cited that also served as a learning experience regarding ''information-motivated'' versus ''informationless'' trading.

The early writings about inventory funds suggested that they would be the answer to turnover.[1] An inventory fund stands willing to take all sells and act as a pool for buys for the managers operating within a multiple-manager fund structure. A number of sponsors thought this was an excellent idea. To my knowledge, there are no inventory funds being run in the original sense today, because sponsors learned a lesson. Those trades were, in fact, all information-motivated trades that resulted in the inventory funds taking in stocks that truly should have been sold and holding onto them. Meanwhile, managers were allowed to buy stocks out of the fund that, in fact, should have been purchased outside. In hindsight, the procedure probably could

---

[1] Wayne H. Wagner and Carol A. Zipkin, ''Can Inventory Index Funds Improve Active Equity Performance?'' *Financial Analysts Journal*, May–June 1978, pp. 1–11.

have worked had sponsors turned the trades around more quickly and put them back on the street under the guise of an informationless trade.

With this brief historical background of the sponsor involvement, let's move forward and examine the factors that generated the heightened interest in transaction costs that began in 1985.

INVESTMENT PERFORMANCE AND TRANSACTION COSTS

Two issues converged on sponsors during the 1985 time frame. One was an evolutionary trend in the professional education of the plan sponsor. This can be termed "fees and transaction costs: expectations versus reality." The second was a regulatory issue involving pronouncements by both the Department of Labor (DOL) and the Securities and Exchange Commission (SEC). The two issues are very different in nature. The first reflects the initiative of the plan sponsor in discharging his duties. The second is more of a reaction to regulation. The primary force is the sponsor's initiative, and that issue will be treated first.

Let's begin by exploring what is meant by "expectations versus reality." Interest in transaction costs has risen because more and more plan sponsors are coming to understand what transaction costs and fees mean in terms of *expectations* for active management versus the *realities* of active management. The progression of diversifying to specialty managers and beyond to multiple managers within asset classes can develop great inefficiencies. A pension plan can end up with many managers who, in aggregate, represent a fully diversified portfolio. When the aggregate portfolio is studied, in contrast to studying the individual managers' portfolios, it becomes obvious that the total fund often takes little risk and is earning commensurately small incremental returns. In other words, the danger of diversification is to diversify away *return* rather than risk. The multimanager structure can breed overdiversification, coupled with high fees and transaction costs. The dilemma is that as additional managers are hired, the best decisions of each of them are dissipated.

The consequences of these problems would be minimal if managers could truly add the hoped-for hundreds of basis points of value over the benchmarks. Comparing managers to a single benchmark such as the S&P 500 creates the impression that active management can add many hundreds of basis points during particular points in the cycle. However, when performance is properly measured against the correct benchmark and correctly attributed to its sources, the resulting numbers are much more modest than sponsor expectations of the prior decade.

The trend toward the establishment of unique "normal benchmark portfolios" for each investment manager increased the sponsor's knowledge of the proper attribution of active return. The normal benchmark portfolio approach traces its roots back to the late 1970s. Because of the complexities of defining normal portfolios and the lack of enthusiasm by the investment management community, sponsor commitment to this approach languished until recently. Significant momentum has developed in the last year as a result of increasing interest in incentive fee structures. As more plan sponsors work to develop better approaches to return attribution (either through their own staff efforts or through the growing expertise of the consultant community), investment managers will be forced to embrace the process. Normal portfolio advocates are not claiming to have found the perfect solution. Still, a strong case can be made that comparing the results of diverse active management styles to a single index will not yield insightful attribution of period-to-period value-added.

At a best guess, the long-term value of active management is probably 50 to 100 basis points over the proper benchmark. Current portfolios average 60% to 70% annual turnover and involve about 1% round-trip commission and market impact. One thus realizes that average portfolio transaction cost drag may be as high as 60 basis points annually. Obviously, if the range of active manager contribution is 50 to 100 basis points, then 60 basis points is a substantial portion and could even exceed the value of active management.

The realization now dawning on pension sponsors is that transaction cost drag may always have been in the 60 basis point range or higher. Compared to an active manager expectation that adds 500 or more basis points of value per year, 60 basis points pales in importance. As Charles Ellis of Greenwich Associates has eloquently expressed many times, it isn't that managers are dumb—quite the contrary: There are too many smart people pursuing too few inefficiencies to sustain current turnover rates.[2] The focal point is not the precise value added by active management, nor is it the accurate measurement of transaction costs. Whatever numbers are chosen, there is an increasing realization that transaction costs are an important determinant of the success of active management.

The evolving trend is, therefore, a shift from overblown expectations to a more subdued reality. This logically leads to a shift in focus from the *return* component to the *cost* component of investment management. Sponsors cannot control expected return. They can, however, exert control

[2] See Chapter 3, "Liquidity and Trading Costs: A Modest Proposal," by Charles D. Ellis.

over the cost structures of the fund. Investment insight leads to small incremental returns awash in statistical variability. Hence, the cost structures are an important component of control over the pension investment process. Sponsors who become more aware of cost structures gain an important advantage in separating fact from myth.

PENSION FUND REGULATION

From the regulatory perspective, two important actions occurred in 1986. A Securities and Exchange Commission ruling extended the array of services protected under Section 28(e), which covered the purchase of research services for directed commission dollars. The previous interpretations that prohibited the purchase of "commercially available" services were withdrawn. As far as money managers were concerned, new ground opened up for soft dollar payments for research services. Almost simultaneously, the Department of Labor released a technical bulletin that imposed transaction cost monitoring requirements on plan sponsors and attempted to define "best execution." These two pronouncements appear to move in completely opposite directions and create a dilemma for plan sponsors. The highlights of these two releases follow.

SEC SECTION 28(E).   Section 28(e) was enacted as part of the 1975 Securities Act Amendments that abolished fixed brokerage commissions. It was intended to provide a "safe harbor" in response to concerns that investment managers would breach their fiduciary duties by paying more than the lowest available commission for brokerage and research services. In 1986 the SEC issued an interpretive release that the safe harbor did not protect "commercially available products." A number of items were specifically excluded, including newspapers, magazines, periodicals, computer facilities and software, office furniture and equipment, and airline tickets. In its 1986 release, the Commission stated that the controlling principle to determine whether something qualifies as research is whether it provides lawful and appropriate assistance to the money manager in the performance of his investment decision-making responsibility. Thus, the test suggests that the actual use to which a product or service is put determines whether it is protected by the safe harbor. The SEC further clarified that soft dollars can be used to pay fees for research conferences and seminars, but not incidental expenses such as airline fares, hotels, and meals.

DOL TECHNICAL RELEASE NUMBER 86-1. The Department of Labor release focused on two noteworthy situations where the relief provided by Section 28(e) would not be available: (1) direction by a plan fiduciary who does not exercise investment discretion for securities law purposes, and (2) the use of commissions to pay for services other than research or brokerage service. The release put forth the plan sponsor's responsibilities regarding the direction and monitoring of brokerage transactions:

> The fiduciary who appoints the investment manager is not relieved of his ongoing duty to monitor the investment manager to assure that the manager has secured best execution of the plan's transactions and to assure that the commissions paid on such transactions are reasonable in relation to the value of the brokerage and research services provided to the plan.

The divergence of these two pronouncements is obvious. The manager can now use the client's commissions to purchase just about anything related to research, including computer systems and services. The plan sponsor, on the other hand, is charged with the duty to monitor that managers act in good faith regarding brokerage, in terms of both reasonableness and "best execution," possibly the most ill defined term in the legislative statutes. The plan sponsors' responsibilities to monitor exist whether or not brokerage is directed for services benefiting the plan. In summary, the Department of Labor has gently warned fiduciaries that they have a duty to monitor the manager to assure that he is acting in good faith regarding brokerage. Meanwhile, the SEC has complicated the process by greatly expanding the services that can be purchased and the tests that can be applied in the endless quest for a workable definition of *best execution*.

The SEC and DOL actions have an important impact on all persons involved in the execution process: the plan sponsor, the investment manager, and the broker. The sponsor must specifically monitor the quality of the executions, particularly when directing brokerage. The manager is reassured by the DOL insistence that sponsors pay better attention to execution, but must be more concerned with improper sponsor direction of commissions. Finally, brokers that can show a record of high-quality, cost-effective executions should find increased sponsor interest.

We have traced the historical involvement of the sponsor in the trading process and cited the two major thrusts that have heightened the sponsor focus. Now we can move forward and examine the period from 1985 through 1988. Although the current recriminations concerning the October 1987 crash disparage the trend toward commoditization of the stock market, plan sponsors have for years been drawn to investment strategies that emphasize trading *portfolios* of stocks in search of the characteristics, tilts, and biases that best fill pension investment needs. This has increasingly been viewed as the best means of coping with the massive size of pension assets and inflows. Obviously, as the focus shifts from individual stocks to factors, informationless trading increasingly becomes more of a sponsor need. This implies a different method of transacting in the marketplace.

The New York Stock Exchange specialist system is rooted in the belief that all trades coming to the post are information-driven. Therefore, specialists and floor traders must hedge against the trades and treat them as an adversarial trade containing potentially harmful information. In fact, an increasing portion of the volume that comes to the floor every day is not based on specific information concerning individual stocks.

One definition of an informationless trade is that there is nothing in the trade that others would want to imitate. Many sponsors believe that these trades do not need risk capital in order to be executed. The open question is whether the Exchange and the major Wall Street trading firms have accommodated this type of trading at sufficiently low cost.

Concerns surrounding the preceding question provide the primary impetus that has led to what are generically termed electronic crossing networks.[3] The New York Stock Exchange and others would do well to study the needs served by the networks that are not filled through the traditional exchange process. To the extent that there is such a thing as an informationless trade (certainly the fact that someone is trading can be valuable information to others), plan sponsors are increasingly interested in the various electronic crossing networks built to accommodate just this type of trade. To a "patient trader," one who does not believe that the trade's information content demands immediate execution, the reduction of both market impact and commissions through the networks is extremely appealing. Although the primary concern of network participants is the apparent lack of liquidity, the trading patterns in mid-1988 have turned the table somewhat on the liquidity argument: With the extremely low exchange trading volume, some traders have found that the networks sometimes present better liquidity.

THE SPONSOR CLAIMS HIS OWN.   The National Investment Sponsor Federation, a federation of plan sponsor groups and individual participants formed in 1985, has created a task force to review the issues surrounding transaction costs. The group has issued an interim report to the membership concluding that trading costs may in fact be the largest controllable plan

[3] See Chapter 16, "Electronic Crossing Markets," by Edward C. Story.

sponsor expense. The report urges plan sponsors to work toward four objectives.

1. *Measure transaction costs.* An active measurement program of commissions and market impact, coupled with a questioning attitude by the plan sponsor, alerts investment managers to sponsor interests and may favorably impact costs.

2. *Require soft dollar accounting from investment managers.* Plan sponsors should request investment managers to itemize all services purchased with soft dollars. This reporting will enable the sponsor to judge whether he is getting full value for the manager's commission directions.

3. *Direct a percentage of trades to discount brokers.* All trades initiated by the investment managers are not of equal difficulty. The sponsor should ensure that the most efficient brokerage services available for various types of trades are utilized to the maximum benefit of the fund.

4. *Support the crossing networks.* Several viable crossing networks exist today. To be fully effective in crossing natural buyers and sellers, they need plan sponsor support. Plan sponsors should ask their investment managers to use these networks to reduce trading costs and collectively gain further insight into their long term viability.[4]

In summary, whether through their own initiative or by admonition of the Department of Labor, plan sponsors are becoming more involved in trade execution and the measurement thereof.

As stated early in this chapter, the fiduciary obligation of plan sponsors is to ensure efficiencies on the cost side, including both transaction costs and related management fees. Obviously, there is a linkage between the development of crossing networks and the use and direction of soft dollars.

Noticeably absent from the National Investment Sponsor Federation recommendations is any comment on sponsor direction of soft dollars. Although the task force report serves to introduce a focus on soft dollars, the views that follow are purely those of the author and not those of the National Investment Sponsor Federation.

SOFT DOLLARS.   These comments are based on two precepts—first, that soft dollars are not a free lunch, and second, that commissions belong to the

---

[4] Interim report of the Transactions Cost Task Force of the National Investment Sponsor Federation, June 1987.

plan. Carrying the implications of crossing networks one step forward obviously suggests the unbundling of research services. The resultant dealer markets would carry the linkage to its extreme, but possibly logical, conclusion.

An editorial in the *Financial Analysts Journal* entitled "Whose Commissions?" succinctly expresses the issue.[5] The comments, which were written not by plan sponsors but by investment managers, flatly state that the manager should provide the research he believes necessary from his own fee revenues and resources. Client commissions should be used either as the client directs or to obtain securities execution at the lowest net cost. The editorial admonished the SEC to reconsider the entire safe harbor concept by recognizing that commissions are an expense to the beneficiaries of the fund and should be expended for their benefit alone. I support this editorial thought and suggest that the commission structure be set to obtain securities execution at the lowest net cost. I do not believe in sponsor direction of commissions. What 28(e) has created is an extremely large off-balance-sheet, off-budget financing not unlike some of our federal government's obfuscated practices.

The process only appears to benefit all constituencies. Plan sponsors buy services outside the normal corporate budget approval process, managers obtain research services they otherwise would buy with their own resources, and brokers create slush money to finance services that would not be bought with hard dollars. In the end, though, someone pays the bill. For a corporate fund, the ultimate payment is made by the corporation through increased contributions to the pension fund. For the public fund, the taxpayer's pocket is the ultimate source of this funding.

Transaction costs and investment management fees have been mixed and confused to the point where neither the sponsor, nor the manager, nor the broker knows who is paying how much for what. They should be separated into their rightful categories. For example, the use of commission dollars to buy research is not truly a transaction cost. It rightfully belongs in the same category as a fee for managing the assets.

Does the investment manager view the expenditure of a dollar of commissions out of the plan in the same way he or she would a dollar of the firm's revenues? Honest reflection by the investment management community would reveal a substantial number of marginally beneficial services that would be dropped if the management firm's revenues were the source of payment. I have asked numerous investment management firms a theoretical question: "If soft dollars ceased to exist Friday at the market close, would

---

[5] Edward Mitchell and Wendell Starke, "Whose Commissions?" *Financial Analysts Journal,* September–October 1986, p. 8.

you purchase the same services on Monday's opening with your firm's resources?'' The answers vary in proportion, but all substantially reduce the amount of purchases when *their* dollars are at stake. Evidently, then, a manager's own dollar is not the same size or shape as the plan sponsor's commission dollar. To quote another money manager who does not believe soft dollar purchases are ethical:

> It is a very dubious practice to charge your customers a fee and then use your commission dollars to buy what in effect are office supplies. If an investment client pays half a million dollars in fees, then the manager should pay for research out of his own pocket. If a manager contracts with vendors to buy pieces of research, he pays excessive commissions which come out of the principal amount entrusted to the fund. That in effect is another hidden fee.[6]

Paraphrasing from a portfolio manager in an editorial comment:

> Without question, in the long term the elimination of soft dollars would be a good thing for the entire investment industry: plan sponsors, money managers, brokers and pure research shops. In the short run, however, many dislocations would take place. These dislocations are the reason that no one will make these changes voluntarily, except the person paying the tab—you, the plan sponsor. If we unbundled and eliminated 28(e):
>
> - *Major brokers*—would not generate unused or marginal research, and would keep this large fixed cost component to a minimum. They would do less research, but at a higher quality standard.
> - *Third-party research*—Marginal research operations would go out of business. Quality research firms would survive on their merits, rather than on how their fees are financed.
> - *Managers*—Would pay lower broker commissions and receive only highly relevant research, thereby increasing performance results. By simply not having to manage the paper flow from the less relevant research, they would save time (which is the biggest cost factor), and thereby increase their profits.
> - *Plan sponsors*—Lower costs from the above three players would be passed on to the plan sponsor; their managers would have more efficient research to work with; and their trades would be more efficiently executed. The result would be cost savings and improved investment returns.[7]

[6] Ivy Shmerken, " 'Soft Dollar Trends' Benefit High Flyers,'' *Wall Street Computer Review*, November 1987, pp. 33–40.

[7] Thomas Quinn, "Eliminating Soft Dollars: A Win–Win Argument,'' *Financial Analysts Journal*, September–October 1988, p. 6.

Section 28(e) and the bundling of commissions is quite similar to two bundling examples that can be drawn from U.S. industry: First, the price of Kodak film used to be bundled together with the processing. Second, IBM once prohibited purchase of its computer equipment in favor of leasing, including "for free" all the necessary software and support. Prices to the purchasers fell significantly when these services were unbundled. The history of bundled services suggests that unbundling universally has revealed efficiencies and cost reductions to be achieved.

Soft dollars are a poor substitute for lower commission rates. In the long run, that's a message our industry needs to examine. I believe everyone would be better served with the elimination of the safe harbor provisions.

The Editor Asks

Q *Some sponsors believe that examining commission costs is akin to going to breakfast and bringing your own eggs for the chef to cook. If the manager is held responsible for his bottom line performance, the argument goes, what is to be gained by examining this one component? How would you respond to this view?*

A Certainly we ought to be mindful that the ultimate measure of the investment management business is the bottom line return. I would, however, make two points in support of plan sponsor involvement in the transaction cost process. First, a subtle conflict-of-interest issue exists in that a portion of the commission is available to the manager to purchase services that would otherwise require expenditure of the firm's assets. If all benefits to the manager were captured by the investment management fee, this conflict would be eliminated.

The second issue relates to the precision of the performance measurement process. Without normal benchmark portfolios, the true attribution of performance is difficult to measure. Given the amount of "noise" in the current process and the tendency for a standard measurement benchmark (currently the S&P 500) to prevail, wide return differences exist that make the true value-added an elusive number. In this environment, examining a controllable cost is a proper activity.

3

LIQUIDITY AND TRADING COSTS: A MODEST PROPOSAL

Charles D. Ellis

Short-term thinking and acting are two of the acknowledged devils giving America such a very hard time these days. To add insult to injury, they confuse and seduce us into doing harm to ourselves.

Everyone seems ready to decry the adverse consequences of politicians concentrating too much on their short-term goal of getting elected and giving too little emphasis to statesmanship and governing over the long term.

Perhaps we should look closer to home.

Automobile manufacturers and television set makers are often criticized for concentrating too much on short-term profits and giving too little emphasis to manufacturing and marketing for the long term.

We can look closer to home.

Investment bankers and arbitrageurs are scolded for concentrating too much on the short-term profits of doing deals and giving too little emphasis to building and financing strong corporations for the long term.

Let's look closer to home.

Pension funds—quite unintentionally—may have become one of the devil's engines, causing our economy to turn its strength against its own best interests and to concentrate too much on short-term trading while giving too little emphasis to long-term investing.

Even more serious and consequential, the great power of pension assets coursing with impressive force and velocity through the capital markets may be driving the behavior of major corporations in ways we will regret.

Consider the situation. Institutional investors compete intensively for lucrative contracts to manage pension funds, and experience shows that

Reprinted with permission from *Financial Analysts Journal,* March–April 1987, p. 4.

awards (and terminations) are driven by recent (three- to five-year) "performance"—measured quarter to quarter.

Striving to outperform their cohorts, the institutional investors—spurred on by Wall Street—are so hyperactive that their average portfolio turnover is nearly 70% (i.e., their average investment is held only 18 months).

This extraordinary activity is both the parent and child of liquidity in the market. (Remember that NYSE volume is five times what it was a decade ago, that NASDAQ and OTC volume has increased even faster, and that trading in stock index futures—which had not even been invented 10 years ago—exceeds the volume of trading on the Big Board every day.)

Liquidity in such extraordinary supply is what makes it possible for even our large corporations to be "put in play" and compelled to scramble out of the way when the "arbs" and aggressive takeover specialists come after them.

Liquidity—and the sure knowledge that other institutional investors will act quickly, whether you do or not—is what causes institutional investors to concentrate too much on short-term movements of stock prices and give too little emphasis to investing for the longer term. They cannot afford to be the long-term investors they want to be because they believe they will lose their pension accounts.

Abrupt institutional response in turn drives corporate management to concentrate too much on short-term profits and give too little emphasis to building their companies for the longer term. They cannot afford to be the corporate statesmen and business builders they want to be because they believe they will lose their companies.

Ironically, our markets' extraordinary liquidity has not, apparently, been beneficial to investment managers. A majority continue to underperform the market because the costs of transactions exceed the profits achieved.

If the market's too fast, let's slow down.

The Editor Asks

Q *Market liquidity is usually viewed as the great good of the markets. According to traditional thinking, liquidity enhances market value and assures all players of rapid transactions at moderate cost. Your comments suggest that this liquidity is costing too much (measured as its results on subsequent performance) and encourages a type* *of institutionalized speculation instead of long-term investment. If institutional investors followed your advice and traded less frequently at a reduced trading cost, do you envision any harm to the functioning of the markets?*

A The question might best be answered by dividing it into its several parts.

First, a liquid market gives investors confidence that they can readily change their investments, and this does justify a higher level of valuation than would be warranted if liquidity were a real problem. Of course, the ratio of increasing valuation versus increasing liquidity is not simply linear, it is asymptotic.

Consequently, starting with the remarkable present situation of extraordinary liquidity, we could give up a fair amount of trading volume without losing much liquidity, *and* we could give up a fair amount of liquidity before you would see any impact on share valuation.

Second, there is a serious question for investment managers—and their clients—as to whether the direct and indirect costs of trading are justified by the incremental reward. The *direct* costs are the costs of executing the extra trades: They appear to some of us to be too much of a drag on performance to be overcome by superior investment judgment—for most managers most of the time.

The *indirect* costs may be more important. To what extent are investment managers getting caught in stocks they really shouldn't be owning and would not have owned except that they assumed they could get out and wouldn't get caught? This cost comes in sudden, irregular, and (mercifully) infrequent lumps—when a stock plunges because its earnings are badly "disappointing." All of a sudden, it's too late to get out. The "liquidity" becomes an illusion. Ouch! It's hard to measure, but it's there. And it's worth thinking about.

Third, while it's clear that providing liquidity is not one of the purposes of fiduciary funds like pensions or endowments, following the advice would not make *any* measurable differences to the functioning of the secondary market—unless, of course, *all* institutional investors made *major* reductions in their trading. Sure, it's possible. But it is *not* going to happen.

4

HOW IMPORTANT ARE TRANSACTION COSTS?

Stephen A. Berkowitz
Dennis E. Logue

Transaction costs are the costs associated with the purchase or sale of securities. They have two significant components: brokerage commissions and market impacts. In addition, there is a tax imposed by the Securities and Exchange Commission (SEC) on the seller of securities and charges from the Depository Trust Company (DTC) to clear transactions.

In aggregate, we have found that institutional trades incur transaction costs of $0.09 per share, representing 0.24% of principal. Of this, $0.07 per share, or 0.18% of principal, was commission costs, and the remainder market impact costs.[1] The latter should correspond to the gross profit of market-makers. Transaction costs have been remarkably stable over the period 1985 to 1987. After measuring trades with a principal value exceeding $300 billion over a three-year period, we have found that market impact costs varied randomly by about $0.01 per share and that commission costs have declined by about $0.005 per share.

Thus, on average, the cost of selling one security to buy another is 0.48% of the principal value of the trades. In an environment where the average aggregate turnover in NYSE-listed stocks can exceed 84% as occurred in 1987, trading is a significant cost of managing money. A portfolio with $100 million invested in equities could expect to incur transaction costs today of $405,211 with turnover rate of 84%.

Commission costs are the costs incurred for brokerage service. For transactions executed on the New York and American stock exchanges,

---

[1] Stephen Berkowitz, Dennis Logue, and Eugene Noser, "The Total Cost of Transactions on the NYSE," *Journal of Finance*, March 1988, pp. 97–112.

these costs are explicit. Where transactions involve bonds or stocks quoted on National Association of Securities Dealers Automated Quotation/National Market System (NASDAQ/NMS) that trade on over-the-counter markets, the commission is implicit and can only be estimated from inspection of the spreads between bids and offers on the day of the trade.

Market impact costs represent a price concession offered to execute a transaction on a timely basis. In theory, the difference between the equilibrium price of a security and the price at which the transaction executes may be characterized as a price concession. This is paid by sellers who execute below the equilibrium price and by buyers who execute above the equilibrium price.

The notion of an equilibrium price is a theoretical construct that allows us to contemplate a world with efficient markets in which all information that affects the value of each security is reflected in the security price. In the real world markets are not perfectly efficient, and we cannot observe directly the equilibrium price for a security.

As the major U.S. equity markets publish daily chronological listings of transactions (and make these data available), we can observe trading patterns. We can determine whether buy transactions made on behalf of a specific investor were executed at *relatively* high prices or sell transactions at *relatively* low prices.

Non-information-based traders who transact frequently should expect to receive execution prices approaching the average of prices observed during the day as weighted by the dollars traded at each price. We use this dollar-weighted average price as a standard. Deviations from this standard are characterized as either *trading costs* (buys in excess of the dollar-weighted average price and sells below the dollar-weighted average price) or *trading profits* (buys below the dollar-weighted average price and sells above the dollar-weighted average price). These trading costs and trading profits serve as a reasonable proxy for the theoretical notion of market impact.

TRANSACTING IN LISTED STOCKS

Transactions are typically initiated by the portfolio manager, either an internal manager (an employee of the sponsoring organization) or an external manager under contract to the sponsoring organization. When the manager places an order with a broker, the order and related instructions are recorded and time-stamped. The stationery and procedures for documenting this process are mandated by the SEC.

Instructions that accompany an order may constrain the broker with respect to the price at which the order is filled, the time available to fill the order, and the settlement terms. Typically, a manager will designate an order to be filled either at the market price or at some specified price (a limit order). In most circumstances, orders are submitted to be filled on a same-day basis.

When an external manager places an order, it could be on behalf of a single client or several clients. Figure 4.1 presents a buy order for 150,000 shares of American Telephone and Telegraph (AT&T) (symbol T) to be purchased on behalf of three clients. The forms that are maintained by brokerage firms enable us to follow this order through the trading process that results in a confirmed trade.

Dewey Square initiated the order with a limit of 22½ and later raised the limit by ⅛ to 22⅝. The broker charged the manager a commission of $0.02 per share for executing this transaction.

When the broker receives an order, any part of the order may be filled from inventory (a principal trade), may be held until an opposing order is found (a cross), or may be communicated to the floor of the stock exchange.

The order may reach the floor of the exchange through the Designated Order Turnaround system (known as the DOT system), which provides for electronic transmission of the orders to the specialist post. The specialist responds to these orders in the same way as to other orders arriving at his post. However, no floor brokerage commission will be charged on DOT market orders of up to 2,099 shares during the trading day or on preopening DOT orders of up to 10,099 shares. DOT currently has the capacity to transmit orders of up to 30,000 shares to the firm's booth for execution by a member.

The member may choose to execute an order or to have the order executed by an independent trader specializing in one or more securities. The physical size of the trading floor, which spans four rooms, makes the use of independent brokers an efficient way to execute orders. When a floor broker (or independent trader) has an order, it may be executed in a transaction with another broker or with the specialist. Specialists were party to transactions involving approximately 12.1% of the NYSE shares traded in 1987.

Although execution may be accomplished in a single transaction, block trades will more often require multiple transactions to execute. The order presented in Figure 4.1 was filled through multiple transactions throughout the day that resulted in 13 distinct prints on the NYSE tape. Transactions involving several participants may have been executed in a single print with the broker on one side of the trade conveying shares to fill standing orders from the book or from other brokers in the crowd.

FIGURE 4.1 A BUY ORDER FOR 150,000 SHARES OF AMERICAN TELEPHONE AND TELEGRAPH TO BE PURCHASED ON BEHALF OF THREE CLIENTS

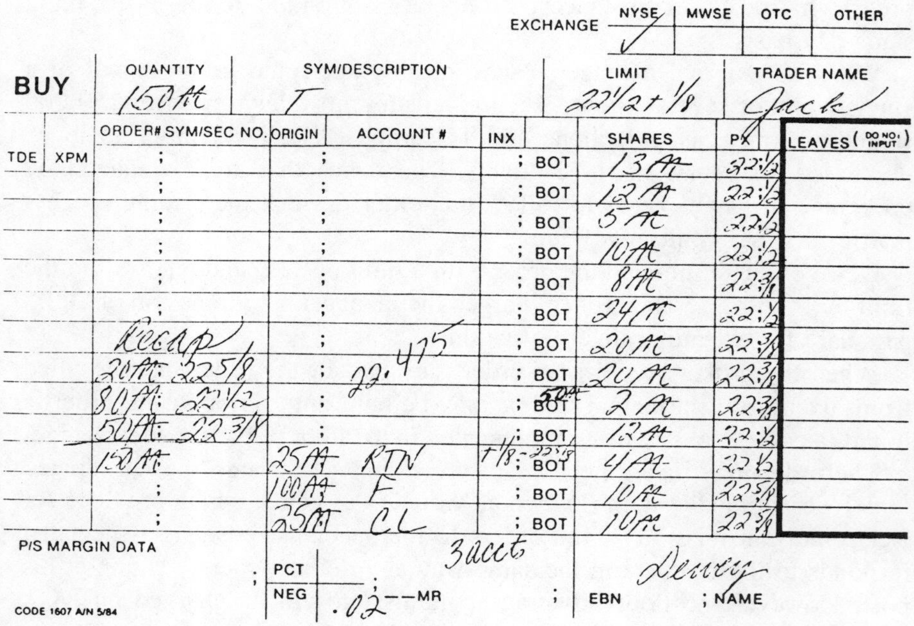

EXCHANGE	NYSE	MWSE	OTC	OTHER
	✓			

BUY	QUANTITY	SYM/DESCRIPTION		LIMIT	TRADER NAME
	150 At	T		22 1/2 t 1/8	Jack

TDE	XPM	ORDER# SYM/SEC NO.	ORIGIN	ACCOUNT #	INX		SHARES	PX	LEAVES (DO NO/INPUT)
		;	;		;	BOT	13 At	22 1/2	
		;	;		;	BOT	12 At	22 1/2	
		;	;		;	BOT	5 At	22 1/2	
		;	;		;	BOT	10 At	22 1/2	
		;	;		;	BOT	8 At	22 3/8	
		;	;		;	BOT	24 At	22 1/2	
		Recap	;		;	BOT	20 At	22 3/8	
		20 At: 22 5/8	;	22.475	;	BOT	20 At	22 3/8	
		80 At: 22 1/2	;		;	BOT	2 At	22 3/8	
		50 At: 22 3/8	;		;	BOT	12 At	22 1/2	
		150 At	25 At RTN		t 1/8 -- 22 5/8 ;	BOT	4 At	22 1/2	
		;	100 At F		;	BOT	10 At	22 3/8	
		;	25 At CL		;	BOT	10 At	22 3/8	

P/S MARGIN DATA

3 acts

PCT; NEG .02 --MR ; EBN ; NAME Dewey

CODE 1607 A/N 5/84

The 13 prints can be summarized by transaction price as follows: 20,000 shares purchased at 22⅝; 80,000 shares purchased at 22½, and 50,000 shares purchased at 22⅜. The price that is confirmed to the manager and ultimately to his three clients is the average of the 13 prints required to fill the order weighted by the principal amount of each print. Thus the manager and his clients will see only one price for this transaction—$22.475 per share (see Figure 4.2).

It is interesting to note that on October 7, 1986, AT&T opened at 22½ with a volume of 27,100 shares. Total volume for the day was 1,101,000 shares on the New York Stock Exchange and 344,000 shares on other domestic markets. The stock closed on the Pacific Coast Exchange at 4:05 P.M. Eastern Time (five minutes after the close in New York) at 22⅞ with a volume of 200 shares.

The dollar-weighted average price for the day was $22.583, with a high of $22.825 and a low of $22.375. Note that the stock closed at the day's high.

FIGURE 4.2 AVERAGE PRICE BILLING

AVERAGE_PRICE_BILLING

3	*But*	*T*	*22.475*
ROUND OUT	S OR B	SYMBOL	PRICE

NAME OF BANK, OR ADVISOR, OR CUSTOMER _____

NEG. _____ : SMT _____
(CENTS PER SHARE)   (ANY TRAILER TO PRINT ON CONFIRM – OPTIONAL)

QTY. EXECUTED	PRICE	ORIGIN	QTY EXECUTED	PRICE	ORIGIN
20 000	*22 5/8*	*NE*			
80 000	*22 1/2*	*NE*			
50 000	*22 3/8*	*NE*			

CUSTOMER ACCT. #	QUANT.	(NEG. TMR SMT) (OPTIONAL)	CUSTOMER ACCT. #	QUANT.	(NEG. TMR SMT) (OPTIONAL)
34006265	*25 000*				
34006221	*100 000*				
34006254	*25 000*				

The order we have been using as an example was confirmed to the buyers of the stock at \$22.475 per share. As the dollar-weighted average price for the day was \$22.583, the execution of this order resulted in a trading profit of \$0.108 per share, or \$16,200 for the entire order. This represents approximately 48 basis points of principal.

MARKET PATTERNS AND THE FAVORITE TRADE SYNDROME

It is tempting to characterize the quality of trading by experience with a single order. In the foregoing example, we might characterize the trading as excellent in that the buy order was filled at a price below the dollar-weighted average price for the day. However, in a trading environment where the trend in portfolio turnover has been increasing steadily over the decade, it is important not to succumb to this temptation. Rather, the quality of trading should focus on the pattern of executions achieved by traders over time.

To examine the pattern of executions, we used data provided by the State Street Bank and Trust Company. The bank provided transaction confirmation data for the equity managers of plans using State Street as master trustee. The data set contained 14,133 NYSE trades involving $3,167,541,933 of principal executed between January 9, 1985, and March 29, 1985. Subsequent measurements involving over $300 billion in principal were used to confirm the findings.

Recent evidence presented by Hasbrouck and Ho suggest that intraday returns (note that a return is merely a percent rate of change in prices) do not fluctuate randomly.[2] They follow a pattern that can be modeled as an autoregressive moving-average process. However, the levels of serial dependence are below the threshold required for a technical trading strategy to be profitable in a world with transaction costs.

Of equal importance in motivating dealer behavior is the Hasbrouck and Ho finding that buy and sell orders also are characterized by a pattern of serial dependence. Without entering the controversy as to whether security prices are generated randomly, it is sufficient to note that, for reasonably liquid securities, the market offers a variety of quotes and transacts at a variety of prices in each issue on each trading day. Thus, we would expect that over a large number of transactions, the deviations between the transaction price and the dollar-weighted average price would appear normally distributed.

If we look at the trading of institutional portfolios in the most liquid stocks by brokers with the largest levels of volume, we find that this expectation is confirmed. Commission costs range from only a few basis points to levels in excess of 100 basis points. Market impacts range from a trading profit approaching 300 basis points to a trading loss approaching 300 basis points of principal.

---

[2] Joel Hasbrouck and Thomas S. Ho, "Order Arrival, Quote Behavior, and the Return Generating Process," *Journal of Finance*, September 1987, pp. 1035–1048.

The plot of transaction costs associated with trades in the most liquid stocks by the brokers with the largest dollar volume of transactions is presented in Figure 4.3. The market impacts, expressed as a percentage of principal, appear on the vertical axis, and commission costs, expressed as a percentage of principal, appear on the horizontal axis.

FIGURE 4.3   PLOT OF MARKET IMPACT COSTS AND COMMISSION COSTS (STOCK SAMPLE: TOP 100 STOCKS; BROKER SAMPLE: TOP 10 BROKERS)

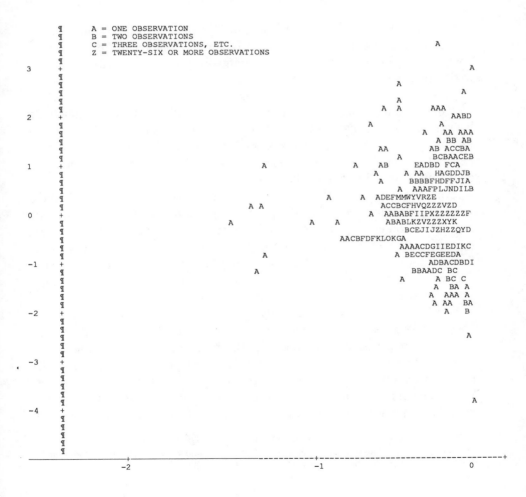

MARKET IMPACT COSTS (AS PERCENT OF PRINCIPAL)

For institutional transactions, market impacts appear (by inspection) to be distributed around a value that approaches zero. In aggregate for all NYSE-listed securities, trading profits will be offset by trading losses thereby creating a zero-sum game. For a large number of institutional trades selected at random, it is not surprising that market impacts approach zero, the level of the market in aggregate.

It is interesting to note that for institutional traders, the market is not quite a zero-sum game—in aggregate, market impacts will sum to a slight trading cost. This occurs because the specialist is privy to order flow information that is not generally available to other market participants. The advantage of the specialist places other market participants at a relative disadvantage. In aggregate, these other market participants incur costs equivalent to 5 basis points of principal resulting from their trades with the specialist.

Our study of market quality on the Toronto Stock Exchange (TSE) confirmed that granting information privileges to market makers results in costs to other market participants.[3] Specifically, we found that the registered trader (the TSE equivalent of the specialist) has a mean positive market impact of 44 basis points. Additional studies revealed that the dollar-weighted average market impact of registered traders was approximately 25 basis points per registered trade. Registered traders participated in approximately 26% of all trades. Consequently, other market participants could expect to incur, in aggregate, trading costs of 6 basis points per trade. This conforms to our findings for NYSE trades.

Commissions appear (by inspection) to be randomly distributed around a value approaching $0.10 per share. One explanation for the large variation in commission costs is the use of soft dollar arrangements. Under the terms of these arrangements, commissions are used to pay for research under Section 28(e) of the SEC act as amended. Outliers, commissions of greater than $0.30 per share, may represent odd lot orders or orders involving a small number of shares of stock.

Similar patterns, with a slightly wider range of market impacts, are observed for transactions in our sample involving brokers outside the top 10 by volume and stocks outside the top 100 by market capitalization.

The range of transaction costs by managed portfolio is substantially narrower than the range of transaction costs observed for individual trades. When the data presented in Figure 4.3 are sorted by manager, the managers with the 10 largest dollar volumes of transactions had total transaction costs

[3] Stephen Berkowitz, Louis Finney, and Dennis Logue, "Quality of Markets Provided on the Toronto Stock Exchange: A Comparison of Automated and Equity Trading," prepared for the chairman of the Toronto Stock Exchange, July 6, 1987.

ranging from $+4$ basis points to -62 basis points. Sorting these same transaction costs by broker yields a range of -91 basis points to -13 basis points.

When we sort the data provided by State Street into manager portfolios, we find that managers with high transaction costs during the first six weeks of the quarter are likely to experience high transaction costs during the second six weeks of the period as well. Similarly, managers with low transaction costs during the first six weeks are likely to experience low transaction costs during the second half of the quarter.

When we perform the same split-sample test with brokers, however, we find that the level of transaction costs observed during the first half of the quarter does not provide any insight into the level of transaction costs that we can expect in the second half of the quarter.

MANAGING THE TRADING PROCESS

The persistent transaction cost trends that we observe in managers were absent among brokers. This suggests that brokerage services may well be characterized as a commodity and that it is the manager who influences the success of the trading process.

Whenever a manager places an order with a broker, the broker receives a short-term option that expires when the order is filled. A broker, receiving an order prior to the market opening, may fill the order at the opening transaction. In this case the market order expires at the open with no particular advantage accruing to the broker.

If the order is a market order and the broker believes that better prices will be available during the day, perhaps none of the order or only part of the order will be executed at the open. If the broker receives an opposing order, thereby making possible a cross-transaction, the option implicit in the first order has generated two commissions.

Assume a broker who is willing to serve as a dealer receives a preopen order to buy at the market price. Later in the day he receives an order to sell at the market price, and the market bid price is $0.25 below the preopen offer price. The broker/dealer could either sell the stock short to fill the original buy order, or sell from inventory at the open and then use the sell order to restore his original position.

In both cases the option would generate not only two commissions, but also the spread between the bid price of the buyer and the offer price of the seller less the clearing cost of the broker/dealer (approximately $125 each for the buy and the sell transaction). The spread of $0.25 per share for a

5,000-share transaction is worth $1,250 to the broker. Broker/dealers can use more complicated transactions involving intraday options and futures positions to hedge broker inventory positions and capture a portion of the spreads between the NYSE and markets for derivative securities.

The diligent money manager can implement successful trading strategies. The success of a trading strategy is largely related to the ability of the manager to ensure that, at expiration, the economic value of options implicit in buy orders or sell orders conveyed to the broker, plus commission costs, is equal to the value of services received by the manager.

Brokers, even those who also act as dealers, must respond to instructions from the principals in a transaction. Thus, the manager can instruct the broker either to be sensitive to price while executing an order or to be sensitive to time while executing an order. By taking time to fill an order, the broker can expose the order to a variety of prices. If immediate execution is required, however, then the broker becomes a *price taker*. A manager may have dramatic impact on transaction costs in the following ways:

- Negotiate commission rates appropriate to the services the broker provides, alert to the fact that higher commission costs may not be offset by lower market impacts.

- Engage in comparative shopping to ensure that the soft dollar prices, as coupled with brokerage costs, do not materially exceed cash prices of services purchased independently.

- Appraise realistically the time required for the information that provides the rationale for urgency to be reflected in market prices to strengthen the negotiating position of the broker.

- Place orders to give brokers the opportunity to obtain as wide a distribution of prices as possible.

- Optimize ticket size with regard to (1) commission structure, (2) exposure to advantageous prices, and (3) the information value inherent in the order.

- Monitor executions to determine if there is a pattern of buying at the high for the day and selling at the low for the day.

Managing the trading process is a matter of common sense. Consider the extreme case of index funds that transact at prices set at the close of the day. This is designed to improve tracking, as indexes are usually priced at the close. However, closing prices were shown to be unrepresentative of the prices available during the day.[4] Moreover, closing transactions represent only 1.5% of the dollar volume of trading in a day.

In 1987 average market impact observed over 670,000 transactions with a principal value of $190 billion was $0.02 per share. For the subset of index fund trades, representing over 28,000 transactions with a principal value of over $4 billion, the average market impact was $0.22 per share. Index fund transactions were executed at an average commission rate of $0.04 per share, compared to $0.06 per share for the entire universe.

CONCLUSION

Transaction costs associated with trades in exchange-listed equity securities are significant and measurable. The data available to money managers and sponsors from transaction confirmations represent the disposition of orders each day rather than the execution of individual transactions. In monitoring transactions, therefore, we have to focus on the relationship between the price at which the order is executed and the prices available during the day.

Sensible trading strategies can improve performance. There appears to be little statistical difference in the ability of brokers to execute transactions. Some managers, however, exhibit a persistent ability to minimize transaction costs. The empirical evidence indicates that proper attention to the trading process can lower portfolio transaction costs.

The Editor Asks

Q *Your estimates of market impact are significantly lower than those of others who have attempted to measure market impact costs. What does this imply to you?*

A When we measure market impact costs, we are asking the following question of our data: "Is there a pattern of executions at prices that deviate from the price that summarizes the trades during the day?" This summary price is calculated as the average of the price of each trade as weighted by the dollar amount of the trade—the dollar-weighted average price.

[4] Robert A. Wood, Thomas H. McInish, and Keith Ord, "An Investigation of Transaction Data for NYSE Stocks," *Journal of Finance*, July 1985, pp. 723–739.

Other measures of market impact costs ask different questions of the data. In our view, other measures may have some theoretical interest. As a practical matter, however, market participants, in aggregate over the entire market, can expect executions equal to the dollar-weighted average price. Consequently, we monitor deviations from this benchmark.

PART THREE

How a Trade Works

5

PORTFOLIO MANAGER TO TRADER

Mark Edwards

In baseball, the phrase "Tinker to Evers to Chance" is recognized as one of the game's great double-play combinations. Through the co-ordination of individual action, reaction, and the confidence that each would do his part, this combination created a niche in baseball history. The same analogy holds true in the investment process. Success is a function of the analyst–manager–trader relationship and the ability of each to work toward a common goal. The analyst–manager relationship has been the traditional focus of attention. The investment process, however, extends beyond research. Implementation, the events leading up to and including trading, has as much impact on returns as does research, but has received much less attention. To manage the portfolio optimally, the manager needs to accept the responsibility for transaction costs and then learn to control them.

Relative performance is determined by the manager's ability to "add value" to a core style. By definition, the S&P 500 is a composite core of the money management universe, and is often used as the standard for comparison. In this case, value-added is the ability to pick stocks or sectors that will beat the S&P 500. Therefore, resources are weighted toward the research function. In Wilshire Associates' Trust Universe Comparison Service (TUCS) equity-only universe, the mean return from July 1982 to June 1987 was 28.7%.[1] The range for the 25th and the 75th percentiles was only ± 5.4%, surprisingly narrow for a period generally considered the most volatile in recent history; earlier studies reveal an even tighter range of

---

[1] Wilshire Associates, Trust Universe Comparison Service, Performance Review, 2Q, 1987. For the five years ending June 1985, the mean return was 16.1% with a standard deviation of 2.7%. The normalized spread between the 25th and 75th percentiles would be approximately + 1.8%.

returns. One may infer from the small difference in returns that the gain from additional research is commensurate neither with the cost nor with the effort that has been applied in the search for undervalued stocks.

Considerably fewer resources have been allocated toward understanding and controlling the implementation process. Previous studies estimate the explicit cost of transacting to be between 2% and 3% of principal on a round-trip basis (even greater if one includes opportunity costs).[2] Commissions and fees account for less than 0.5% of principal; market spread and impact constitute the remainder. Figure 5.1 graphically represents the potential impact that transaction costs have had on relative performance over those five years. Assuming a mean cost of 4%, a fund with 50% turnover would experience a shortfall of two percentage points. Over the same five-year period, the S&P 500, measured without the cost of transactions, realized a 29.9% compounded rate of return. To match the market, an average manager would need a return of almost 32% before costs. As turnover increases, the required ability to pick superior investments also increases. It's no wonder that, in bull markets, active management is universally maligned.

If the cost of transacting could be reduced 1% of principal, the average manager would no longer be average. In the TUCS comparison, the manager would move up to the 29th percentile; and, relative to the S&P, the manager would be able to show value-added. The potential return of reallocating a greater portion of attention toward implementation is obvious.

Control over transactions starts with understanding the role of trading in the investment process. With the understanding of the trading–investing relationship comes an understanding of why costs exist. Although some costs are an economic fact of life, others are variable and often can be controlled. Once the controllable costs are identified, the management process can proceed in a more profitable fashion.

---

[2] Explicit measurement has been conducted by various researchers using various methods, with one-way results ranging from 1% to 1.8%. See G. Beebower and R. Surz, "Analysis of Equity Trading Execution Costs," presented at the Seminar for Security Prices, November 1980; K. Condon, "Measuring Equity Transactions Costs," *Financial Analysts Journal,* September–October 1981; and H. Demsetz, "The Cost of Transacting," *Quarterly Journal of Economics,* February 1968. Implicit costs are based on estimates of impact that results in actual portfolio performance lagging paper results. See K. Ambachtsheer and J. Farrell, "Can Active Management Add Value?" *Financial Analysts Journal,* November–December 1979. Also, an unpublished study was conducted in 1987 by John Brush of Columbine Capital to determine the expected returns net of transactions for internal management. Based on Street estimates of the most likely concession necessary to ensure implementation, the expected cost approximated 5%.

FIGURE 5.1 POTENTIAL IMPACT OF TRANSACTION COSTS ON RELATIVE PERFORMANCE, 1982–1987

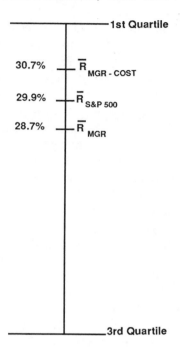

TRANSACTION COSTS/TRADING COSTS

One of the primary difficulties surrounding the discussion of transaction costs is that the investment community has adopted a perception of trading as an autonomous function. The epitome of this thinking is the description of trading as a zero-sum game.[3] Trading is compared to a poker game, with commissions as the house fees and the residual as either the gains or the losses of the participants. All of the participants are assumed to have a common time horizon and motivation, allowing expert traders to be identified by their consistent ability to win.

The key to the analogy lies in the caveat that the delineation of expertise holds if the trader is "unconstrained by investment directives."[4] In practice,

---

[3] Beebower and Surz, "Analysis of Equity Trading Execution Costs," pp. 2–3.
[4] Ibid.

trading is not an isolated function, but exists as part of the investment process. The true definition of expertise can be made only within the context of the entire process. Thomas Loeb has described the measurement process as "measur[ing] a combination of (1) the cost of using the market mechanism and (2) the behavior of the institutional trader."[5] Loeb continues: "[T]he real cost of trading, however, can be determined solely by the particularly market mechanism through which an institution transacts."[6] The trader's behavior is a reflection of the management process and should be measured as such. In the same way that management styles vary with respect to time horizons and objectives, so must trading desks. The trading game is not the investment game. Managers desiring liquidity may be required to pay a concession to ensure execution. Other managers providing liquidity may require price compensation before choosing to transact. In neither case are there necessarily gains or losses due to trading. The investment world is imperfect, fraught with inadequate time and exogenous influences. The game is dynamic, not static like poker, where the players need only to concentrate on their capital and their cards. Measurement should be similarly dynamic and adapted to the variables of transacting.

The idea of measuring the cost of trading is laudable. The trade process should be given the same scrutiny as any other input in the investment process. Beneficial analysis, however, needs to discriminate between costs attributable to trading (the market mechanism) and costs attributable to the management process (the trader's behavior).

WHY COSTS EXIST

Transactions do not always precisely match supply and demand. When an imbalance exists, either the buyer or the seller is forced to offer some price concession in order to complete the trade. Transaction costs are determined by the degree of concession. To determine why, where, and when costs occur, one needs to understand the components of a trade, the variability of each component, the relative contribution of each to overall costs, and how each component can be controlled.

COMMISSIONS.   Commissions are simply the cost of using a vendor to facilitate a trade. The institutional marketplace offers three options for

[5] T. Loeb, "Trading Cost: The Critical Link between Investment Information and Results," *Financial Analysts Journal*, May–June 1983, p. 39.
[6] Ibid.

trading: (1) trade directly with a broker (principal), (2) use the broker network to find another buy side transactor (agent), or (3) seek the other side directly. Commissions in the third option reflect the base cost of processing the trade, seldom exceeding a penny (or 0.025% of principal). The use of a broker requires either human or capital resources to enable timely facilitation. As agent, the broker seeks to compensate its labor; as principal, the broker seeks to hedge against adverse price risks. In either case, commissions at the institutional level are not likely to exceed 0.15% to 0.20% of principal, a relatively small component of trading costs.

THE SPREAD. The second cost component is the spread, the difference between the bid and the asked prices for simultaneous execution. The determinants of the spread are:

1. *Price:* The usual minimum spread for a listed stock is $0.125 either side of the last price, creating higher percentage spreads as prices drop.
2. *Volume:* The level of activity is an indication of trading competition. As competition increases, the spread decreases.
3. *Holding risk:* The fundamental beta. High betas require high spreads.
4. *Insider risk:* The risk that another transactor may have information that would have a significant impact on the stock price. An alternative definition is "information risk."
5. *Number of market-makers:* For competitive purposes, this is the depth of the broker–dealer network.[7]

Price and liquidity (volume and the number of dealers) are explicit (physical) spread determinants; the risk factors are implicit (psychological or experiential) spread determinants.

For each stock, there is a normal or base spread that reflects the consensus attitude toward the risk of immediate execution. Marginal buyers and sellers constantly adjust prices to minimize their risks while satisfying their desire to transact. Why and how quickly the normal spread changes is a function of the relative importance of each of the five determinants. The relative importance is, in turn, determined by the participants in the trade process.

MARKET IMPACT. The third and most significant component of transaction costs is market impact, the price movement beyond the base spread.

[7] G. Benston and R. Hagerman, "Risk, Volume and Spread," *Financial Analysts Journal,* January–February 1978, pp. 46–48.

Depending on the motive, transactors will determine an acceptable trade-off between time and liquidity. Market impact reflects an imbalance in the available supply or demand for stock within a given time horizon. When the desired transaction is more than the marketplace can accommodate, a new price will be found which gives additional participants an incentive to trade. Impact will be determined by the ability of the initiating transactor to reach a sufficient number of participants. The degree of price concession is proportional to the available time. As time is increased, the number of participants is potentially maximized and the spread is minimized; as time is decreased, additional risk compensation is required, commensurate with the participants' mutual perception of information risk.

THE RATIONAL TRADER

There are three general trading strategies in the marketplace. The choice of strategy and the resulting cost are determined by the participant's transaction motive. The first alternative is to "work" the trade and match time with liquidity. Although this option has the least impact, it also carries the highest degree of opportunity risk. Other transactors may enter the market and adversely move either the stock price and/or the entire market, requiring the decision either to (1) continue trading within the confines of the market, (2) step up and pay the price required to complete the trade, or (3) discontinue trading and create potential opportunity risk. The second alternative is to ascertain the level of available supply and demand and then offer a price that attracts other traders. The third alternative is to avoid the auction market altogether and, instead, negotiate directly with a dealer. A concession will be demanded, but the use of the dealer provides immediacy while reducing other competitive pressures.

Jack Treynor has identified and classified five participants according to their motives.[8] The two best known are the *information-based* and the *value-based* investor. A third participant is the *liquidity-based* investor, possessing neither information nor an opinion of specific value, and transacting primarily on the desire to effect changes in the characteristics of the underlying portfolio. The fourth participant, the *pseudo-information-based* investor, tends to behave as one privy to information with as yet unrealized

---

[8] J. Treynor, "Implementation of Strategy: Execution," in Maginn and Tuttle, eds., *Managing Investment Portfolios: A Dynamic Process* (Boston: Warren, Gorham and Lamont, 1983), pp. 27–34; W. Bagehot, "The Only Game in Town," *Financial Analysts Journal*, March–April 1971, p. 13; J. Treynor, "What Does It Take to Win the Trading Game?" *Financial Analysts Journal*, January–February 1981, pp. 55–60.

value but which, in fact, is either erroneous or already reflected in the price of the stock. The final participant, the *dealer*, has attributes encompassing each of the other participants at varying times. Usually, the dealer acts as a passive provider of liquidity, but in certain markets the dealer's actions are more typical of the information- or pseudo-information-based transactor.

Because the need for immediate liquidity is low, the value-based transactor would generally prefer to "work" a trade and minimize impact. Should prices move adversely and exceed acceptable norms, trading will be suspended until value is reestablished. Similarly, the liquidity-based transactor has little sensitivity to stock-specific information. Greater sensitivity to market or systematic risk, however, may result in time constraints and, consequently, higher costs.

The information-based transactor, conversely, has a rationale for incurring market impact. Because trades must be done quickly, a concession is usually required to ensure implementation. (By definition, pseudo-information-based transactors will act in a similar fashion.) Trading in the auction market, rather than requesting broker capital, would be the least costly route. Within the investment community, opinions of value are extremely divergent, resulting in the probability of a low-cost trading counterpart somewhere in the system. The perception of immediacy, however, often precludes the willingness to seek the least costly trading partner. To guarantee implementation, the trading partner of preference has become the broker/dealer.

The dealer acts in a dual capacity. The primary role is as a market functionary, using capital to intermediate when excessive auction spreads discourage trading. Position risks are reduced by both the broker's ability to find a suitable trading partner quickly and by the ability to absorb short-term positions into inventory. The dealer may also act as an active investor, adjusting inventories to reflect existing positions and expectations. If forced to initiate trades to adjust inventory, the dealer will often be captive to the auction spread. Conversely, when responding to requests for liquidity, the incentive is to maximize the acceptable spread.[9]

When facilitating immediacy, the dealer must be careful. Couched within the request for dealer capital is a de facto admission that time is of the essence—that is, that the requesting party has information to exploit. If the dealer's risk premium is too low, a loss may result when the position is reversed. If the premium is too large, the trade may not occur and/or ill

---

[9] For a discussion of the spread when the dealer takes an initiating role, see J. Treynor, "The Economics of the Dealer Function," *Financial Analysts Journal,* November–December 1987.

feelings by the customer may jeopardize future business. Adding to the dealer's dilemma is a communication gap that has developed between the buy side and the Street.[10] Without knowledge of the motive to trade, the full extent of risk is unknowable. Even with knowledge, positioning is risky. Regardless of transactor type, the relevance of information and the potential impact on supply and demand require prudent risk assumptions.

The dealer cannot consistently decide whose information is valid or what the impact on liquidity will be. The prudent response, then, is to do what an insurance company does and allocate costs over the entire customer base. Ideally, spreads would reflect each transactor's motive and liquidity. In lieu of the ability to discriminate between motives, the dealer is forced to create uniform spreads relative to volume that reflect neither motive nor true economic impact.[11] The irony of this situation is that the information-based transactor may be trading with a lower spread in the dealer network than would be available in the auction market. Immediacy requires a cost, and the auction market tends to extract a fair cost with respect to time constraints. By utilizing the dealer network, where risks are shared, the trader with the largest potential reward is compensated by all other users of dealer capital. Pogo was right when he said, "We have met the enemy, and they is us."

THE MANAGER'S IMPACT

Although transaction costs have been studied for over two decades,[12] they have only recently become a hot topic in the plan sponsor and portfolio management communities. The interest by plan sponsors is in response to the previously mentioned performance shortfall, amplified by discount broker claims that non-research-oriented commissions paid to primary dealers are not justified by trading performance. Use of a discount broker is theoretically justified as a cost-saving practice, both with respect to

---

[10] "The Buyside–Sellside Relationship: Assessments and Predictions," *Institutional Investor Trader Forum*, 1987. Respondents to a survey emphasized the deteriorating relationship within the trading community. The underlying issue was the communications breakdown that has developed as a result of a mutual lack of trust.

[11] Loeb, "Trading Cost," pp. 41–42. The normal spread tends to remain relatively fixed once a median capitalization level is achieved. The drop in percentage costs corresponds directly with an increase in the average price. Loeb's observation of spread cost with respect to market capitalization and block size reveals an almost linear relationship, rather than the logarithmic relationship expected as a result of relative liquidity changes.

[12] Demsetz, "The Cost of Transacting"; C. Ellis, *Institutional Investing* (Homewood, Ill.: Dow Jones–Irwin, 1971), pp. 34–53; Bagehot, "The Only Game in Town"; see also Chapter 2, "A Sponsor Looks at Trading Costs," by Robert E. Shultz.

returns and via rebated commissions. In fact, there is reason to believe that overall commission reductions brought on by the discounters' claims have actually hurt performance—a subject addressed later in the chapter.

The managers' interest is based on fear: Inadequate returns from active management have led to a loss of market share to passively managed index funds. The problem is considered a trading problem, not a procedural problem. Therefore, to protect business, managers have been forced to take an active interest in trading, an area previously considered off limits. In reality, the trading community understands and has adjusted to transactional difficulties in an economic and rational fashion. The problem is not in trading, but in management.

Although the portfolio manager's primary responsibility is often the value and the timeliness of a research idea, interest must extend also to the trading desk, or the underlying rationale will be at risk. As a process, investment may begin with research, but the end cannot occur until the security is sold and the proceeds collected—if then. The proper implementation of a trade is as essential as stock selection and timing.

The trader's behavior, and the resulting transaction cost, must directly reflect the manager's transaction motive. The motive determines how much to transact, how quickly to transact, and with what acceptable concession. The only cost components not de facto determined by the motive are the initial stock price and the number of available dealers. When the trader's actions are inconsistent with the actual rationale for the trade, unnecessary costs are created, and performance suffers. Efficient and effective trading requires that the trader and the manager act as one.

THE SUCCESSFUL COMBINATION

The "Tinker to Evers to Chance" analogy is arguably unfair. Reaction in baseball is a function of practice, and the number of practical options in a given situation is limited. Not so in investing. There is no right or wrong way to invest; one acts in response to one's perception of what is required for each particular fund. In lieu of universal rules, benchmarks need to be established to serve as guides for the manager to identify which actions or perceptions actually add value. Change is good when it corrects an undesirable route. Change without direction only results in costly mistakes as one emotional action is reversed by an equally emotional reaction.

Because styles can and do vary, consistency of process is extremely important. Occasionally, every management style is out of sync with the market, either in stock selection or in timing. The winning manager is the one who accepts these periods as unavoidable, to be viewed as an opportunity to learn or to take a vacation from the market—both routes have been highly recommended. What the manager should *not* do is to change to a currently successful style. Reorienting one's stock selection process is extremely difficult, and the risk is compounded by a potentially mismatched trading style. Excessive transaction costs combined with an unfamiliar or uncomfortable style are humbling to the manager and, more important, potentially costly to the client.

KNOW THYSELF

Control over transaction costs means the ability to distinguish between a necessary input and an unnecessary impact. Where and how a transaction takes place determine the cost and are, in turn, justified by the underlying rationale for the trade. The rationale itself is determined by the manager's investment philosophy and style. To "know thyself," the manager must understand what makes a particular management style both unique and valuable.

The holding period, the time required to realize the expected return, is the crucial variable that binds the investment and the trading styles. Although each investment has a distinct but indeterminate holding period, portfolios tend to reveal patterns over time. A value-oriented manager may require years before maximum value is realized from a particular holding. Conversely, an information-based manager may have a time horizon measured in weeks or even days, depending on the theme or situation.

Liquidity concession, the trade-off between time and available market supply and demand, is determined by the holding period. As a cost, it is amortized over the life of a holding. Consequently, the longer the holding period, the smaller the cost and the higher the acceptable concession. Because immediacy is low for long-term investments, the ability to absorb additional spread may present the long-horizon manager with attractive opportunities in the "illiquid" universe. Though not confined to this universe, the manager may find sources of excess return due to the ability to transact on favorable terms.[13] As the holding period shrinks, so does the

---

[13] The "small cap" effect as discussed by M. Reinganum ("Misspecification of Capital Asset Pricing: Empirical Anomalies Based on Earnings, Yields and Market Values," *Journal of Financial Economics,* March 1981) has been the subject of a variety of subsequent analyses to explain the phenomenon. With respect to this paper, see Y. Amihud and H. Mendelson, "Liquidity and Stock Returns," *Financial Analysts Journal,* May–June 1986, pp. 43–47, describing the effect of the holding period on expected returns.

ability to spread costs, forcing the manager to become more liquidity-conscious. The practical universe is reduced to an institutionally efficient core, and illiquid investments require significantly higher returns in order to offset the spread concession.

The importance of the holding period on the available universe and on return expectations is not well accepted by institutional managers. A common error is mismatching, resulting in costs inconsistent with expectations. Managers need to understand what they do, develop a process compatible with their style, and then implement that process in a consistent fashion to prevent mismatching of the investment horizon and trading horizon.

AM I WHO I THINK I AM?

In recent years, benchmark portfolios have become an accepted reference for a manager's stock selection.[14] With respect to a given orientation, however, there are a variety of styles, which allows each manager to add value. Just as a benchmark portfolio provides the manager with an asset reference, a transaction benchmark needs to be established to provide a reference both for the investment rationale and for the implementation of that rationale.

Table 5.1 presents a comparison of four managers used by the state of Minnesota.[15] Although two primary orientations, growth and value, are represented, each manager reveals a distinctive style, which would not necessarily be revealed in a benchmark portfolio. Three critical variables are used to identify the firm's style: holding period, relative liquidity, and information sensitivity. Other variables may be equally applicable; the key requirement is an objective nature and sufficient history to allow comparison over time. The category definitions are:

1. *Turnover:* Annualized, using quarterly transaction data.
2. *Average holding period:* The inverse of turnover adjusted for cash.
3. *Relative liquidity:* The average market capitalization relative to the Wilshire 5000, divided by the average daily trading volume per

---

[14] Most commonly associated with the concept of benchmark portfolios is Barr Rosenberg, e.g., "The Capital Asset Pricing Model and the Market Model," *Journal of Portfolio Management,* Winter 1981, pp. 5–16. See also J. Bailey, "Benchmark Portfolios and the Manager/Plan Sponsor Relationship," unpublished, 1988.

[15] The analysis covers portfolio and trade data from January 1984 through June 1987.

TABLE 5.1   MANAGER STYLE AND TRADING STYLE

	GROWTH 1	GROWTH 2	VALUE 1	VALUE 2
Turnover (%)	114.30%	47.20%	46.00%	235.00%
Holding period (months)	10.50	25.30	26.00	5.20
Relative liquidity	3.07	2.99	0.56	0.79
Impact (%)	0.37%	−0.25%	−0.01%	0.05%
20-day (%)	−1.09%	1.21%	−1.44%	0.79%

position. A number above 1 can be considered a fair approximation of relative liquidity.

4. *Impact:* An estimated measure of price movement created by the trader's presence in the market. This number is net of commissions and is adjusted for market activity.[16] High levels of information sensitivity should be reflected in medium to high impact costs and low levels of sensitivity reflected in low to negative impact costs. However, reduced liquidity or holding period decreases may be reflected in increased costs.

5. *Twenty-day return:* The price change 20 days after the trade is completed. Both buys followed by price increases and sales followed by price decreases are given positive values, reflecting value-added in the timeliness of the transaction.

Although interpretation of the data is dependent on the manager's stated objectives, the table should provide clues to the following:

Is the observed holding period consistent with the assumed style? Are the stock selections consistent with the holding period and the fund size? Is the trading impact consistent with the motive and the relative liquidity?

Most important, are these observations complementary or do they reveal conflicts in style and perception, both by the manager and by the trading desk?

An example of comparative analysis follows.

GROWTH. The emphasis is on above-average capitalization with consensus expectations of above-average growth. GROWTH 1 is a

---

[16] SEI Evaluation Services. There are a variety of trading evaluation services available, each with its own respective merits and flaws. The key observation is the direction and the magnitude of the measurement relative to investment style.

cyclically oriented manager, utilizing extensive in-house research to seek unexploited stocks. Turnover is relatively high, reflecting a perception of timeliness when investing. Trading is often triggered by opportunistic price moves, but the trader's influence on supply or demand results in price reversals. Positions are relatively liquid, so impact appears to be due to a perception of timeliness. However, the negative posttrade returns would suggest that immediacy may be unwarranted.

GROWTH 2 is secularly oriented, as reflected in the longer holding period. Trading often occurs once a price trend is established, but relatively passive trading combined with sufficient liquidity virtually eliminates measurable impact. The 20-day results suggest that excess value is captured by the manager's timing. Although both portfolios usually have similar sector and even stock concentrations, over the measurement period, GROWTH 2's annual compound rate of return exceeds that of GROWTH 1 by over 3 percentage points.

VALUE.   The two value managers concentrate on stocks with below-average consensus growth expectations and above-average value character-istics. Although the representative portfolios may reveal similar characteristics, the management styles are extremely dissimilar. VALUE 1 is a traditional value manager, both in holding period and in the willingness to take very specific individual stock bets. Though still a concern, the impact of illiquidity is offset by the relatively long holding period. Another offset is the tendency of this manager to buy into weakness and to sell into strength, as noted in the 20-day returns. ''Premature'' trading, a trait endemic to long-term value managers, usually results in opportunity costs that rival the potential impact of more timely transactions. In this case, it is extremely important to resist any liquidity concession deemed necessary to ensure implementation. There is, apparently, always another opportunity.

VALUE 2 is a short-term contrarian; although stock selection features relative value consistent with market underperformers, implementation is triggered by excessive market overreaction. In this case, the manager is able to use illiquidity as a bargaining chip in exchange for a price concession. For both managers, the measured impact is overstated. Price concessions in the manager's favor are often realized immediately prior to initiating the trade, but price reversals often lag in out-of-favor stocks. VALUE 2 does seem to be able to exploit trading opportunities very well, whereas VALUE 1 may want to become more spread conscious before transacting.

Once each contributor in the investment process is able to ''know thyself,'' he must learn to ''know each other.'' The double-play combination was Tinker to Evers to Chance, each planning his actions contingent on his knowledge of what the others were doing.[17] In this respect, investing is the same. Because the process involves interdependent decision making, communication is essential.

Interaction by each participant in the process is a mutually beneficial exercise. As the participant involved with the day-to-day realities of the marketplace, the trader is a valuable source of research information. Often, the dilemma of information validity can be resolved by listening to Street gossip or by analyzing the trade tapes for unusual volume or spread changes. When time or liquidity is a concern, the knowledge of pending trades can aid the trader in determining the most efficient potential market. Because the trade process begins long before the trade is submitted, the manager may want to elicit feedback from the trader as part of the decision process. The marketplace ultimately determines practical position limits, and the trader should provide estimates and insights with respect to both liquidity and timeliness.

NONMANAGER COST INFLUENCES

Transaction costs are not always reflective of the investment process; they may instead be a result of indirect pressures that have an impact on management decisions. Within the management firm certain structural barriers may exist. A primary barrier is organizational—either a cultural barrier, resulting in a "Chinese Wall" between managers and traders, or the adherence to an "investment committee" structure that restricts the free flow of information. Although these barriers are surmountable, they present risks to the delicate balance between research and implementation.

Outside the firm, costs are influenced by the plan sponsor's intervention in either commission allocation or commission levels. Historically, directed commissions for research purposes were considered necessary, and any related transaction costs were considered unavoidable. In recent years, the question of the cost of trading compared to the value of Street research has led to increased emphasis on execution ability to maintain market share. At the same time, the use of designated "soft dollar" brokers has proliferated as a means for plan sponsors to reduce overhead through commission rebates. As with Street research, the benefits of this relationship may not

---

[17] Joe Tinker, Johnny Evers, and Frank Chance played for the Chicago Cubs from 1905 to 1909. Of note is that Tinker and Evers had to be forcibly separated following an incident in 1906, and seldom spoke with each other thereafter. Regardless, their on-field behavior suggested a far greater degree of communication than would be expected. If investment behavior was as well integrated, there obviously would be no need for this chapter.

justify the costs, especially at the manager level. A 1985 study by Gilbert Beebower and colleagues concluded that the trading impact by the soft dollar brokers was understated because of the average level of liquidity per position traded relative to Street firms.[18] Beebower's premise was that the rational trader would designate only the most liquid trades to soft dollar brokers in order to minimize potential costs. The effect of this liquidity skimming is a residual with increased risk for facilitating brokers, accompanied by higher spreads.

Compounding the situation is the recent thrust toward commission reduction. Prior to deregulation, commissions provided a profit source for principal positions. Reducing commissions has forced the broker to reallocate risk back to the customer. Unfortunately, this has led to the phenomenon of risk sharing. Increased pressures on commissions by plan sponsors have a balloon effect: When one end—the commission—is squeezed, the other end—the spread—expands. The problem is that squeezing is done in pennies, but the expansion occurs in the spread, which moves in eighths. Not only are costs not reduced, they are likely to be increased. Pogo's words are echoed.

CONCLUSION

Transaction costs are widely viewed as a trading problem. However, transactions are the culmination of the entire analysis–management–implementation trilogy. All the steps are interdependent, and none must be viewed as separate. Trading costs are a reflection of the economics of the marketplace. Transaction costs occur when the desire to trade exceeds the economic limits.

The analysis–management relationship is defined by the investment philosophy of a manager or a firm. The management–implementation relationship is defined by the manager's style, the mutual perception of the motivation to trade. Certain philosophies and styles require costs to be incurred to ensure implementation, and the imposition of trading constraints may result in suboptimal returns. It is in the manager's best interest to develop benchmarks that reflect both the investment philosophy and the style. Optimal management calls for the ability to monitor the investment process against a reference point, both to ensure consistency and to allow concentration on value-adding areas. The philosophy and the style must be

---

[18] G. Beebower, R. Surz, and V. Kamath, "Commission and Transaction Costs of Stock Market Trading," SEI Corporation Study, July 1985.

complementary, and so must be the benchmarks. Any change reflected in a benchmark must be reviewed with respect to the whole process to avoid unnecessary costs.

Finally, nonmanagerial influences on the investment process must be minimized if optimal results are to be achieved. The manager who fails to acknowledge the need to integrate and to monitor implementation jeopardizes future returns and, consequently, future business. When the ability to implement is exogenously impeded, returns suffer despite the manager's abilities. The choice, however, should be up to the manager.

The Editor Asks

Q *A trader spends most of his day, day after day, talking on the telephone to the Street. He develops strong personal relationships and a trust and dependency on the Street to fill his needs. You argue very convincingly that he should pay more attention to what his managers are saying, yet a wide gap exists between the portfolio manager and the trader on an intellectual, a communication, and a cultural dimension. In practical, day-to-day terms, what would you suggest be done to narrow this gap between trader and portfolio manager?*

A The gap that exists is neither intellectual nor cultural; rather, it is perceptual. It appears that roles are often assigned each participant in the investment process, defining what is expected and protecting all from overall performance responsibility. Unfortunately, a well-designed organization may result in a disjointed investment process. Barriers have been created and must subsequently be eliminated if the communication gap is to be bridged.

The firm can help by modifying the performance barrier. Distinct responsibilities and objectives may contribute to expectations, both by the firm and by the individual, but they do not necessarily contribute to returns. Because each job is mutually dependent, performance must be oriented toward a common objective. If any participant is not contributing or is acting askew, it is the responsibility of the other participants to reorient that individual before returns are affected. Similarly, the firm should recognize this mutuality and deemphasize mismatched orientations.

Within the performance barrier there is a time barrier. The portfolio manager and the trader are often viewed as operating with dissimilar time horizons and judged accordingly. The rationale for transacting, however, has a distinct (albeit fuzzy and occasionally incorrect) horizon, and trading should be handled accordingly. Differences need to be reconciled to accommodate the investment objective, not the performance objective.

At the individual level, the perception group is addressed through "know-one-another." In a growing number of firms, either the portfolio manager is also the trader or the trader serves as a co-manager. In either case, there are no gaps. Each participant understands the overall objective and operates accordingly. Most firms, however, maintain the traditional structure of separate roles. In these cases perceptions and expectations must be mutually understood, and differences reconciled. The trader must be integrated into the analyst–portfolio manager link, both to understand the investment objective and to provide a rational sense of the market. Similarly, the portfolio manager needs to become an active participant on the desk, providing input and feedback when pertinent.

Finally, the portfolio manager and the trader should make a practice of reviewing all transactions on both an a priori and a post hoc basis. The a priori analysis should include the trade rationale, prevailing market conditions, relative liquidity, and any potential events that could affect relative price performance. The post hoc analysis should focus on how the trade was conducted relative to the a priori discussion and actual market conditions. Transactions are neither homogeneous nor solely a function of trading, and reviews must consider both execution and expectations. Through a trader–portfolio manager alliance, performance should improve and the communication gap disappear.

6

TRADER TO BROKER

Stanley S. Abel
Eugene A. Noser, Jr.

Professionally managed investment portfolios as a class have not outper-formed the S&P 500 average. There is general agreement that trading costs are the reason overall performance of all professionally managed portfolios lags the S&P 500.

The reduction of trading costs has become the number one concern of both pension plan sponsors and the senior executives of the largest investment management companies. They now realize that the only way large organizations can outperform the S&P 500 is through superior trading.

Investment management company traders control their firms' daily trading activity. The decisions these professionals make largely determine the quality of the trading their clients will receive. If they miss the right price on only 15,000 shares of stock by one-quarter of a point, they will lose the total pension of one pensioner for one year. This illustrates in human terms how large the buy-side trader's responsibility is.

The major decisions a management company (buy-side) trader makes are:

1. When to place the order.
2. How many shares to place at one time.
3. Type of order to place.
4. Broker to use.
5. Time frame in which to execute the order.

WHEN TO PLACE THE ORDER

We will use the term *order* to mean the entire amount of one stock to be purchased or sold through one broker on one day. The market is open from

9:30 A.M. to 4 P.M. Eastern Time. (There is some overnight trading worldwide, but it is minimal.)

The average daily range of all stocks, from low to high, was 2.23% in 1986. Therefore, the time of order entry during the day plays a great part in the cost of the execution received. The most prudent way to enter orders is before the market opening, with the execution taking place throughout the trading day. If orders are not placed before the opening, part of the day's trading is missed and there is less opportunity for a good trade.

Occasionally, when traders believe they have information that will influence stock price movement almost immediately, they may attempt to time the order placement. In today's climate of volatile program trading and international computer-connected markets, this is a very challenging procedure. When and how the management company trader places the order largely determines the execution he will receive.

THE NUMBER OF SHARES PLACED AT ONE TIME

Should the management company trader open up to a stockbroker, informing the broker/dealer company of the entire intention (program) to buy or sell sometimes massive positions over days or weeks, or should he parcel smaller orders to different brokers in turn, in order to keep his plans confidential? Trading data from the third quarter of 1987, as shown in Table 6.1, demonstrate that 60.2% of all dollars traded in NYSE-listed companies occurs in the largest 200 companies, 84.9% of trading occurs in the largest 500 companies, 76.3% of trading occurs in trade sizes of 25,000 or less, and

TABLE 6.1   CROSS-TABULATION OF MARKET CAPITALIZATION BY SHARES PER TRADE, THIRD QUARTER 1987 (IN PERCENTAGE OF TOTAL DOLLARS TRADED)

Shares	1–10,000	10,001–25,000	25,001–100,000	100,001 and over	Totals	Cumulative
Top 100 Market Capitalization:	27.9	6.0	6.3	2.9	43	43.1
Second 100:	10.1	2.7	3.0	1.4	17.1	60.2
Next 300:	14.0	4.1	4.3	2.2	24.7	84.9
Next 500:	6.3	1.7	1.7	0.7	10.4	95.3
All Others:	2.6	0.8	1.0	0.4	4.7	100%
Totals:	61.0	15.3	16.2	7.5		
Cumulative:	61.0	76.3	92.5	100.0%		

Source: Francis Emory Fitch, Inc.

FIGURE 6.1   NYSE TRADING BY MARKET CAPITALIZATION

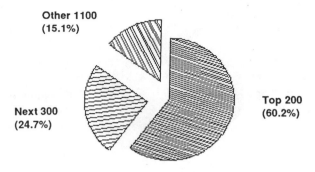

92.5% of trading occurs in trades of 100,000 shares or less. These data are practically identical to similar data for the first quarter of 1985 taken from the Department of Labor study of ERISA plans, proving that trading by share size and market capitalization is remarkably stable over time.

In spite of all the publicity concerning large block trades, only 7.5% of the dollars traded in NYSE stocks occurs in the superblock size of 100,001 shares or more.

From Table 6.1 showing trading in NYSE-listed stocks, we can derive Figure 6.1 showing trading by market capitalization, and Figure 6.2 showing trading by share size.

These two figures make it clear that buy-side traders are careful about the amount of information given and trading done by one broker at one time. This is a wise precaution because information concerning large potential trades gives the broker/dealers a free option to use such information for their own purposes.

FIGURE 6.2   PERCENTAGE OF DOLLARS TRADED IN NYSE STOCKS BY SHARE SIZE

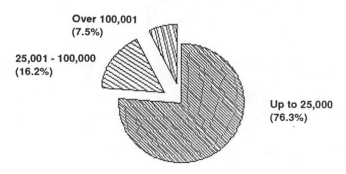

FIGURE 6.3   WHO IS ON THE OTHER SIDE OF YOUR TRADES?

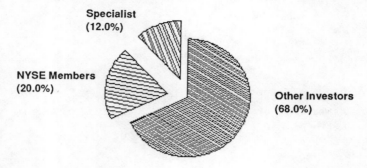

A *Pension and Investment Age* article in the issue of December 14, 1987, entitled "Front Running Assailed," found that over 50% of institutional traders and 40% of brokers considered *front running*—that is, the misuse of information on pending trade—to be a problem. Front running occurs when a broker who has advance knowledge of a trade positions himself so that he may benefit from that trade at the expense of his client.

The December 1987 issue of *Institutional Investor* features an article on front-running research recommendations entitled "Drawing the Line on Front Running." It warns managers that it is possible to front-run the broker's published research reports.

Data taken from the 1987 *New York Stock Exchange Fact Book* show that members of the NYSE are on the other side of the management company trades 32% of the time (see Figure 6.3).

Fortune recently revealed that the return on capital of one of the five largest specialist firms varied from 34% to 95% over a five-year period.

FIGURE 6.4   NYSE MEMBER INCOME, 1986

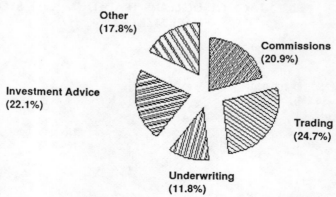

Trading System Technology stated on March 14, 1988, that one large broker was making 30% to 40% return for its firm on capital using a proprietary trading system. Figure 6.4, compiled from the *New York Stock Exchange Fact Book,* shows that trading revenue of members was 27.4% of income versus 20.9% for commissions in 1986.

A study commissioned by the Toronto Stock Exchange showed that market intermediaries make 48 basis points on average when they buy and 38 basis points when they sell. This evidence warns the prudent buy-side trader to follow President Reagan's arms-control maxim, ''Trust but verify,'' when placing orders. The safest method of trading is to give as little information to the broker as possible. This will help prevent front running.

TYPES OF ORDERS AND RELATED TRADING TERMS

The manager/trader uses a wide variety of instructions in placing orders to accomplish his purposes. Following is a list of some of the types of orders and terms traders use to control their brokers.

All or None (AON).   Execute the entire order or none of it within the price limit, if any. (It does not have to be the same price.) It does not have to be executed immediately, and it has no standing on the book.

Book.   Specialist book that maintains precedence of orders waiting for execution.

Cap Order.   A percentage of volume order with instructions to participate if possible as sales take place. This order cannot initiate any sales, and it may not be possible to participate in all sales.

Clean or Do Nothing (Cross-Clean).   Try to cross stock without losing any to other buyers or sellers, or else do nothing.

Cross.   To buy and sell equal amounts of the same stock at the same price.

Day Order.   An order to buy or sell, which, if not executed, expires at the end of the trading day on which it was entered. All orders are assumed to be day orders unless otherwise instructed.

Do It Away.   Execute the entire order in another marketplace, usually another Exchange.

Fill or Kill (FOK).   Execute an order in its entirety immediately, or cancel.

Give Up.   A term with many different meanings. For one, a member of the Exchange on the floor may act for a second member by executing an order for him with a third member. The first member tells the third member that he is acting on behalf of the second member and "gives up" the second member's name rather than his own. All independent (two-dollar) brokers give up the names of other members when acting as their agents.

Go Along.   Try to participate in sales as they occur but not to initiate them.

Good 'Til Canceled Order (GTC) or Open Order.   An order to buy or sell that remains in effect until it is either executed or canceled.

Held Order.   Order that must be executed as trades take place.

Hit the Bid.   Sell what you can at the prevailing bid up to the total amount of the order.

Immediate or Cancel (IOC).   An order to be executed immediately or else canceled. *Note:* Part of the order may be executed and the balance canceled on an IOC.

In Line/In Here.   Execute within the current quote (within quotation based on issue spread).

In Line or Work.   Execute the entire order within the current quote or work not held.

In Touch With (ITW).   Do not have a working order, but the trader does know that a particular account has an interest and should be shown any situations.

Leaves.   The unexecuted balance of an order.

Limit, Limited Order, or Limited Price Order.   An order to buy or sell a stated amount of a security at a specified price, or at a better price, if obtainable after the order is represented in the trading crowd.

Liquidity.   The ability of the market in a particular security to absorb a reasonable amount of buying or selling at reasonable price changes. Liquidity is one of the most important characteristics of a good market.

Lose Stock. Has three different interpretations for different situations:

1. "O.K. to sell stock."
2. When putting up a print, the statement "O.K. to lose stock" would refer to allowing a buyer or seller on the floor to participate on our print, resulting in our losing part of the buy or sell side of the trade to the floor.
3. If we have a position on a trade, the trader handling the trade might say "O.K. to lose stock," meaning that if someone comes in after the trade he may then take over our position.

Manipulation. An illegal operation. Buying or selling a security for the purpose of creating a false or misleading appearance of active trading or for the purpose of raising or depressing the price to induce purchase or sale by others.

(Market) Coming In. Prices dropping (bear market).

(Market) Coming On. Prices moving up (bullish market).

Market On Close (MOC). Execute on the close or as near to the last sales as possible, but it is not guaranteed the last sale.

Market Order. An order to buy or sell a stated amount of a security at the most advantageous price obtainable after the order is presented in the trading crowd.

Market Price. The last reported price at which the stock or bond sold or the current quote.

Match. Participating in sales with the book or another broker or brokers.

Minimum Lots. Volume restrictions set by traders specifying one time or continuous minimum lots—that is, minimum of 1,000 to start, lots of 1,000, and so on.

Natural Buyer/Seller. Customers on both sides of a cross-trade; or, agent transactions—natural interest as opposed to specialist (for principal) interest.

Not Held. Broker will not be held to sales on the tape; it is O.K. to "work" the order.

Odd Lot.   An amount of stock less than the established 100-share unit or 10-share unit of trading: from 1 to 99 shares for the great majority of issues, 1 to 9 for certain inactive stocks.

Off-Board.   This term may refer to over-the-counter transactions in unlisted securities, or to a transaction of listed shares that is not executed on a national securities exchange.

Offer.   The price at which a person is ready to sell, as opposed to *bid,* the price at which someone is ready to buy.

On Print Only.   Execute only if a large block trades, usually of a specified size; the order has no standing (no position on the book).

Opening Only.   The order is to be executed on the opening sale only and, if not, is canceled.

Over-the-Counter.   A market for securities made up of securities dealers who may or may not be members of a securities exchange. The over-the-counter market is conducted over the telephone and deals mainly with stocks of companies without sufficient shares, stockholders, or earnings to warrant listing on an exchange. Over-the counter dealers may act either as principals or as brokers for customers. The over-the-counter market is the principal market for bonds of all types.

Participate Do Not Initiate.   Do not initiate a trade, only go along if it trades.

Positioning.   Refers to the act of going long or short for a firm account— that is, taking the other side of the customer's trade.

Primary Distribution.   The original sale of a company's securities; also called *primary* or *public offering*.

Pull Back.   Withdraw from the current bid or offer.

Quote.   The highest bid to buy and the lowest offer to sell a security in a given market at a given time. If you ask your broker for a "quote" on a stock, he may come back with something like "25¼ to 25½." This means that $25.25 is the highest price any buyer wanted to pay at the time the quote was given on the floor of the Exchange and that $25.50 was the lowest price which any seller would take at the same time.

Round Lot. A unit of trading or a multiple thereof. On the New York Stock Exchange the unit of trading is generally 100 shares in stocks and $1,000 or $5,000 par value in the case of bonds. In some inactive stocks, the unit of trading is 10 shares.

Scale. Execute all increments up or down—that is, try to sell continually into a rising market or buy into a declining one.

Scale Order. An order to buy (or sell) a security that specifies the total amount to be bought (or sold) and the amount to be bought (or sold) at specific price variations.

Scattered. No one buyer or seller; implies various buyers or sellers.

Seat. A traditional figure of speech for a membership on an exchange.

Short Covering. Buying stock to return stock previously borrowed to make delivery on a short scale.

Short Position. Stocks sold short and not covered as of a particular date. On the New York Stock Exchange, a tabulation is issued once a month listing all issues on the Exchange in which there was a short position of 5,000 or more shares and issues in which the short position had changed by 2,000 or more shares in the preceding month. Short position also means the total amount of stock an individual has sold short and has not covered, as of a particular date.

Short Sale. A transaction by a person who believes a stock will decline and sells although he does not own any. For instance: You instruct your broker to sell short 100 shares of ABC. Your broker borrows the stock so he can deliver the 100 shares to the buyer. The money value of the shares borrowed is deposited by your broker with the lender. Sooner or later you must cover your short sale by buying the same amount of stock you borrowed for return to the lender. If you are able to buy ABC at a lower price than you sold it for, your profit is the difference between the two prices, not counting commissions and taxes. But if you have to pay more for the stock than the price you received, that is the amount of your loss. Stock exchange and federal regulations govern and limit the conditions under which a short sale may be made on a national securities exchange. Sometimes a person will sell short a stock he already owns in order to protect a paper profit. This is known as *selling short against the box.*

Specialist.   A New York Stock Exchange member responsible for making the market in a stock. He has four functions:

1. Auctioneer
2. Agent for other brokers
3. Dealer when necessary
4. Uniting buyers and sellers

Specialist Market.   When the specialist is both the bidder and offerer in the stock for his own account.

Stay on the Bid Side.   Do not "pay up" for a stock, but buy only on the bid side.

Stay on the Offer Side.   Sell only on the offer side; do not hit any bids.

Stock Ahead.   Sometimes an investor who has entered an order to buy or sell a stock at a certain price will see transactions at that price reported on the ticker tape while his own order has not been executed. The reason is that other buy and sell orders at the same price came in to the specialist and were placed on the book ahead of his and had priority.

Stop Limit Order.   A stop order that becomes a limit order after the specified stop price has been reached.

Stop Order.   An order to buy at a price above or sell at a price below the current market. Stop buy orders are generally used to limit loss or protect unrealized profits on a short sale. Stop sell orders are generally used to protect unrealized profits or limit loss on a holding. A stop order becomes a market order when the stock sells at or beyond the specified price and, thus, may not necessarily be executed at that price.

Strict Scale.   Execute at predetermined increments up or down; do not make an exception.

Third Market.   Refers to the over-the-counter trading of listed securities.

To Come.   The remaining shares to be bought.

To Go.   The remaining shares of an order to be sold.

Top or Low Limit. The highest or lowest price restrictions—that is, buy top/sell low.

Trading Post. The structure on the floor of the New York Stock Exchange at which stocks are bought and sold. About 100 stocks are traded at each post.

Try to Lift. Try to scale an order up.

Unlisted Stock. A security not listed on a stock exchange.

Up Tick. A term used to designate a transaction made at a price higher than the preceding transaction. Also called a *plus tick*. A *zero plus tick* is a term used for a transaction at the same price as the preceding trade but higher than the preceding different price.

We can see from this glossary of trading instructions that the management company trader can control the broker he selects. The stockbroker is a "mechanic," who executes the order he receives according to the instructions given him.

An important question is: With this arsenal, how does a buy-side trader decide what broker and what type of order to use?

SELECTING A BROKER

Greenwich Research Associates has done a great deal of research on why investment managers select brokers. They find that about 40% of the time a broker is selected because of research. About 10% of the time a sponsor directs the pension fund manager to use a certain broker. The other 50% of the time the order is given to a broker for "execution capability" by the management company trader.

Buy-side traders select brokers for a variety of reasons. They may be paying for their research or their willingness to commit capital to facilitate a fast trade, or because the broker may have a natural buyer or seller for the other side of the trade. The primary differences among brokers executing orders on the floor are in the amount of service, the rapidity of reports of execution, and the care with which the order is executed.

Interestingly, there seems to be little effort to obtain more attractive commission rates through price negotiation among brokers with similar execution capability. The Department of Labor study showed that the largest brokers trade at all rates between $0.01 per share and $0.37 per share. Therefore, lower commissions are available from all brokers to those clients who insist on them. Yet most managers pay an average rate of $0.06 to $0.07 per share for all trades without using lower rates for unbundled execution-only trades.

When a broker receives an order he can take three possible actions:

1. He tries to find the other side of the trade. Brokers do this because it turns one commission into two. To get the other side of the trade, brokers often favor the side they are seeking by giving the needed side the benefit of the spread between the bid and asked prices.

2. If a broker can't locate the other side, he may become the other side himself. If his client wishes to buy 25,000 shares of XYZ Company, the broker may become the seller of XYZ stock either from his inventory or by selling the stock short, intending to buy it back later or at a lower price. When brokers commit their capital in this manner, they intend to add a capital profit to their commission charge. If brokers lose money in committing capital, they often request additional commissions to offset losses.

3. Most of the time the broker will take the order to the trading floor and execute it according to customer instructions.

TIME FRAME IN WHICH TO EXECUTE THE ORDER

There are only two variables to which a management company trader can be sensitive in placing orders: *time* or *price*. If a trader needs to accomplish a large amount of trading in a short period of time, he will have to make price concessions. If a trader wishes to trade at a specific price, he will have to be patient until the price is available in the market.

It is in the economic interest of brokers to do as much trading as possible in the shortest time possible. Therefore, brokers tend to promote the necessity for speed at the expense of price. Most manager/traders are very much aware that brokers encourage hurry-up, one-price trading for the "best" of all reasons—broker profits as well as the appearance of rapid servicing.

The average stock listed on the NYSE trades at about $40 per share. The average share volume per day in NYSE-listed stocks on all exchanges is about 250 million shares per day. Thus, the average daily dollar volume is about $10.0 billion. There are 252 trading days in a year. Therefore, in 1989, trading in NYSE-listed stocks should exceed $2.5 trillion.

TABLE 6.2   NEW YORK STOCK EXCHANGE–LISTED STOCKS:
DAILY TRADING BY CAPITALIZATION

Capitalization	Percentage of Trading	Average $ (millions)	Shares @ $40 (thousands)
Top 200 stocks	60%	30.0	750,000
Next 300 stocks	25%	8.3	208,000
All others (1,100) stocks	15%	1.4	34,100

TABLE 6.3   DAYS NECESSARY TO TRADE
ONE MILLION SHARES AT 25% OF
DAILY VOLUME

Capitalization	Days
Top 200 stocks	5.3
Next 300 stocks	19.2
All others (1,100) stocks	117.3

From the foregoing data and data taken from Table 6.1, we can derive Table 6.2. From the measurement of billions of shares of trading over three years, we know that it is rare for an institution to do more than 25% of the volume of trading in a stock in one day. It is also rare for an institution to trade more than one million shares of a stock in a short period of time.

Table 6.3 shows the amount of time necessary to trade one million shares of stocks at 25% of the daily volume by capitalization size. It is crystal clear that large orders in anything but the top 200 capitalization stocks must be handled with great patience and care. Any attempt to emphasize quick executions over the price of the transactions must result in very costly trading in all but the largest 200 stocks traded.

OBTAINING BEST EXECUTION AT THE BEST COMMISSION RATE

We cannot leave the subject of manager–broker relationships without describing the economics of the brokerage business.

A trade for a broker has two cost components. The first is paperwork and record keeping. This is called *clearing* and is comparable to check clearance. It runs no more than $25 per transaction. The second is the actual trading or brokerage costs. These costs amount to no more than one cent per share, with a maximum of $100 per transaction. Therefore, no single trade can have a direct cost of more than $125, regardless of the number of shares involved. (The average brokerage transaction has a direct cost of about $85 to $90 a trade.) The average institutional trade is about 7,500 shares in size. It produces revenue of about $450 (at six cents per share) and provides a gross profit margin of about 300% of maximum cost.

For example: If your transaction is 25,000 shares and you pay eight cents per share commission, that is a total charge of $2,000, or about 1,600% over the maximum direct cost of $125 per transaction. That same transaction done at four cents per share would cost $1,000 and would still be a very profitable ticket at 600% of broker maximum cost. Stockbrokers calculate their profit in terms of dollars per transaction. Since the unbundled cost per trade rarely exceeds $125, this unbundled broker cost is the key number to remember when considering commission payments to brokers.

Finally, we come to best execution. Everyone involved in trading is seeking best execution. Can everyone get it? There are two sides to every trade. If one side is getting best execution, what is the other receiving?

It may be unrealistic to expect best execution on every trade, but it certainly is not out of order to expect at least average execution from investment managers and their brokers. Although best execution may be difficult to define and measure, average execution is not. Average execution is the volume-weighted average daily price at which a stock trades. It is the equivalent of the average price account, which all managers use to distribute fairly stock bought for more than one client. Below-average executions combined with high commissions result in out-of-control transaction costs.

Trading costs can be controlled by adopting the following measures:

1. Make sure you are benefiting from the lowest commission rates available. In examining master trustee reports, we have found that all brokers are willing to execute trades at unbundled rates. Those that insist on the lowest available rates will get them.

2. Measure your transaction costs against the volume-weighted average price available in the market. This will detect those brokers whose trading departments seriously limit your chance of outperforming the market.

Finally, it's important to remember that the customer (buy-side trader) controls the order by means of the way it is placed with the broker. Brokers follow customer instructions precisely. For example: A buy-side trader may place two orders in the same stock with a broker with each order having a different time frame and set of instructions. Perhaps one order requires immediate execution, whereas the other is to be accomplished over a period of five days. In the end, it's the instructions and careful supervision provided by the buy-side trader that produce superior trading.

The Editor Asks

Q *Suppose a buy-side trader has two orders. One is a sell from a portfolio being liquidated, with funds required in two weeks. The other was called in by a portfolio manager in response to a news wire item. How should the trader respond to these different trading situations in terms of timing, sizing, type of order, selection of broker, and time to completion?*

A There is a common thread that links the methods used to execute orders with apparently different time requirements. That thread is care and caution.

In the case of the two-week situation, a prudent method would be to execute the order over that period of time in increments—in other words, do the same amount every day for the two weeks.

The order in response to a tape announcement should be handled with caution. Brokers take advantage of portfolio managers who wish to sacrifice price for speed of execution. In general, once the announcement is out, it is probably best to let the dust settle before trading even if this takes a day or two. Benjamin Franklin said, "Act in haste, repent at leisure." This is especially valid in trading. Don't follow the herd by acting in panic. It's too expensive to your trading result.

7

BROKER TO FLOOR

Wayne H. Wagner

When it comes to trading common stocks, the floor of the New York Stock Exchange is the big leagues. There are many alternatives to trading on the NYSE floor, including regional exchanges, third market, crosses, and upstairs principal trading. Although some of these are substantial in size, they all take their pricing cues from the dominant market, the New York Stock Exchange. If a stock price changes on the NYSE, all the other markets usually change in short order by a similar amount.

The interaction that occurs on the floor sets the price for securities because most trades in NYSE-listed securities occur on this floor. The prices set here are the best because they represent the widest and deepest array of buyers and sellers. *Best* in this sense means fairly determined in a deep, well-informed, interactive marketplace. *Depth of market* means that transaction costs are lower, in terms of bid–ask spread, than in any other market for stocks. Buyers and sellers can trade inexpensively, with two important effects:

- Buyers and sellers can trade on smaller bits of information and are thus likely to trade more frequently. Therefore, prices will be more representative of current value.
- Investors are more willing to hold securities because they can readily dispose of them whenever they choose. As a result, buyers will pay more for listed securities. This enhances the value of the company whose shares are traded and reduces its cost of capital. This is why the vast majority of large companies pay the Exchange for the privilege of having their stocks listed and traded there.

The author is grateful for the assistance of Arthur Frumkes, William Lupien, and Eugene Noser in writing this chapter.

There are two more reasons that most investors prefer to trade on the NYSE: fairness and professionalism. *Fairness* means that every customer receives equivalent treatment. *Professionalism* means that every customer's order will be handled with skill and competence. The floor community does not tolerate cheats or fools.

THE PLAYERS ON THE FLOOR

Unlike some other markets, the NYSE is a physical location. General Motors trades at a specific longitude and latitude, and not 10 feet away from that precise location. Buyers and sellers of GM have their orders represented in the one location where they are most likely to encounter the contra side of the trade. Floor traders believe the eyeball-to-eyeball contact on the floor is essential to advantageous trading.

Standing at the center of that focus is the *specialist,* whose job it is to conduct the market for GM shares (as well as any other stocks that may be assigned to him). No other individual on the floor is empowered to conduct the market in GM stock. The specialist is self-employed and earns his living by earning fees for trading services and, more important, trading for his own account. The exclusive right to trade GM on the floor comes with a set of obligations. The Exchange imposes onto the specialist the responsibility to maintain "a fair and orderly market" within the constraints of his capital and his ability. He is evaluated continually according to a set of rules, procedures, and criteria established by the Exchange to ensure fairness and professionalism.

The specialist is an independent businessman, buying and selling goods from his own inventory and performing services for a fee. However, the specialist is not subject to some of the risks of small businessmen: He has been granted a unique privilege, the exclusive right to trade his stocks on the floor of the NYSE. This is a substantial privilege, worth significant monies, but it comes with obligations imposed by the Exchange. These obligations are not all money-makers per se; in fact, the specialist is required to perform these functions without compensation. Fulfilling these obligations will at times result in losses to the specialist's inventory account.

The specialist conducts the auction market: Transactions occur at the crossover points between the buyer willing to pay the most and the seller willing to accept the least. When there are no buyers willing to accommodate the seller at a price that satisfies the NYSE definition of continuity, the specialist is *required* to step in and accommodate the public order. *Continuity* is defined as price adjacency; over 90% of all NYSE trades occur within one-eighth of the previous trade. This requirement to maintain continuity is called the *affirmative obligation* of the specialist.

What happens when stock prices move sharply downward? If possible, the specialist tries to move the stock price downward in an orderly sequence, with each trade priced near the previous price. If that proves impossible, as it will at times, the specialist needs Exchange permission before allowing a price gap.

At first glance, it appears that the specialist is in an unenviable position. He is required to buy stock on the way down and to sell it on the way up. Furthermore, the specialist is not permitted to trade for his own account in front of a public order; public orders always take precedence. So how does the specialist make money?

Specialists make some money on the spread between the bid price and the asked price. In this function, the specialist is like any other merchant, buying inventory at a low price and hoping to sell it at a higher price. Another opportunity for profit is the opening of the stock: The specialist accumulates buy and sell orders that arrive before the opening bell and matches them off. If there is an imbalance that is not too great to be handled, the specialist is expected to absorb it into his own inventory. The Exchange watches this activity very carefully: If the stock opens up, the specialist is not allowed to be a seller out of his own inventory. Still, the specialist is the only one allowed to see the order flow, and has an excellent view of how overnight events are affecting investor sentiments.[1]

Specialists also earn money by acting as brokers: A floor broker can leave an order with the specialist for the specialist to execute whenever possible. Most orders in thinly traded issues are handled this way. For this service, the specialist earns a fee in the neighborhood of two cents a share. Similarly, the specialist can serve as catalyst, acting as the neutral location where trading intentions and indications can be stored for later potential use.

Although these more or less mechanical functions are significant sources of specialist revenue, the specialist also profits by buying at propitious times—when prices are low—and selling later at higher prices. He does this partially through an information advantage that comes with the exclusive right to trade a stock but also, more importantly, through a developed and refined sense of short-term market trends.

This is not an automatic source of profit, although the odds are definitely (and deliberately) stacked in favor of it. Think of it as the enticement investors offer an individual to make him want to become a specialist.

Sometimes the specialist makes money in spite of himself; he is, as they

---

[1] See Chapter 22, ''The Single-Price Auction,'' by Steven Wunsch.

say on the floor, ''forced to make money.'' The operative principle here is that stock prices forced up or down by good or bad news tend to overreact. The specialist, because of the affirmative obligation, often buys stock that no one else wants and sells stock that everyone wants to own. Though often a frightening proposition at the time, this works out well enough often enough to net out as a money-making proposition.

If he had his preference, the specialist would make his money in small increments at frequent intervals. He sleeps better if he goes home neither short nor long a significant amount of stock.

THE FLOOR BROKERS

The specialists are the kings of the jungle, but the floor brokers are the dominant species on the NYSE floor, far outnumbering the floor brokers of the large brokerage firms and the specialists. They are mostly independent businessmen, living by their wits and reputation. The specialists are the Anointed Ones, whereas the more numerous floor brokers survive by doing whatever needs to be done.

For all his responsibilities, the specialist is still a person, with the reactions and responses of any human being. His responses to the risks he must bear and the returns he hopes to gain will differ from those of other specialists and will vary from time to time. For example, he may be sure about one stock's trading situation but highly uncertain about another. One stock may be highly predictable and another wild and crazy. In subtle ways, all these factors affect how he will respond to the market at any given moment. This flavors the trading characteristics of the stocks he trades.

All these subtleties affect buyers and sellers as well. The key to effective trading is to know *how different specialists react*, which is another way of saying *how different stocks trade*. The job of the floor broker is to read these multitudinous and conflicting signs and respond appropriately.

There are two ways an order can be brought into the sphere of the specialist. Smaller orders can be presented to the specialist electronically via the Designated Order Turnaround (DOT) system. This electronic access allows market orders and limit orders to be handled efficiently, but more or less mechanically, by the specialist.

Orders that require more finesse are usually handled by a person retained to represent that order on the floor. Large orders, orders in a volatile or thinly traded stock, orders whose buyer or seller is concerned about the ebb and flow of the market—these all represent situations where some discretion is desired.

These orders arrive on the Exchange floor by telephone or computer workstation from the customer's brokerage firm. The call is taken by a clerical employee of the brokerage firm permanently assigned to the Exchange floor. He may hand the order to a floor broker employed by the brokerage firm, but few brokerage firms retain enough floor members to handle the maximum order load at all times. More often than not, the order is passed to a freelancer known as a two-dollar broker. This interesting name derives from the fact that these individuals used to handle a 100-share order for two cents a share. This figure is now substantially lower per share—the broker makes it up on volume—but the name has stuck.

The Exchange is far too large to be covered by one individual. The floor spreads out to the size of eight basketball courts in four different rooms. It would take several precious minutes to walk from one end to the other. Accordingly, the floor brokers are usually zoned. *Zoning* means that a floor broker will usually handle orders only within a certain physical floor proximity. He may handle orders in the stocks traded within his zone for several brokers. Even though he does not know the identity of the client for whom he is trading, he may know as much about the order flow in a given stock as the specialist does.

Most often, "good execution" occurs when an order is well handled by the floor broker.

WORKING AN ORDER

The skills of a floor broker are hardly challenged by the limit orders and market orders that represent the bulk of trading in terms of number of orders. No discretion is required, or even permitted, for these types of orders. Limit orders are delivered to and watched over by the specialist. Market orders place primary emphasis on rapid execution at the prevailing market price. The DOT system, through which orders up to as much as 30,000 shares can be transmitted, can easily handle most limit and market orders. The specialist is required to execute DOT orders up to 2,099 shares.

Sometimes the floor broker will be involved in program trades,[2] which are trades executed in many stocks simultaneously. No discretion is involved; all that is required is the physical presence to carry orders to where they can be filled.

The floor broker's specialty is handling orders where discretion is needed. The discretion concerns the balance of buyers and sellers at the time when

[2] See Chapter 14, "Package Trading," by Patricia C. Dunn.

the order is to be executed. Whatever subtleties were considered by the portfolio manager and his buy-side trader in deciding to purchase this stock at this moment, all orders look much alike by the time they get to the floor. *Why* an order is coming right now is not the concern of the floor broker. As far as he is concerned, orders fall from heaven.

Most often, the order handed to a floor broker will be stated as a "market not held" order. This means that he has been given discretion to work the order according to the present trading situation as he sees it. He is "not held" to fill the order at any specific price, nor is he held to participate in all trades that print on the tape. He has been retained to use his skill to obtain the best price for his client.

A good floor broker calls upon his experience, his feel for the market. A visitor accompanying a floor broker through the execution of the order might notice the surges and swells of information afloat on the floor, but he could hardly appreciate the subtlety of the messages being processed.

Let's walk with a floor broker through the execution of a trade and listen in to his thoughts. Our floor broker has just been handed an order by one of the major Wall Street firms to buy 30,000 shares of Ford, market not held. Since his stall is near Ford, he sees a lot of orders in this stock. The post is only a few steps away.

Without thinking about it, he registers the noise level: "The tempo must be picking up. Not too many brokers standing around." Noise level is such an important barometer of market activity that the different trading rooms are audially connected.

As he walks over, he glances up at the tape to check for any last-second trades in Ford. What happened 10 minutes ago is ancient history. The situation can—and does—change every few seconds. What matters is the situation at the post during the time he is working the order.

"Timmy, what's the picture?" Timmy is the Ford specialist. (One of the charms of the place is the continued use of nicknames that most people leave behind in grade school. But then, 80% of the floor members do not have a college degree.)

Timmy answers: "Seventy by seventy and a quarter. Seventy thousand to buy, twenty-five thousand to sell." These are the orders on the book, sent to the specialist by DOT or handed to him by the floor brokers in front of him.

Timmy and the floor broker have known each other for 15 years. They deal with each other every few minutes, day after day. They trust and respect each other, which means that they reveal a little more than they might to someone they didn't know as well. Remember, they have interacted every few minutes for years and are likely to continue meeting for years into the future. Neither wants to make the other look bad. This trust and familiarity eases the trading process.

Our broker sees the Merrill Lynch broker in the crowd. Merrill Lynch has been a net buyer in Ford for days, and our order is going to have to compete with the Merrill broker in the crowd. The biggest order usually commands the market, and our broker wants to see that his buyer gets a piece of any significant size for sale. To accomplish that, he either has to get the Merrill Lynch broker to agree to let him participate, or he has to compete with him on price by offering to buy at a higher price. "I'm fifty." "I'm in for thirty." As is typical, they agree to split any available supply. This "making room for everybody" is practiced most of the time.

"Five thousand to buy," our broker says to Timmy. By placing an order with the specialist, our broker secures a place for himself in the queue. By not revealing to public display the full size of his order, he keeps his options open. Now, if any sellers appear, this order has a chance of being partially filled. Partial fills are looked upon very favorably by the floor brokers.[3] A series of partial fills clearly demonstrates that the order was "worked," and it also protects the floor broker and his client from a bad execution. For example, if the price were to drop after a one-ticket fill, it would look as though the shares were bought at a higher price than necessary. If he scaled down, filling the orders a bit at a time, the average price paid would decline with each lower priced partial fill. Importantly, it requires no omniscience, yet the broker is protected from filling an order at a price that may appear unattractive because of subsequent, unforeseeable events.

The floor broker may bid awhile and then step back awhile if he feels he may get a better execution by doing so. If the situation is not particularly to his liking, he may even get back to the customer to update him on the situation and perhaps receive amended instructions. If he leaves the post, however, he will most likely hand his order to another floor broker in the crowd so as not to miss an opportunity.

Because the floor broker is paid only on shares transacted, he prefers to complete the order as quickly as he can so he can move on to the next ticket. He knows, however, that the Wall Street firm and the customer are watching the tape and will judge him on how well the order was handled.

In a stock like Ford, orders move through almost continuously. It usually takes no more than a few minutes to fill the order through participation. If more urgency is required, the floor broker may bid more aggressively, stepping ahead of the rest of the crowd to be the first to trade against incoming sell orders. If the client's instructions so provided and no other

[3] See Chapter 6, "Trader to Broker," by Stanley S. Abel and Eugene A. Noser, Jr.

orders stood in the way, he could engage in a transaction with the specialist's inventory.

After the trade, an Exchange clerk called a *reporter* enters the trade into a card reader, where it is validated and transmitted to the electronic ticker tape. Typically, within 30 to 40 seconds of execution, the whole country knows about the trade.

The floor broker writes down his record of the trade and then reports back to the clerk so the brokerage firm can call the client with the completion. The brokerage firm also initiates the bookkeeping entry that starts the accounting and settlement process.[4] The floor broker's record serves as a check in case of a mismatch between buyer record and seller record. It also serves to account for the services the two-dollar brokers bill out to the brokerage firm.

The next morning, the trade will show on the books of the brokerage firms representing the buyer and the seller. A mismatch could occur if one of the parties had jotted it down wrong in haste. If there is any mismatch—a QT or questionable trade—the brokers involved will try to set the record straight. If they cannot come to an agreement, they can take their disagreement to a *floor governor,* a senior floor broker with special powers granted by the Exchange to arbitrate disputes. The floor governor also grants permission to halt trading in a stock or to allow a trade to occur that is uncomfortably far from the previous price for reasons such as company news.

LEARNING BY DOING

Where do these specialists and floor brokers acquire the skills to handle stock trading with finesse? They learn by doing, on the floor of the Exchange. Most traders start out as clerks or runners on the floor, working for either a broker or a specialist. As they progress beyond the rudiments and show some talent and integrity, they move on to more difficult tasks.

As more skills are acquired, the young broker finds himself wanting to buy a seat of his own. This is a major purchase: Seats have sold for well over $1 million. Few floor brokers have the creditworthiness to finance a seat, so a seat is almost always leased from a larger firm. In mid-1988, lease rates were around $165,000 per year. Brokers carrying that much fixed operating cost are motivated to work hard.

The Exchange floor is not unlike a medieval guild, where recruits progress from apprentice to journeyman to master. Often the skills are passed down from father to son or from brother to brother. A remarkable

---

[4] See Chapter 8, ''Transaction Settlement: The Final Step,'' by Vincent Walsh.

percentage of the floor community had fathers, grandfathers, and other relatives who also worked the Exchange floor.

The average experience among NYSE members is twenty years. This longevity is quite a contrast to other trading professionals. For example, most floor traders trading their own capital on the futures exchanges succumb to the pressure in just a few years. As Mike Heeger, a market maker on the floor of the Chicago Mercantile Exchange, quipped: "Those fellows you see in that pit with gray hair? Don't be confused. They're twenty-eight years old, too."[5] The pressure on NYSE floor members is not as great.

As would be expected, there is not a great deal of movement of people onto and off the floor. The number of floor members has been fixed at 1,366 since the early 1950s. Once a person has the knowledge and the credentials, he is likely to stay within this tightly knit community. If the volume's good, nobody leaves except feet first.

CHANGE ON THE FLOOR

The New York Stock Exchange did not become the preeminent market by sticking to outmoded practices. This is not to say that the impetus for change comes from the floor; change comes about in response to pressure from members, clients, regulators, or other exchanges. But once the change is inevitable and the initial resistance has been overcome, the Exchange can implement change with amazing speed. Some examples:

1. The ticker tape was created way back in 1867 and fully automated in 1975–76. The tape truly makes a difference. This public record gives every investor information on recent trades and an indication of exactly how many shares he could trade right now and at what price. This information has greatly increased knowledge and confidence among the investing public and added greatly to the liquidity of the market. If anyone—quite literally *anyone*—sees a price that he thinks is too cheap, he can easily enter an order at that price.
2. When the Securities and Exchange Act was passed in 1934 to "put a policeman on Wall Street," the Exchange quickly became that policeman, and took over most of the functions of regulatory oversight.
3. When pressure from institutional investors for lower commission costs became irresistible, negotiated commissions quickly became

[5] Quoted in Martin Mayer, *Markets* (New York: Norton, 1988), p. 27.

the standard. Increased volume led to greater prosperity on the Street.

4. When small order flow threatened to swamp the Exchange, a major development effort led to the DOT system. The DOT system followed the lead established by the Scorex system developed by the Pacific Coast Stock Exchange. By reducing the workload on high processing cost/low commission orders, the Exchange community improved profitability.

5. When Congress mandated a National Market System in the early 1970s, the New York Stock Exchange took the lead and implemented the Consolidated Tape and the Intermarket Trading System (ITS). Even though all orders introduced on any exchange theoretically have equal visibility and equal price priority, the NYSE easily retains its traditional role as the source of the best price information.

6. When growing institutionalization threatened to swamp the Exchange, the major brokerage firms stepped in to do "upstairs" trading. Upstairs traders try to find the contra side of the trade away from the Exchange floor so that supply and demand can reach the floor simultaneously, thereby avoiding mistiming and steep price movements. If the other side cannot be found, the major brokerage firms stand ready to commit capital to complete the trade to the client's satisfaction. A satisfactory process evolved so that these block trades could speed through the market without disruption.[6]

SUMMARY

The stately classical façade of the New York Stock Exchange building at 11 Wall Street masks the modernity of the Exchange process that lies within. But the solidity suggested by the noble columns accurately represents the strength and solidity within.

The whole world takes its major cues about the health of the United States and world economies from the actions on the NYSE. Although the Tokyo Stock Exchange now far outstrips the NYSE in terms of shares and monetary trading volume, it has not yet acquired the NYSE's reputation for fairness and solid value.

Markets are not made of buildings, but are made by the give-and-take interactions of the inhabitants of those buildings—the market participants.

[6] See Chapter 12, "Upstairs, Downstairs: The Block Traders and the Specialists," by Donald L. Luskin.

The greatest thing that can be said of the Exchange community is that *it works*. It doesn't work by government order, and it doesn't work because of some economist's classical grand design. It works because it delivers what is asked of it at a reasonable cost. It works because people believe it works and can see it working. It works by a delicate balancing of opposing interests, all of whom are accustomed to trusting that they will be treated fairly. The public exposure of interests and trades, the rules of fairness, the certainty that the trade will be completed, and the genuine concern for the interests of the investing public all contribute to the preeminence of the New York Stock Exchange.

Mostly, the Exchange works by the experience and dedication of the professional men and women who make it work—minute by minute, year by year, and century by century.

The Editor Asks

Q *The adequacy of the Stock Exchange systems and procedures were severely tested by the October '87 crash. What do you think the response of the Exchange should be?*

A The Exchange quickly moved to work on the capacity problem to ensure that in the future it would be able to handle the volumes seen in October. This was a vital and important step, since some of the most alarming aspects of the crash were that the market mechanisms could not cope: Telephones weren't answered, computer communications backed up, and program traders shut out smaller investors.

On a less positive note, the gut-level reaction was to deny that there was anything wrong with *their* part of the mechanism and to point the finger of guilt at other parties, such as the program traders and the futures exchanges. (Sadly, the Exchange was not the only market constituency to try to absolve itself of responsibility or even complicity in the crash.)

Some important and nagging problems remain.

The primary base on investment now is institutional, and the floor hasn't totally adapted to that reality. Institutions need to trade in amounts that are too large in time frames that are too short for the floor to digest. This problem has been handled to date by the block trading desks, yet this leads to isolated pockets of information. Also, the rules that ensure fairness on the floor do not apply equally upstairs; for example, an upstairs block desk *can* step ahead of a public order. The Exchange needs to reassert the importance of centralizing the market in one location with equal information access to all participants.

Institutions increasingly think in terms of strategic moves, whereas the Exchange is still focused on individual issues. As Robert Shultz has suggested,[7] the prime concerns of pension sponsors are with such macro-issues as stocks versus bonds, small stocks versus large stocks, and similar broadly defined strategic deployments. The difference between holding stock A versus stock B, which remains the focus of the floor, can be little more than a minor detail to the institutional investor. It is important for the Exchange to recognize and create accommodations for this type of trading.

Finally, the commitment to computers and telecommunications still lags behind. This technological lag increasingly results in cost inefficiencies and speed of execution problems for the investment managers and their clients. Quite literally, there are investment managers who can—and do—make computerized buy/sell decisions faster than those decisions can be executed on the Exchange. Information flow is still slowed to the pace of a walk on the Exchange. Many observers believe this difference between institutional action time and Exchange response time was a major problem in the October '87 crash.

The importance of the ticker tape in widening the distribution of trading information has been identified. The next step is to embrace fully the universal electronic distribution of trading information. Location is no longer paramount; the institutions that survive and dominate in the future will be those that recognize the global village characteristics of the market.

[7] Chapter 2, "A Sponsor Looks at Trading Costs," by Robert E. Shultz.

8

TRANSACTION SETTLEMENT: THE FINAL STEP

Vincent Walsh

Operations efficiency is important to maximize portfolio return. Generally, investment managers prefer to assume that clearing and settlement will be automatic because problems are disruptive to the smooth flow of the investment process. Unfortunately, however, this is not always the case, and the profitability of the best investment decision can be undermined by the costs of inefficient settlement. At the same time, through awareness of potential problems and effective responses when they occur, settlement costs can be minimized.

No interest is earned and reinvestment of funds is constrained for the investment manager on sales of securities until securities are delivered versus payment. Conversely, brokers lose interest and will sometimes make claims against clients when purchases of securities are not settled on the original settlement date because of the institution's DK (''don't know'') of the delivery and the corresponding failure to pay.

Also, an institution's satisfaction with an investment manager or broker can be severely affected by trade-processing and settlement problems. When problems occur, it often may suggest a lesser degree of care in the original investment decision or the execution and follow-up, as well as detracting from investment and trading decisions. Also, when cancels and corrects occur frequently, balancing of the institution's position with its custodian to his in-house portfolio system is made more difficult.

HOW ARE TRADES IN DTC-ELIGIBLE SECURITIES PROCESSED?

In this section, we focus on the processing flows for institutions and broker/dealers associated with book entry settlements typical of U.S. corporate securities via Depository Trust Company (DTC) and other interfaced U.S. depositories. These securities typically settle on a standard five-business-day clearance and settlement cycle. DTC-eligible securities include most equities publicly traded in the United States, such as American Depository Receipts (ADRs) and most corporate as well as many municipal fixed-income instruments. ADRs are certificates issued by banks that represent investments in foreign securities but are denominated (and pay dividends) in dollars rather than a foreign currency, and that settle in the DTC. ADRs can be very cost-effective for institutions that want to make overseas investments without the cost commitment of establishing a global custody arrangement.

The DTC holds securities in its vault and permits book entry settlement among brokers and custody bank members. Certificates there are stored in security order and underlie book entry records of ownership. This reduces the issuers' cost of printing and transferring certificates and of making dividend and interest payments. The DTC has a large common vault holding securities registered in "street name," and updates its records to change ownership of shares from one DTC participant to another. This improves settlement efficiency by eliminating the need for physical deliveries and reregistration.

INSTITUTIONAL TRADE FLOW. The NYSE's Rule 387 requires members who deal with institutions on a cash-on-delivery (COD) basis to utilize DTC's Institutional Delivery System (DTC-ID) for the confirmation and affirmation of securities trades. The rule also requires the use of a depository for book entry settlement. Because of its inherent efficiency, and encouraged by this rule, nearly all institutional trades are confirmed and settled between brokers and investment managers through this system. COD settlement means that DTC will record on its books the transfer of ownership of securities held within its vault at the same time that the value of the transaction is transferred. Of course, this depends on the agreement of both parties and the availability of funds and securities for against-payment settlement.

In contrast, individual investors typically maintain holdings through a bank or broker but also may choose to hold securities themselves. In that case, the broker will instruct the issuer's transfer agent to register them in the purchaser's name after settlement. The certificates will be provided to the customer upon receipt.

Figure 8.1 diagrams a simplified institutional trade flow. On the trade date (TD), in response to an institutional order, the broker provides an execution report to the investment manager. The investment manager will update his portfolio system and send instructions for all trades to his

FIGURE 8.1   INSTITUTIONAL TRADE FLOW

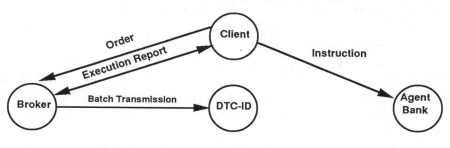

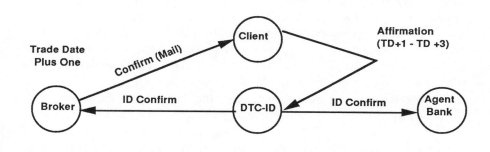

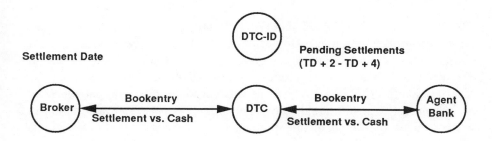

institutional client's agent bank. The broker will prepare a trade ticket and input it into its own bookkeeping system. Then the broker's system sends trade confirmations to DTC's Institutional Delivery System (DTC-ID) in a tape at the end of the trade date.

On TD + 1, DTC-ID will process inputs from all brokers and will make available to the investment manager ID confirmations (printed in hard copy, batch transmission, on-line, and so on) of each trade done. Copies are sent to the broker, the institution's agent bank, and other interested parties if appropriate. This ensures that all parties possess the details of the trade generated from a single source. Although it is the ID confirmation that is primarily relevant for settlement, typically the broker will also mail a confirmation directly to the investment manager as well as to the underlying investing institution, if different.

The investment manager acknowledges, or "affirms," each trade to DTC either directly or through the institution's agent bank, indicating that the confirmation agrees with its own records and that settlement may proceed. This step may occur as early as TD + 1 or as late as TD + 3 without delaying settlement.

On the basis of affirmations, the DTC-ID system will produce lists of pending deliveries (normally on the morning after affirmation) for each agent bank and broker, which DTC will then settle on the settlement date unless buyer's funds or seller's securities are unavailable. Brokers and custodian banks may also send exception lists (normally on TD + 4) to DTC indicating trades not to be settled automatically on the settlement date.

When the settlement date arrives, a book entry movement of securities versus payment takes place at DTC. This protects both parties by allowing them to retain control over their assets until they obtain the assets of the contra-party. Shares are transferred by book entry between the depository accounts of the delivering and receiving agent banks and brokers, with appropriate payment being credited to the selling party and debited to the purchasing party.

BROKER–DEALER TRADE FLOW. Figure 8.2 outlines a simplified broker-to-broker settlement. Broker trades are first *compared* locally in the market where executed and then *settled on a net basis*. The "street side" or broker trade input will be reported to the National Securities Clearing Corporation (NSCC) or a regional clearing corporation for comparison. This is in contrast to institutional settlement, which is based on affirmation of broker input by the investment manager and trade-for-trade settlement versus payment through an agent bank.

Trades between broker/dealers on the NYSE, American Stock Exchange (AMEX), and NASDAQ markets are cleared and settled through the Trade Comparison, Clearance and Settlement System run by the NSCC. NSCC is owned equally by the NYSE, AMEX, and the National Association of Securities Dealers (NASD). The regional exchanges use similar interfaced systems at regional clearing corporations.

NSCC speeds up the clearance process and reduces credit risk by comparing all the trade details (security number/symbol, price, quantity, trade date, contra-party, etc.) submitted by buying and selling brokers to each transaction. If the trade details match, a comparison is reported to both

FIGURE 8.2 BROKER TRADE FLOW

TRADE DATE

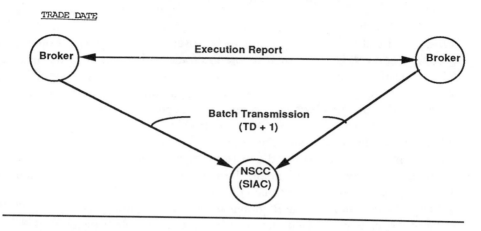

Trade Date Plus Two

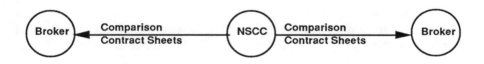

Settlement Date

contra-parties on contract sheets, and there is a binding contract for settlement from which neither party can withdraw without agreement from the contra-party. Comparison appears on contract sheets on TD + 2 (or later) on nonautomated NYSE and AMEX floor executions and NASDAQ over-the-counter (OTC) executions based on matching of tape input on TD + 1 by each broker to NSCC with the contra-brokers' and reporting the next day.

If the trade details submitted to comparison do not match (e.g., if one of the brokers fails to write a ticket, or an error is made in trade input), NSCC contract sheets indicate each submitting broker's unmatched input as an "uncompared" to the submitting broker and as an "advisory" to the contra-party identified in the input. The brokers' purchase and sales (P&S) departments then review these items against original input to resolve any differences on the contract sheets. The party in error will then accept the correct details of the contra-party, or, if necessary, both sides will resubmit to comparison. NSCC will then report the trade as compared in the next daily cycle if the details have been matched. Once a trade is reported as compared, NSCC interpositions itself between the broker contra-parties for the remainder of the clearing process. NSCC guarantees settlement and assumes credit risk in the event of contra-party failure from midnight following the report of a compared trade.

Following comparison, on the various exchanges and NASDAQ, all settlements are consolidated in the broker's NSCC (or other designated clearing corporation) clearing account. To accomplish this, the regional exchanges will submit via the Regional Interface Operation (RIO) to NSCC or the appropriate designated clearing corporation on behalf of the broker.

Settlement between brokers is done through the NSCC and interfaced regional clearing corporations through the Continuous Net Settlement (CNS) system for CNS-eligible securities. Here, compared trades are settled in a net environment, where each broker will settle with NSCC the accumulated net long or short securities position in each DTC-eligible issue for the trades that the participant is settling that day. The CNS system then receives or delivers the net quantities each day within the broker's DTC account. NSCC settles with each participant directly and guarantees all CNS net settlements.

A net money settlement is done between NSCC and each participant in a clearinghouse funds payment received or paid once a day for the net principal value of all buys and sells.

WHAT ARE THE BROKER'S ROLES?

The investment manager's contact with the broker is initially with the sales assistant or the sales trader covering the account. At the same time, most institutions have staff dedicated to follow-up on trade input through settlement. Close coordination within a brokerage firm between salesmen or traders and trade support staff is therefore necessary. This helps ensure input of trade details and customer accounts. It also is key to follow-up on unaffirmed trades or settlement problems.

Effective liaison between investment managers and brokers is key to effective transaction processing and to new product flexibility. It also tends to take advantage of system capabilities of some brokers, such as computer-to-computer interfaces, short name reference files, and communications networks. It starts with initial setup of accounts from the investment manager and continues through trade processing and settlement.

BROKER FUNCTIONS. To an investment manager, the four most visible and important (after execution) functional areas of a broker are trade support, purchase and sales, institutional bookkeeping, and cashiering. Other functional areas such as dividends and proxy and stock record affect institutional trade processing, but their roles are behind the scenes or invisible under most circumstances.

The trade support function handles trade input. It also facilitates the setting up of new accounts for the investment manager whenever necessary. Contact may be direct or through the broker's coverage staff. Upon execution, trade tickets are written, figuration is added, and then tickets are input upon execution.

Most firms have automated the input of customer accounting information and the preparation of confirmations, which historically occurred in the purchase and sales department. P&S still takes responsibility for reconciliation of trades from the evening of the trade date up until settlement. Customer trade details and "street side" comparisons are reviewed and balanced.

For investment managers trading in COD accounts, institutional bookkeeping performs credit-related functions. It monitors and follows up on the broker's exposure due to unaffirmed trades as well as attempted deliveries that are refused or DK'd (a "don't know" response) by the investment manager. This department is typically the link between the customer and the cashiering function when querying the status of or attempting to expedite a delivery. Often the new accounts function is part of margin and institutional bookkeeping, responsible for ensuring accurate customer account information and related documentation.

The "cage" or cashiering function is responsible for receiving and delivering securities versus payment. Payments are made upon instructions from the margin or institutional bookkeeping departments. The securities movement and control function in cashiering will endeavor to maximize the efficiency of deliveries made by the broker in COD accounts. This involves securities borrowing as necessary to supplement available inventory needed for deliveries. The bank loan area is another key function responsible for funding the broker's daily cash flow requirements and balancing to external bank accounts.

SETTLEMENT EFFICIENCY. The choice of a brokerage firm will be affected by its settlement efficiency. Efficiency of settlement is most clearly associated with a broker's consistent ability to deliver securities on institutional purchases.

Because brokers make their living through velocity of turnover, numerous buy and sell trades will take place in the same issue in a large firm. Broker deliveries are dependent on available inventory and, otherwise, on the ability to borrow the security issue to be delivered. Typically, in a broker's settlement department or "cage," the aggregate position is managed without reference to which specific buys and sells were originally related. This is often true even if an investment manager crosses a trade through a broker between two subaccounts. For example, settlement of a purchase can be delayed even though the seller may have delivered on the settlement date. Inventory may not be available to deliver to the buying institution if open customer or firm short positions or other customer deliveries absorb the inventory received and if stock borrows cannot be arranged.

Inefficiencies in settlement can also occur for brokers with substantial retail businesses. Small retail deliveries can preempt and thereby delay large institutional deliveries depending on delivery priorities. This problem is generally most serious with issues that cannot be borrowed as a result of illiquidity or large-scale short selling in the market. Efficient use of computers to determine optimal delivery priorities helps maximize the efficiencies of cage operations. At the same time, specialized institutional firms generally avoid most conflicts in settlement priorities. They are also in a better position to expedite or give special handling to large deliveries.

CREDIT CONSIDERATIONS. An investment manager's choice of a broker for specific transactions is based not only on expertise and service concerns but also on credit issues. Particularly in volatile markets, until settlement occurs, there is a risk of loss of principal if the counterparty goes out of business. In liquid instruments, in a delivery-versus-payment environment, this risk is generally limited to the market price movement in the securities because stock is held on sales and cash is held on purchases until settlement occurs. In the worst-case situation of firm failure, however, trades may remain unsettled for an extended period of time before action can be taken to resolve them. At the same time, with less liquid instruments or large blocks of stock, the cost of closing out positions can be far more than the difference between cost and market.

Assessing credit exposure requires awareness of the capitalization of the broker (and its parent, if appropriate) as it relates to the riskiness of the business. The events of Black Monday have emphasized the risks inherent in the securities business. The two most serious categories of losses of the October 1987 market break were among option market-maker clearing firms and block trading firms. Large losses were also borne by retail firms with clients holding large naked option positions.

In contrast, brokers who dealt almost exclusively as agents or intermediaries between buyer and seller without taking a principal position were nearly unhurt by the immediate events of the market break. Although some agency brokers are much less well capitalized, the nature of their business does not put capital at risk.

Most brokers have a mix of principal and agency businesses. Obviously, principal trading brokers put capital at risk to a much greater extent than agency brokers do. Block trading firms on any given day may have hundreds of millions of dollars of exposure in the equities markets. In the event of a market move against them, large trading losses can occur. At the same time, if there is a sudden reduction in the availability of credit facilities that necessitates the closing out of positions and the realization of inventory losses, the broker may be subject to failure. This also can be exacerbated by the tightening of capital requirements and margin rules in these markets.

All retail brokers are exposed to their individual clients who sell naked options, trade in futures contracts, or to whom they lend money through margin accounts. In the event of a sudden decline in the market, client portfolio values may decline precipitously, eliminating the equity in their customers' accounts. If the client cannot meet his commitments, then the broker carrying those accounts must assume the liabilities and residual losses for the defaulting customer.

If the broker uses a clearing agent, that agent may assume the liabilities of the correspondent in the event of failure. Therefore, capital and credit exposure is reduced to the extent of the equity of the clearing firm as well as the capital of the broker itself. A clearing firm's reputation depends on its willingness to do business on behalf of its customer brokers, so it is inclined to meet commitments on behalf of its correspondents. There is, however, little or no regulatory guidance requiring a clearing agent to continue to settle for a correspondent in the worst case of a firm failure.

The institution should carefully consider the firms with which it does business and should ask for copies of focus reports and financial statements to evaluate exposure if it is concerned about specific brokers. It must trade off the flexibility, variety of ideas, market intelligence, and pricing competition associated with numerous relationships against exposure to firms involved in inherently riskier lines of business.

WHAT ARE THE CUSTODIAN'S ROLES?

The custodian or agent bank of an institution provides a wide range of functions in support of securities transaction processing. The nature of the services and the cost of transactions are important to the decision. At the same time, the choice of an agent is often driven by overall banking relationship considerations.

CUSTODIAN FUNCTIONS. This section focuses on the role of the custodian in investment management of a domestic U.S. portfolio. The role of the custodian is to carry out accurately or fulfill the instructions of the customer and to provide the best possible service in processing transactions and accounting for the investor's portfolio. Besides transaction settlement and activity reporting, the custodian provides safekeeping and custody of securities including income collection, conversions and reorganization processing when needed, cash management services, and activity reporting. These functions are closely integrated with each other in providing an overall service. In turn, the investment manager is responsible for providing the account manager with complete and accurate instructions.[1]

The custodian typically is compensated on a combination of transaction fees and a percentage of securities holdings. These charges are negotiated on the basis of the specific characteristics of the institution, including expected transaction volume, the value of securities (and funds) being invested, the types of investments and locations where investments are held, and the level of reporting and services desired.

Custodians or agent banks respond to their customer instructions to receive and deliver securities and funds on behalf of the institution. Deliveries are generally done versus payment unless there are specific instructions otherwise. Book entry settlement minimizes the potential for delivery problems. If physical securities are received, inspection is needed to verify and detect lost, stolen, or forged securities. Then securities can be reregistered into the name of the nominee.

Safekeeping and custody involve the maintenance of securities holdings, including continuous monitoring of changes affecting the instruments and, above all, protecting the principal value of instruments. Physical instruments require efficient bank vault storage. Often this involves coordination of subcustody agents for investments in different markets or different types of

---

[1] Julie Ann Ben-Susan, "Global Clearance and Custody Issues," presented at the International Operations Association Symposium on International Equity Compliance and Clearance Strategies, New York, June 24, 1987.

instruments. Custody for depository-based securities is generally done through a nominee company through which the custodian acts as the nominal holder for the investor.

Efficient income collection of dividends and interest is a crucial part of safekeeping and custody. For depository securities such as U.S. equities, payment is received through the agent bank's settlement account. Because of DTC's efficiency of making dividend and interest payments, customers are typically credited on the payable date. Also, in the case of physical bearer bonds, coupons are clipped and presented to the paying agent. Internationally, in contrast, it is often typical to credit dividends and interest only upon receipt because of the limited sources of accurate and consistent corporate action information available and the greater risk of delay in receipt.

Related to sources of corporate action information is the less formal information and advice that some custodians offer to investment managers. This refers to advice on local market regulations regarding the handling of assets.[2]

The custodian reports capital changes and reorganizations in a timely way to the investor and acts on the basis of the investment manager's instructions. Stock dividends and splits are recorded when they occur. Also, new shares offered as a result of mergers or spinoffs are credited. Beneficial holders are advised of pending tender offers, and the bank will tender for the client prior to expiration if so instructed. Finally, conversions or exchanges between warrants, convertible bonds, preferred stock, or ADRs and common stock or other instruments are processed.

A key part of efficient settlement is timely advice of all securities movements. This includes transaction journals and daily statements. The mode of these communications varies widely. On-line terminal data communications are common for domestic U.S. instruments among major institutions. Progressively, this is becoming available between custodians and investment managers internationally as well. Advice can also be provided by mail, telex, or computer interface. Direct communication between a responsible account administrator and the investment manager is important for less routine matters. Finally, to varying degrees, custody agents provide periodic statements of deposited securities, often indicating measurements of performance.

Some form of cash and collateral management is important to the efficient custody service. Integrating cash management with securities custody services can improve the return on the portfolio through securities lending income and investment of excess cash.

[2] International Society of Securities Administrators (ISSA), *ISSA Handbook* (Zurich, Switzerland, 1986), pp. US1–US41.

THE CUSTODIAN RELATIONSHIP. The choice of a custodian depends on a variety of factors. The investment manager needs an agent to settle transactions, hold securities, collect dividends and tax reclaims, and administer corporate actions. The investment manager also needs a bank to support its specific cash management needs, including foreign exchange if necessary. Over and above other functional requirements, safety of assets must be guaranteed. Finally, the benefits of the overall banking relationship should be considered.

The mutual responsibilities of the investment manager and agent bank are generally included in a contract that defines the relationship. This includes the form of instructions (phone versus written). The contract may also spell out dividend, corporate action, and pricing services that will be utilized through the agent, and will state the cost of the service and the risks and exposures of the relationship. Beyond the contract, it is important for the investment manager to develop a strong working relationship with the custody agent to convey its system and procedure requirements.[3]

HOW CAN TRADE-PROCESSING PROBLEMS BE AVOIDED?

Settlement efficiency can be maximized with little additional cost. The most important factor is accurate and timely input of trade information at the various stages. This section focuses on the common problem areas in providing institutional account information, the broker's trade input, and posttrade follow-up. Attention and care in these areas require little more than common sense but can pay substantial benefits in settlement efficiency.

SETUP AND MAINTENANCE OF SUBACCOUNT INFORMATION. Each broker has its own bookkeeping system in which each investment manager's institutional subaccounts are set up. One frustrating trade problem occurs if a trade is booked to what appear to be the correct subaccounts but no ID confirmation is received because of inaccuracies in the broker's bookkeeping system. Avoiding this problem depends on the original setup of the accounts as well as on accuracy of account input.

It is common for investment managers, when first establishing a relationship with a broker, to provide data on a number of subaccounts for the

---

[3] Gerald Doyle, "Global Clearance and Custody Issues," presented at the International Operations Association Symposium on International Equity Compliance and Clearance Strategies, New York, June 24, 1987.

various accounts under management. Although trading may never occur in some of these accounts with a particular broker, setting them up in advance greatly facilitates accurate input and timely trade processing. The original setup of accounts needs to be accurate, which depends on effective broker trade support and consistent information from the investment manager.

When a trade is done in a new subaccount or fund, or with a broker that is new to the investment manager, standing instructions must be communicated on the trade date for each subaccount. Trade input cannot be entered without account information. It is best to convey this information to the broker as early in the day as possible to avoid rushing the broker's input process.

COMMUNICATION OF BREAKDOWN INFORMATION.   Investment managers often allocate portions of a large trade to more than one account. The broker will then split the trade on the basis of the investment manager's decisions. Problems in communicating subaccount information between the investment manager and the broker are common. When possible, investment manager account information provided during trading hours maximizes the time for careful input and double checking and also provides more time to resolve any questions that arise.

In contrast, some investment managers specify subaccount information only after the close, when all execution reports have been received. At that time, the broker's trade support staff is busiest, working under strict evening processing deadlines to complete all input. The broker often may have insufficient time to check for accuracy.

In extreme cases, the broker may not even be able to process input until the next day, thereby delaying the confirmation process. In this situation, the broker must input trades to a suspense account and rebook them to the client the following day.

PROCESSING BROKER TRADE INPUT.   Institutional trades are much larger, on average, than retail trades and demand a special level of care and customer service. Brokers often establish separate trade support units for handling institutional trade input.

The most common problem in institutional trade processing is the failure of the broker to input trade details accurately. In this situation, the investment manager will see either no confirmation or a confirmation with inaccurate details, so that affirmation will be delayed. Trade affirmation can also be delayed if the investment manager records the execution inaccurately. The broker, however, creates DTC's trade input for the investment manager and the custodian. If appropriate, the broker will cancel and correct the trade to modify input to DTC-ID, and the investment manager or institution will reinstruct its agent bank.

Breakdowns and average pricing of trades are common in institutional equity trading. Large block agency trades are often executed in multiple pieces with different prices, necessitating calculation of shares for the average price per share that is applied to each breakdown.

The booking of average-price trades often results in input errors, which must be corrected. First, the average price can be miscalculated because most brokers determine the average manually. Also, missing pieces such as late execution reports will change the average price, necessitating correction of every ticket or subaccount piece. Second, designation of subaccounts requires free-form communication between the investment manager and the broker to specify how many shares are associated with which subaccounts. Also, since most brokers input trades manually and average pricing is generally done through a house or trading account, the simplest trade requires multiple trade input on both sides, with the possibility of booking trades on the wrong side, the wrong stock, or the wrong price. The best way to avoid this problem is to automate it back to the client's own input and the original executions.

Another common problem area is entry of commissions for agency transactions. Multilevel commission schedules require manual calculation on each trade. For example, different rates may apply depending on trade size and whether the trade was executed OTC or on an exchange. Commission problems can be minimized by sophisticated systems to automate complex commission calculations.

The Instinet Trading System facilitates breakdowns, average pricing, and complex commission calculations. The potential for error is sharply reduced because an institutional execution through Instinet is electronically captured from the original client's keystrokes without manual entry. Each execution is held during the day in Instinet's Clearing Interface System (CIS) and updated for commission changes and client account information. This gives the investment manager unsurpassed trade input quality. Average pricing is automatically facilitated on-line. Also, client trade lists are balanced each evening to original client information to ensure accuracy. Finally, the CIS provides institutions with same-day confirmation of breakdown details on-line via the trading system. This permits real-time review on trade date of data as it will be confirmed to the depository and custodian.

POSTTRADE FOLLOW-UP.   On the morning after the trade, an ID confirm will be produced by DTC and sent in hard copy or data transmission to the broker, the investing institution, the institution's custodian, and other interested parties. It is the investment manager's or institution's responsibility to compare this confirm to its own records and affirm if appropriate. Depending on the investment manager, affirmation may be done directly or through the custodian's network. If there is disagreement with the confirm, the investment manager shares responsibility with the broker to follow up and resolve any differences. Settlement will be delayed if affirmation is not done before the end of TD + 3.

For his part, the broker receives lists of unaffirmed trades starting from TD + 3, and telephone calls are made to institutions to request affirmation or resolve differences as appropriate. The broker's exposure to unsettled trades is minimized if aggressive follow-up on unaffirmed trades is carried out.

The investment manager must also ensure that the custodian has the information required to complete settlement. Depending on the institution's standing instructions, the custodian needs accurate instructions on each trade in the proper format and with a full security description to minimize the potential for error. Also, the source of the funding for settlement must be clearly reported unless it is understood from a standard instruction.

Normal industry practice is to make delivery versus payment on the fifth business day. Despite the best efforts, however, settlement is delayed on some COD transactions. The broker is constrained by regulations and also exposed on unsettled transactions. When a broker attempts to deliver purchased securities to an institution versus payment but the delivery is rejected, it is called a DK or "don't know" trade. Delivery is rejected by the agent bank on behalf of the institution, since the institution "doesn't know" the trade under the stated terms. Often this situation causes the broker to incur interest expense if the stock must be financed overnight.

Typically, on institutional purchases, the broker will attempt delivery repeatedly and follow up with the client and his bank on DK'd deliveries. The agent bank will refuse to take delivery unless affirmation of the trade or delivery instructions have been received from their client. Meanwhile, the position may have to be financed by the broker who holds the undelivered securities, incurring interest expense. If the customer is at fault, the broker may subsequently attempt to recover interest expense based on delayed settlement.

On institutional sales, an investment manager sometimes may not have securities available to make a delivery on a selling execution on settlement date. For example, the investment manager may have purchased the securities from another broker who has not yet delivered them. Alternatively, physical certificates may be in transfer or lost. If a loss is incurred that is wholly or in part the institution's responsibility, the broker may absorb it but also may choose to go to arbitration or to take legal action against the client.

Under the most extreme circumstances, when a customer has failed to deliver a security sold in a COD transaction, the broker may close out the unsatisfied sale with a buy-in. A *buy-in* means offsetting a customer sale with a customer purchase at the current market price. Thus, any profit or loss is due to the customer. Although this is a legal option on any unsettled fail-to-receive, buying in essentially means giving up on a client and is done only when necessary because of the strain on the continuing business relationship. Thus, buy-ins are typically a last resort on trades that have been unsettled for several weeks. It is most often necessary when an agency broker is himself being bought in or forced to make delivery on a stock that cannot be borrowed. It also can arise as a result of the Regulation T rule requiring settlement within 35 days if the trade remains outstanding after repeated extensions have been filed. Under special circumstances, however, buy-ins may be forced much sooner than this.

A monthly reconciliation by the institution between the custodian and its own records is essential. This is needed even more frequently with active trading accounts. Institutions share responsibility with the executing broker to follow up on unsettled trades. If, for example, a trade is not booked by the broker (therefore producing no confirmation), the investment manager should advise the broker of the oversight.

SUMMARY

In this chapter, we have overviewed postexecution processing and settlement for DTC-eligible securities. Because of DTC's and NSCC's well-developed clearing processes, DTC settlement can be virtually automated among institutions and brokers once the trade has been input accurately. Manual processing is necessary only for exceptions or input errors. Therefore, efficient settlement depends on effective communications among brokers, custodians, and investment managers.

The investment manager generally makes the original investment decision and then, based on this decision, chooses which brokers to use for execution. In addition, the investment manager must be prepared to follow up on posttrade processing. The broker is responsible for initial trade input based on the terms of the execution, allocated according to the investment manager's discretion. Then the broker will settle the trade with the agent bank through DTC. The agent bank or custodian is responsible for carrying out the instructions of the investment manager to maintain institutional portfolios of securities and to settle transactions in a timely fashion.

The Editor Asks

Q *Do you see any momentum for reducing the standard five-day settlement period? What are the impediments? What would be the advantages?*

A The technical capability to consider a shorter cycle is either under development or already implemented, so it is likely to become a serious issue in the next year or two.

The current cycle has the advantage of consistency and sufficiency for settlement of U.S. equities given the current state of posttrade processing mechanisms. Technically, at least three or four (if not five) business days are needed to process U.S. equity trades in light of current batch-processing systems. Between brokers, it permits sufficient time to compare trades in a given market and shift the liability to the designated clearing corporation for settlement. At the same time, it is not uncommon for institutions to need three or more days for affirmation to be recorded. Shortening the settlement period would increase the uncertainty and increase the rate of DK'd deliveries in this environment. It would also be extremely expensive to change all the domestic bookkeeping and trading systems built based on a five-day cycle to adopt to a shorter period, so a major initiative would be required.

Another advantage of a five-day cycle over a shorter period is related to conversion across international borders. Conversion of instruments between markets becomes less efficient when settlement periods vary. In fact, some foreign markets with longer settlement periods, including the United Kingdom, are considering the advantages of a five-day rolling cycle. In an increasingly global environment, establishing consistent standard cycles across markets may become more important than shortening the cycle in the United States.

On the other hand, since the crash of October 19, 1987, a great deal of interest has grown in management alternatives to reduce risk in the securities business. There is no doubt that credit risk is far greater the longer the time between trade date and settlement date. Institutional trades in U.S. equities average over $250,000 and can be up to several million dollars in value. There is significant exposure for a contra-party to go bankrupt between trade date and settlement date on a five-day period. Also, the following initiatives have reduced the potential technical constraints on a shorter settlement period:

- *DTC's same-day funds:* This creates the potential for routinely selling DTC-eligible instruments versus payment in Fed funds rather than clearinghouse funds in an integrated environment of securities and money.

- *DTC's international ID:* This initiative will provide an intraday capability for confirmation and affirmation. Its intent is to facilitate processing of foreign securities trades for institutions with short settlement cycles. The same process could be applied to permit a shorter settlement period in the United States in the future.

- *Locked-in trade reporting:* NYSE, AMEX, and NASDAQ each have initiatives intending to eliminate the comparison process in favor of Trade Date submission of "locked-in" two-sided input. In addition, NSCC has service bureau and qualified special representative programs for locked-in submission of input from trading systems. These initiatives will reduce the exposure and shorten the time frames needed for comparison.

In conclusion, although the benefits of movement toward shorter settlement periods are relatively clear, when that is realistically likely to occur is very uncertain.

PART FOUR

The Costs of
Transacting

9

A TAXONOMY OF TRADING TECHNIQUES

Wayne H. Wagner

Taxonomy is a term borrowed from the biological sciences that refers to the classification of organisms according to their basic characteristics. A taxonomy classifies together organisms that are similar and separates those that are different. Like organisms, trading techniques exist within and adapt to their environment in order to survive. Accordingly, this chapter begins with a description of the trading and exchange environment.

Visitors to the floor of the New York Stock Exchange (NYSE) inevitably hear an Eden-like comment that "this is the best of all possible markets." *Best,* on the Exchange floor, usually means best *liquidity,* but also implies an ability to (1) rapidly adapt to changing market conditions and (2) evolve toward better mechanisms as new technologies and new investor demands arise.

MARKET LIQUIDITY

The great advantage of market liquidity is that traders and investors can trade in reasonable volume without a major impact on stock price. Many factors contribute to making a market liquid. Clearly, the most important factor is the continuous interaction of a *large number of buyers and sellers.* This large pool of investors is both the cause and the effect of liquidity: Investors are willing to hold shares because they can dispose of them whenever they choose.

The material for this chapter was originally presented at the Conference on Trading Strategies and Execution Costs sponsored by the Institute of Chartered Financial Analysts in New York City on December 3, 1987.

Obviously, all investors cannot share the same opinion about the value of a stock. They would either all want to own the shares, or none would want to hold shares. The price would head toward infinity or zero. So a key factor in building liquidity is *a diversity of opinion,* information, and investment needs among market participants. A large pool of investors enhances the probability of diverse opinions.

Liquidity presupposes a *readily accessible location:* either a physical exchange floor or electronic medium. Similarly, liquid markets need to be readily accessible in time, which implies *operating continuously* during convenient market hours. Continuous operations implies that someone, such as an assigned specialist or a group of market-makers/dealers, is present to maintain market continuity.

Liquidity also implies *a reasonable cost of transacting* so investors can trade and adjust portfolio positions without excessive loss of value. High transaction costs destroy market liquidity since investors would not trade except on information of great significance. Liquidity, in turn, lowers trading costs. If a dealer expects to turn his inventory quickly, he can operate at narrower profit margins.

Market *integrity* makes for more liquid markets. Investors who receive fair and honorable treatment in the exchange process will trade again.

Liquidity is enhanced if investors are assured of the *sanctity of the contract:* certainty of trade completion. Proper trading safeguards make investors feel secure about the financial ability and guaranteed commitment of the contra trader. Exchanges limit membership to parties that pass standards of financial strength, knowledge, and integrity. Contract assurance also underlies the "know your customer" requirement placed on exchange members.

Diversity, location, continuity, low cost, integrity, and sanctity of contract all enhance the creation of a large pool of buyers and sellers. Value also flows to the companies whose securities are listed on the exchange. Investors who believe their holdings possess the valuable trait of liquidity will pay more for new securities. Higher stock prices enhance the value of the corporation and lower its cost of capital.

Obviously, not all companies are large enough to support an extensive pool of buyers and sellers? How do markets for thinly traded securities function?

If markets have little "natural liquidity," they must be *made* liquid artificially, and a need is created for a functionary to *make* the market. A market is made when a market-maker stands willing to provide *bridge liquidity* by buying stock offered and holding it until a buyer arrives. This is also the mechanism that allows markets to operate continuously.

The need for artificially supplied bridge liquidity attaches a cost to liquidity. A market-maker must be compensated for providing bridge liquidity. Like any merchant, he makes money by selling inventory for a higher price than he paid for it. The seller takes a little less than he believes the stock is worth in order to complete his side of the trade. Similarly, the buyer pays a little more than it is worth to get the stock when he wants it. The difference is market-maker profit.

This market-maker spread is one of the major costs of trading. The presence of large blocks creates market-maker risk and strains market-maker capital. As a result, spreads widen and trade prices are impacted. When pressure is put on commission levels, more trading costs shift to the less observable spreads and impact.

That liquidity creates value has been demonstrated. Here we see that it also costs to create liquidity. The costs of liquidity (e.g., brokerage firm profits and manager shortfall) are readily observed. The value added to company securities (and investment performance) through liquidity is more difficult to measure. Techniques that reduce transaction costs but compromise value-enhancing liquidity do not serve investors' basic objectives.

This discussion suggests another question: Can markets become so liquid that they no longer require the expense of market-maker services? With a very liquid security, natural buyers and sellers would arrive frequently. None would be much inconvenienced by a short wait until the contra-party wished to trade. This can be described as a not-quite-continuous market. For this dealerless market to operate effectively, qualified natural investors would need access and standing equivalent to that of the market-makers. In effect, natural buyers and sellers would perform as bridge market-makers, even though it is not their principal business to "make" markets. This would increase competition for market-makers and reduce the profitability of market-making. This would not appeal to the current designated market-makers.

THE MARKET WE HAVE

The New York Stock Exchange has lasted for 200 years precisely because it has continually changed to meet investor needs. The basic market exchange has evolved into an *agency auction with affirmative obligation*. *Agency* means that only exchange members represent orders on the floor. *Auction* means that buyers compete by raising the price offered in order to attract sellers. The NYSE imposes an affirmative obligation on a specialist to maintain an "orderly" market by absorbing temporary trade imbalances into his personal account.

Most of the time, this mechanism provides the specialist with an opportunity to earn market-maker inventory profits. At times, however, the affirmative obligation will force a money-losing proposition onto the specialist. To balance the requirement that the specialist absorb an occasional financial loss, the Exchange grants several valuable privileges:

1. The specialist has an exclusive right to his assigned stocks. This monopoly gives him the right to collect an inventory spread between market order sellers and market order buyers. The Exchange establishes rules and standards to ensure that these inventory profits do not become excessive.

2. The specialist has exclusive access to valuable information concerning investor trading intentions. His physical presence represents the spot where investors must go to trade in his assigned stocks. He can develop a feel for the market by his interaction with the crowd. He also has the exclusive right to maintain and view the limit order book. This presence and knowledge help protect him from assuming money-losing inventory positions.

3. The specialist has exclusive knowledge of the balance of buy and sell orders at the opening—and, recently, at the close—of the market. Since the specialist often accommodates the imbalance out of his own inventory, he can establish an opening price that greatly increases his chance of an inventory profit.

This venerable procedure has been considerably strained by the growth of institutional investing. The personal capital available to any specialist is trivial compared to the buying power of institutional investors. Thus, an informal support system has arisen to augment the specialist and fill needs that are otherwise not well served.

Some examples:

1. Specialists on other regional exchanges participate electronically in market-making, independent of where the trade is originally presented.

2. Upstairs brokers commit their own capital to principal a trade (for a price concession) to accommodate their clients.

3. A host of accommodations are available on or near the floor to absorb imbalances beyond the carrying capacity of the specialist—all for an accommodation profit, of course.

4. Investors can use the so-called third and fourth markets to approach the other side of the trade, circumventing the exchange floor entirely.

These ancillary arrangements are vital to the survival of the major exchanges in their present form. Without these, the shortcomings of specialist capital would become all too apparent, and the Exchange could not continue to function as it does now.

Even with all the ancillary support functions, critics fault the system for not being adequately capitalized, accommodative, or accessible, particularly in times of strain. The system is designed to avoid fast markets and gap prices. It appeared not well prepared to function when these are unavoidable, as happened during October 1987.

In addition, a new constituency, the pension plan sponsor community, is beginning to question whether the system is cost-effective. This skepticism stems from many motivations:

- Average investment manager performance continues to disappoint plan sponsors. The open question is whether the cost of completing a trade exceeds the information value that motivates trading.
- The Department of Labor is pressuring plan sponsors to assure that trusteed funds are used exclusively for trust beneficiaries. Specifically included are assets spent in the transaction process.
- Sponsors and corporations (as well as investment managers) voice concerns about adequacy of market-maker capital and responsiveness.
- Sponsors and government agencies express concern over system abuses such as insider trading and frontrunning.

ALTERNATIVE MARKET STRUCTURES

Most discussions of market structures focus on the existing markets and implicitly accede that this is "the best of all possible markets." This may be true; yet there are other methods of organizing securities markets, many of which are described in other chapters of this book. These other market structures are used in different locations throughout the world for various types of securities. Some operate in parallel with the organized exchanges in this country.

The important characteristics that distinguish one market from another are as follows:

- Markets may operate *continuously* or on the basis of periodic *calls-to-market,* in the manner of some European markets or the crossing networks.
- The market-making function may be delegated to agents, dealers, or specialists. In contrast, dealerless markets provide direct trading between natural buyer and natural seller.
- An affirmative requirement to operate an "orderly" market contrasts to an open outcry market organization such as that used by the futures exchanges.
- Market-makers may compete as in the over-the-counter market, or they may operate under a NYSE-like trading monopoly.

Market structures evolved in different directions as they sorted out the interests of their constituencies. In different markets, the floor community, the brokers, the investment advisors, the security issuers, the beneficial owners, and the governing bodies have different degrees of power and relative sophistication. This has led to differing trading solutions in different securities and locations.

As a result, markets differ in their responsiveness to timing, size, and imbalance of trade. They differ with respect to who has access to trading information and in the uses to which that information can be put. They differ in the cost of providing the trading facility. They differ in terms of whose capital supports bridge liquidity: that of the specialists, the dealers, or the investors themselves.

TRADING MOTIVATIONS

Markets exist to accommodate investors who wish to trade. Trading motivations differ, but investors can be broadly summarized into two categories: information-motivated investors and liquidity-motivated investors. Information-motivated investors act on information or strategic decisions that they believe will lead to superior investment performance. Liquidity-motivated investors trade on a desire to convert between investment or consumption, or on a reassessment of long-term policy.

Information traders, often referred to as *active traders,* usually stress speed of execution. They are more likely to use market orders and rely on market-makers to provide bridge liquidity. Liquidity traders, sometimes called *passive traders,* are more concerned with the cost of trading. They like to use less time-sensitive trading techniques in the hope of trading time indifference for a lower cost execution.

Information traders are more likely to trade issues in large blocks than are liquidity traders. They are also more likely than liquidity traders to trade *with* market direction—to sell into a down market. Because information traders trade on their own insights or evaluations, they are far more interested in anonymity of identity and intended action.

Thus, a trader must first examine the urgency or importance of rapid execution of the trade. Is the trade based on information? Will the value of doing the trade disappear or dissipate if it is not done immediately? How big is the trade relative to the liquidity and market direction? How much shock absorber capability does the market have in the face of a trading imbalance?

Trades that are not motivated by information, however, have much more flexibility to use different, perhaps lower cost, trading techniques. These techniques are also available to active managers who are not executing information-based trades.

TYPES OF TRADES

The most common type of trade is the *market order,* which instructs the broker to execute promptly at the best price available. A similar order, but one that gives the broker greater discretion, is the *market-not-held order. Not held* means that the broker is not held to any specific trade price. *A best-efforts order* gives the broker even more discretion to work the order when market conditions are most propitious.

Some types of orders are designed to execute at specific times. *Market-on-open orders* execute at the opening price, a time that many investors feel provides maximum liquidity. At certain times of the quarter corresponding to futures and options expirations, it is possible to use *market-on-close orders.*

Other orders are designed to execute at specific prices. A *limit order* will execute only when the market price reaches the limit.

Some orders place high importance on immediacy of execution. *Principal trades* require bridge capital and often require a price concession. *Program trades* have similar characteristics except that they apply to many issues traded at once, and the broker is paid through higher commissions rather than price concessions.

By contrast, some orders are deliberately low-key and designed to respond to favorable market conditions. In addition to the market-not-held and best-efforts orders mentioned before, traders can use *participate (do not initiate) orders.* These orders are designed to respond to initiatives and indications made by active traders on the other side of the trade.

Orders that openly display their nature, such as *secondary offerings* or *"sunshine" trades*, attempt to entice the other side of the trade to respond to availability.

Finally, traders may avoid the exchange entirely and seek out the other side directly in a dealerless market. *Third-market trades, fourth-market trades, direct crosses,* and *crossing networks* are some of the trading mechanisms used.

THE TAXONOMY

Trading motivation is the major axis on which the taxonomy is drawn. Categories are scaled between extremes of active and passive trading. The reader is cautioned that, as with any taxonomy, it is the taxonomist who gets to choose the names for the classifications. Also, economics as a science is not as replicable as biology. The finer differences may be in the eye of the beholder, and reasonable people disagree with the appropriateness of the characterizations and the categorizations.

The taxonomic categorizations are as follows:

1. Liquidity, whatever the fair price (most active).
2. Costs are not significant.
3. Possibly hazardous, need agent.
4. Gravitational pull.
5. Low cost, whatever the liquidity (least active).

For each of these classifications, the following sections address uses, advantages, costs, and potential weaknesses.

LIQUIDITY, WHATEVER THE FAIR PRICE. Types of orders include *principal trades, program trades,* and *market-on-close orders.* Information traders who believe they need to trade with immediacy and often in size use these trading techniques. The trader quickly secures a guaranteed execution at a guaranteed price. The major cost of these trades arises when the broker is placed at risk and must receive a fair compensation for bearing that risk. Also, these trades demand high liquidity on short notice. They may overwhelm the available liquidity and cause prices to move as their presence is detected in the market. Traders using these techniques usually recognize that these methods are expensive, but they are willing to pay the price in order to achieve the desired execution.

Some readers may be surprised that program trades are included in this category. Weren't program trades invented to serve the needs of index funds, surely among the most passive of investment techniques? But program trading shares the shifting of risk to the broker and the inattention to market liquidity typical of the most aggressive traders. Program trades are also used to secure arbitrage profits between equities and the futures or options markets. (They are usually called *basket trades* in this context.) With these trades, prices and execution cost are irrelevant; what counts is securing the spread between the markets. Market-on-close orders can serve much the same purpose.

COSTS ARE NOT SIGNIFICANT. Types of orders are *market orders* and *market-on-open orders*. The majority of investors, particularly noninstitutional investors, seldom consider any other kind of orders than these when trading securities. As mentioned in the preface, this type of order indicates the classical view that trading costs are not significant. Traders who use market orders trust the competitive market to generate a fair price. Active control of the order is not required. For many orders, fair market price is a reasonable assumption. Indeed, many Exchange floor procedures are specifically designed to encourage market orders and to ensure that these orders receive fair prices. Spreads received from executing market orders are an essential part of specialist income.

These orders work best for smaller orders and more liquid stocks. They are sometimes called "no-brainers" in that they require little trading skill on the part of the broker. They are often used to pay soft dollar commissions in exchange for valuable services. Traders who use these orders accept that they will pay a reasonable spread and commission to have their orders executed. Trade costs are accepted without question; indeed, they are seldom even considered.

The weakness of these orders is that all discretion is surrendered. The trader has no control of the trade, and the broker is expected to exercise only the most rudimentary cautions.

POSSIBLY HAZARDOUS, NEED AGENT. Types of orders are *best efforts*, *market-not-held*, and *participate*. Traders who use these orders recognize that their orders may create an impact unless they are handled carefully. They engage the services of a carefully selected broker to work the order to the best of his knowledge and skills. These orders are often used for larger orders, frequently in more thinly traded issues. They are very popular among small to medium-sized institutional money managers.

The advantage of these trades is that they may do better on price than orders that demand quick execution. This is particularly important when the order must be completed through a series of sequential trades. Obviously, timely execution is not of primary importance. These orders often carry a higher commission, because executing the order is more work-intensive for the broker. The assumption is that the higher commission offsets the higher transaction costs that would probably be extracted elsewhere.

Implied in this type of order is an authorization to do some low-level advertising. Advertising lets the market know that a willing buyer/seller is standing in the wings. Again, the trader loses control of the order. When he executes and the price at which he does so are in the hands of the broker. The trader frequently doesn't know how much has been done until after the market closes. Another danger is that the agent may serve multiple masters: other clients and possibly his own brokerage firm. The valuable information that a buyer or seller exists is released to the broker. It is difficult for the trader to discern where and how that information may have been used, and whether any of those uses were detrimental to his interests.

GRAVITATIONAL PULL.   Types of orders are *secondary offerings, sunshine trades,* and *call markets.*

Gravitational pull is a term coined by Cohen, Maier, Schwartz, and Whitcomb.[1] It describes how the public acknowledgment of a desire to trade will draw out the other side of the trade, hopefully at attractive prices. As Cohen et al. describe it, "If a trader's price is close enough to a counterpart offer, he will 'jump' his price and transact with certainty via a market order."

The major advantage is that it draws attention and liqiduity to itself. If enough contra-side traders are attracted, the trade may execute with little or no market impact. If a surplus of contra-side traders becomes interested, the initiator may garner a trading profit.

These orders often require substantial orchestration, implying high broker operating costs. This difficulty of administration is one of their greatest weaknesses. Another weakness can occur if sufficient other side is not drawn out, and shares remain unsold and are tinged with a shopworn character.

LOW COST, WHATEVER THE LIQUIDITY.   Types of orders are *limit orders, third-market orders, fourth-market orders,* and *crossing networks.* Low cost of trading is the primary interest of traders who use these types of order. There may not be a contra party to his order willing to trade with him

---

[1] Kalman J. Cohen, Steven F. Meier, Robert A. Schwartz, and David K. Whitcomb, *The Microstructure of Securities Markets* (Englewood Cliffs, N.J.: Prentice-Hall, 1986), p. 4.

on the terms he suggests. He takes the chance that the order may not execute at all. This is best suited to noninformational liquidity trading situations.

The advantages are low commissions, low impact, and possibly the elimination of the market-maker spread. The major weakness, of course, is the uncertainty of whether any trades will be done at all. Traders fear that they may end up "chasing the stock" if they are unable to find the other side in these "meet" markets.

SUMMARY

Table 9.1 summarizes the uses, advantages, costs, and weaknesses of these trading techniques. The spectrum runs from fastest execution to slowest, from highest expected cost to lowest. This suggests the sequential use of these techniques, moving up to more expensive strategies only after trying less costly methods.

Different types of orders exist to serve different market segments. The ability of the exchange system to adapt and create solutions to real investment problems is truly impressive. In general, traders get what they demand in terms of trading services. In exchange, they usually pay a fair and competitive price to the brokers and exchanges for the services provided.

It is not productive to argue that trading costs are too high. Given the demands, and given the intensity of competition and readiness to adapt, trading costs are likely as low as they can be—unless a change is made in the nature of the services demanded.

Traders who insist that they must have the facilities and conveniences that the exchange community now provides must be prepared to pay the costs. To reduce costs, sponsors and investment advisors may have to assume more of those costs and risks within the trading process. The traders may have to work harder and retain more responsibility. They may need to make do without some of the services they are accustomed to receiving for free. They may need to make do with less bridge liquidity and to centralize trading at specific call-to-market times.

Most fundamentally, investors and traders are accustomed to a market that readily assumes the duties, costs, and risks of trading, and delivers a plethora of valuable but dimly related services at no additional charge. They are less accustomed to the thought that it is expensive to run such a market. In the future, sponsors will demand of traders that they make clearer choices, which reconcile trade costs with the benefits received. Sponsors pay the cost of trading and are entitled to—and are demanding—a clear accounting of the benefits derived.

TABLE 9.1   A TAXONOMY OF TRADING TECHNIQUES

	Uses	Advantages	Costs	Weaknesses
Liquidity, whatever the cost: Principal trades Program trades	Immediacy, in size	Guaranteed execution; guaranteed price	Places broker at risk; creates impact	Pushes the market around
Costs not important: Market orders Market-on-open orders Market-on-close orders	Certainty of execution; suited to simple trades	Competitive price	Pays the spread; may create impact	Loses control of trade
Possible hazards, need agent: Best efforts trades Market-not-held orders Participate orders	Larger size; low scale; advertising	May do better on price	Higher commission; lower impact	Loses control of trade
Advertised orders: Secondary offerings Sunshine trades	Large size; advertising; "gravitational pull"	Competitive price	High operational, organizational costs	More difficult to administer
Low cost, whatever the liquidity: Limit orders Third-market trades Fourth-market trades Direct crosses	Noninformational trading; indifferent to timing	Low commission; no spread; low impact	High operational cost	Uncertainty of trading; "chasing" the stock

The Editor Asks

Q *In terms of evolutionary development, the market grew out of what you describe as higher immediacy strategies, with lower cost strategies evolving later as an embroidery on the basic Dutch auction market. How do investors think about the cost–benefit trade-off of moving from one level to another? How do you think they do or should address this question?*

A Carl Sagan, in his book *The Dragons of Eden*, describes how man's more advanced brain evolved in three major evolutionary steps, all of which we retain today and each of which serves a different function.[2] In the process, the ancient brain structure did not wither away; quite the contrary, it maintained its functionality and grew to encompass new functions. So it is, I believe, with the evolution of the markets.

The basic Dutch auction that occurs on the exchange floor still performs essential functions without which investors cannot survive. There will always be a need for immediacy in trading, and the liquidity, whatever the fair price, trading strategies best meet those needs.

I do not view the evolution of additional techniques as an impairment to the basic market order exchange transaction. Rather, I see the added techniques as serving needs that are not well served otherwise. I do not see these as sapping liquidity from the Exchange; rather, they encourage more trading from parties that might not otherwise trade if they perceived trading to be too costly. In the process, stability and liquidity are provided to the markets.

Most traders are aware of the lower cost alternatives and use them when they are advantageous. A problem occurs, however, when a higher cost alternative is selected even though the advantages of immediacy are not required. This is probably the greatest shortcoming of soft dollar usage: The advantages of alternative trading techniques are obscured by the desire to get the bills paid.

---

[2] New York: Random House, 1977.

10

TRADING COST: THE CRITICAL LINK BETWEEN INVESTMENT INFORMATION AND RESULTS

Thomas F. Loeb

Some active managers can demonstrate that their stock selection processes have added value before trading costs. After allowing for these costs, however, most probably find that their portfolios fall short of performance expectations. Obviously, an appraisal of trading costs is critical for determining the ultimate value of stock selection or market timing skills.

A number of institutions have endeavored to measure the cost of trading.[1] Studies of trading costs to date have generally measured a combination of two factors—(1) the cost of using the market mechanism and (2) the behavior of the institutional trader. The measurement procedure is complicated by the subjective timing and block size decisions of the individual trader and by the need to eliminate from the result the effects of general market movements, new information about a stock or other ''news'' in order to capture the real cost of trading.

The *real* cost of trading, however, can be determined solely by the particular market mechanism through which an institution transacts. Because institutional traders' approaches to the market mechanism will vary significantly, appraisals of trading costs that include trader discretionary behavior

[1] See Gilbert L. Beebower and William W. Priest, ''An Analysis of Transaction Costs in Equity Trading,'' Seminar on the Analysis of Security Prices, Chicago, November 3, 1978; Larry J. Cuneo and Wayne H. Wagner, ''Reducing the Cost of Stock Trading,'' *Financial Analysts Journal*, November–December 1975, pp. 1–28; and William L. Fouse, ''Risk and Liquidity: The Keys to Stock Price Behavior,'' *Financial Analysts Journal*, May–June 1976, pp. 2–12.

are likely to produce a wide range of results. In fact, traditional measurements of trading costs may provide information about the skill or luck of the traders studied, but little insight into the actual costs levied by a particular market mechanism, and even less insight into how trading might best be accomplished.

THE MARKET MECHANISM

There are two types of market mechanisms through which stock trades may be executed—the auction market and the negotiated market. The auction market is comprised of one market-maker (specialist) per listed issue on each stock exchange. The negotiated market is characterized by more than one competing market-maker in each issue (i.e., over-the-counter markets). The "upstairs" dealer market is a special form of negotiated market where highly capitalized stock exchange members compete to make their own markets in both listed and over-the-counter issues.

The upstairs dealer market provides the best arena in which to measure trading costs. First, this market covers a larger number of stocks than the auction or OTC markets taken separately; in fact, it provides uniform trading data across all publicly traded U.S. issues. Second, it is the most liquid market when dealing with a single issue or large groups of stocks simply because of its access to larger quantities of risk capital. Third, the upstairs dealer market mechanism provides ready markets in all issues, thereby precluding the possibility that we will "miss" a trade and fail to know what the trading costs would have been.

The key advantage of measuring trading costs in the upstairs dealer market is that one can capture the full cost impact of an investment decision without having to adjust for intervening factors. The market-maker's bid or offer covering the investor's entire stock position will contain a risk premium that is implicitly adjusted for block size, trading liquidity, the potential impact of unannounced news and possible special information effects known only to the transactor. On the other hand, the results of this approach remain time-period dependent; changing market and liquidity conditions will limit their usefulness as a predictive tool.

COMPONENTS OF COST

Trading costs in the upstairs dealer market may be divided into three components of cost charged by the market-maker. First there is the

FIGURE 10.1   COMPONENTS OF TRADING COST

market-maker's spread, which is the basic cost component reflecting the difference between the bid and offer prices of a stock in a market made for at least 100 shares. Second is the price concession—the incremental cost subtracted from the existing bid price on a sale transaction or added to the existing offer price on a purchase transaction when the market-maker is asked to buy or sell more shares than are indicated at his basic bid–offer spread. Third is the brokerage commission, which is typically charged explicitly in the negotiated market and is generally the smallest of the three components. (Securities and Exchange Commission fees and transfer taxes occur only on sale transactions and are small enough that they may be ignored for the purpose of measuring trading cost.)

Figure 10.1 diagrams these three cost components. The basic market-maker's spread is flanked on either side by the price concession. The price concession is shown for both purchase (offer side) and sale (bid side) transactions. Brokerage commissions are added to either side of the figure to reflect the explicit brokerage charges on purchase or sale transactions.

By starting at the "mid-price" of the basic market-maker's spread and measuring the cost to the right, one can estimate the one-way purchase cost. By measuring the cost to the left of the mid-price, one can calculate the one-way selling cost. Although the transactor may incur more or less of the one-way trading cost shown when purchasing or selling a particular block of stock, he would incur the full measure of the spread, price concessions and brokerage commissions for the "round trip" if he purchased and immediately turned around and sold the same block of stock across a large number of transactions.

ESTIMATING THE COST OF TRADING

Using the Wilshire 5000 Index Stock Universe as our base, we calculated data on the relationship between company size, stock price and the basic market-maker's spread for stocks across the entire U.S. equity market. The market-maker's spread for a minimum of 100 shares was based on a 10% sample of 4,416 stocks; we obtained listed stock spreads from the appropriate stock exchange specialist and over-the-counter stock spreads from NASDAQ. Table 10.1 shows the results by market capitalization sectors (shares outstanding times price). The average price, average spread, and spread/price cost of each stock in each sector are equally weighted.

The high positive correlation between stock price and company size is clearly recognizable. The average price of a stock in each capitalization sector, taken at the midpoint of the market-maker's spread, increases with increasing market capitalization. Interestingly, however, the average market-maker's spread (for what nominally is 100 shares) is higher for small companies than for large ones. This difference forms the basis for the very large spread/price cost differential between small and large companies and is the source of the difference in trading costs for round lot trades (before the incremental costs associated with block size). The spread/price cost for the smallest companies is about 12.6 times the spread/price cost for the largest companies. This may reflect the difference in liquidity, but it may also be partially due to the fact that stocks are quoted, at minimum, at one-eighth of one dollar intervals, rather than in cents per share. For very small stocks, an incremental 12.5 cents may be a very large additional cost as a percentage of market price.

To obtain an estimate of the *total* cost of trading for share amounts of 100 or more, we obtained the market-maker's spread, price concessions, and brokerage commissions from the block quotes of a number of market-makers selected for their experience in making dealer markets involving

TABLE 10.1   MARKET CAPITALIZATION AND MARKET-MAKER'S SPREAD

Capitalization Sector (millions of dollars)	No. of Issues	Percentage of U.S. Market	Average Price	Average Spread	Spread/Price Cost[a]
0–10	1,009	0.36	$ 4.58	$0.30	6.55%
10–25	754	0.89	10.30	0.42	4.07
25–50	613	1.59	15.16	0.46	3.03
50–75	362	1.60	18.27	0.34	1.86
75–100	202	1.27	21.85	0.32	1.46
100–500	956	15.65	28.31	0.32	1.13
500–1,000	238	12.29	35.43	0.27	0.76
1,000–1,500	102	8.87	44.34	0.29	0.65
Over 1,500	180	57.48	52.40	0.27	0.52

[a] Round-trip trading cost for 100 shares *excluding* commission costs.

very large capital commitments across a broad range of stocks of varying liquidity and company size. In order to control for variable negotiated commission rates, we assumed that explicit commissions would be paid on all transactions including those involving over-the-counter issues. Explicit brokerage commission costs are purely negotiable, hence will vary depending upon a particular institutional investor's requirements with respect to broker capital commitment, security research and small-order handling, to name a few factors. For the purposes of the study, we applied an average of commission rates actually experienced to the block quotes.

We drew from the Wilshire 5000 a sample of approximately 180 issues spread across the market capitalization structure outlined in Table 10.1. Actual bid-offer markets were quoted for blocks of stock ranging from $5,000 to $20,000,000 in value. The minimum trade was 100 shares in any company, and the maximum did not exceed 5% of a company's market capitalization. The dealer's market was quoted at approximately the same time for each issue assigned to him at each block size level. Each dealer provided markets in a sample of Wilshire 5000 issues spanning the entire universe. The samples were taken over the period of March to August 1982.

Table 10.2 provides the spread/price cost (including commissions) for the entire sample arrayed by market capitalization versus dollar block size. Each capitalization sector includes approximately 20 different issues. The spread/price cost shown at each block size level is the equally weighted average of those observations. There are approximately 1,200 observations in total.

IMPLICATIONS

The results given in Table 10.2 are noteworthy for a number of reasons. When more shares are required for puchase or sale than the amount indicated at the basic market-maker's spread (100 shares), dramatically higher trading cost differentials between the smallest and largest capitalization sectors result. At the $5,000 level, the round-trip trading cost is 15.7 times greater for the smallest issues than for the largest; at the $25,000 level, the multiple is 22.7. Although the cost drops rapidly as company market capitalization increases, it is still very costly to take even relatively small positions in companies of up to $75 million capitalization. Given typical active portfolio sales turnover rates of 35% per year, it would in general be unreasonable to expect small-stock strategies to exhibit positive performance after adjustment for risk and transaction costs.

Note also that high market capitalization stocks (over $1.5 billion) can be

TABLE 10.2   MARKET CAPITALIZATION, BLOCK SIZE, AND TOTAL SPREAD/PRICE COST

Capitalization Sector (millions of dollars)	Block Size (thousands of dollars)								
	5	25	250	500	1,000	2,500	5,000	10,000	20,000
0–10 ($4.58)[a]	17.3%	27.3%	43.8%						
10–25 ($10.30)	8.9%	12.0%	23.8%	33.4%					
25–50 ($15.16)	5.0%	7.6%	18.8%	25.9%	30.0%				
50–75 ($18.27)	4.3%	5.8%	9.6%	16.9%	25.4%	31.5%			
75–100 ($21.85)	2.8%	3.9%	5.9%	8.1%	11.5%	15.7%	25.7%		
100–500 ($28.31)	1.8%	2.1%	3.2%	4.4%	5.6%	7.9%	11.0%	16.2%	
500–1,000 ($35.43)	1.9%	2.0%	3.1%	4.0%	5.6%	7.7%	10.4%	14.3%	20.0%
1,000–1,500 ($44.34)	1.9%	1.9%	2.7%	3.3%	4.6%	6.2%	8.9%	13.6%	18.1%
Over 1,500 ($57.48)	1.1%	1.2%	1.3%	1.7%	2.1%	2.8%	4.1%	5.9%	8.0%

Note: Round-trip trading cost *including* commission costs.
[a]Average price of issues in capitalization sector.

traded in blocks of between $1.0 million and $20 million at one-way trading costs of between approximately 1% and 4%. This suggests that active investment strategies based on relatively low quality information should be restricted to the large capitalization sectors of the equity market. It furthermore suggests that institutions with unusually large managed equity asset pools will find it difficult to execute efficiently individual stock transactions of significant value in any but the largest capitalization companies.

Of course, the quotes on which these results are based are average spread/price costs (including commissions) across a number of market-makers, each of whom provided a universe-wide sample of quotations at a different point in time. The results, therefore, do not necessarily represent the "inside," or best, bid and offer in each market capitalization and block size sector. Traders will naturally attempt to execute at the best bid or offer available at the time. The difficulty here is that the best bid and offer for a stock in a particular sector, which includes about 20 different issues, is likely to be an extreme or outlying occurrence based upon a particular market-maker's current position in that stock. It would be unrealistic to suggest that transactions attempted in the indicated block size and company size over this period could have been executed at the spread/price cost implied by the best bid and offer prices available at those points in time. The average is likely to be more representative of the typical trade.

It is also possible that a trader might set as his objective purchasing stocks only on the bid side of the market-maker's spread and selling on the offering side in whatever quantity is required. In this way, he can avoid the largest portion of the trading cost. There are occasions when supply and demand conditions present such opportunities, but they are only possible when there is a significant imbalance on the supply or demand side of a particular market. Thus, although lower total round-trip trading costs are no doubt achievable at times, this dealer market cost information reflects conditions that permit the markets to clear. For every winning trader in a particular transaction, there is a losing trader. Because stock market trading is dominated by professional institutional traders, there is no one else to win from! Thus, on average, the typical round-trip block trade will incur the full measure of the market-maker's spread, price concessions, and brokerage commissions.

EVALUATING TRADING TECHNIQUES

Our trading cost results suggest how trading techniques for the implementation of an equity investment decision can be evaluated. Consider, for example, two separate managers holding the same 50 issues, Manager A operating with $250 million and Manager B with $1.0 billion. For simplicity, assume that each issue carries equal weight in the portfolio: Manager A's average dollar position would be $5.0 million and Manager B's $20 million.

Has Manager A any particular advantage over B when taking his position in stocks averaging about $35 per share with between $500 and $1,000 million in market capitalization? Given the spread/price costs for this capitalization sector, the round-trip cost of taking a full position in one trade and disposing of it in the same way is 10.4% for Manager A and 20% for Manager B.

Although the market-maker's cost estimates for these two managers differ significantly, a trader might argue that A has no appreciable advantage over B. The trader may well take the view that the normal trading block size for the particular stocks in his portfolio will vary from $500,000 to $1,000,000 based upon his assessments of liquidity and his familiarity with the markets for these stocks. In this case, he might argue that the expected round-trip trading cost would be between 4% and 5.6% for both managers, taking full account of the fact that the managers must accumulate $5.0 million and $20 million, respectively, in each individual stock position. He may argue that purchasing the stocks slowly, $500,000 to $1,000,000 at a time, will produce relatively low trading costs.

Note, however, that the schedule of spread/price costs provided in Table 10.2 represents the market-maker's implict forecast of the trading costs he would incur in trading increasingly larger blocks of stock. This in fact reflects the same problem confronting the traders representing Managers A and B. It would seem more realistic to use the market-maker's forecast of the trading cost for the full investment position rather than to base cost estimates on the particular block size the trader deems best suited to the trading liquidity of a stock.

Using the "tradeable" block size to estimate trading costs may be misleading because trading blocks of a stock serially produces certain barriers to achieving the lowest trading costs on an entire stock position. When a trader purchases only that portion of the total transaction requirement that he feels is the tradeable amount and does not disclose his full intention, he may give the impression that he will not be the source of additional pressure on the stock. Acting on that impression, a market-maker who uses his capital to facilitate the trade may be subjected to unexpected risks and costs. As the trader places additional purchase orders of the same issue with other market-makers, either to accumulate rapidly the full stock position or to create a competitive environment, pressure on the stock's price will increase. The market-makers, however, will be quick to recognize this deception and will act to protect themselves by increasing, perhaps dramatically, the spread/price cost charged for providing trading liquidity to that particular trader.

Whether the trader executes the required investment decision in individual $1.0 million trades, in some series of larger trades or in one trade is entirely a matter of judgment. To evaluate the total cost of taking the required position, whatever the technique chosen, one should start with the current mid-price of the stock, take into account opportunity gains and losses produced by market changes over the period of accumulation, add commission costs, and compare the result with the market-maker's forecast of that cost. The results of such a comparison will highlight the value of trading discretion versus the cost of the upstairs dealer market mechanism.

CONCLUSION

The selection of an institution's equity investment strategy should depend not only upon how much excess return is expected to be available from perceived market inefficiencies, but also on a careful assessment of the liquidity of the equity issues used to execute the strategy and the size of the commitment required to implement individual investment decisions. This may appear to be merely a matter of common sense. But how many organizations have a firm idea of what it costs to trade into and out of their particular stock positions? How many can provide a well-reasoned approach to measuring whether or not their traders add value to the process by virtue of their discretionary behavior?

The Editor Asks

Q *Most traders agree that the concepts of your study are correct, but they believe the numbers apply only to capital-at-risk trading and are unrealistically large for any actual trading experience. In your opinion, how should these cost estimates be used? How do these numbers relate to typical trading cost expectations? Do you believe that anything has changed since you wrote your paper five years ago?*

A In my 1982 research, dealer spreads were used as a proxy for trading costs expected to be incurred in the process of implementing an investment decision. This method has been criticized for inflating the results by including certain costs that can be avoided by avoiding the dealer. Such criticism reflects a prevalent, yet inadequate, view of the components of total trading cost. The dealer quote proxy appeared to be useful precisely because it went beyond simple statistical measurement of market impact at the time of a block trade to the broader issue of opportunity costs inherent in any trade. The concept was that these quotes would capture the full cost impact of an investment decision, including broad market movements, unexpected news announcements, and the opportunity costs associated with the passage of time. In actuality, these costs, reflected in dealer spreads, confront all traders whether they utilize the dealer market or transact through another market mechanism.

The research also concluded that trading costs were dependent on the market capitalization and the block size of the particular stock being traded.

I continue to find support for these original propositions, although certain refinements in the use of these trading-cost estimates will make them more useful today. For example, the relationship of market capitalization and block size to total spread/price costs presented in Table 10.2 should be extended to accommodate the higher market capitalization companies in which the predominant portion of institutional trading occurs. In addition, the explicit brokerage commission cost imputed in the estimates should be adjusted downward by approximately 50% to reflect current conditions more adequately.

The following functional relationship accommodates an extension of the original spread/price cost table along both market capitalization and block size lines and is comparable to the extension proposed by Sharpe and Grossman.[2]

$$T_c = \exp\left(a_0 + a_1 \cdot \ln(b/m) + a_2 \cdot [\ln(b/m)]^2 + a_3 \cdot \ln(b)\right)$$

where: T_c = spread/price cost
  b = block size
  m = market capitalization

This formulation also provides an approach to estimating the spread/price cost for any particular portfolio consisting of issues with varying market capitalization and block size characteristics.

Since 1982, the market capitalization structure across the entire equity market has expanded dramatically as market values have appreciated. In order to determine how the original estimates relate to current trading-cost expectations, the spread/price cost for various dollar-size portfolios of S&P 500 issues (capitalization-weighted) were estimated with the foregoing formula exclusive of commission cost. Each result was divided in half to produce a one-way estimate of trading cost. In addition, dealer bid–ask spread quotes were collected recently from a number of major market-makers and spread/price cost estimates produced. Interestingly, the ascending relationship between portfolio size and trading cost evidenced in the 1982 results was again observed. There also appears to have been a decline in the relative cost structure, however, reflecting a reduction in expected trading costs (see Table 10.3).

As a point of reference, in 1982 the S&P 500 stood at about the 123 level during the period of the research, while its nominal bid–ask spread was

[2] W. Sharpe and S. Grossman, "Financial Implications of South African Divestment," *Financial Analysts Journal*, July–August 1986, p. 20.

TABLE 10.3   UPDATED SPREAD/PRICE COST ESTIMATE

Portfolio Size	1982 Spread/Price Cost (One-Way)[a]	1988 Spread/Price Cost (One-Way)[b]
$10	0.33%	0.22%
$20	0.37%	0.26%
$30	0.38%	0.30%
$40	0.41%	0.32%
$50	0.43%	0.35%

[a]Original data with extensions.
[b]Recent spread/price cost data.

about 70 cents, reflecting a 0.35% one-way spread/price cost. Recently, with the S&P 500 at the 270 level, the bid–ask spread was 1.30, reflecting a 0.24% one-way spread/price cost. The reason for the reduction in expected trading costs is that dealer spreads have widened by 86% while the market value has increased by more than 170%, so that the spread/price cost has actually declined in percentage terms.

In the course of my experience in trading the S&P 500 issues since the study, timely spread/price cost estimates have provided remarkably effective indications of actual trading cost. Dealer spread/price cost calculations have also proved useful in estimating the cost of trading smaller stock universes, though with somewhat less accuracy. In fact, the estimate of expected trading costs derived from current market prices and dealer spreads may be a useful measure of market liquidity for trading across a broad spectrum of equity issues.

11

EVALUATING TRANSACTION COST

Gilbert Beebower

The measurement of transaction cost has assumed more importance as the investment community and its clients have come to understand the extreme competitiveness in the search for superior risk-adjusted returns. In a world where (1) investors in aggregate will receive the market return minus the costs of implementing all investment strategies; (2) one investor's value-added must be achieved at the expense of other investors; (3) realistic estimates of value-added are likely to be on the order of only 1 to 3 percentage points per annum; and (4) the most advanced performance measurement techniques require unacceptably long periods of time to identify the presence of any value-added at all, the measurement and control of transaction cost must concern every investment manager and fiduciary.

The measurement and evaluation of transaction cost is a complex process. Total transaction cost has been identified as being composed of three distinct components. The first, commission/fee payment, is the easiest to identify and measure. The second component, execution or market impact cost, has become amenable to measurement and analysis by virtue of the availability of specific data associated with an executed trade. For the third component, opportunity cost, the data required to measure and analyze it have not generally been collected. Both execution and opportunity cost measurement are subject to statistical uncertainty, unlike commission/fee cost, which can be measured precisely and absolutely.

An ideal thorough evaluation of total transaction cost is, like most or all evaluations of other complex real-world activities, probably not attainable. Nevertheless, meaningful measures have been developed, some of which have been implemented with a degree of success. As the importance of transaction cost becomes more apparent to investors and their investment managers, more detailed data will become available to be analyzed in more sophisticated ways.

TOTAL TRANSACTION COST

Both Jack Treynor in 1981 and Andre Perold more recently have suggested that total transaction cost might be measured by the difference in return between the manager's ideal portfolio and his actual portfolio.[1] The ideal portfolio is defined as the paper or model portfolio wherein all of the manager's portfolio decisions are executed at strike prices observed shortly after the decisions are made. These prices might be the average of the bid–ask spread obtained from a quotation source, the next actual execution price reported through an execution reporting service, or the actual execution prices of the next series of trades that equal the desired number of shares.

This performance difference would include the three components of transaction cost. One is any explicit commission or fee. The second is the execution or market impact cost wherein the buyer's gain is the seller's loss and vice versa. The third is an opportunity cost. For trades that have been executed, this cost is the difference between the decision strike price and the fair price (zero execution cost price) at time of execution. For trades that never get executed (unexecuted orders), the opportunity cost is open-ended, thus changing with each measurement period.

This definition of total transaction cost requires the continuous management on paper of an ideal portfolio, regardless of how much the actual portfolio diverges over time from this ideal. The paper portfolio should be managed within the confines of actual portfolio constraints and client preferences in order to maintain its relevance as a correct and valid benchmark.

The difference between ideal and actual portfolio return would be decomposed into the three cost components mentioned before. This decomposition would permit the portfolio manager and his trader to consider the trade-off and interaction among commission/fee, execution, and opportunity costs. The reduction of any one component might well have an adverse impact on the others.

The analysis of transaction cost, including opportunity cost, as described

[1] Jack L. Treynor, "What Does It Take to Win the Trading Game?" *Financial Analysts Journal,* January–February 1981, pp. 55–60; Andre F. Perold, "The Implementation Shortfall: Paper versus Reality," *Journal of Portfolio Management,* Spring 1988, pp. 4–9.

is complex and requires the collection of data that are rarely if ever currently available. The first two components of cost, commissions/fees and execution, are more readily measured and analyzed with available data.

It is these two components of cost that are discussed in some detail in this chapter.

KEEPING TRANSACTION COSTS IN PERSPECTIVE

The normal reason for transacting in an investment vehicle (stock, bond, property, etc.) is to achieve a desired investment objective. All three components of transaction cost must be considered and balanced if transaction costs are to be minimized. Driving commission/fee costs to zero may well be expected to increase execution and possibly opportunity costs. Striving for zero or negative execution costs may be expected to increase opportunity costs for many investment strategies. Zero execution cost can be guaranteed by the simple expedient of not trading, with a concomitant loss of opportunity associated with active investment judgment. Minimizing opportunity costs (as exemplified by guaranteed blind package trading) may be expected to increase execution cost.

As mentioned before, just as in so many other areas of real-world endeavor, the measurement and analysis of transaction cost is complex and characterized by uncertainty. Nevertheless, the potential savings to large pools of investment capital from modest reductions in total transaction cost are substantial and essential to the realization of superior investment returns.

EVALUATING VERSUS MEASURING

WHAT IS A GOOD MEASURE? Before discussing specific measures of transaction cost, it is essential to consider the attributes of any valid measure. Too often, measures are designed to accommodate available data, ease of calculation, or—perhaps worst of all—preconceived notions of which specific process of implementation should produce superior results.

Certainly there are endeavors where form is considered an important criterion of the performance to be measured. A quantitatively measured value may or may not be of substantive concern. Music competitions, high diving, and ice skating (especially free-style) are some obvious examples.

The measurement of transaction costs, however, does not fall into the same category. The end results, quantitatively measured, are all that is of concern or interest. A similar, familiar area of measurement is total portfolio rate of return. Measurement of elapsed time, distance, and height are common ways of assessing performance in athletic competition.

All these measures of performance measure results quantitatively, not qualitatively.

A singular characteristic of these measures is that the measured results are of no value, in and of themselves, in instructing the participants how to perform better, or worse.

Knowing how a stopwatch works, how a tape-measure was constructed, or the most arcane aspects of the dollar-weighted (internal) rate-of-return formula and calculation are all of no value to the runner, high-jumper, or portfolio manager in the pursuit of superior results. This aspect of a good measure means that each participant in the contest is free to exercise his or her best judgment and creative and intellectual powers in the pursuit of a measured excellence.

An often stated negative aspect of a good measure is that it necessarily lacks any value in directly suggesting remedial action or in defining how to improve future results. That is not to say that a careful and thorough understanding of the process that resulted in the measured performance (not the measurement) may not be valuable. It may even be the only way in which the participant can hope to alter the process to produce better results in the future.

Observing the means by which others excel as determined by a good measure is often valuable. In the 1968 Olympics, Dick Fosbury was the first man to win the high jump by going over the bar with his *back down*. This not only proved his creative genius but also set a new standard of measured performance. Since his feat was public, others quickly learned to do the same. In investment management and trading, one is left mostly to one's own resources. The detailed process is almost always considered proprietary and is unavailable to public view.

The extremely competitive nature of the investment management business drives practitioners to disclose the minimum necessary to gain and retain business. Helping one's competitors learn to do better rarely gives one a competitive advantage. This understandable secrecy makes valid measurement all the more important. In effect, the results as measured are all that may be available for review.

The importance of using a valid measure when evaluating transaction cost cannot be overstated. As will be seen, several bad measures have been promoted and used. Bad measures should be rejected outright rather than dressed up as practical or useful alternatives. The thesis espoused in this chapter is that a bad measure is worse than no measure at all. A disturbing notion offered in defense of many bad measures is that *any* measure consistently applied to all participants must have some value. This is patently absurd.

On the contrary, a bad measure consistently applied to all participants is worthless at best (if ignored) and harmful if believed. For in every bad measure there is an explicit definition of the process whereby "excellence" can be achieved, a definition devoid of relevance to the achievement of true value.

MEASURING THE COST OF AN EXECUTED TRADE. The conceptual and implementation difficulties of measuring opportunity cost have prevented any meaningful empirical research to date. Measuring the cost of an executed trade, though still daunting, has been attempted by several researchers and commercial vendors. Each of the promoted methodologies bases the measure of execution cost on the concept of a *fair price*. That is, if one looks at a trade as always involving two parties, a buyer and a seller, only three results are possible: (1) both the buyer and the seller trade at a fair price; (2) the buyer pays a premium and the seller receives that premium; and (3) vice versa. No matter who is on the other side of your trade, be he a market-maker, speculator, or investor, your gain is his loss or your loss is his gain.

The concept of a fair price has embedded in it the idea that trading is a zero-sum process. All the money involved in a trade is accounted for by knowing the trade price, the shares traded, and the explicit commissions and taxes paid, if any. This assumption of a zero-sum process is basic and realistic when measuring the cost of executed trades, but it ignores the issue of opportunity cost. A portfolio manager may well feel that a trade that was delayed and executed later at a then-fair price was very costly in terms of lost opportunity.

THE HIGH–LOW MIDPOINT MEASURE OF EXECUTION COST. An early commercial application of an execution cost methodology used the highest price transacted and the lowest price transacted in a given security on a given day. These data are readily available in the *Wall Street Journal* and the financial sections of many other newspapers. The "fair" price benchmark used was the midpoint, or the average of the high price and the low price. Since *any* single fair price benchmark meets the criterion of conforming to a zero-sum process, this methodology might appear to have merit. This measure is characteristic of all prespecified single- or multiple-day benchmarks in that it assumes the entire order was available to be executed by the trader or broker *prior* to the measurement period, *and* that the entire order had to be executed within the measurement period. Under these well-defined but generally unrealistic constraints, the lower the price of purchases and the higher the price of sales, the better.

Certainly, those traders or brokers who were given an order to execute before the day began and were required to complete the total order that day, and who in doing so achieved prices favorable to the benchmark—that is, buying below the average high–low and selling above the average high–low—have traded at advantage to those who traded otherwise that day. The problem arises when the entire order was not available prior to the measurement period and/or the entire prespecified order need not be executed prior to the end of the measurement period.

It is not fair to measure a trader or broker against prices that occurred prior to the receipt of the order. All trade orders do not arrive on the trader's or broker's desk before the opening on the day(s) over which he is to be measured. Nor is it fair to permit the trader or broker to delay the execution of a portion or all of an order until a measurement period in which he knows he will look good by the specific measurement methodology applied. The first condition unfairly penalizes the trader or broker, and the second permits the gaming of the execution cost measure, unfairly making the trader or broker look good.

If the low of the day occurs before the order is submitted to the trader or the broker, it is not fair to penalize him for not being able to transact at such favorable prices. If the trader or broker is free to delay the trade until a day on which the price looks good but is materially worse than on previous days on which he had the order and could have traded, the effectiveness of the trading is misrepresented.

The high–low methodology embodies most of the weaknesses found in bad measures. To the extent that the measurement period precedes the actual trade (and therefore possibly the actual order to trade), opportunity costs are imprecisely and incorrectly being mixed with actual execution costs. To the extent that the trader or broker can "game" the methodology (wait until he knows he will "look good," regardless of trading effectiveness), the measure of cost is irrelevant at best and misleading, wrong, and detrimental at worst.

A valid test of any good measure, and more relevantly of any execution measure, is to ask yourself: "Could I arrange to look good with no skill at all, knowing that I would be measured in this fashion?" Every trader (and investment manager) can determine what the current high–low of the day for any (and all) stocks is at any point of time. Should they wait until late in the trading day, it is obvious and simple to determine whether current prices are safely below (for buys) or above (for sells) the current midpoint of the high and low prices. If you know you are being evaluated by this measure, you either trade in the knowledge that the trade will be measured as a good one, or wait until tomorrow to try again when the trade may look better (but in fact may be worse if the stock moves in your favor relative to the previous day). If you truly believe that this measure correctly assesses the cost of trading, you can fire your trader(s) and pay your brokers as little as possible—it takes neither intelligence nor skill to produce good trading by this measure.

THE TRADE-WEIGHTED AVERAGE PRICE OF THE DAY AS A MEASURE OF EXECUTION COST.

As data and computing power became more widely available, there were those who, not understanding the flaws and deficiencies in the high–low methodology, exacerbated the weaknesses of that methodology by defining the "fair" price as the average price of the day—that is, the price derived from the total dollars traded divided by the total shares traded. This methodology has all the weaknesses and flaws of the high–low methodology plus an additional one. Whereas there is no systematic way to trade in a manner to guarantee or approximate the actual high–low midpoint price of the day, there is a way of approximating the average price of the day.

If only 100 shares trade at the low of the day and all the rest of the trades occur at the high of the day, the high–low midpoint will be below the price at which most trades occurred. Only the buyer of the 100 shares would look good.

Using the average price of the day, however, introduces another mechanical system of trading. If you participate in every trade, the results will measure average. That may not be great, but it certainly won't be bad. And, again, you can fire your trader and pay your broker next to nothing.

The average price of the day also introduces a particularly unique constraint. All buyers *and* all sellers on a given day achieve zero trading cost. To illustrate this, imagine that one buyer is determined to buy all the stock available in a given period. This might well be presumed to be a high-cost strategy. Indeed, this investor always pays more than anyone else is willing to pay and is, in fact, the only buyer for the period. He has *made* the average price of the day. Ergo, he has incurred no cost. The sellers will also be measured as having sold at "fair" prices even though the buyer outbid all other buyers. This would seem to be counterintuitive. If you want average costs, participate all day. If you want superior costs, wait until the end of the day to decide whether to trade, or else take as much of the day's trading volume as possible. The more of the day's volume your trade represents, the greater its impact on the benchmark price and the nearer to zero your execution costs will be.

A PREVIOUS PRICE USED AS A BENCHMARK FOR THE MEASURE OF EXECUTION COST.   The extensive research associated with the various forms of the efficient market hypothesis has lent substantial support to the idea that any actual transaction price is an unbiased estimate of the fair price of a security at the time of transaction. This thesis has led some practitioners to structure computerized trading systems to consummate trades only when the price of transaction is equal to or better than some previous price. This is another obvious case of defining what constitutes good trading rather than measuring a result. Trades executed at, or better than, the specified price are good. Trades executed unfavorably are bad. Again, the art and skill of trading (knowing markets and market conditions) are reduced to a formula.

Here the market (everyone else) determines what and when trades occur. Even if, on average, prices are unbiased estimates of fair prices, might it be possible that such a trading system will find it has only traded specifically when such prices are not "fair" prices. It is very likely! One should always be suspicious of someone's motivations to trade with you. Again, if one defines good trading in a manner that requires neither intelligence nor skill and that can be mechanically executed, then by definition the results will be good. What happens if everyone agrees that any of these trading strategies is in fact the right one? If no one will buy or sell at prices worse than the previous price, then the price can't change. Think back to the high–low and average price measures. *No* trading should take place until someone else has set the range of price. In extremis, all of those measures would preclude trading except at one price for the day.

The only solution is to measure execution costs using a methodology that is independent of all specific concepts of what constitutes good trading.

AFTER-TRADE MEASURES OF EXECUTION COST.   The only measures that qualify as legitimate and equitable are those that do not specify beforehand how to achieve superior results—that is, measures made using only after-trade data. This concept was espoused by Myron Scholes in 1972, by Wayne Wagner and Larry Cuneo in 1975, and by Beebower and Priest in 1978.[2] This thesis of after-trade measurement is that relative price movements following the trade are the only valid measure of the cost of a trade. Price reversals after a trade indicate positive cost. Price reinforcements

---

[2] Myron Scholes, "The Market for Securities: Substitution vs. Price Pressure of the Effects of Information on Share Prices," *Journal of Business,* April 1972, vol. 45, no. 2; Larry J. Cuneo and Wayne H. Wagner, "Reducing the Cost of Stock Trading," *Financial Analysts Journal,* November–December 1975, pp. 35–44; Gilbert L. Beebower and William W. Priest, Jr., "An Analysis of Transaction Costs in Equity Trading," presented at the Seminar on the Analysis of Security Prices, November 3, 1978.

after a trade indicate negative cost. Neutral price movements after a trade indicate fair prices.

The terminal point of measurement must lie beyond the influence or impact of the transaction(s). This raises the issue of when the measurement period should be closed. A case can be made that the measure should extend somewhat beyond the point at which the trader has ceased to be interested in trading.

Here, as with the measurement of opportunity cost, the problem of data collection arises again. A commercial service that has been in use for nearly 10 years employs an after-trade measurement that assumes market equilibration occurs within one trading day after the last execution in a single- or multiple-day series of executions in any given stock. This is clearly an approximation. Ideally, one would like to know the total order size on the trading desk, the exact position of each executed trade in the flow of executed trades, and the point in time at which the marketplace should or might have recognized that the specific trader was no longer interested in transacting. Where the trade was "positioned" by a broker, one would like to know when the broker had "unwound" the position. It is unlikely that these data will be available in the foreseeable future. Therefore, as in most real-world situations, approximations are made. To a limited extent, these approximations can be tested by reputable researchers.

Specifically, the service just referred to measures after-trade price reversals using stock return as measured from (1) trade price to trade day closing price linked to (2) trade day close to next-day close minus the return of an equal weighted industry index associated with the traded stock. This next-day "residual return" is included to prevent trades made at the closing price (often preferred by index fund managers to minimize tracking error) from being defined as zero-cost trades. The use of second-day residual returns instead of unadjusted returns helps to reduce some of the noise introduced by the additional time period. The use of raw returns is acceptable but requires a larger sample size to obtain statistically reliable results.

An objection that has been raised to this after-trade measure is that closing prices are involved in the calculation. Research by Wood, McInish, and Ord has shown that closing (and opening) prices appear to be generated by a different process than intraday prices.[3] None of these researchers has suggested that closing or opening prices are biased estimates of fair prices. From a researcher's standpoint, opening and closing prices are superior

[3] Robert A. Wood, Thomas H. McInish, and J. Keith Ord, "An Investigation of Transactions Data for NYSE Stocks," *Journal of Finance*, July 1985, pp. 723–741.

points of relative prices across the universe of securities. It is at these times that more stocks trade simultaneously, or more nearly so, than at other predetermined times of the trading day. Performance measurement, valuation models, and so forth all prefer to use the best estimate of contemporaneous prices. Likewise, the after-trade measure of price reversal uses the closing price of the traded security as compared to the closing prices of a peer group of securities. Price reversal is determined by the relative movement of the traded stock to the movement of a large number of stocks in which one didn't trade.

This specific after-trade measure becomes less valid when the organization being measured trades in several hundred security names a day. The measure becomes useless when applied to an extended-market, index fund package trade covering a thousand or more securities, because there is no peer group of stocks in which no trades were made.

The after-trade measurement concept, however, is still valid. The measure must be applied to a large number of independent packages over time to determine the magnitude of any systematic price reversal. The question is: Do prices reverse with greater than random frequency after one's trading in baskets?

Ten years of analysis of the complete trading activity of a number of money management organizations has identified a phenomenon that is still not satisfactorily explained: Purchases are systematically measured as less costly than sales. An anecdotal explanation suggests that selling is more urgent than buying because you can only sell what you own, and when you become disillusioned with a stock you want it out of your portfolio, whereas buying is more discretionary. Unfortunately, if this were always true, no one would be able to detect this permanent disequilibrium. Treynor has proposed a reasonable explanation but one that seems unlikely to account for the magnitude of the disparity. Market-makers who find themselves with excessively long positions are known to announce their situation broadly and to be willing to sell at relatively favorable prices. On the other hand, market-makers who find themselves excessively short in a stock are known to keep it as secret as possible.

To compensate for the fact that purchase results are generally lower in cost than sale results, it is recommended that purchase and sale results be measured and compared separately. Round-trip (purchase and sale) results should be computed giving equal dollar weights to the purchase and sale results, respectively. This approach can be compared to a time-weighted return, which places all parties on an equal footing relative to uncontrolled cash flows.

Researchers who have applied the average dollar-weighted price methodology to trading data have reported a similar bias in their results. This is doubly mystifying because that methodology guarantees not only that purchases and sales will net to zero, but additionally that all purchases and sales separately must aggregate to zero.

The after-trade measure must be designed to minimize or eliminate the possibility of gaming—that is, defining a priori what "good trading" is. The only possibility of gaming an open-ended after-trade measure is to rig the closing prices associated with the measurement of the trade. That is, if one purchased a security over a three-day period, the first day's trades would be measured against that day's closing price and against the relative return as measured from that closing price to the closing price four days later (one day after completed trading in the stock). Gaming could occur if either the traded security's closing prices or a meaningful number of peer group closing prices, or both, were manipulated. The investment manager's trader would have to accomplish this since any broker would risk making customers who traded on the other side of the security look bad. Most brokers would have to charge an additional fee for maintaining the administrative system necessary to make selected clients look good.

A more serious question can be raised concerning the period it takes for the market to equilibrate after an organization stops trading in a stock. Tests have been made using periods of two, three, four, and five days after the last trade in given stock. The longer periods of measurement add noise (variance) to the results but do not appear to change the relative ranking of trading performance among measured investment organizations, most of which are very large and are therefore candidates for experiencing more protracted disequilibrium effects after trading. The marketplace might be expected to have imprecise information about when these organizations have actually stopped or completed their trading programs in a given security.

WHO SHOULD MEASURE TRADING COSTS?   There is no question that each investment management organization should incorporate a transaction cost analysis into its standard operation. Only through measurement, evaluation, and feedback can a process improve.

In the last several years, transaction cost measurement services that are designed for plan sponsors have become common. Of necessity, these services analyze only the portions of trades that have been allocated by the various money managers to the sponsor's portfolio. The data are provided by the plan custodians.

Great care must be exercised with these analyses. The manager's actual trade size is not known, and the manager may well have aggregated several client positions together in order to give the trader maximum flexibility in managing the execution. Since actual trade sizes are not known, analyses of trading cost versus trade size or percentage of the day's volume are unwarranted and potentially misleading. These data may mask both the number of days in which the manager traded for other accounts in the same stock, and the actual daily participation in the stock's traded volume. Only when trading is viewed from the perspective of the management organization's trading desk can trading size and percentage of trading volume analyses be properly evaluated.

Analyses of broker results by each manager are even more complex because they reflect the interaction of portfolio manager requirements, buy-side trader judgment, and the manner in which the broker delivers an execution with the buy-side trader's approval. As much as brokers offer the easiest target for abuse, it must be kept in mind that no manager or buy-side broker need consummate any execution. This caveat concerning broker evaluation also applies to investment organization analyses where the totality of the trading data is available. Here trader input is essential to the understanding of how each broker is utilized.

Measurement of execution costs should be kept in perspective. Trading is an integral part of the investment process, and its costs should not be taken out of the investment context. If trading costs were paramount, we could achieve a zero execution cost by the simple expedient of not trading. Such an approach, however, is not consistent with the charter of most active investment managers. An investment manager who truly receives the first call, or the first insight, may correctly judge that an eighth or quarter of a dollar given up in execution will more likely than not be exceeded by the capture of immediate or near immediate opportunity. That is what an active manager is being paid to do.

Evidence that a manager has traded well, although perhaps expensively, can be evaluated by measuring the short-term investment performance of the traded positions. If within a relatively short time the portfolio performance has been improved by the trading activity, a high measured cost need not be considered bad. The after-trade performance measurement period should be longer than the trading horizon and shorter than the manager's investment horizon; it may reasonably vary from 10 to 30 days. It should be noted that this short-term performance measurement will include the benefit of minimizing the cost of missed opportunity.

COMMISSION COSTS

The measurement of commission costs is straightforward, but evaluating their appropriateness is considerably more difficult. Almost without exception, commissions associated with pension plan trading are used not only to pay brokers for execution, but also to pay for Securities Exchange Act of 1934, Section 28(e), eligible services, and for ERISA-approved or otherwise lawful plan expenses. Because only a portion of the commission paid for these trades might properly be attributed to execution, one would not expect any systematic relationship between execution cost and the total commission paid for the trade. Brokers accept a wide range of commission rates as expressed in cents per share. The services they provide in return are more likely to be related to the total quarterly or yearly commission dollars received than to the specific commission rate paid. The brokerage industry is primarily driven by *relationships,* which often include services and compensation beyond those related to equity trading alone.

The increase in the trading of over-the-counter equities by institutional investors to a level representing 10% to 15% of all equity trading has heightened the importance of measuring execution cost correctly. Institutional trading in over-the-counter equities is done on a net cost basis. That is, no explicit commission is recorded. No one should be so foolish as to suppose that the equivalent of a commission is not being paid when these trades are executed. Institutional investment managers are known to impute a commission charge for net trades. They apply this amount to their calculation of commissions paid to brokers when discussing how much the broker has received in payment for 28(e)-type research services.

The after-trade measured reversal (or reinforcement) will include the consequence of the widened bid–ask spread quoted in the over-the-counter market, which is required by the market-maker/dealer when no explicit commission is to be paid. Empirical analysis of over-the-counter trading using an after-trade execution measurement methodology confirms the presence of this unrecorded commission.

SUMMARY

Trading is a necessary and integral part of all investment strategies. Minimizing the total cost of trading directly enhances the wealth that has been allocated to a strategy. The measurement and analysis of total transaction cost and its components, though complex, is vital to the transformation of investment research and judgment into an actual portfolio wherein their value will be realized. No one component of the total transaction cost should be measured or controlled in isolation from the other two components.

Any and all measurements that are applied to the analysis of transaction cost must pass muster as "good measurements." A good measurement is one that measures results but in no way defines or dictates how good or predetermined results can be achieved.

As with investing in general, the zero-sum nature of execution cost means that one trader's gain is another trader's loss. Only by constant and expert attention to the details of trading can one expect to add value through the investment process.

The Editor Asks

Q *You have probably looked at more data evaluating trading prowess than anyone in the world. What, in your opinion, distinguishes a great trader from a good trader? Have you noted any common mistakes that could be avoided?*

A Trading is necessarily an integral part of the investment process. The ability to demonstrate exceptional skill as a trader depends to a large extent on how much trading flexibility the demands of the portfolio manager permit. Demands for immediacy are likely to be costly, albeit less costly, for the expert trader. A "great" trader is one who makes an effort to be a part of the investment decision-making process, thus bringing his understanding of market liquidity and trading opportunities to bear before, during, and after investment decisions are made. A "good" trader only satisfies the portfolio manager after the decision has been made.

A common mistake that lesser traders often make is to second-guess the portfolio manager as to when the trade should be executed on the basis of predicting where the price will be tomorrow or days later, not on the basis of current liquidity. If a trader can predict where prices will be tomorrow or some days later, he should be in charge of the investment process.

PART FIVE

Current Trends in Trading

12

UPSTAIRS, DOWNSTAIRS: THE BLOCK TRADERS AND THE SPECIALISTS

Donald L. Luskin

In 1903, architect George B. Post designed the New York Stock Exchange building's grand classical façade at the corner of Broad and Wall Streets to suggest that this was a temple of finance and the national capital of the U.S. equity market. For many years it was indeed the capital, and its ever-increasing trading volume would suggest that it remains so. But the volume records belie a gradual decrease in the Exchange's dominance. Today, although the Exchange continues as a dominant clearing mechanism, its central role as a marketplace has become largely symbolic.

No single institution has arisen to replace the New York Stock Exchange as the dominant provider of a common facility in which trades can be negotiated and as the maintainer of fair and orderly markets. Instead, gradually, and invisibly to the public, these functions have scattered from their single origin "downstairs" with the specialists on the Exchange's trading floor and come to rest "upstairs" among the block traders of brokerage firms in New York and around the world. Of course, the specialist continues to control the execution of the majority of orders cleared by the Exchange, but these are mostly small public and arbitrage-related trades, many sent to the floor via the Designated Order Turnaround (DOT) system. It is the upstairs traders, not the specialists, who control most of the huge institutional block trades that make up the bulk of the value.

The evolutionary migration from downstairs to upstairs began in the 1960s, the "go-go years" when the mutual funds, pension plans, and bank trust departments that controlled an increasing concentration of the United States' investable wealth began actively and aggressively to trade the market. As orders sent to the Exchange became larger and larger, the specialists found themselves hamstrung by three self-imposed constraints limiting their effective adaption to the new institutional market.

First, specialists traditionally worked alone, with neither partners nor competitors, so there was no community of fellow risk-bearers through which to diffuse large orders. Second, specialists were prohibited by Securities and Exchange Commission (SEC) rules from doing business directly with non-Exchange members—that is, public investors. They had no direct means to seek natural counterparties to offset large orders. Third, Exchange rules prohibited specialists from affiliating with the large brokerage firms that handle public underwritings, so they were denied this much-needed source of new risk-bearing capital.[1] The leading brokerage firms, on the other hand, were under no such constraints. They had no limitations on their access to partners, competitors, customers, or capital.

The brokerage firms had one more natural advantage as well: regulated commissions mandated by the Exchange. Originally designed for small individual customer orders, the Exchange's commission schedule was a windfall for brokers handling huge institutional trades that cost no more to process. With lucrative regulated commissions cushioning possible trading losses, the brokerage firms were perfectly positioned to step in and act as off-floor pseudospecialists. Subsidized by regulated commissions, the major brokerage firms aggressively competed with the specialists and with each other to build market share in the booming new business, and a generation of Wall Street culture heroes was born—legendary traders such as Gus Levy and Bob Mnuchin of Goldman Sachs, Jay Perry of Salomon Brothers, and Cy Lewis of Bear, Stearns.

Despite the manifest advantages of the upstairs traders, the Exchange specialists—still technically in charge of any trades cleared on the Exchange—played a vital role in the trading process. For the first time, however, they had competition. In a recently published reminiscence on the origins of upstairs trading, Will Weinstein, then an upstairs trader at Oppenheimer & Company, explains the uneasy symbiosis between the upstairs traders and specialists: "You'd rather not be in a war; you'd rather be helping each other. We had that with some specialists, but in the beginning it wasn't the norm. They resisted as hard as they could. We ultimately had the upper hand because we had the clients. You knew you would win ultimately, but it was often a very expensive trip. . . ."[2]

---

[1] Twenty years later, in the wake of the stock market crash of October 1987, this third constraint was removed.

[2] "The Way It Was: An Oral History," *Institutional Investor*, June 1987, p. 41.

In May 1975, upstairs traders lost one of their key advantages over the specialists when the Exchange's commission schedule was abandoned in favor of competitively negotiated rates. As Alan Greenberg of Bear, Stearns and Company observed, "People who continued to do block trading found out that the percentages were now against them. It was just a losing, losing proposition, because the commissions were sliced so much that the vigorish was gone."[3] Nonetheless, upstairs block trading has continued to be a central feature of most large brokerage firms' equity trading efforts. Brokers generally maintain that upstairs trading is not profitable in and of itself, but it is deemed to be a necessary loss leader to attract profitable business in other trades that do not require risking the firms' capital.[4]

Just at the time the upstairs traders lost the advantage of regulated commissions, they acquired a new one to take its place: the advent of the listed stock options markets. Whereas the specialists were prohibited by SEC rules from trading options on stocks in which they made a market,[5] the upstairs traders could use options to reduce and restructure the risk of their positions. Additionally, the upstairs traders were positioned to monopolize a new customer base: investors who specialized in combined stocks-and-options trading (such as simultaneously buying stock and selling a call option).

The growth of options trading gave rise to a new class of specialized upstairs options traders: large private trading companies with names virtually unknown to the general public. At the most sophisticated of these companies, trading is conducted entirely by computers. Their terminals prominently display bids and offers in the trading crowds of the various options exchanges. Floor traders wishing to trade with such a computer simply point to the appropriate bid or offer on its terminal's screen, and the trade is automatically consummated. The computer then considers the trade in the context of its overall position and marginally adjusts all its other bids and offers accordingly. These computers are said to account for upwards of 15% of daily trading volume in the several classes of options in which they are active.

As the 1970s drew to a close, yet another evolutionary force in the U.S. equity market emerged that would further consolidate the supremacy of the upstairs equity trader. Pension plan sponsors were increasingly favoring indexation and other quantitative, highly diversified investment strategies, calling for techniques of "package trading" that would allow entire portfolios of stocks to be executed all at once, rather than one at a time.

---

[3] Ibid., p. 118.

[4] On the other hand, some claim the exact opposite—that in today's razor-thin commission environment skillful upstairs trading is the only way to make an institutional equity brokerage operation profitable.

[5] This restriction has since been removed.

Whereas the specialists were bound to the time-honored system of market-making in individual stocks, the more flexible upstairs traders innovated techniques for facilitating simultaneous trades in thousands of stocks.[6]

Although the upstairs traders have certainly deprived the specialists of their historical role as the center of the U.S. equity market, the specialists have by no means been entirely replaced. They continue to fulfill two unique and vital roles unaddressed by the upstairs traders. First, the specialists mastermind the massive daily flow of small public and arbitrage-related orders; the upstairs traders ignore these almost entirely, concentrating instead on large block trades. Second, the specialist has an affirmative obligation to make a fair and orderly market day in and day out; the upstairs trader, on the other hand, can always choose to stand aside if he does not wish to risk his capital.

Let's examine the structure and functioning of a typical upstairs trading operation of a large U.S. brokerage firm. It is located in the firm's New York headquarters, although the firm has offices around the country and around the world. A staff of a dozen traders, each specializing in stocks belonging to particular industry groups, is orchestrated by a single chief trader who, by virtue of his power to risk millions of dollars of the firm's capital (and by virtue of his forceful personality) is a member of the firm's most senior management. Each trader's position's size is governed by a risk limit calculated as the absolute value of the difference between the market value of his long and short positions. The aggregate risk posture of the entire trading staff is monitored by sophisticated software that helps the chief trader hedge with risk-reducing stock, option, and futures positions.

The success of this trading operation is contingent on obtaining and immediately acting on superior information. Therefore, the trading staff is seated within eyeshot and earshot of the firm's New York institutional sales desk, ceaselessly monitoring the information stream flowing through the salesmen from the firm's largest customers. The staff is connected by a two-way public address system to the firm's local and international offices. The traders' desks are stacked with video terminals constantly displaying, updating, and analyzing stock, bond, commodity, and currency quotations from around the world. The Dow Jones and Reuters news tickers march tirelessly across large wall-mounted display boards. There are open lines to the firm's booths on the New York Stock Exchange and the Chicago Mercantile Exchange floors, where the latest stock and stock index futures quotations are orally relayed to the trading staff even before the electronic quotation screens can display them.

---

[6] A recent study by the New York Stock Exchange has suggested that the Exchange may wish to consider developing a multistock specialist post.

The typical upstairs trade begins on the trading desk of an institutional investor, let's say a mutual fund in Boston. The fund's trader has been instructed by the fund's portfolio manager to promptly buy 500,000 shares of XYZ. The trader can see on his quote screen that the last trade in XYZ was at 52, and that the market is currently 51¾ bid, offered at 52¼. On average, XYZ trades only 200,000 shares in an entire day, so the trader is justifiably concerned that if his large buy order were simply dropped on the New York Stock Exchange, it might move the stock significantly higher. So he calls his broker and asks where the firm's upstairs trader will sell him half a million shares.

As soon as the broker receives the inquiry, he relays it to the block trader responsible for XYZ's industry group. The trader shouts to the other salesmen to recall any selling interest in XYZ that they may have heard recently from their customers. He consults an institutional holdings database to see the XYZ positions held by banks, mutual funds, and pension funds who might be persuaded to sell. He may call his firm's research analyst to learn if there are any special news developments recently announced or closely anticipated in XYZ. He will consult his firm's borrow desk to make sure that XYZ is available to be borrowed (since the trader has no existing long position in XYZ, he will have to borrow shares in order to sell them short). He will consult his firm's floor broker on the New York Stock Exchange to see if there has recently been any special interest in the stock on the floor. He will glance at a screen on his desk that tells him how S&P stock index futures on the Chicago Mercantile Exchange are trading relative to the actual index, hoping to get a clue as to the tenor of short-term market sentiment. He will call his floor broker on the Chicago Board Options Exchange to see if there has been any unusual trading activity in the options listed on XYZ. Ultimately, relying as much on sheer guts and knowhow as on any objective information he has just received, the trader will make an offer: He will sell half a million shares of XYZ at 53.

The broker relays the offer back to the customer, the trader at the mutual fund in Boston. Now the customer must decide whether to accept the upstairs trader's offer of 53—three-quarters of a point higher than the current New York Stock Exchange offering of 52¼. To accept the offer, the customer would have to believe that he would move the stock up even higher if he tried to buy it without the upstairs trader's intervention. Yet the customer knows that the upstairs trader is no fool—the upstairs trader must believe that he himself can buy the stock for 53 or less (otherwise he would end up taking a loss on the position). In making his decision, the customer will probably consider the fact that he is in a hurry to buy the stock—his portfolio manager believes he has valuable information about XYZ. On the other hand, the upstairs trader will be in no special hurry to unwind his position, so he will likely have less price impact; and the longer he gives himself to unwind, the greater the chance he will find an interested seller of XYZ through his salesmen's worldwide network of institutional investors. Ultimately, the customer's decision will be intuitive, based primarily on a commonsense assessment of whether three-quarters of a point is a fair premium to pay for what amounts to "execution insurance."

When the customer accepts the offer, the trade is consummated for all practical purposes. Technically, however, there remains one very important step: printing the trade on the New York Stock Exchange tape. Even though the trade has truly been completed away from the Exchange, the upstairs trader's firm, which is an Exchange member, is bound by rules requiring that all trades be formally executed on the floor. To accomplish this, the upstairs trader instructs his firm's floor trader to execute the trade with the specialist. The floor trader approaches the specialist and announces that he has 500,000 shares of XYZ to cross at 53. First, however, because 53 is higher than the current offered price, any offers to sell at 53 or less that are on the specialist's book, or held in the order decks of the floor traders congregated at the specialist's post, will have to be accommodated. These competing orders pose no obstacle to the orderly completion of the trade: They simply sell to the customer at 53, receiving a somewhat better price than they expected (the upstairs trader, consequently, ends up having to sell fewer shares than he originally anticipated).[7]

The advent of upstairs trading has transformed the traditional relationship

---

[7] Will Weinstein ("The Way It Was," p. 40) recalls an amusing incident in which a specialist forcefully showed a new block trader at Lehman Brothers the rules of the game:

In the early days when Lehman had no floor brokers because it was beneath their dignity, . . . one of the senior partners at Lehman—it may have been Bobby Lehman himself—called, I think it was Morty Marcus [the specialist in Litton], and said, "Dear Mr. Marcus, this is, ahem, So-and-So at Lehman Brothers. We have both a buyer and a seller of Litton Industries, one of the stocks you make a market in down in the, ahem, New York Stock Exchange. And we were wondering what the procedure is for executing this transaction."

So Morty Marcus said: "Well, we have a public outcry system here, Mr. Lehman. The procedure is simple. You have your broker—you do have a broker." "Well, we don't have a broker, but we have a partner here who is a member of the New York Stock Exchange." And Marcus said: "Have Mr. Member come down to the floor, and have them ask for me. They all know where I am, and have him come into my crowd. . . ."

The guy walked into the crowd and he said, "Is this where Litton is traded?" And someone said, "Yes, it is," and he said, "200,000 Litton at 61," and Morty Marcus said, "Take 'em." And he bought the 200,000 in front of Lehman's buyer. When the guy said, "You can't do that. Why did this happen, this isn't what you told me," Marcus said, "You forgot to ask me if I wanted any."

between brokers and customers, both for good and for ill. On the positive side, there is no question that upstairs trading would not have evolved if it did not well serve customers' needs for liquidity. Thanks to upstairs trading, customers now have access to a quality and variety of market-making services that would otherwise be unavailable. Seeking facilitation from a single Exchange specialist limits an investor to a single possible counter-party who may have no motive to trade at a price favorable to the customer. By accessing multiple upstairs traders, however, an investor can expose his order to a diverse set of potential counterparties, one or more of whom may be highly motivated to trade. Even when there is no investment motivation for an upstairs trader to facilitate a particular trade, there may be business motivations: competition between upstairs traders to facilitate particular blocks, for prestige and market share and to create a quid pro quo that will capture a customer's other business.

Upstairs trading's most important long-term benefit for investors is that it brings them closer to the trading process by combining brokerage and market-making functions in a single operation. Over time, customers and upstairs traders can evolve fruitful working relationships that would be impossible if the customer were constrained to dealing with the anonymous specialists mediated by brokers, who never have a personal stake in the outcome of the ultimate customers' trades.

On the negative side, upstairs trading throws the brokerage industry into certain unavoidable conflicts with its customers. Most fundamentally, the upstairs trader who initiates original trades for investment profit only, rather than to respond to a customer's needs for liquidity, is in essence an investor, in competition with all other investors for a finite number of opportunities. Conflict is inevitable even when upstairs trading is carried out only to facilitate customer orders, for trading is a zero-sum game: The more profitable the trade turns out to be for the broker, the more opportunity cost is implicitly paid by the customer.

An alert investor will not overlook these potential conflicts in his dealings with upstairs traders. But if we take a more philosophical view of the progress of market evolution, these conflicts can be seen largely as the disintegration of traditional—though not necessarily inevitable—class distinctions between different types of market participants. When not-too-distant advances in data-processing and telecommunications technologies grant all participants equal access to one another's order flow, we can begin to imagine a model for a marketplace of the future built on a level playing field, where the distinctions between *customer, broker,* and *specialist* are blurred beyond meaning. What today are dangerous conflicts will tomorrow be healthy competition.

The Editor Asks

Q *What you have described is a dealer market, quite similar in substance to the dealer markets in bonds. What are the virtues and shortcomings of a dealer market relative to a centralized market from the viewpoint of the investor? How does he know which dealer to call?*

A The notions of *exchange* and *dealer market* exist at opposite ends of a continuous spectrum of institutional cohesion. At the extreme left end is total anarchy, a freewheeling dealer market without formal lines of communications, and in which any investor can choose to act as a dealer at any time. At the extreme right end is a complete monopoly, a single exchange that totally dominates the dealer function and requires that all communications be channeled through it. In between these extremes are hybrid structures. For them, the distinctions between *dealer market* and *exchange* are largely semantic. To the extent that upstairs traders compete as dealers with the New York Stock Exchange, they move our prevailing market structure to the left by thwarting the potential dominion of the Exchange and casting it in the role of just another competing dealer. At the same time, however, as the upstairs traders and the Exchange become inevitably linked by customers, facilities, and technologies shared in common, they become an ad hoc electronic exchange, moving our market structure toward the right.

Market structures toward the left end of the spectrum are strengthened by the Darwinian discipline of unfettered competition, but are cursed by the waste and inequality implicit in any understandardized information environment. Those toward the right are blessed by the efficiency and fairness of centralization and standardization, but are cursed by the inevitable flabbiness of monopolies. Our current market structure is close enough to the center of the spectrum to allow investors a choice, based on their predispositions and preferences, as to which of the blessings and which of the curses they would like to attach to their transactions. Those who trade actively and intuitively may prefer to deal exclusively with upstairs traders, basing their selection of traders on the quality of trust in their professional relationships. Those who trade passively and mechanically may prefer to deal exclusively with exchanges, simply sending "sunshine trades" into the marketplace on the belief that market efficiency will produce a fair, if not brilliant, execution.

13

ELECTRONIC TRADING ON THE EXCHANGES

George M. Spehar

Despite the fact that many unknowing market participants have only recently been made aware (often painfully so) of the widespread use of computer technology in modern execution, electronic trading is not a new concept on Wall Street. A few large firms, particularly those with extensive retail brokerage operations, have long been accustomed to the convenience, cost savings, and streamlined processing and comparison provided by systems such as the NYSE's DOT and SuperDOT, the American Stock Exchange's PER, and NASDAQ's SOES (Small Order Executive System). These organizations, when faced with the challenge of efficiently processing thousands of small retail orders daily, quickly realized that automation was a much more elegant solution than an army of bleary-eyed, expensive, and error-prone back-office clerks.

Although few could possibly have foreseen it at the time, this initial foray into the realm of technology and automation laid the groundwork for the sweeping changes in form and function that would eventually result in today's equity markets. Along the way, it amplified and received amplification from several other major trends:

- The gradual metamorphosis of stock market from a public to a largely professional arena.
- The advent of passive management and program trading in the 1970s.
- The introduction of stock index arbitrage in the 1980s.
- The geometric progression of modern technology.

EVER-GROWING INSTITUTIONAL DOMINANCE

If we were to journey back in time to the 1960s, we would find a stock market where professional investors accounted for roughly 50% of the trading volume on the NYSE. By the early 1980s, the growing reliance of individuals on the professional expertise provided by the mutual fund industry, along with public and corporate pension plans, had increased that percentage to approximately 75%. Recent studies indicate that an even larger portion, at times 90%, is now accounted for by institutional investors.

Correspondingly, NYSE volume, not only of shares traded but of actual daily transactions, exploded, prompting the exchanges themselves to introduce (and continually enhance) technological improvements such as computerized automatic order routing and processing systems, electronic specialists' books, and list processing.

THE ADVENT OF PASSIVE MANAGEMENT

The publication in 1973 of Burton Malkiel's thesis on efficient markets, *A Random Walk Down Wall Street,* which pointed out that most "expert" investors continually underperformed the broad market averages, proved to be a seminal event in the history of pension management.[1] Armed with this knowledge and a growing body of supporting academic research, plan sponsors began to put their fund managers' results under a microscope. Malkiel's efficient market banner aroused professional interest and confirmed the earlier work of pioneers like Bill Fouse and Tom Loeb.

Initially, Malkiel's thesis spawned intense debate in the investment community as to the representative validity of various market averages. Then, an increasing acceptance and a growing awareness on the part of plan sponsors led many professionals to focus on portfolio management and broad market aggregates rather than on fundamental analysis and the selection of individual securities.

At the same time, the total pool of institutional capital available for investment was expanding. Investors and sponsors alike discovered that the available supply of securities with the market capitalization and liquidity sufficient to absorb these vast sums was extremely limited. Attempts to invest only in stocks that passed muster often proved to be prohibitively expensive in terms of both price impact and the time required to accumulate

[1] Burton Malkiel, *A Random Walk Down Wall Street* (New York: Norton, 1973).

a meaningful position. This eventually forced even many disbelievers into "closet indexing"—that is, holding broad portfolios that essentially mimicked a stock market index. The combination of all these factors finally culminated in an industry where, today, hundreds of billions of dollars are either overtly or "closet" indexed in the United States alone.

THE ADVENT OF PROGRAM TRADING

At the time the first index funds were created, no readily available mechanism existed that would allow passive managers to act on their portfolios in the same manner in which they thought about them—that is, as indivisible investment aggregates. This presented some important problems, most notably:

- The logistical inefficiencies implied by the purchase of hundreds of stocks piecemeal over an extended time frame.
- Variance between the performance of the index portfolio and the benchmark it was designed to replicate.

This variance, dubbed *tracking error,* was introduced primarily by the manner in which the portfolios were traded. Since, at the time, the only available trading technology was the traditional one of trading stocks one at a time, passive managers were able neither to achieve correct relative stock weightings nor to capture closing prices used for valuation. Put very simply, the inability of passive managers to trade simultaneously and proportionately prevented them from capturing the very attributes that defined their investment strategy.

To eliminate the deficiencies imposed by prolonged periods of trading, index managers began cooperating with their brokers to devise methods that ensured the simultaneous execution of a properly weighted portfolio at a precise value.

Originally this merely took the form of a client sending a list to a broker, who had tickets prepared manually in advance for distribution to strategically positioned counterparts on the exchange floor. These counterparts were then given instructions to execute at closing prices. Wall Street lore abounds with stories of huge boxes of color-coded buy or sell tickets being wheeled through the massive trading rooms of legendary brokerage firms on their way to the floor for execution. One can only imagine the raised eyebrows and piqued interest this must have generated in the rooms, as well as on the floor, not to mention the rumor-mongering on a national scale. As time passed, some houses added a level of "sophistication" and began sending *both* buy *and* sell tickets to the floor for *each* program in order to confound and confuse would be front-runners and rumor-mongers. The feeling was that even though the world might know something material was imminent, only a select few would know the market side until the moment of execution. In retrospect, this seems almost comical in the context of an industry that prizes information so highly. Inevitably, confidentiality was compromised, sometimes resulting in higher costs for the client and a damaged reputation and loss of repeat business for the broker.

A variation that has survived to this day was to divide the list up according to NYSE rooms. Each block trader would then be assigned the stocks trading in a specific room and would phone orders to the floor via direct telephone wires. Corresponding postexecution reports for those stocks would come back to the same trader, who would then prepare a ticket for processing and trade comparison. Although this method certainly eliminated the "Hey, what's in the box?" syndrome, it often had the undesirable side effect of tying up the trading desk at the expense of the normal flow of institutional business.

It is obvious, then, that even these "improved" methods presented a number of formidable obstacles for both the index manager and the executing broker. For both parties, the process was very slow and labor-intensive, often requiring tremendous preparation and long lead times. The possibility of costly errors in execution resulting from both the manual transposition of the original list and the confusion generated by armies of frantic floor brokers scurrying about executing hundreds of stocks were made painfully apparent on numerous occasions. After all, depending on haste and handwriting, 20,000 FDX can easily be read as 20,000 FOX. To all this, add cumbersome, expensive processing, and it is easy to understand why these methods, though all that were available at the time, came to be viewed as less than optimal solutions to the problem of transacting indexed portfolios.

Although the (initial) requirements were that these trades be simultaneous as well as proportionally correct, in reality they were probably more price-sensitive than purely time-sensitive. That is, other than the broad requirement of trading at, say, month end, fund managers were most concerned with accurately capturing the prices reflected in a particular close. Because they found that the impact of their own trading often caused plan participants to pay higher prices, strategies eventually proliferated where brokers, at their own risk, would guarantee closing prices on an after-the-fact basis. This, of course, presented its own unique set of circumstances, which are beyond the scope of this chapter.[2]

THE INTRODUCTION OF STOCK INDEX ARBITRAGE

The contribution of index arbitrage trading was primarily its focus on time-sensitive trading—that is, the ability to get broad portfolio trades done almost instantaneously. By the time stock index futures began trading in February 1982, the NYSE's DOT (Designated Order Turnaround) system, introduced in March 1976, had long since been incorporated into the daily order flow of most large brokerage firms. Those whose significant retail businesses demanded the daily processing of thousands of public orders were particularly heavy users. What remained was a golden opportunity for the few bright individuals scattered around Wall Street who understood the mystery of index arbitrage. Coordinating data-processing and trading functions would eventually result in the creation of immensely profitable and, for its time, technologically advanced transaction machinery.

At first, because of the gross mispricings provided by the new futures markets, arbitrageurs were able to trade portfolios of as few as 30 to 50 stocks and still realize enormous profits. These stocks were executed in the same fashion as a typical index program—that is, one by one.

As time went on and word spread, more players emerged, bringing more capital to bear on this profitable new business. This began to enforce the theoretical pricing relationship between the stock and futures markets, causing spreads to contract. Arbitrageurs began to notice significant and costly tracking error when their incomplete sample baskets failed to converge perfectly with the underlying index at expiration. Contracting spreads and the high cost of manual trading provided the arbitrage community with economic incentives to develop automated trading capabilities. This eventually led to the use of perfectly weighted arbitrage portfolios, rebalanced nightly and poised for trading on a moment's notice. Able to operate well beyond the constraints of stock-by-stock trading, arbitrageurs were able to eliminate tracking error and profitably continue to exploit the ever-contracting stock/futures spreads. With its emphasis on instantaneous execution and the backing of deep-pocketed professional traders, index arbitrage provided the link joining the methods of the past with the reality of modern technology.

[2] See Chapter 14, ''Package Trading,'' by Patricia Dunn.

WHERE WE ARE TODAY

Largely because of the flexibility and sophistication derived from modern technological improvements, market participants now have the benefit of previously nonexistent trading alternatives. In view of this, it might be worthwhile to compare some of the characteristics of purely manual order submission and execution with those encompassing electronic enhancements.

Nowadays, a list is seldom "faxed" to a broker or read over a telephone. Rather, it is much more rapidly and accurately transmitted via computer-to-computer telecommunications links. Once stored in computer memory, the list can be screened in numerous ways, yielding valuable pretrade information that can be used to achieve a better execution.

Electronically transferring orders to the exchange floor, where they are automatically parsed to the appropriate trading post, drastically reduces the preparation workload and lead time necessary to get the orders on the floor. Once they are there, the execution itself is accomplished much more quickly. No tickets need be written, and floor personnel need only be used on an as-needed basis. Consequently, there is much less confusion, and confidentiality is more likely to be preserved. Furthermore, the elimination of manually copying the list onto trading tickets reduces the risk of errors in transposition.

Hundreds of individual reports can be processed in a matter of minutes, giving those responsible a much better feel for the progress of the overall execution. And (as locked-in trades) electronic comparison procedures are quicker and more accurate than those available for manual executions.

Finally, automation provides greater productivity for both broker and client. Personnel are more effectively able to manage even the minutiae of a massive portfolio restructuring, and to concentrate more fully on their normal daily responsibilities.

IMPLICATIONS

It would be difficult to overstate the impact that sophisticated computer technology and instantaneous telecommunications have had on modern investment and decision-making processes. The evolution of an electronic infrastructure has made possible the swift and efficient exchange of assets across a broad spectrum. This has gone a long way toward satisfying the institutional demand for more liquidity in the marketplace. The very fact that a professional investor can: (1) make the decision to trade a portfolio, (2) identify the particular combination of assets making it up, (3) transfer the list to his broker, and (4) have the orders being worked on the floor, all within the span of minutes, amounts to nothing less than a quantum leap forward in the cycle of liquidity. The tools now exist to trade entire portfolios of stocks in much the same manner as a trader following a more traditional approach would trade an individual stock.

Indeed, some have reached the point of almost taking this liquidity for granted. The ease and convenience with which portfolios can be transacted has caused some institutional investors to forget that liquidity may not be a free good. The old computer maxim ''garbage in, garbage out'' can acquire a previously unthinkable dimension. Some have maintained that once start-up costs have been borne, electronic order handling places few demands on a broker's human or risk resources. To the contrary, a handful of unfortunates on *both* sides of the Street can testify to the excruciating and embarrassing consequences of complacency. The potential for one major buy program to be misidentified as a sell, or for missorted share values to be attached to a list of tickers has resulted in higher levels of responsibility and compensation. Personnel who might previously have been classified as ''support'' are now raised to the level of ''professional.''

Electronic pathways linking member firm order rooms directly to the trading floor have created the capacity to process vastly increased trading volume at lower cost. The massive expenditure of time and money on plant and personnel suggest that, quite to the contrary, Wall Street and the exchanges themselves have paid dearly to create this sort of liquidity. Speed, automated efficiency, enhanced productivity, and increased reliability of comparison and clearance procedures (not to mention the skyrocketing volume of recent years) have helped to offset start-up costs. However, the continuing expense of development that will provide tomorrow's investors with markets of unequaled quality and efficiency, where information flows unimpeded, bespeaks a financial challenge that only the most committed, well capitalized, and resourceful may be able to meet.

We find ourselves witnessing the fundamental changes that electronic trading has brought to the institutional equity business. The burgeoning passive management industry, index arbitrage, and the emergence of quantitatively driven investment strategies seek to capitalize on group, rather than individual, security attributes. These have all resulted in expanded applications for the techniques of portfolio trading. Electronic trading continues to account for an increasingly larger share of the institutional business, promoting new and different relationships between brokers and their institutional clients, partnerships that hinge on computer expertise and quantitative prowess.

The Editor Asks

Q *The disadvantage of electronic order submission is the loss of "feel" or the supply and demand of an individual stock. What are the implications for investors?*

A Today, portfolio traders have at their fingertips sophisticated technological tools that permit them to trade groups of stocks in substantially the same fashion as individual stocks have always been traded.[3]

But as long as there are stock pickers who believe they can beat the market on an absolute or even a relative basis, there will continue to be a need for skilled, knowledgeable, and above all experienced traders who can pick up a phone and accurately convey their wishes to the trading floor. Electronic trading and manual trading should not be mutually exclusive. Rather, in the best of situations, the different disciplines should complement each other to produce new meaning and practical relevance for that overworked and possibly underachieved concept *best execution*.

Contrary to popular belief, computers don't make trading decisions, the people who control them do. Computers and technology merely aid the decision-making and management process. The result, one would hope, is more productive people and more economically beneficial solutions.

Who knows how much of the promise of AI (artificial intelligence) will be fulfilled and in what direction it will lead us? One thing, however, is clear: Professional investors are most willing to pay for what is often termed *value-added*—and value, like beauty, is in the eye of the beholder. In trading, as in any endeavor where the outcome is uncertain, judgment is what ultimately separates the winners from the losers. Computers don't have judgment. Computers don't have "feel." They don't have customers, either.

Many investors have voted with their pocketbook that "feel," or performance of individual stocks, is not paramount in their investment plan. This does not, however, absolve those administrating transactions from the responsibility of doing them in as cost-effective a manner as the framework of the execution permits. Obviously, from a *purely* trading perspective, the "best" solution might be to have each stock assigned its own trader, who would devote his total time, energy, and concentration to that execution. In today's world of megafunds and broadly diverse core portfolios, however, it could be argued that this is not realistic, practical, or relevant.

[3] See Chapter 24, "Intelligent Trading Systems," by David Leinweber.

For example, when a market timing decision is made and the vehicle of implementation is a diversified portfolio, a feel for individual stocks is probably not the appropriate focus. Perhaps a "market feel" is what's called for, and a more macro approach to how this particular execution may relate to or affect the market might be more relevant. By the time you try to figure out what's going on with 850 stocks, your opportunity has in all likelihood slipped away. Admittedly, there will be $\frac{1}{8}$s and $\frac{1}{4}$s lost along the way to someone with better "information," but the ability to get the trade done and put the idea to work is probably more important. If everyone has done his homework, if the investment strategy and means of execution are aligned and the appropriate systems and people are in place, a more important cost will probably be that of missing the trade. I don't believe electronic trading has inherent disadvantages versus manual trading except as they are perceived in specific situations. I don't believe hammers have inherent shortcomings versus saws, either. If I want to cut a piece of wood, I use a saw. If I want to drive a nail into it, I use a hammer. The perceived disadvantages most likely result from the inappropriate use or misunderstanding of electronic trading techniques.

14

PACKAGE TRADING

Patricia C. Dunn

When the history of the markets in the 1980s is written, the emergence of "package trading" will likely be identified as the most significant new trend of the decade. Like block trading in the 1970s, package trading has come to be the dominant execution method of a new class of institutional investors who use the market itself, and not just the individual securities that make it up, as their basis for investing. This chapter will review the rationale of package trading as a phenomenon of the changing environment in the modern investment era.

PACKAGE TRADING: A DEFINITION

In concept and definition, package trading is exceedingly simple. It is the purchase or sale simultaneously of an entire portfolio or cross-section of a portfolio. The subtleties and complexities in the implementation of package trading will be discussed later. Those who employ the technique most frequently are index fund managers, index arbitragers, hedgers, and broadly diversified semiactive equity managers, who all use package trading to maintain the diversification they seek in their portfolio holdings throughout the trading process.

BACKGROUND

One of the key developments in investment practice during the decades of the 1970s and 1980s has been the growth of portfolio strategies recognizing that well-developed capital markets tend to be "efficient" in their pricing of individual securities. Although debate continues as to the *level* of efficiency of the U.S. stock market, few professional investors have been untouched in their thinking by the implications of capital market theory unleashed in the late 1960s: In markets where information flows freely, prices move quickly to reflect all known factors affecting security valuation. Therefore, portfolio management strategies designed to "beat the market" are destined, on average, to fail because stock prices don't reflect exploitable values—they incorporate all known information already.

Although few investors believe in "strong-form" notions of efficient market theory, and evidence abounds of short- to long-term stock price effects that belie the purist's view, the general case for market efficiency is a powerful one. It is particularly true for very large investors, like pension funds, whose size alone makes it difficult to successfully exploit stock price inefficiency: If the price wasn't efficient before they traded, it will be when they do!

As a practical matter, reasonably efficient markets motivate investors to seek broad diversification in their portfolios. If it is not possible to exploit inefficient prices on average and earn rewards for incurring specific stock risk, then it is rational to diversify away as much specific risk as possible and achieve reward for taking the systematic risk of the market itself. Along with important subsidiary benefits, it is primarily on this notion that index funds—portfolios designed to match the performance of all or part of the market—developed and grew in the 1970s and 1980s.

The history of indexing and its impact on investment practice is outside the scope of this chapter, but the need for indexing as an investment alternative leads directly to the need for package trading as the implementation method for index funds and other broadly based portfolios. Package trading is merely the manifestation of investors' desires to hold diversified portfolios—in fact, package trading is the trading implication of efficient markets.

THE RATIONALE FOR PACKAGE TRADING

Just as block trading was an outgrowth of the institutionalization of the stock market in the 1970s, package trading has been an outgrowth of the 1980s trend toward investing in broadly diversified portfolios. Although block trading is accepted today as conventional practice, so deeply embedded in the marketplace as to seem preordained, in fact, like package trading, it evolved out of the needs of a group of investors whose importance emerged along with that of institutions as the dominant market force.

Block trading was a controversial development in the marketplace of the 1970s, as package trading has been during the 1980s. It begged many questions about the purpose of organized stock exchanges and potential harm befalling the little guy who did not have access to "upstairs" block market-making facilities. Block trading took hold and flourished because it met a legitimate set of investor needs: Large institutional portfolio managers, attempting to add value through stock selection, needed to be able to buy and sell large blocks of stocks in one transaction, whereas the natural order flow to the exchange specialists came in small, unpredictable fragments. The growing capital base of the major Wall Street investment houses gave them the capacity to make principle markets in large blocks of stock, as desired by institutional traders. In its development, block trading angered many who felt it would forever change the nature of the market for the worse, but in the end a formal set of block trading rules emerged to govern the practice and mollify its critics.

Most of what has developed in the last 20 years as the infrastructure of stock market trading is built on the needs of investors who use specific security selection as the premise for their investment approach. If the dominant motivation of traders was to buy and sell stocks based on their potential to add or subtract value, then it followed naturally that market-making and operational capacity developed to serve that dominant need. But what if information-motivated, stock-by-stock trading decisions played no part in a portfolio's objective? This is the situation faced by index fund managers attempting to trade the first benchmark-tracking portfolios in the early 1970s.

GROWTH AND DEVELOPMENT OF PACKAGE TRADING

When index funds received their first commitments of institutional assets in the early 1970s, there immediately arose the need to find a trading style that would help assure their objective to track the performance of the broad stock market (defined by many then, and yet today, as the S&P 500 Index). An active portfolio manager receiving new assets could take a time-extensive approach to buying the desired stocks, using block trading or market orders to the floor of the exchange to accumulate the desired stocks one by one. In contrast, the index fund manager was responsible for providing a rate of return to match the S&P 500 exactly, minus the unavoidable costs of trading. But accumulating all the stocks in the index one by one would subject the portfolio to unwanted performance deviation, arising solely from randomness in the timing of stock purchases over time.

The ideal trading style was apparent: Buy all the stocks desired as of the same moment in time. In that fashion, the positions taken would reflect the pricing of all the stocks in the Index at once, and the portfolio could begin tracking the Index properly from the start.

The straightforward objective of the trading style was not met with its complement in the marketplace. In fact, the major barrier to package trading was, in the early 1970s until the early 1980s, its physical feasibility. For example, the normal means of order transmission from the manager to the broker is a phone call announcing the stock or handful of stocks to be bought or sold. When 500 stocks are involved, however, that is impractical. The normal means of order transmission from the broker to the exchange floor is a handwritten paper ticket—no problem when a few orders are involved, but 500? The established means for order execution requires a floor broker to go to the specialist's booth, reach a price, and consummate a trade. How does a limited group of floor brokers handle 500 orders at various locations around the exchange floor at once?

The uneven tracking performance of the early index funds reflects in part the difficulty of executing package trades. In response to the need for close tracking of performance, arrangements between index funds and brokers were developed to execute package trades at "guaranteed" prices. In these trading programs, brokers accept the price risk of executing hundreds of stocks at the same prices used to compute the index (such as the NYSE closing price) in exchange for a potential share of any trading profits, plus commissions.

A wide variety of guaranteed price programs developed, significantly motivated by the lack of market infrastructure available to index fund managers to execute efficiently at target prices across a broad list of names. Guaranteed price programs were a means of passing on to the executing broker the risk and difficulty of acquiring or disposing of hundreds of stocks through the market's established mechanisms, built to accommodate individual stock traders.

For most of the 1970s and into the early 1980s, the existence and development of package-trading techniques went almost completely unnoticed by the investment community. Use of the style was limited to a small handful of index fund managers and well-capitalized brokers who were willing and able to undertake these unusual trades. The vast majority of institutional brokerage continued to be dominated by the needs of active managers, involving stock research to motivate trades, block trading to accommodate them, and well-trodden paths of distribution among brokers, exchanges, and money managers.

Interest in the trading needs of indexers was limited during this period to two or three major brokerage firms, which undertook the investments in procedural and operational infrastructure necessary to support them. These investments included developing electronic means for transmitting tradelists from the index manager to the broker, ticket generation, and order confirmation. All were accomplished with little fanfare, reflecting a belief on the part of those investing in the infrastructures that diversification through index-like funds was the wave of the institutional investment future.

Functionally, package trading evolved mostly through the interaction of index fund managers and those brokers interested in their business. For example, early package trading typically involved a competitive bidding process in which the manager sought bids to complete the package of trades at the lowest commission cost, using price guarantees and profit-sharing incentives.

Once the winning bidder was determined, the manager electronically transferred a tradelist to the broker, with the specific names and share amounts unknown except to the winner. From that point, the broker prepared tickets for execution on the floor of the NYSE. Once all the executions were completed, usually over a number of trading days, the actual executed price of the trades was totaled and compared to the guaranteed price. Negative differences, or trading losses, often accrued entirely to the broker, whereas trading profits were shared between the broker and the account. Over time, an almost infinite variety of guaranteed packages were developed based on different profit-sharing rules, disclosure rules, time to complete the package, and/or trading restrictions. Each program type attempted to achieve the ideal trade-off between commission costs and market impact or spread costs for a given package to be executed.

As an aside, the term *package trading* was almost unknown until the mid-1980s. Index fund trades were known as *program trades* or, later, *basket trades*. Today, *program trading* has become synonymous with index arbitrage (to be discussed later) as a result of misuse of the term by the press once it began noticing the trend in the late 1980s.

THE WAVE HITS: PACKAGE TRADING IN THE 1980S

While index fund managers and the few brokers supporting their trading needs toiled in relative obscurity, important events were developing in the investment industry that brought their activities to the forefront of professional and public attention. These events included the introduction of stock index futures in 1982, the release by the NYSE of its DOT and

SuperDOT order-routing system in 1986, and the growth of index funds throughout the 1980s.

STOCK INDEX FUTURES AND PACKAGE TRADING.   It is surprising to most who became familiar with program or package trading as a result of the October 1987 market decline that the use of these trading techniques far predated the introduction of stock index futures. In fact, as noted, the term *program trading* has forever changed as the result of press coverage of the market break. But it is crucial to understand that package trading is a means to an end, not an objective in itself—where the goal is to move into or out of an entire slice of the market at once. That goal itself serves a broader objective—for example, to track the market in an index fund or to trade efficiently between the stocks in an index fund and their nearly perfect substitute, S&P 500 Index futures.

Stock index futures based on the S&P 500 Index began trading on the Chicago Mercantile Exchange in April 1982. They represented an important breakthrough in the development of the capital markets because, for the first time, traders and investors could take a position in or against the entire S&P 500 through one single transaction—buying or selling the S&P 500 Index futures. They were, in effect, a prebundled package of stocks, in concept representing a full flowering of the implications of efficient markets and the value of diversification.

Index fund managers were quick to recognize that the existence of S&P 500 Index futures begged an evaluation of their attractiveness relative to an investment in the 500 underlying stocks themselves. After all, if the duty of the index fund manager was to replicate the performance of the Index, then it follows that the replication should be gained in the most cost-effective manner. Stock index futures differed significantly in their trading characteristics and institutional features, but a careful evaluation of their price versus the prices of the stocks—adjusted appropriately, as will be described—could potentially yield nearly riskless profit opportunities relative to an investment in an index fund.

A full treatment of the development, use, and characteristics of stock index futures is outside the scope of this chapter, but a simple description of their substitutability for an investment in S&P 500 stocks is necessary. First, a futures contract on the S&P 500 represents the promise to deliver or take delivery of the stocks in the Index at a preset future date. The contracts cover quarterly delivery cycles and have an important cash settlement feature, requiring the exchange of cash instead of the stocks themselves to fulfill a short or long position to the buyer or seller of the contract. All cash movements are handled through a clearing corporation, capitalized by futures market participants, which is responsible for daily settlement of all monies owing or owed to both sides of the contract based on its daily price movements.

Upon their quarterly expiration date, the price of the expiring S&P 500 Index futures contract is set equal to that of the Index itself. During the quarter, the prices of the contracts are established by supply and demand, and they occasionally become "mispriced" relative to the underlying stocks in the Index. An evaluation of their mispricing rests on analysis of the price of the futures contract relative to the Index at a given moment in time, minus the dividend that will be foregone for not investing in the stocks, plus the interest earnings that can be achieved because the investor need only deposit a small fraction of the value of the Index as initial margin to buy (or sell) the contract.

The price adjustment to the futures described dictates the theoretically fair value of the contracts relative to an investment in the stocks. The difference, or *basis,* between the futures contract and the stocks in the S&P 500 Index can be tracked using real-time price feeds to detect when the basis is under- or overpriced. Occasionally, the basis becomes sufficiently cheap that it will cover all the costs of selling the stocks owned by an index fund (including commissions and the market-maker's spread), the costs of buying the futures, and the costs of repurchasing the stocks when the futures expire, with enough mispricing left over to yield a small profit. Conversely, the basis occasionally becomes sufficiently rich that an investor can cover all the costs of buying the S&P 500 stocks, selling the futures against them, and later reversing the trade at a profit. This investment creates a substitute money market instrument with an above-market yield.

The numerous forces that lead to the mispricing of the futures relative to the stocks are not necessarily well understood, but futures market participants in general react to the same forces for market valuation as do investors in individual stocks. In a formal sense, index fund arbitragers are the mechanism for maintaining proper alignment of the markets, transmitting between them price information reached at different points in time by both.

As the market for stock index futures has grown and deepened, rivaling and at times exceeding trading volume in the stocks themselves, it has become an important means of price discovery for the broad market. Because trading in futures is about one-tenth as expensive as trading in stocks, they may be the first place investors go to express their opinions about the market in general. If so, the occasional mispricing of the basis between the futures and the stocks can be thought of as a leading indicator of where the market in general is heading. Through index arbitrage, that information is quickly transmitted back to the stock market, which by its fundamental nature does not trade to new levels all at once, but stock by stock.

A small fraction of index fund investors, representing between 5% and 10% of the estimated $150 billion invested in stock index funds in early 1988, instruct their managers to monitor systematically the relative price levels of S&P 500 stocks versus the futures for arbitrage opportunities. At least once per quarter (on contract expiration date), the price of the futures will be equal to that of the index, creating a nearly riskless return enhancement for an index fund if the futures underpricing is captured. The opportunities for profit from index arbitrage have been variable, ranging from 4% to 6% per year in the first months of 1982 to 1% or so in the mid-1980s. This level of value-added is equal to much of what is hoped for from active management, but index arbitrage delivers it with much higher certainty and less risk.

The major risk in index arbitrage is execution risk, and package trading plays a crucial role in assuring, through simultaneous purchase or sale of all stocks in the portfolio, that the substitution of futures for stocks can be made successfully. In the early years of index arbitrage, the package trading techniques used to execute this intermarket trade were identical on the stock side to those used to execute "plain vanilla" index fund trades: Large institutional brokers with significant floor brokerage facilities would disseminate, as efficiently as possible—given the physical limitations of people and space—orders to be executed in the crowd at the specialists' booths.

PACKAGE TRADING AND SUPERDOT.   Introduction of the NYSE DOT and SuperDOT system, permitting electronic routing of entire lists of stocks to specialists for execution within known price parameters, was an important development in the market infrastructure supporting index fund trades. SuperDOT has been the principal modification of the NYSE's order execution capacity that directly serves the needs of broadly diversified investment managers. It permits them to trade in a manner consistent with their portfolio objectives, based on the entire market instead of selectively within the market.

The DOT system itself (Designated Order Turnaround) was an innovation by the New York Stock Exchange intended to alleviate the burden of handling small retail market orders. The system operates under a defined set of rules and allows for the execution of small orders electronically at prevailing market prices, relieving the specialist of a great deal of routine order handling.

SuperDOT includes a tradelist-processing feature that permits the Exchange member entering orders to direct more than one stock at a time to the specialists' booths. Its applicability to index fund traders was immediately apparent because it provided a cost-efficient method for executing a large cross-section of stocks at once. SuperDOT meant that the capacity to execute package trades was no longer limited to brokerage firms with the largest or most experienced floor brokerage resources. Its existence increased competition among brokers for package-trading business. In its way, the development of the tradelist-processing feature of SuperDOT is analogous to the development of the personal computer: Those who had neither the capital nor the expertise to install a mainframe computer found themselves merrily computing on spreadsheets as soon as the technology became available and cheap.

In addition to being cost-efficient for handling the routine orders of index fund managers trading in small positions across hundreds of names, SuperDOT took much of the execution risk out of index arbitrage trading. Recall that the success of index arbitrage rests on achieving substitutability between the stocks and the futures. The multiorder handling capacity of SuperDOT permits higher assurance that the intermarket trade is consummated at the relative prices that motivated it. Stock-by-stock manual execution of index arbitrage packages continued, particularly for handling larger orders outside the parameters of DOT system execution.

Quite beyond its application as a package trading mechanism for index arbitrage, SuperDOT provides an efficient, low-cost means of executing any order involving several or hundreds of stocks. The needs of passive traders are often best met through SuperDOT, which remains the closest link between the needs of broadly diversified investors and the trading liquidity of the New York Stock Exchange. (Comments on the limitations imposed on the use of SuperDOT in reaction to the October stock market decline will follow in the chapter summary.)

THE GROWTH OF INDEXING.   It is impossible to separate the growth and use of package trading from the growth in popularity of indexing, principally because index fund managers invented it to meet their specific investment objectives. Package trading is becoming more widely used by active managers as well, particularly those with quantitatively based investment styles that tend to be widely diversified. After all, information is not the sole motivation to trade for any manager—liquidity needs arise independent of news likely to affect stock valuation. For example, an active manager satisfied with the structure of a portfolio might be required to invest new cash or to supply cash to his client. Rather than be forced to tinker with the individual's holdings, he can use package trading to increase or decrease the portfolio's holdings pro rata, preserving its characteristics during the trading process. Under this scenario, the active manager is very much like the passive manager in his trading objective: The benchmark is his current portfolio, and preserving its performance during and after trading is the goal.

Nonetheless, index funds and package trading go together, hand in glove, nearly all the time. The growth of indexing in the 1980s (to about $150 billion, or 6% of the value of the equity market) has brought the trading style much more attention, some critical of its impact on the market. Criticism of package trading today is remarkably similar in content to that of block trading 20 years ago. The charges against it include concern that it interferes with the smooth functioning of the market and that it is inherently unfair because small investors can't use it. Much of this criticism strikes index fund managers as ironic: After all, isn't passive management the ultimate recognition of the market's superiority as a whole to any small part of itself? And don't the little guys benefit when their retirement funds are invested at lowest possible cost using package-trading techniques?

ARE PACKAGE TRADES ALWAYS USEFUL?

Even for those whose trading objectives are met well by package trading, this method may not be the lowest cost or most appropriate trading style under many circumstances. Several factors must be considered by the manager contemplating a package trade:

- How packageable is the merchandise to be traded? While a pure S&P 500 portfolio maps well into the liquidity of the marketplace, packages of unrelated stocks or non-market-weighted tradelists may be more expensive to trade as a package—particularly if price guarantees are required from the executing broker.
- Does the manager have any specific information on the stocks to be traded? Package trades imply informationless or liquidity-motivated decisions. If the trader believes he has information about the stocks to be traded, then perhaps it can be used successfully to execute the trades individually.
- How much time does the trader have to execute? In general, the less immediate one's demand to trade, the lower trading costs can be, particularly if large size is involved. Executing a large package immediately may be more costly than attempting to trade in smaller pieces over time. The best alternative for pure index traders,

however, may be to avoid the opportunity costs of *not* trading but packaging reasonably sized slices.

- What is the cost of package versus traditional trading methods? The agency commission costs of package trades are generally very low, but price guarantees can be expensive, particularly for information-motivated traders. Cost alternatives must always be considered.

SUMMARY

Rather than attempt a how-to approach to package trading, this chapter is intended to deepen the reader's intuitions about the motivations for and development of portfolio trading. The specific methods and mechanisms of package trading are so dynamic, and the institutional features of the marketplace in such flux, that a cookbook for how to make a package trade would become outdated nearly instantaneously. As a case in point, the events of October 1987 and their aftermath have altered much of market reality—particularly for those whose investment objectives are best met through package trading.

Assuming the continued growth of index funds and related investment strategies based on the principles of modern investment theory, one can assume that package trading is a permanent fixture in the marketplace. Whether the marketplace will adjust smoothly or with difficulty to the existence of package trading remains to be seen, but there is little doubt that the legitimate trading needs of diversified investors will be met by counterparties who seek opportunity in doing so.

AFTERWORD

Certainly a review of the crash of 1987 is outside the scope of this chapter. Informed readers no doubt know that a great deal of new attention has focused on program trading as either the cause of, a contributor to, or—a minority view—a mitigator of the market decline. Although it is difficult to say for certain because of confusion in terminology and understanding, it appears that most attention is aimed at the practice of index arbitrage as a prime culprit.

The level of concern and fear that index arbitrage has engendered is very real and important merely because it exists, representing an image problem of significant proportion for those who use package trading. Yet the many official reports on the market break contain much information supportive of the practice of index arbitrage, especially the Brady Commission's introduction of the one-market concept. Index arbitragers embrace this concept wholly because it contains a crucial notion needed to make an unemotional assessment of the strategy's market effect: If, indeed, the marketplace for stocks and futures trades as one, then a purchase in one-half the market (i.e., in futures) offset by a sale in the other half (i.e., in stocks) is neutral in its impact on this "one" market.

The debate over whether index arbitrage exacerbates market volatility is likely to continue for some time, in large part because the existence of these so-called informationless trades is seen by many investment professionals as threatening to the "true" function of the market—to direct capital efficiently in the securitized economy. Many critics, decrying the development of stock index futures as serving no useful economic purpose, represent them as means for mere bets on the market as opposed to vehicles for fundamental investment decisions. In its way, the argument is a bread-and-butter issue for that part of the investment industry that depends for its economic well-being on the existence of winners and losers (as there must be!) on each side of stock-by-stock trades.

Index fund managers and index arbitragers argue that, in fact, market risk *is* a commodity that can be taken or hedged away through futures—and that to choose to do so is reasonable and prudent, as well as cost-effective, relative to doing so through conventional investment management. Given that most investment outcomes are explained by market forces, not stock selection, it is not surprising that stock index futures have grown so in popularity. But they would not be nearly so useful in the absence of arbitrage, which is a necessary condition for their pricing to remain viable relative to that of stocks. To curtail index arbitrage is tantamount to removing futures from the investment landscape, forcing investors to use more costly stock trading to manage their exposure to the commodity component of investing, market return, and risk.

To label index arbitrage trades as disruptive because they are not based on "fundamental" investment decisions begs many ancillary questions about what constitutes legitimate trading: Should dividend capture trades be banned? Should trades motivated by technical analysis be removed from the market? All are informationless relative to company fundamentals, but true fundamentalists should welcome the trading volume represented by these activities as opportunities to trade profitably. A market in which only fundamental traders existed would, in the extreme, point out the limitations of winning the zero-sum game of trading, given that wealth is not created by markets but merely traded among their participants.

Fundamental investors should, in any case, not be cowed by intradaily market volatility, even if it is created by the neutral buy/sell trading of index arbitrage. Such daily market machinations are of no consequence to longer term investors, but market professionals may understandably regret the loss of clients trading for short-term advantage who may be discouraged by volatile markets. Whether these shorter term traders are needed for the market to do its job of capital allocation is another matter entirely. That their lessening numbers would allocate capital away from the brokerage and money management industry is, however, undeniable.

Notwithstanding the foregoing, concern persists that index arbitrage creates excess market volatility. This proposition remains the subject of a great deal of research and little consensus among academicians, practitioners, and market regulators. In response, the NYSE moved in early 1988 to limit use of its SuperDOT tradelist routing facility when the Dow Jones Industrial Average of 30 stocks trades a given number of points above or below the previous day's closing level. The curbs on the SuperDOT system are aimed at index arbitrage traders as opposed to routine index fund package trades, but nonetheless represent the removal of a valuable tool for efficient order handling under specific market conditions.

Of more concern to pure package traders is the potential misconstruction of their motivation and objectives by those unfamiliar with the precepts of indexing, especially those empowered to limit means for diversified portfolio trading. Those who are committed to investment innovation must recognize the discomfort their innovations may create. The next few years will no doubt bring a wholesale increase in the practice of modern investment strategies and, one may hope, an increase in the market's comfort with their existence.

The Editor Asks

Q *In discussing passive trading, Steve Manus suggests some techniques that he believes trade off immediacy for reduced trading costs (see Chapter 15). Could you discuss when you would choose the package-trading techniques as opposed to the techniques suggested by Steve?*

A No single trading style can possibly be ideal under all circumstances, even for those, like index funds, with very straightforward investment objectives. Package-trading techniques are valuable because they eliminate much of the *unmeasured,* and perhaps unmeasurable, costs of trading—the opportunity cost component of *not* trading when one is charged with providing instantaneous exposure to the equity market. The art or science of trading-cost measurement has not advanced to capture the effect of waiting to trade, which can be expected, on average over time, to be a positive cost because equity markets rise on average over time. Packages neatly avoid this cost by assuring that all desired exposure is gained quickly and efficiently.

In addition, it is the rare trader who is able to "win" consistently against the other side of the trade when a masterminded, stock-by-stock trading approach is used. Since index fund managers presumably operate without information, they are not typically in a good position to avoid buying or selling first the stocks that are in excess demand or supply in the market. Packages avoid that adverse selection problem.

These points are most applicable, however, when one is trading in position sizes that map well into the natural liquidity of the marketplace, such as capitalization-weighted index fund tradelists. When one is trading out of or into positions that do not fit well into natural trading liquidity, time-extensive trading may be the best alternative. Good traders, be they index fund managers or active managers, recognize the characteristics of the portfolio to be traded and choose a package or nonpackage approach accordingly.

15

PASSIVE TRADING

Stephen P. Manus

The traditional equity trading style depicted by the phrase "buy low, sell high" suggests an ability to determine at least the approximate value of a particular issue of stock. The emergence of alternative styles of money management, which deemphasize the importance of determining specific stock values, has also prompted the development of corresponding trading strategies. Indeed, properly utilized passive trading techniques give further credence to the definition of ignorance as bliss; that is, an equity trader may be better off with no opinion rather than an established view of a stock upon entering the marketplace.

HISTORICAL PERSPECTIVE

The single event that has had the greatest impact on the professional investment community during the past half-century was the passage of the Employee Retirement Income Security Act (ERISA) in 1974. The direct results of this legislation were:

1. The establishment of minimum funding standards for qualified pension and profit-sharing plans.
2. Minimum standards of fiduciary behavior for plan sponsors and trustees. The indirect result of this legislation was the explosive growth of the money management business. Corporations adopted a longer term view of their pension plans and turned to the stock market in search of greater returns. The period since 1974 has seen a change in the stock market from a retail to an institutional market, dominated by tax-exempt assets that could be aggressively traded without regard for tax consequences.

An ever-increasing portion of these assets has been placed in *index funds*. These funds are broadly diversified portfolios designed to match market averages, such as the S&P 500 Index. Index funds are said to be passively managed; that is, the portfolios are constructed on a buy-and-hold basis in order to mirror the structure of the market index.

The need for index funds grew out of the idea of market efficiency. The growth of the institutional market brought a steadily increasing number of skilled professionals analyzing companies in greater detail. Efficient market theory suggests that the sum of this analysis is reflected in the price of a stock at any time. The more that is known to the public, the harder it becomes for any individual manager to find bargains and thus outperform the market.

Another view of this problem was presented by Charles Ellis, who used the term "loser's game" to describe the investment business. Ellis argues that institutions cannot expect to outperform the market because they *are* the market. Because transaction costs are incurred by managers but do not affect market averages, managers can expect to underperform the market by the amount of these costs. Thus, the stock market can be viewed as a game that will be won not by the person making the most correct decisions, but by the person making the fewest incorrect decisions.[1]

ACTIVE TRADING: ASSESSING THE VALUE OF INFORMATION

For a better understanding of passive trading, let us first consider more traditional trading styles associated with active management. The typical active manager evaluates a fairly stable universe of stocks and makes value judgments regarding each stock. For the most part, these judgments will be similar to those made by the rest of the market. Occasionally, the manager's judgment will deviate from consensus sufficiently to justify a buy or sell of the stock.

The stock market brings together potential buyers and sellers, few of whom have exactly the same opinion of the stock's true value. When buyers and sellers cannot agree upon a price at which to trade, *market-makers* (specialists or broker/dealers) will provide liquidity, thus clearing the market. The party initiating the trade incurs costs both tangible (commissions) and intangible, in the form of a market-maker spread. Although market-maker spreads are difficult to measure, everyone agrees that they are greater than zero and are at least as important a component of transaction

[1] Charles D. Ellis, *Investment Policy* (New York: Dow Jones–Irwin, 1985).

costs as commissions. This, no doubt, accounts for the survival of market-makers in the aggregate.

The market-maker spread is the amount paid to the market-maker for accommodating a trade when no natural buyer or seller exists on the other side of the trade. Thus, the party that initiates the trade must be convinced that his information is sufficiently valuable to warrant compensating a market-maker. Those who pay market-maker spreads are, in effect, paying an insurance premium against adverse price movement.

PASSIVE TRADING TECHNIQUES

Passive trading techniques are an outgrowth of the development of index funds. Because these funds purchase stocks solely for reasons of diversification, without regard for fundamental valuation, the index trader should be unwilling to pay market-maker spreads to compensate anyone for accommodating his trade. In order to reduce or eliminate these spreads, he must trade in a manner that attempts to reverse the traditional roles of initiation and accommodation.

Passive trading is not a short-term affair. Passive traders do not set out to make each trade the ''best'' possible trade (however that might be measured). Rather, their goal is to avoid systematically losing more than one has to lose on the aggregate of their trades over the long run. To succeed at this game, a passive trader must:

1. Be willing to share information about his potential trades with the investment community.
2. Be flexible regarding the time his trades are completed.
3. Be flexible regarding the specific price level at which he is willing to trade.

Although each of these points is important, the first is especially crucial. Active traders are typically reluctant to reveal much, if any, information to the marketplace, probably for two reasons. First, they don't want anyone else to know what it is that they know about a particular stock. Second, they fear that the awareness of their intentions will influence the existing price. Passive traders do not face the same problems. They have no information regarding the valuation of the stock and, given their time flexibility, could withdraw their trade interests in the event of unacceptable price movement.

The ideal situation for a passive trader is to participate in *cross-trading*. Cross-trades occur when two passive traders discover that they are on opposite sides of a potential trade. In such a case, they will usually agree to accept a randomly determined price, such as the market close of a certain day, and will pay a broker a minimal commission rate to assure proper reporting and securities movement.

The most important element of cross-trading is finding a partner with whom to trade, whether through structured or informal channels. There currently exist electronic crossing networks, which allow traders to reveal information about their impending trades to other system users.[2] Traders can also input actual trade interests into these systems, which will automatically generate trades when buy and sell interests on the system match. Although the electronic networks are clearly the wave of the future, informal crossing networks have functioned for quite some time. For example, index fund managers involved in portfolio restructuring may call other index managers in search of the other side of their trades. It is clearly advantageous to a passive trader to use crossing networks as much as possible. The greater challenge to the passive trader is what to do when cross-trading does not appear practical—that is, when the natural other side cannot be found.

When cross-trading is not an option, the passive trader attempts to function as a provider of liquidity to the market. He accomplishes this by making it known that, as a passive buyer or seller, he is willing to trade a certain stock or stocks. He is thus attempting to attract the other side of the trade, which might have been reluctant to deal with the specialist or with other market-makers.

It may be easier to understand the actions of the passive trader by comparing him to another passive trader, the typical house seller. Sellers of houses rarely seek bids from brokerage or equity firms in order to sell immediately. Such an action would imply a need for cash, or a judgment that the housing market was overvalued. This would be comparable to the actions of an active trader who believes he has information regarding a stock.

The typical house seller behaves in a more passive fashion. He might post his own "For Sale" sign in front of his house, hoping to catch the eye of an interested buyer. More often, he will enlist the services of a broker, who will charge a commission. In return for this commission, the broker will expose the house to potential buyers in his network, or those being serviced by other brokers. The trade-off implicit in using a broker is that the exposure provided will increase the ultimate sale price by at least the amount of the commission charged. The seller is free to pull his house off the market at any time, or to alter the price he is seeking, on the basis of market conditions. If the seller

---

[2] See Chapter 16, "Electronic Crossing Markets," by Edward C. Story.

is truly passive, he will attempt to receive his perceived fair market value and will not be under time pressure to accept anything less.

The passive seller of stock behaves in much the same way. When he has exhausted any cross-trading possibilities, he must expose his sell interest to other potential buyers. He does this through a broker, paying a commission for exposure and execution rather than for the assumption of risk by the broker acting as market-maker. The selection of the particular broker will depend on a number of factors:

1. Perception of the broker's ability:
    *   Has the broker handled passive trades before?
    *   Does the broker understand the proper time constraints placed on the order?
    *   Can the broker give the order proper exposure without adversely affecting price?

2. Composition of the broker's order flow:
    *   Is the broker familiar with the stock? Has he traded it frequently in the recent past?
    *   Is the broker in touch on a regular basis with enough potential buyers?
    *   Is the broker in touch with buyers of appropriate size? (Many discount brokers may not be able to locate buyers of 10,000 or more shares.)

Commissions paid will reflect the difficulty of the trade. Again, as with the house seller, the broker earns the commission by increasing the ultimate sale proceeds by reducing market impact.

A crucial element of such a passive trading strategy is the need for flexibility regarding the timing of trades. The passive trader and/or broker must communicate that, as the provider of potential liquidity, he is under no pressure to complete the trade within a certain period, and that any bids or offers made could be withdrawn without consequence. The greatest potential risk in such a strategy is the risk of the overall equity market moving against the passive trader while waiting to complete the trade. This market risk can be hedged in a cost-effective manner using stock index futures. Eliminating market risk does not account for specific risk, that chance of price movement based on events affecting the specific stock rather than the whole market. The true passive trader is willing to accept some specific risk, which historically is less than market risk. This is justified in pursuit of lower trading costs because specific risk is random, while market-maker spreads are not.

The pricing of a passive trade will vary depending on the particular time and stock. Passive traders cannot be ignorant of market swings and fundamental changes in stock prices. For example, a passive trader interested in buying stock at the bid side of the market may be faced with a sudden $2.00 increase in stock price. The obvious question is whether or not he is wise to increase his bid accordingly, and the answer will depend on the circumstances.

If the price move is consistent with a positive trend in the market, it would be wise to increase one's bid. The original bid level is now unrealistically low, and increased cost should have been offset through hedging with futures. If there is a significant and widely publicized change in fundamentals (e.g., takeover rumors or a change in earnings forecast), such an occurrence would also prompt an increase in bid. Unexplained price increases specific to the stock in question, however, should raise a caution flag, as some of the activity may be in response to the presence of the passive trader's bid. In such an instance, it is wise to maintain the original bid level or possibly to withdraw the bid for a period of time to reduce the potential for gaming the strategy.

As a summary of passive trading, consider again the traditional methodology employed by most traders. The aggressiveness of any trader will be defined by how he views the trade-off between two factors:

1. The potential value of the information that has caused the trade to be initiated.

2. The potential market-maker spreads he may pay if he insists on trading sooner rather than later.

Passive traders have no information regarding the future values of the stocks they are trading. Thus, they are justifiably the least aggressive traders. Because they have no underlying reason to initiate trades, they act instead to accommodate the trade interests of others.

PASSIVE TRADING BY INDEX FUNDS

The most attractive means for an index fund manager to complete informationless trades is to avoid the traditional equity marketplace and attempt to find an equally passive trader on the other side of his trade or program, thus creating a so-called cross-trade. However, even with electronic crossing networks attempting to facilitate this type of trade, index funds must frequently go to the marketplace to buy or sell stock.

Because of the large number of holdings in their portfolios, index fund managers are frequently forced to trade hundreds of issues in one program. The index fund manager may elect to trade all of the stocks at a given time through one broker, a practice referred to as *package* or *program trading*. Generally, the broker will guarantee that actual executions will be at least as good as the prices at a designated point in time, usually a market close. In some cases, the broker will have knowledge of the specific contents of the program prior to the designated time of pricing. At other times, the broker may have only a general description of the program and will bid "blind" of the actual contents.

It can be argued that program trading is not truly passive because it does not take advantage of the time flexibility afforded a passive manager. Nonetheless, program trading is popular with index fund managers because it accomplishes three ends. First, it eliminates a lot of busy-work by executing hundreds of trades at one time. Pricing and reporting procedures among broker, fund manager, and custodian are streamlined. Second, it eliminates specific risk as well as market risk by completing all trades simultaneously. Finally, program trading purports to eliminate market impact by obtaining the market closing price on all trades.

Whereas the first two benefits are obvious, the transactions cost picture is less clear. Commissions on these programs are higher than those charged on most other passive trades. These commissions reflect an insurance premium being charged by the broker in order to guarantee executions at the market close. In addition, the closing price may be adversely affected by the very activity generated by the program during the day. This adverse price impact can be eliminated by giving the broker little or no information about the contents of the program, thereby forcing a blind bid and guarantee after the close has occurred. Doing so, however, will result in higher commissions being charged by the broker. This reflects an appropriate increase of the insurance premium for guaranteeing the executions with limited knowledge.

A common misconception is that index funds are always trading hundreds of stocks at a time. In reality, this is not the case. In fact, the most difficult trading situations for index managers involve fewer names and are those where passive trading is most helpful:

1. Changes in the composition of the index.
2. The conversion of former actively managed portfolios into index funds.

In the first instance, consider an example where company A is added to the S&P 500 Index, and represents 0.2% of the total weight of the Index (the mean weight for any stock in a 500-stock index). Given an estimate of $200 billion indexed in 1988, and an average share price of $40, index fund managers would need to hold 10 million shares of company A, a stock that was not previously held in their funds. Thus, during the trading day when company A's addition is announced, all index managers must compete for those shares of company A for sale. The price of company A stock will rise dramatically to induce existing holders to sell to indexers.

Some index fund managers might purchase their quota of shares at the first opportunity in order to assure tracking. This can result in the payment of sizable spreads to market-makers willing to accommodate such a trade. In addition, most of the upward price movement occurs between announcement and the next opening of the stock, rendering early buying mostly futile. The more rational approach is to adopt a passive view, placing an order after the opening and attempting to accumulate stock over a number of weeks. This approach will give any holders who are considering selling an opportunity to evaluate their situation and perhaps come to market.

TRANSITION MANAGEMENT: TURNING ACTIVE PORTFOLIOS INTO INDEX FUNDS

When active managers are terminated, clients often turn to an index fund manager to dispose of the assets in the existing portfolio. This would seem to be a wise choice, in that index managers usually demonstrate lower trading costs than active managers. If the index manager chosen is unversed in passive trading, however, the choice may prove costly to the client.

Active portfolios and index funds are, to borrow a phrase, apples and oranges. Active portfolios generally contain relatively few concentrated holdings, representing aggressive bets by the manager. In addition, index funds are capitalization-weighted; that is, companies are represented in these funds in proportion to the total dollar value of their outstanding shares. Active portfolios face no such constraints: Some of the largest holdings in an active portfolio may be the smallest and least liquid stocks. The trading costs associated with selling the active portfolio will almost always exceed the cost of buying an index fund. Thus, whereas program trading may be an acceptable means of building an index fund, it is not the correct way to dispose of most active portfolios.

A passive trading strategy is, however, appropriate. Because the active manager has been terminated, the portfolio can be assumed to have no "information content." That is, there is no reason to expect these stocks to perform either better or worse than the overall market in the future. Liquidating the active portfolio is almost always more difficult than buying the stocks that make up an index fund. The index manager should thus proceed to sell off the existing portfolio in a passive fashion, with no time constraints. As buyers for these stocks are found, the more liquid index fund stocks (or stock index futures) can be purchased to preserve the level of market risk.

PASSIVE TRADING OF SMALL STOCKS

A great deal of attention has been paid in recent years to the *small-stock effect*—the idea that an unusual amount of a stock's historical performance, relative to market averages, is an inverse function of its size or company capitalization. That is, not only have small stocks tended to outperform large stocks, but the greatest relative performance has come from the group of the smallest companies. Although a number of ideas have been advanced as causes for this phenomenon (e.g., taxes and the January effect, misallocation of risk), its actual cause remains a mystery. This has not served to stem the increasing tide of institutional money being invested in this sector of the market. The growth of institutional interest in small stocks is being met by two groups: passive managers, offering highly diversified portfolios with an outstanding track record, and active managers seeking excess returns in an area that should theoretically be less efficient than the more popular stocks of larger companies.

The major problem associated with investing in small stocks is inordinately high trading costs. Although small-stock prices are generally lower, market-maker spreads are usually at least as large in the absolute sense and thus much greater as a percentage cost. Since the goal of a passive trading strategy is to eliminate the market-maker spread, knowledge and use of passive trading strategies become more important with small-stock trading than with the more liquid stocks of larger companies.

Perhaps the most critical element in successful trading of small stocks is the ability of the portfolio manager and trader to eliminate, or at least minimize, the need for any specific stock to be bought or sold. Indeed, since most small-stock funds contain more than 100 issues, the impact of any single issue on performance is small. Thus, it is wise to avoid active trading strategies, such as market orders, which assure completion of a trade. Such strategies can realistically generate trading costs of 5% to 10%, enough to offset any excess returns projected by the fund manager.

When flexibility exists with regard to specific names and time of execution, a win–win situation can be established between trader and dealer. Armed with the information that a passive buyer of a stock exists if stock turns up for sale, the dealer may be able to make a riskless profit on the other side of the trade, knowing that he is acting not as a holder of inventory but as a conduit between buyer and seller—a finder, if you will. The amount of profit made by the dealer depends on how actively or aggressively the seller of the stock behaves. This profit or finder's fee is of no concern to the passive buyer, who should be able to purchase the stock with little or no true market impact.

PASSIVE TRADING FOR ACTIVE MANAGERS

One of the most widespread misconceptions within the financial community is that informationless trades that are so identified will always be accommodated in the marketplace at less cost to the trader than will information-based trades. Thus, flows the argument, index funds can and do trade at lower cost than active managers do. Although the latter conclusion may be true, the reasons behind it are less obvious. That is, the higher active trading costs are more a function of trading style than of management style.

As an example, imagine two identical buy orders for 50,000 shares of XYZ company stock. One order is placed by a passive or index manager, based perhaps on a change in his universe or some other factor creating a need to purchase the shares. The passive manager is neutral on the prospects of XYZ relative to the market, and advertises this fact. The second order is placed by an active manager who feels that XYZ will outperform the market in the future. Also, let us assume that the two orders, passive and active, represent the entire position to be traded at that time.

If, in this instance, natural sellers of XYZ exist, they are delighted to see the influx of buy interest and will not be deterred by the potential presence of information held by the active buyers. Indeed, if one of the natural sellers is an active manager, he certainly should have more confidence in his own opinion than in that of others. When no natural sellers exist, a market-maker would be more concerned about the risk he is taking by assuming a short position in XYZ than about the potential validity of the active information. Thus, the major concern of the market-maker is the total amount of stock to be traded rather than the reasons behind the trade.

This suggests that the active manager should be able to trade at a similar level of cost to that incurred by the index manager. The fact that most active managers do not trade as cheaply is less a function of their species than of their trading style. An index manager is relatively unconcerned about the price movement of a specific stock and thus can buy patiently, using time to his advantage. But the active manager's ex ante belief is that a stock to be purchased is underpriced. Thus, fearing an adverse price movement in the stock, he will be less patient.

This does not imply that active managers should completely abandon the idea of using passive trading strategies. The idea of market efficiency suggests that the value of the active manager's information is probably closer to zero than he believes. In theory, the degree to which an active trader behaves passively should be inversely proportional to the level of confidence held in one's information.

One simple way for active managers to trade passively is to use the existing automated crossing networks. These networks would allow them to expose orders to the marketplace at low commission and market impact. In addition, the identity of the trader would remain a secret, as would the proposed trade interest unless executed. In the past, active traders have complained about the low percentage of their trades that are completed by the crossing networks. In fact, passive managers as a group do not trade enough to keep these networks alive. The acceptance of these networks by active managers will result in more opportunities for passive and active managers alike.

Some passive managers, fearing that information could work against them, are opposed to cross-trading with active managers. This is probably an overreaction, because active managers will respond to their information and move prices accordingly whether or not index fund managers are willing to trade. Also, in theory, an information-based trader should be more highly motivated than a passive one. Thus, in some ways, informationless traders should be more willing than other passive traders to trade with them.

SUMMARY

The key to successful money management may be who is the smartest or who develops the best information. It may be, however, that neither of these is as crucial as it may seem. Over the last two decades money managers as a group have failed to outperform the market averages. This is not very surprising when one considers that money managers in the aggregate *are* the market averages. Thus, the major factor contributing to underperformance must be the transaction costs that managers incur but averages or indices do not.

Buying or selling stocks is not essentially different from buying or selling anything else; the more convinced a buyer is that something is underpriced, the more willing he will be to pay the asking price immediately. Thus, having information, whether good or bad, can lead to more aggressive trading and higher trading costs. If markets are efficient, information will, on average, be worthless, but higher trading costs will persist.

Passive trading involves minimizing the importance of much of the information that one has. Although this may seem illogical, in the long run the lower costs resulting from passive trading will more than offset the foregone value of unused information.

The Editor Asks

Q *Many of the stock exchange rules and procedures are designed to ensure that all investors are treated fairly. The net result is that orders tend to become indistinguishable at the point of execution, regardless of the motivation for trading. Can you suggest any changes to market structures that would simplify trading for passive investors?*

A It is not clear that simple changes could be made to existing exchange rules to benefit passive traders. After all, if traders were asked to label their orders on the floor as *active* or *passive,* I can think of no reason that anyone would benefit from identifying his order as active. Traders are not considered passive merely because they say they are. Their behavior over a period of time establishes their style and reputation in the trading community.

Because stocks do not trade continuously on exchanges, at any given time a bid and an offering exist on a stock. The goal of the passive buyer at that time is not necessarily to buy at the bid side or lower, but to *avoid* buying at the offering side or higher. He would be willing to accept the average of the bid and the offering, as would a passive seller. Placing a bid at that average price, however, might move the existing offering higher. Thus, the passive trader, like everyone else, must play a cat-and-mouse game.

The advantage offered to passive traders by crossing networks is that the participating parties generally accept the neutrality of the existing prices. This is true whether using a closing price after market hours, or picking a particular random point such as the last sale at 11:00 A.M. As a result, crossing networks are a natural haven for passive traders.

16

ELECTRONIC CROSSING MARKETS

Edward C. Story

A *cross* is a transaction between a buyer and seller who agree between themselves on the price, shares, and time of a securities trade. Historically, most of the efforts of the block trading desks have been to arrange crosses.[1] Recently, new computer-based electronic crossing systems have been developed to facilitate crossing between institutional investors without the intervention of a broker.

Direct crossing began 10 years ago as a simple form of trading, with phone calls between friendly and trusting traders of money management and pension institutions. They read lists of stocks to each other and checked off trades with a pencil. The entire process was somewhat informal. Whoever had the shortest list would read first. Stocks were checked off one by one by hand. The clearing was turned over to a mutually designated broker or to a custodian to print the trade and complete the accounting of the transfer. It was very simple. It was also awkward and time consuming.

The advancement of computerized investment operations and the demand for low-cost execution have forced crossing to take a more prominent role among the tools of the modern trader. There are a number of trends that have prompted this evolution:

- The fourth market of the 1960s set the stage, along with the development of the block houses and the third market.
- Indexing introduced a more cost-conscious approach to trading.
- Program trading further expanded the practice of computer-to-computer order transfers and the handling of large blocks of stocks at one time.

[1] See Chapter 12, "Upstairs, Downstairs: The Block Traders and the Specialists," by Donald L. Luskin.

- Electronic trading came into its own in the 1980s through the computerization of the major brokerage firms and increased activity among firms such as Instinet that execute trades electronically.
- Pension funds increasingly pressed their money management firms for accountability in performance and in transaction costs. In neither area were managers meeting expectations, and frictional costs were viewed as a culprit.

From these developments have come many widely practiced pension investment solutions, including broad-based indexing, incentive fees for money managers, moves by pension plans to reduce costs and increase performance of money managers, soft dollar scrutiny, accountability of money managers, and changes in trading procedures. One of those changes has been the formalization of crossing.

Crossing is the matching of natural buyers and natural sellers at a predetermined or externally determined price. Liquidity is supplied by the transactors themselves and not by middlemen or market mechanisms. There are at least three different types of crosses: the external or regular cross, the private or arranged cross, and the internal cross.

External crosses involve trading between multiple entities without private prearrangement between trading entities. Prior arrangements specify a time of day and provide a mechanism for advertising of the contents of a trading list if so desired.

Private or *arranged* crosses involve trading stocks between two or more institutions who wish to trade only among themselves. This is done by private agreement between the two parties. A third type of cross, the *internal* cross, provides for trading stocks from one account to another within the same institution. It can occur when one account is reducing commitment at the same time another account has received an increase in assets.

A typical external cross would operate something like this. First, a time of day is set, say an hour after the close of the market. All users have been informed that closing prices will be used to price any matches. Each of the participants who wishes to enter trades builds a list on his own trading room personal computer (PC). A modem is used to create a dialup connection to a secure account on the main computer. Orders are then transmitted, along with any instructions concerning the display of the order.

At the specified cross time, users are locked out of the main computer, which then proceeds to match sell orders against buy orders. When the process is completed, the users are allowed to log on, download their completed trades, and provide clearing information. Completed trades are then submitted for public record. Orders that are not completed are canceled and kept confidential. These orders may be resubmitted at the time of the next cross, or they may be executed through more standard trading mechanisms.

HOW DOES CROSSING COMPARE WITH AUCTION SYSTEMS?

There are numerous structural differences between crossing and the auction process. Foremost is the price-setting mechanism. In the auction, price is set by the continuous ebb and flow of supply and demand. When a willing buyer meets a willing seller, a trade takes place. In crossing, the price is produced outside the crossing mechanism, most usually by an exchange auction process. A certain instant of time acceptable to the participating traders is chosen for the recording of exchange prices. This time may be the market opening, the close, or some time in between. Neither the cross nor the crossing mechanism determines the price. Although it is theoretically possible for the crossing traders to agree on a price other than an exchange-related price, this is not usually done for fiduciary and legal reasons.

A second major contrast between the auction process and crossing is the continuous trading on an auction market compared to the snapshot, all-at-once trading that occurs with a cross.

Both agency trades and principal trades are accommodated in the auction market. Crossing is distinguished by the *direct* connection between buyer and seller. Brokers are not required to supply principal for trades in a crossing network; the only principal required is supplied by pension plans trading for their own accounts. Direct and internal crosses create no agency relationship, but an agency relationship is created if the buyer and seller meet in a crossing system. The agency function, however, is accomplished more by the simple provision of a meeting place than by the personalized search for the other side of a trade.

The auction system creates a natural scattering of information, which is difficult to avoid: Trading intent must be revealed in order to attract the other side of the trade. This information is gathered by eager traders, who use it to position their own trades advantageously. Some of the information flows through limited channels, but much of it flows instantaneously, and almost unrestricted, from coast to coast. Such information flow is the motor of market impact.

The control of information is of particular interest to the block trader. The block trader is walking the tightrope of releasing just enough information to attract the natural other side to the trade and yet not giving away enough information to have an impact on the ultimate trading price. Crossing involves a high degree of control over information flow. In the formal crossing systems, information scattering can be eliminated: A total blackout can be imposed by the trading institution. Alternatively, the institution can provide a limited release or display of information, as occurs in private crosses between parties known to each other. Display of such information might also occur on the bulletin boards supplied by the formal crossing networks. Finally, total release of the information can be made in a manner similar to "sunshine" trading, in which all relevant trading information is broadcast to the world.[2]

The flexibility of crossing to allow for the controlled release of information is a significant difference in comparison to auction systems. It provides security to the trading institutions and prevents information regarding their trading intentions to be used against them.

Normal auction markets grew up in less mechanized, less electronic times. They retain many holdovers of an age in which time could not be easily compressed and shoe leather was used abundantly. Crossing, in contrast, was developed within the last 10 years. It is much less labor-intensive and, in its system or network form, almost totally electronic in operation. In the auction market, the trade is effected by humans, sometimes assisted by computers. In a crossing system, however, the computer effects the trade with minimal human interaction.

Because a cross occurs in a microsecond and at a predetermined price, there is no need for market stabilization or continuous market-"making." There are no specialists and no market-makers (and thus no spreads). Crossing does not lend itself to the payment of soft dollars for research services. It is a service business, competing on commission price and trading advantages. It was not developed in the manner of brokerage businesses in the auction market, which frequently involve the supply of soft dollar services. The costs of these services would camouflage—if not destroy—the most visible advantage enjoyed by crossing: low commission prices.

ATTRACTIVENESS OF CROSSING

The greatest attraction of crossing stocks is the elimination or reduction of market impact. Market impact, normally considered the largest cost asso-

---

[2] See Chapter 18, "Sunshine Trading," by Steven Bodurtha.

ciated with any large trade, occurs when large orders or careless trading upset the supply-and-demand relationship of a stock. Market impact adversely affects the price obtained by the trader initiating a trade. A sell order that swamps the market with a very large percentage of the float is likely to depress the price of that stock. A buy order large enough to exhaust the available supply will most certainly raise the price of the stock.[3]

Crossing eliminates such price movement because a predetermined price is used. Orders can be of any size whatsoever; size in and of itself will not affect the price. The significant variable of price fluctuation is largely eliminated by the cross.

The *spread* is the difference between what the highest bidder is willing to pay and what the lowest seller is willing to receive in a given trade. If the bids and offers are those provided by the specialist, the spread constitutes a profit for the market-maker or specialist. Unless it is negotiated down or eliminated, it represents a "frictional cost" paid to the specialist as compensation for operating the market.

Spreads are thus a by-product of the stabilization process in an auction market; they are irrelevant to the crossing process. There is no stabilization process to provide continuous liquidity in a cross. Trades done by cross, therefore, eliminate the spread and provide additional cost savings.

The appeal of crossing can be even greater with smaller stocks than with the larger, more frequently traded variety. With less frequently traded stocks there is a greater danger of creating impact by altering the more delicate balance of supply and demand. Over-the-counter (OTC) stocks have larger spreads; when these spreads are divided between the buyer and the seller (as is done in at least one of the formal crossing systems), both buyer and seller experience lower costs than in an OTC market.

The largest *visible* cost in effecting a trade is the commission. Auction market commissions have stabilized in a 2- to 20-cent range. Typical commissions average around 7 cents, with an inside range between 5 and 12 cents.[4] Crossing occurs at or below the lowest point of this range. Depending on the system or process used, crossing will cost no more than 2 cents per share traded and may cost one cent or less.

This low cost reflects the enviably simple cost structure of crossing networks. A central computer, a few people, a PC terminal already in common use on any typical trade desk, telephone lines, and a clearing

---

[3] See Chapter 10, "Trading Cost: The Critical Link between Investment Information and Results," by Thomas F. Loeb.

[4] See Chapter 4, "How Important Are Transaction Costs?" by Stephen A. Berkowitz and Dennis E. Logue.

process are all that's needed to run a crossing network. This stands in contrast to the labor and equipment intensity of the broker/exchange system.

Crossing results in a reduction of errors. There is ample time before the trade to make sure all information is entered correctly, and ample time after the trade to process clearing instructions correctly. As a result, errors rarely occur. This represents a significant source of cost savings to the operator.

LIMITATIONS TO CROSSING

An order placed in a crossing system may not find its counterpart. There is no party "making" the market, and no guarantee of execution. By mid-1988 order volume had grown to between 15 and 40 million shares per day, yet only a few hundred thousand to 5 million shares a day actually executed. This can be a significant discouragement to action-oriented traders who view rapid execution of orders as a measure of the value they add to the investment process.

The recurrent concern for participants in crossing systems is this limited liquidity. From the viewpoint of the network operator, achieving increased liquidity is the classic chicken-or-egg difficulty: Liquidity will draw more traders, but the only source of liquidity is more traders. Once the crossing systems pick up additional participation, completion rates will move sharply upward.

Crossing does not, in itself, provide liquidity, but the existence of a system for crossing can attract "crossing liquidity"—that liquidity seeking the cautious trading of large blocks of stock without market impact. Current crossing systems attract this liquidity by providing a formalized means for crossing and a daily or more frequent schedule of crossing opportunities.

In the past, crossing was available only to the larger institutions, in particular the passive investment managers. The introduction of the crossing systems expanded the opportunities to cross to smaller and more varied institutions.

Before a trader can use a crossing system, he or she must overcome the feeling of awkwardness that stems from unfamiliarity with the mechanical procedures of using a personal computer to trade, as well as unfamiliarity with the benefits and nuances of using crossing as a tool in the trading process. Any new product or procedure falling outside a user's normal experience will be accepted only slowly. This learning-curve process has slowed the acceptance of crossing networks.

Crossing initially appears to limit the trader's control over the trading process. In the extreme, the trader believes he has lost control and is degraded to a simple order taker. In fact, however, the trader has gained one more opportunity to complete the trade on favorable terms. This represents an expansion of the options available to the trader and raises the skill level required.

Keyboard phobia is common among the older traders, who much prefer telephone conversations. A friendly tone of voice and the "joke of the day" are still the *lingua franca* of the trading fraternity. In the extreme, the trader views crossing as a threat to his livelihood. It not only relieves him of a large portion of the human contact that gives him a feel for the market, but also eliminates the negotiation function and much of the judgment needed to gain advantage in trading stocks.

Crossing relies on a balance of buyers and sellers to be effective in finding a match. During periods of substantial market volatility, one side or both tend to disappear as traders are uncertain whether the exchange prices represent reasonable estimates of true value. As a result, matching frequency fades. Reduced activity on the formal crossing systems was experienced in October 1987 and other periods of high market volatility.

Crossing is not well suited to soft dollar payments and, therefore, is not as attractive to money managers who use soft dollars to pay their research costs. At one or two pennies per share, the pricing structure of crossing does not provide a lot of slush for ballgame tickets, Bruce Springsteen concerts, limousines, and even more enticing favors.

Some of the bell-cow pension plans find this to be a breath of fresh air.[5] One of the major recommendations of the National Plan Sponsor Federation has been to support lower cost trading systems like crossing. Nonetheless, the majority of the pension plans have been slow to exert pressure on their managers to experiment with the crossing systems.

The managers who have been quickest to adopt the crossing systems are those who are less dependent on the Street for research ideas. Index funds, quantitative managers, in-house funds, and organizations capable of performing their own research have been the first to embrace the concepts.

A weakness of crossing from a theoretical perspective is the lack of an intrinsic price discovery mechanism. The current price is externally determined, and crossing is therefore dependent on the existence of an exchange to determine prices. Crossing, however, does not upset the existing market stabilization procedures in the exchanges. It has no perceptible effect on stabilization of specialists or market-makers.

---

[5] See Chapter 2, "A Sponsor Looks at Trading Costs," by Robert E. Shultz.

CROSSING SOURCES

Despite the emergence of formal crossing systems, crossing is still being done directly between institutions today. Crossing is also done by brokerage firms, whose upstairs or block desks are frequently responsible for whole baskets of stocks being traded. These large trades can be considered crosses when the participants choose an externally determined price and simply allow the broker to take care of the paperwork. Upstairs and block desks are more likely to do private crosses and some internal crosses.

The first organized system open to all market participants was The Crossing Network, released by Instinet Corporation in 1986. This system was designed at the request of pension plans and investment managers who had been crossing among themselves and desired a more formal system to replace the awkward one-on-one telephone method. The system was completed in the fall of 1986 and was taken to the market by Plexus Group in December of that year.

The Crossing Network provides internal, private, and external crosses. It uses as a price-setting mechanism the closing price on the primary exchange for listed stocks and the mean bid–ask at the end of the day for OTC stocks. The Crossing Network operates one cross once each day at approximately 5:00 P.M. Eastern Time.

At the same time that Instinet was building its system, Jeffries and Barra had formed a joint venture to develop POSIT (Portfolio System for Institutional Trading). POSIT was announced shortly after Instinet and Plexus brought The Crossing Network to market, and commenced operations within 10 months.

POSIT has more dimensions of flexibility than The Crossing Network. The system is designed to operate at any time of day or night and currently operates between 7:00 A.M. and 7:00 P.M. Most important, it provides the opportunity for the trader to choose one of an almost infinite number of trading prices: the open, the close, noonday, 11:32 A.M., 2:16 P.M., or any other mutually acceptable time–trade price combination. A minimum number of 10 stocks per entry is required, emphasizing the desire to facilitate trading of portfolios or composite assets.

Both systems provide participants with a facility for advertising their trading desires. Although advertising on the bulletin boards tends to increase order flow, most users of both systems are hesitant to release their trading intentions to other participants. Both systems operate on central DEC-VAX computers tied to IBM PCs or similar equipment by dialup telephone lines. Both provide anonymity and confidentiality of trading intent. Both can separate classes of traders and limit the trading partners to a particular group or class.

POSIT offers the additional service of integrated residual handling. The left-over trades that were not done through crosses can be turned over to the Jeffries trade desk. A commission quote is provided electronically, which takes into consideration the residual handling fees. Instinet's trading desk does not provide a similar integration of residual handling.

The Crossing Network charges one cent a share. With substantial annual volume, this price may go as low as 0.75 cents per share. POSIT charges 1.5 cents or more for the cross and additional fees for the handling of the residual. As of mid-1987, both systems continued to survive and to grow slowly.

The marketplace includes anyone that trades in reasonable size and frequency. Money management institutions are the major sources of this trading. Some pension plans that manage their own funds use one or both of the formal systems. Even brokers use the systems.

COMPARISON TO OTHER COMPUTER-ASSISTED SYSTEMS

The features of a crossing system can be illustrated by comparison to any auction market. However, we will take this opportunity to introduce another approach to computerized trading, that of the Computer-Assisted Trading System (CATS) in use at the Toronto Stock Exchange and also installed at the Tokyo Stock Exchange. The Tokyo CATS is patterned after the Toronto System and has achieved the greatest volume, but the Toronto CATS has computerized more of the trading functions.

CATS is a fully automated exchange. The system was created by the exchange for the exchange. CATS only executes trades in the more thinly traded stocks.

Crossing is a trading system. It is not an exchange; it is an added tool to institutional traders as well as to members of an exchange. Trading is done in any stock tradable in the United States. Crossing was created largely by institutional traders, with eventual help from entrepreneurial trading organizations (Jeffries and Instinet) as well as advisory and marketing firms (Barra and Plexus).

ALTERNATIVE FEATURES. The most obvious difference is that the CATS is a continuous/auction market, whereas the crossing systems are both calls to market. In The Crossing Network, the call is made once a day, at 5:00 P.M. In POSIT, the call is flexible; it may occur at the opening, at the close, or at any time during the trading day or night between 7:00 A.M. and 7:00 P.M.

Although CATS does not guarantee execution, execution can be expected during the trading day if price is not a consideration. Supply will adjust to demand. In crossing, supply cannot adjust to demand; the result is that crosses will not likely have full completion rates. Completions range between 0% and 60 + %, with the direct mode in the 10% to 15% range on The Crossing Network.

CATS allows all order types: market, limit, stop loss, short sells, and so forth. Crossing systems are far simpler. In a crossing situation there is no need to tailor the trade to attract (or repel) the other side. Rather, it is assumed that the other side is desired and it is up to the system as a whole to attract the other side in sufficient quantity to satisfy each user.

In one sense, orders placed on crossing systems are "double-limit," as the price is either known ahead of time (The Crossing Network's use of major markets' closing prices) or determinable by mutual agreement of the parties involved (POSIT's multiple pricing alternatives). Users have the distinct advantage of accepting or vetoing a given price prior to execution. If the price is not acceptable, the order can be canceled.

CATS provides multiple sources of information to the floor users of that system, whereas crossing systems provide little or no market information. The prices to be used are not displayed; it is assumed that the trader has access to this information. Even when the bulletin board features of the crossing systems are used, orders are displayed only on the specific instructions of the user submitting these orders. The institution's name is held in confidence. Where institutions do not wish to reveal specific names, they may attempt to attract interest with advertised generalized descriptions of the trading intentions. Frequently no information at all is publicized.

CATS supplies continuous order and spread information to Toronto Stock Exchange members and to anyone with a terminal. The same information is provided to all firms using the CATS terminals, but those with terminals have a clear information advantage over those without them. Essentially, the exchange traders have an advantage. Crossing systems, however, equalize all players, exchange traders or not, with respect to information provided.

APPEAL.   CATS was built to fit an important part of an exchange into a limited physical space. Its appeal was its space-saving characteristics. The appeal of crossing is to reduce trading costs for large-volume trades having low time sensitivity.

CATS, like most other auction exchanges, provides a very high probability of execution. Crossing systems do not.

AVAILABILITY.   CATS is available to everyone on the exchange, but only to exchange members. Crossing systems in the U.S. market are available to all institutional traders plus retirement systems that wish to trade their stocks directly. Crossing systems might eventually become available to the general public, but at present this is limited by the credit and clearing risk considerations of all participating parties.

ACCEPTANCE BY TRADERS.   CATS has been accepted by traders, for two reasons. Its coverage is limited to the thinly traded stocks, and it was built in response to the need for space, literally the real estate on the floor of the Toronto Exchange. It has been generally accepted despite the unfamiliarity of the system compared to manual tickets for traders. Because it is simply the only way to trade certain stocks, utilization has been widespread.

Crossing through the crossing systems has been slow to take hold. It is a different concept, less so with the POSIT model (during the day) than with the Instinet model (after hours).

Crossing was an entrepreneurial response to a perceived market need; it is backed by no exchange monopoly or structure of special privileges. It was a response to the growing desire for alternative low-cost markets, in the spirit of providing a less expensive service for certain commodity-like trading of stocks. As such, it is only a tool for the professional trader and must be actively marketed to him.

CATS *is* its own marketplace and therefore has experienced substantial use. Crossing in its marketplace is still the domain of the leading-edge traders and those who adapt to innovation quickly. The initial weakness of having no established exchange protection is countered by the necessity of adapting to the needs of the marketplace. This may be the Darwinian factor that provides for the survival of crossing systems. Certainly, the crossing systems have gone through significant market-expanding adaptation since inception.

CATS is "the way" to trade certain stocks in Toronto. Therefore, it must achieve only bare acceptability to be used. In contrast, crossing systems must compete for liquidity. Such systems must ultimately be more attractive to the user than alternative means in order to survive.

SUMMARY

Crossing as a trading tool is a niche product. It will never replace or overwhelm the volume of trading done on auction markets. It does, however, provide a low-cost complement to the existing market structure. Its use so far is limited to innovative trading institutions and to traders who adapt early to new trading tools. As liquidity increases, greater numbers of users will be attracted, which will, in turn, provide greater liquidity.

Evolutionary changes that may be built into crossing systems include price-setting mechanisms that remove the dependency on major auction markets for fair pricing. Systems to "pay up" for liquidity are a possibility. International crossing systems are a distinct possibility once they have been proved in the U.S. markets.

Crossing has for a decade provided low-cost trading opportunities, but only for a limited number of participants. The number of participants has now increased dramatically and will likely continue to do so. The cost structures and resulting commission prices are low relative to the Street alternatives. Crossing provides pension plans with an effective tool to lower trading costs, especially in situations involving large portfolio changes. Already, numerous quantitative money management firms are changing their procedures to incorporate crossing for direct, computer-to-computer trading without human assistance.

On the stage of trading, crossing has grown from a sideshow to a formal act. But it will never be the main event.

The Editor Asks

Q *There are two criticisms that have been directed toward the concept of crossing networks:*

1. *They thin liquidity by drawing supply and demand away from the central market.*
2. *They rely on the Exchange to establish prices but do not participate in price setting.*

How do you respond to these assertions?

A The only supply and demand that is drawn away is equally matched supply and demand. In other words, the supply or demand that is left over will likely end up on a formal exchange, both providing liquidity and helping to establish prices. The assumption underlying the question is that somehow market participants have an affirmative obligation, as specialists do, to maintain liquidity or participate in price setting. They do not.

There are various types of liquidity. A significant portion of crossing liquidity consists of impact-sensitive trading in which immediate execution is not crucial. If this trading did not have the tool of crossing to use, it is likely that it would be doled out quietly, slowly, and laboriously so as to have minimal market impact and probably minimal effect on liquidity.

In the extreme Armageddon scenario where crossing takes over the marketplace, there would be violent fluctuations in price and little if any capacity in the marketplace(s) to stabilize prices. It is far from likely that crossing will ever achieve such a central and significant role in the marketplace as even to approach remotely such a dire set of circumstances. History shows that there is an underlying judgment in the marketplace that ultimately provides a very desirable balance. A dynamic balance, yes, but balance, nevertheless.

17

TRADING ILLIQUID STOCKS

Jeanne Cairns Sinquefield and Cem Severoglu

There is extensive literature on how various portfolios of stocks and other investments have performed over time. For example, *Stocks, Bonds, Bills and Inflation* examines returns of major asset categories since 1926.[1] These return series and others are often used to make general asset allocation decisions. Such return series, however, implicitly assume that one can purchase stocks and the like in unlimited amounts at closing prices. On a practical basis, there are limits both to the amount one can invest during a given period and to the effect of trading size on prices. Therefore, any portfolio manager needs to consider how his portfolio strategy interacts with his trading strategy.

Liquidity is a major factor in designing a trading strategy. We believe that strategies for trading illiquid stocks differ from those for liquid stocks. Trading strategies for illiquid stocks also depend on the portfolio strategy. In this chapter, we will first examine the liquidity of the U.S. stock markets. Next, we will discuss the strengths and weaknesses of various trading strategies for illiquid stocks, and how they vary depending on the portfolio strategy used.

MEASURING LIQUIDITY

What is an *illiquid* stock? Miller and Grossman, in an unpublished paper entitled "The Determinants of Market Liquidity," define liquid markets as "those providing a high degree of immediacy of large order execution at a low cost. A market is a low cost provider of immediacy in our sense when

---

[1] Roger Ibbotson and Rex Sinquefield, *Stocks, Bonds, Bills and Inflation: The Past and the Future* (Charlottesville: Financial Analysts Research Foundation, 1982).

a customer can trade a large amount very rapidly without suffering an adverse price response."[2]

Many different measures have been used for comparing and quantifying the liquidity of stock markets. Table 17.1 provides some common and uncommon measures of liquidity for common stocks. In our tables, stocks are categorized by market capitalization. Previous studies have shown that smaller companies are less liquid than big companies.[3]

Market capitalization is calculated as the number of shares outstanding times price. The capitalization breaks used first rank all New York Stock Exchange (NYSE) companies into 10 deciles. Then these breaks are used to categorize American Stock Exchange (AMEX) stocks and National Market stocks (NMS) on the NASDAQ. The data include 4,945 companies: 1,603 on the NYSE, 771 on the AMEX, and 2,571 on the NASDAQ/NMS.

For each of these companies we obtained data on bid and ask price, average number of shares traded per day in the past 10 days, and shares outstanding. Data to calculate decile breaks were based on January 31, 1988, data from Interactive Data Corporation (IDC). Price and volume information was obtained from Bridge Trading Company data using February 10, 1988, data. Using these data, we were able to calculate for each company (1) mid-price—the average of the bid and ask prices; (2) spread—the difference between the ask and bid prices; (3) percentage spread—the spread divided by the mid-price; (4) average dollars invested—the average number of shares traded per day times the mid-price; and (5) the percentage of shares outstanding traded—average shares traded divided by shares outstanding.

Let's consider the sensitivity of various measures of liquidity. A common measure of liquidity in the trade press is the bid–ask spread—the hypothetical cost if one traded in and out on the same day and paid the offer and sold at the bid. This measure, however, provides little differentiation. The only differences are between the largest and smallest companies (deciles 1–5 and 6–10). However, Table 17.1 shows that the smaller the company, the smaller the price of stocks. This is important because a bid–ask spread of $0.25 on a $50.00 stock is relatively smaller than the same spread on a $10.00 stock.

A variable that provides more differentiation between small and large companies is percentage spread. The percentage spread measures the cost in a return sense of buying and selling a stock in a single day, with zero

[2] Merton Miller and Sanford Grossman, "The Determinants of Market Liquidity," unpublished paper, University of Chicago, 1987.

[3] Thomas Loeb, "Trading Cost: The Critical Link between Investment Information and Results," *Financial Analysts Journal*, May–June 1983, reprinted as Chapter 10, this volume.

TABLE 17.1 BID–ASK SPREAD AND AVERAGE DAILY VOLUME BY MARKET CAPITALIZATION DECILE, 2/10/88

Decile	Number of Names	Average Mid-price	Average Spread	Percent Spread	Average Shares	Average Dollars	Percentage of Shares Out
1	172	49.34	0.29	0.76	458,000	$21,388,000	0.27
2	181	36.05	0.26	0.84	237,000	$ 7,275,000	0.30
3	190	31.29	0.30	1.03	145,000	$ 3,748,000	0.31
4	230	26.22	0.30	1.23	88,000	$ 1,812,000	0.25
5	270	24.22	0.35	1.55	64,000	$ 982,000	0.23
6	361	21.55	0.34	1.42	33,000	$ 426,000	0.18
7	367	17.11	0.43	2.36	24,000	$ 263,000	0.17
8	479	14.43	0.48	3.07	19,000	$ 172,000	0.18
9	649	10.97	0.38	4.03	12,000	$ 93,000	0.16
10	2,046	6.31	0.41	8.22	6,000	$ 23,000	0.12

Source: Data from Bridge Trading Company.

commission. Here the difference is strongly correlated with capitalization. For example, a decile 1 stock has an average cost of 0.76%, whereas a decile 10 stock has an average cost of 8.22%. Obviously smaller capitalization stocks can be more costly to buy and sell.

In addition to the percentage spread as a measure of trading cost, investors must also consider the cost of brokerage commissions. Comissions are usually paid on a cents-per-share basis. This means that lower priced stocks will be more costly to purchase than higher priced stocks. A 10-cent commission would add a cost of 0.2% to an average decile 1 stock and 1.5% to an average decile 10 stock.

Percentage spread, however, is only a partial measure of liquidity and trading cost. It examines the cost of a limited amount of shares if one bought at bid and sold at offer. *Liquidity* refers to executing a large order at a low cost. What is a large order? Some authors define a large order as the cost of buying 50,000 or some other arbitrary number of shares. Since there are wide differences among prices of stocks, however, this is misleading. A better measure of liquidity is the dollar amount that can actually be traded. A decile 1 stock, on average, trades $21.3 million a day, whereas a decile 10 stock trades an average of $23,000 a day. Not only does it cost a lot to trade a single share of smaller capitalization stocks, but only a small amount of money can be invested per day.

This measure of size of order, however, only focuses on the dollars available to be invested. Sometimes the strategy is to obtain a certain percentage of a company. Therefore, another measure of liquidity of a company is the percentage of shares outstanding that are traded on a daily basis. The percentage of shares outstanding that trade per day is double for large companies over small companies. It ranges from 0.3% to 0.12% of shares outstanding being traded. It is somewhat easier (ignoring the dollars involved) to obtain a 5% holding in larger companies than in smaller companies. This is a good measure for comparing liquidity among small companies.

The foregoing liquidity comparisons can also be made across exchanges. Tables 17.2 and 17.3 provide these data. Given the small number of top-half stocks that trade on the AMEX and NASDAQ/NMS, we will focus on differences by exchange in deciles 6 to 10.

First, prices on NYSE stocks are, unexpectedly, slightly lower than on NASDAQ/NMS and AMEX stocks. The bid–ask spread, however, is lowest on the NYSE and higher on the AMEX and NASDAQ/NMS. This results in percentage spread being lowest on the NYSE. Importantly, the negative relationship between capitalization and percentage spread occurs on every exchange. It costs more to trade in smaller companies than in larger companies, because of both higher spreads (execution costs) and lower prices (brokerage costs).

The difference in average dollars traded per day again is positively correlated on every exchange. Again, the NYSE is more liquid as measured by higher daily volume on both a share and a dollar basis. Percentage of shares outstanding traded also shows the same relationship by exchange and capitalization. Larger capitalization stocks are more liquid on both a cost and a volume basis than are those of smaller companies, and NYSE companies are more liquid than AMEX and NASDAQ/NMS companies.

Of additional interest is how these measures look for the OTC nonnational market stocks. There, the average percentage spread is 24%, the average mid-price is $3.45, and the average amount that can be invested per day is $4,000. Ignoring trading costs in such markets can have a dramatic impact on returns.

Tables 17.1 to 17.3 examined various ways of measuring liquidity. A manager in designing a trading strategy should examine (1) trading cost using measures such as percentage spread as a measure of potential market impact and price as a measure of brokerage cost; and (2) capacity using average dollars and percentage of shares outstanding traded that can be traded. Of interest in Table 17.1 is that the average company in the smaller half has a trading cost of greater than 2% ignoring brokerage, whereas the average decile 9 or 10 stock absorbs less than $100,000 per day. We consider most stocks in the bottom-half size range of the NYSE to be moderately to highly illiquid.

TABLE 17.2 MEASURES OF LIQUIDITY BY MARKET CAPITALIZATION DECILE AND BY EXCHANGE, OTC VOLUME DIVIDED BY 2, 2/10/88

	Variable: Average Spread									
	Decile									
Exchange	1	2	3	4	5	6	7	8	9	10
OTC	0.21*	0.24*	0.40*	0.39	0.45	0.30	0.51	0.65	0.50	0.49
NYSE	0.29	0.26	0.26	0.24	0.25	0.26	0.25	0.24	0.22	0.21
AMEX	0.13*	0.22*	0.80*	0.59*	0.72*	0.78	0.78	0.47	0.25	0.21

	Variable: Average Mid-price									
OTC	41.77*	32.31*	35.31*	30.97	23.92	21.27	17.34	15.77	11.45	6.57
NYSE	49.88	36.89	30.13	24.44	23.30	18.83	16.36	12.69	9.78	6.35
AMEX	7.38*	18.42*	48.63*	29.95*	36.85*	33.93	21.57	15.79	12.04	6.39

	Variable: Percentage Spread									
OTC	0.61*	0.82*	1.17*	1.33	1.80	0.99	2.71	3.61	4.33	9.12
NYSE	0.76	0.82	0.98	1.14	1.39	1.66	1.76	2.38	3.24	5.49
AMEX	1.69*	1.97*	1.61*	1.83*	1.93*	2.08	3.26	2.91	4.16	6.14

	Variable: Average Shares (thousands)									
OTC	719*	231*	102*	56	38	28	26	17	10	5
NYSE	455	241	154	104	78	37	23	25	20	13
AMEX	223*	64*	76*	36*	55*	34	19	14	8	6

	Variable: Average Dollars (thousands)									
OTC	29,622*	5,803*	2,872*	1,226	661	400	262	162	82	22
NYSE	21,358	7,523	3,974	2,107	1,185	492	286	209	126	41
AMEX	1,643*	1,835*	1,442*	748*	557*	271	166	115	84	21

	Variable: Percentage of Outstanding Shares									
OTC	0.67*	0.24*	0.23*	0.18	0.16	0.17	0.17	0.17	0.15	0.11
NYSE	0.27	0.31	0.33	0.29	0.27	0.20	0.19	0.21	0.21	0.16
AMEX	0.01*	0.11*	0.10*	0.10*	0.15*	0.11	0.10	0.12	0.14	0.12

	Variable: Number of Names									
OTC	3	13	23	57	83	155	179	240	364	1456
NYSE	168	165	160	160	169	162	154	172	159	134
AMEX	1	4	7	13	18	44	34	67	126	457

*$N < 30$

Source: Data from Bridge Trading Company.

TABLE 17.3 OTC NONNATIONAL STOCK UNIVERSE BID–ASK SPREADS AND AVERAGE DAILY VOLUME

	Number of Names	Aver-age Bid	Aver-age Ask	Average Mid-price	Aver-age Spread	Per-centage Spread	Average Shares (thousands)	Average Dollars (thousands)
Value	1414	3.22	3.68	3.45	0.46	24.21	11	8

Source: Data from Bridge Trading Company

TRADING STRATEGIES

Obviously, the trading strategy used for investing in IBM will be different than that for a small company. The practical issue is how to modify one's trading strategy to account for liquidity. First, one must consider the portfolio strategy. The extremes of portfolio strategies are stock indices and stock picking. In the first, a manager wants to own a small but exact number of shares in a large number of companies. In the second, a manager wants to own a large number of shares or percentage of a very small number of companies.

CONTROLLING TRADING TIME AND DOLLARS.   After the portfolio strategy, the three key variables in trading illiquid stocks are (1) time, (2) dollars, and (3) flexibility of portfolio/trading strategy. Basically, trading illiquid stocks is not easy. In many cases, these three variables can constrain one's ability to implement a portfolio strategy, without increasing major cost.

Time is a major factor in trading illiquid stocks, for several reasons. First, by definition illiquid stocks do not trade very much, either not at all or in small amounts. The liquidity pattern is also for stocks to trade in large blocks every so often. Therefore, because the trading is skewed, stocks normally trade in amounts significantly smaller than the average volume. Lynch, Jones and Ryan demonstrate this fact in their monthly "Market Impact and Liquidity Report" that examines both the average and median volume of stocks.[4] For all NYSE and AMEX stocks the median volume is approximately 60% of the average volume. This implies that a significant amount of block trading occurs off the exchanges. Normally brokers will call known holders or size players of the company to try to place the trade before showing it on the exchanges. A manager can therefore miss participating in some blocks. The missing of blocks seems more prevalent in illiquid stocks than in liquid stocks. This has the effect of increasing the time it can take to trade illiquid stocks.

Second, the average daily volume in an illiquid stock overestimates the maximum amount that a single participant can trade on a given day. This is especially true for the OTC market, where there are multiple market-makers for each stock. In the OTC market, the volume is not channeled through a central marketplace such as the specialist's booth. A trader usually submits his order to a single market-maker and cannot always get access to the entire order flow, which may be executed through other market-makers. Moreover,

---

[4] Lynch, Jones, and Ryan, "Market Impact and Liquidity Report."

an aggressive buyer who insists on participating in every trade may make it impossible for any other trader to be the total volume for the day. Thus, regardless of the trading strategy, the amount of an illiquid stock that a single participant can trade in a given day may be limited and is usually significantly less than the average daily volume in the stock.

Dollars are another constraint when trading illiquid stocks. A relatively small order in terms of dollars may translate to an amount larger than 100% of the average daily volume for an illiquid stock. The amount of money that can be invested in a given portfolio strategy within a given time is a very important issue for an investor in illiquid stocks. For a stock picker, that depends on whether one can find a seller of the specific stock. For a stock index strategy, it depends on which companies are in the universe.

Dollar constraints should be examined explicitly before trading. Table 17.4 provides information on the total market capitalization by decile and by exchange, as well as the total size of the stock market universe and the total dollars traded daily. Clearly, regardless of time, one cannot invest $5 billion in a $2 billion universe, nor can one expect to invest more than a reasonable percentage of the daily volume in a given day.

TABLE 17.4 MEASURES OF CAPACITY BY MARKET
CAPITALIZATION DECILE AND BY EXCHANGE, OTC VOLUME
DIVIDED BY 2

Exchange					Decile					
	1	2	3	4	5	6	7	8	9	10
Variable: Total Market Capitalization (in billions of dollars)										
OTC	13.4*	27.8*	27.3*	38.7*	33.4	38.2	26.6	22.6	20.2	26.3
NYSE	3,144.8	405.1	198.1	114.1	71.5	38.7	23.0	16.2	9.0	3.3
AMEX	11.5*	8.8*	8.4*	9.5*	7.1*	10.8	5.2	6.3	7.1	7.6
Variable: Amount Traded Daily (in millions of dollars)										
OTC	89.1*	76.9*	65.7*	69.8*	54.5	63.1	46.6	39.1	29.6	31.6
NYSE	3,663.2	1,249.3	641.8	334.2	192.9	78.4	43.4	35.2	19.3	5.3
AMEX	1.7*	7.6*	10.1*	9.9*	10.4*	12.1	5.4	7.9	9.7	9.2
Variable: Investable Amount for a Balanced Program (in millions of dollars)										
OTC	77.5*	61.7*	40.1*	42.8*	33.4	37.6	28.1	22.4	17.7	18.4
NYSE	1,535.7	878.2	432.7	211.7	127.3	54.3	29.0	22.3	12.1	3.7
AMEX	1.7*	2.0*	4.9*	5.1*	5.3*	6.3	2.9	4.4	5.5	5.5
Variable: Investable Percentage for a Balanced Program										
OTC	86.9*	80.2*	61.0*	61.3*	61.2	59.6	60.4	57.1	60.0	58.3
NYSE	41.9	70.3	67.4	63.3	66.0	69.3	66.9	63.3	62.7	69.6
AMEX	100.0*	26.5*	48.3*	51.3*	51.2*	51.8	52.5	55.0	57.1	59.2

* $N < 30$

Source: Data from Bridge Trading Company.

Let's examine the implications of the data for a portfolio strategy that attempts to construct a market value–weighted index. Assume that on a practical basis it was decided that, on a given day, the portfolio should invest an amount equal to the average dollars traded daily. Table 17.4 also provides the dollars and percentage of this money that the portfolio could actually invest in a day. The portfolio cannot invest the total amount in a given day because, for some stocks, the market value–weighting requirement will result in orders that are larger than what is normally traded in a single day. The data summarized in Table 17.4 are very interesting. For example, a portfolio strategy of decile 10 NYSE stocks only would limit the amount that one could invest to $3.7 million, assuming one had a balanced buy program of $5.3 million and was willing to be 100% of the volume on a single day. The amounts increase by capitalization, whereas—because of skewness of liquidity—the percentage tradable doesn't.

Obviously, dollars can be a serious constraint in trading illiquid stocks, as can time. The issue is to be realistic about the size of programs that can be put into the market. For illiquid stocks, the larger the program, the higher the trading cost and the lower the completion rate.

TRADING FLEXIBILITY.   Flexibility is another issue when trading illiquid stocks. A pure index strategy, with no flexibility on time, and sizable dollars, can be very costly when trading illiquid stocks. Yet this same strategy would have low costs for liquid stocks. A real-life example of trading in small-capitalization stocks can illustrate the magnitude of trading costs.

In a research paper entitled "Package Trading," Wayne Wagner published trading data associated with the construction of a Wilshire 5000 Index fund using a sample of 1,100 stocks.[5] The stocks to be traded were divided into two groups. The first group consisted of liquid stocks whose average daily volume was significantly higher than the amount to be traded for this program. This group was traded using package trading, where the broker guaranteed a strike price for a negotiated commission. The second group consisted of the less liquid stocks, which could not be efficiently traded using package trading. This group was traded on a best-efforts basis using block trading houses. The cost of trading the first group was small (under 0.5%). The cost of trading the illiquid group was strikingly higher, especially for the smaller capitalization issues. For stocks under $100 million in market capitalization, the market impact (excluding commissions) was 7.5%. Paying the offer should have had a market impact of only approximately one-half the percentage spread, or 3%. This provides some strong evidence that trading costs for small-capitalization issues can be extremely high.

We recently conducted a survey among the major brokerage firms to see what they might currently charge to do programs of illiquid stocks. Few would agree to undertake a guaranteed program, where they would have to deliver a basket of stocks at previously determined prices. Those who would quoted commissions as large as $1.00 per share on a $10.00 stock. The reason for this reluctance is the large losses a few brokers have incurred in executing previously guaranteed packages. Our survey and the Wagner data both indicate that program trading (short-term trading strategies) for illiquid stocks is extremely costly regardless of whether the broker or the manager executes it.

Flexibility, however, refers to more than time and dollars. It also refers to discretion on (1) how orders are worked, (2) responding to blocks, and (3) generating cash through selling. Trading illiquid stocks requires some common sense.

Portfolio traders and their brokers should have some discretion when working orders. Not all orders should have to be completed in a day. This requirement can result in poor or even absurd executions. Even a small order in an illiquid stock can easily have an impact on its market. Giving discretion to the trader and the broker allows them to use their subjective judgment on the amount and timing of trades.

The ability to respond to blocks of illiquid stocks is also important. Illiquid stocks may not trade every day. The sellers are often willing to sell at a discount if they are under time pressure, or have large size. Severoglu, in an unpublished 1987 paper,[6] measured the impact of being misbalanced on a real-life small-capitalization portfolio consisting of over 1,000 stocks, most of which were under $100 million in market capitalization. It deviated considerably from a perfectly balanced portfolio. Yet the monthly differences in returns between a perfectly balanced portfolio and this real portfolio were small. Over a cumulative two-year period, the returns were identical. Yet, as measured by SEI Corporation, this same portfolio had slightly negative trading costs. Trading blocks reduced trading costs but did not cause significant variation from the returns of an index.

The generation of cash through selling is another area where flexibility is required. Care is needed in executing sell orders as well as buy orders. For

---

[6] Cem Severoglu, "The Costs of Deviations from Perfect Balance," unpublished paper, 1987.

a portfolio of illiquid stocks, it is important to match the rate at which stocks are sold to the rate at which stocks can be purchased. Given the dollar constraints in investing in illiquid stocks, cash should not be generated unless it can be reinvested within a reasonable period of time. The return on cash (short-term instruments) is normally lower than the returns on stocks.

SUMMARY

Liquidity is directly correlated with the size of a company as defined by its market capitalization. Smaller capitalization stocks are very illiquid and can be extremely costly to trade. A good proxy for liquidity is the percentage spread. An average decile 1 stock (the largest capitalization group) has a percentage spread of 0.76, compared with 8.22% for an average decile 10 stock (the smallest capitalization group). Another measure of liquidity is the average daily volume of a stock expressed in dollars. According to this measure, if an investor is willing to be 100% of the trading volume on a given day, he can invest in excess of $20 million in a typical decile 1 stock, but only $23,000 in a decile 10 stock.

The most cost-effective way to trade small-capitalization stocks is to use a passive trading strategy. Aggressive trading strategies require that a fixed amount of a certain stock be traded within a short period of time. Price is only a secondary concern for aggressive trading. For a small-capitalization strategy, aggressive trading can result in exorbitant trading costs. A passive trading strategy refers to responding to a trade initiated by another party so that the other party bears the costs. This strategy requires a high degree of flexibility in which stocks are traded and in when they are traded. It can be readily applied to a small-capitalization index fund, which typically has a greater degree of flexibility than an actively managed portfolio.

The Editor Asks

Q *Your data indicate that a larger portion of volume in smaller issues trades in proportionately larger blocks. This implies that a buy-side trader must be opportunistic and able to respond to availability when and if it occurs.*

What procedures would you suggest a trader use to secure an opportunity to participate in the available supply? Are there any dangers to be aware of in the use of these procedures?

A In our chapter we have illustrated that an aggressive trader of a small-capitalization stock will usually incur a high market impact. Trading, however, is a zero-sum game, and the cost to one party is a benefit to the other. Thus, the lack of liquidity of small-capitalization stocks can actually serve as a benefit to a small-capitalization index fund.

The question addresses a specific application of this idea to a buy-side trader responding to blocks. On any given day, there will be distressed sellers of large blocks of small-capitalization stocks. Most of the sellers recognize the difficulty of trading these issues and may be willing to sell their blocks at a substantial discount.

There are four elements that are essential to running a block trading operation to take advantage of these opportunities. First, the manager must have the flexibility to deviate from a perfectly balanced market value–weighted portfolio. On any given day, the manager must be willing to substitute one stock for another or to overweight a particular stock in the portfolio. Our own studies show that for a widely diversified small-capitalization portfolio, small deviations from a perfect balance have a negligible effect on the returns.

Second, the manager must keep a constant pool of cash equal to the anticipated amount of daily block trading. If the cash level is too low, then the manager may miss a portion of the blocks. If the cash level is higher than the average amount spent on purchasing blocks, then the excess cash may have an adverse impact on the returns.

Third, the manager must have established relationships with an extensive network of brokerage houses. Unlike blocks of large-capitalization stocks, which are traded through a handful of brokers, the small-capitalization block orders are dispersed among hundreds of brokerage houses, including many small regional brokers. A successful block trading operation must have the manpower and the administrative and computer capabilities to receive indications from and execute trades with a large number of brokers. It is also important to provide brokers with sufficient incentives because they usually make their first call to their most favored clients. These incentives include attractive commissions, a short response time, and a list or description of the stocks in which the manager may have an interest.

Finally, the manager must have certain safeguards to avoid purchasing blocks from sellers with insider information or bidding on blocks with artificially inflated market prices. Although on average blocks are sold at a discount from fair market prices, occasionally the seller may possess some information that is not reflected in the current market price of the stock. Successfully screening out information-motivated blocks requires extensive experience in trading small-capitalization issues. Some factors to consider include the recent price–volume history, current holders and their recent trading activities, and any pending news such as earnings announcements.

18

SUNSHINE TRADING

Steven Bodurtha

Since its inception in 1982, the stock index futures market has become known for its liquidity and convenience. In implementing global investment decisions, plan sponsors and investment counselors have come to rely on stock index futures (SIFs) as an efficient, low-cost alternative to the often-cumbersome practice of trading large portfolios of stocks.

The growing use of stock index futures has been accompanied by a heightened interest among asset managers in trading larger amounts of SIF contracts relative to daily volume and average trade size. For the most part, the futures market has accommodated this interest admirably. Nonetheless, the emergence of SIF blocks has forced institutions and brokers to think harder about trading strategy in futures markets. At the heart of this thinking lies a commitment to minimize transaction costs and improve investment performance.

"Sunshine trading"[1] is a direct response to these developments. Begun in early 1986, sunshine trading envisions an auction-like procedure in which the details of an institutional order are publicized, ideally well in advance of the actual trade. Under the purest version of this preannouncement, specific details of the desired transaction would be disclosed, including the particular contract to be traded, the size of the order, and the precise time at which the trader is willing to transact. By broadcasting these details throughout the brokerage and investment communities, the institution ideally attracts the best prevailing bids or offers from interested contra-parties.

This chapter analyzes the results of 12 sunshine trades, with an aggregate value of more than $1 billion, that have been executed in the SIF market. Single transactions involving more than $300 million have been executed by

---

[1] Leland O'Brien Rubinstein Associates, Inc., originated the term *sunshine trading* and was the first (and, to date, the only) institutional user of this technique.

this method, and sunshine trades have accounted for as much as 50% of the total day's trading in a futures contract. All sunshine trades were executed on behalf of an institutional money manager.

Although most sunshine trading has occurred in the futures market, some experts believe that this execution technique can have its most favorable effect on the stock market. Some of the key market reforms proposed in the wake of Black Monday embrace the fundamental principles that underlie sunshine trading.

THE LOGIC OF SUNSHINE TRADING

Sunshine trading is designed for institutions whose trading is not motivated by expectations about futures values of traded assets. Most index fund managers, being invested passively in portfolios that are meant to track some market index, qualify as "expectationless" traders. Their primary mandate is to match the market's performance, not to beat it through active stock picking. The trading activity of portfolio insurance vendors also is not based on expected equity market returns. Likewise, a pension fund that wishes to change its asset allocation may buy or sell stock index futures without making any statement about market direction.

These market participants have a perspective on trading that is quite different from that of expectation-motivated parties such as active money managers. In executing a trade, an active money manager must be concerned about revealing his trading intentions, which may convey a valuable opinion (based on research, for example) about future asset prices. If this information is revealed, then asset prices may change before the money manager can take advantage of his own research. For example, a widely respected money manager who discloses his decision to buy IBM may watch the price rise beyond his reach simply because his endorsement induces others to buy before he can.

In contrast, expectationless traders are not compelled to conceal their intentions because they reveal no fundamental information and express no opinion about future asset values. In fact, as regular buyers and sellers of large asset positions, passive investors can be viewed as bringing valuable liquidity to the market, allowing other parties to transact in substantial volumes with someone who is not trading on the basis of expectations, and without incurring a lot of market impact costs.

Sunshine trading was developed to help large expectationless traders capture the value of the liquidity they bring to the marketplace. By preannouncing the precise time and size of a trade (for example, a portfolio insurer's sale of 3,000 S&P 500 futures contracts at 11:00 A.M.), a passive investor could ideally encourage all liquidity seekers (buyers, in this example) to bid simultaneously on the asset being offered. These liquidity seekers might be drawn to the sunshine trade because their conventional trading alternative would tend to drive prices up and away from them. By concentrating the bidding at one time, the expectationless client may be able to obtain attractive execution prices. In essence, the passive trader attempts to auction off a valuable asset—its liquidity—to the highest bidder.

WHY NOT BLOCK TRADING?

In equity markets, the traditional response to an institution's desire to buy or sell large positions has been the block or program trade. In these transactions, institutions pay brokers to commit capital in order to guarantee executions at specific prices or times. For example, an active money manager may not want to disclose his intentions to more than one broker. In such a case, the money manager may ask a broker to commit capital and guarantee execution of the entire order at a negotiated price. Or, an index fund that wants to sell a diverse equity portfolio quickly may employ a program trade to achieve the liquidation at the close of trading.

At present, however, there are regulatory constraints on block trading in futures. Unlike block transactions in the debt and equity markets, futures trades may not be negotiated "upstairs" or prearranged. Federal regulations and exchange rules require that all futures trades be executed by the open, competitive outcry of the futures pit.

Aside from these regulatory limitations, there are economic reasons that block trading may be inappropriate for the expectationless trader. Although broker capital is important to the facilitation of many trades, it should not be employed casually. In fact, for a large expectationless trader with valuable liquidity to offer, broker capital may be unnecessary. Rather than paying for the use of broker capital, an expectationless trader may instead be able to capture the value of its liquidity by preannouncing its intentions. This potential opportunity is the driving force behind sunshine trading.

SOME CRITICISMS OF SUNSHINE TRADING

The most commonly heard criticism of sunshine trades is that they can be "front-run" by opportunistic traders. For example, if a savvy market participant knows precisely when a large sell order is arriving on the exchange floor, he may try to sell the futures short before the specified time, thereby driving the price down. At the preannounced time, he will then buy the futures (cover his short position) from the sunshine trader at lower prices, and book a tidy profit. Of course, this type of opportunistic trading would come at the expense of the institution conducting the sunshine trade.

Although front running is a very legitimate concern, there are some natural safeguards built into the sunshine-trading mechanism. First, advance knowledge of sunshine trades is given to all market participants. When all participants have the same information about order flow, it becomes far more difficult to front-run successfully. For example, when all opportunists are armed with the same knowledge about a sunshine trade, they may sell short more contracts than are being offered in the sunshine package. Then, at the time of the sunshine trade (and afterwards), they may wind up bidding against each other to cover their short positions, in addition to competing with liquidity seekers attracted to the market by the sunshine trade. Faced with these prospects, the would-be opportunists may be deterred from front running in the first place. Furthermore, even if front running is temporarily depressing prices prior to a sell transaction (for example), shrewd traders may see an opportunity to buy, thereby pushing prices back up before the sunshine trade is executed.

Another criticism of sunshine trading is that universal knowledge of large supply or demand will "overhang" the market, creating unfavorable pressure on futures prices. Until the bulk of the sunshine trade volume is transacted, skeptics argue, this pressure will result in unattractive execution prices. Although this criticism merits consideration, futures traders should remember that incomplete information about supply and demand can drive the market to extremes. For example, if an institution wishes to sell 1,000 futures contracts, it might begin by submitting three separate but sequential orders of 200 contracts each. Although the institution may find comfort in not having disclosed its total interest, the traders in the futures pit may assume that the institution has 1,200 more contracts to sell, rather than the actual balance of 400. As a result, the institution may end up putting more pressure on futures prices than it would have had it been completely open about its intentions.

Skeptics also suggest that the sunshine-trading format is not consistent with the needs of liquidity seekers. By dictating precise and limited times at which liquidity will be available, the sunshine trader may miss the opportunity to trade with contra-parties who desire liquidity during other periods. If there are no liquidity seekers at the specified time of a sunshine trade, then the expectationless trader may end up trading at less attractive prices. Of course, the goal of trading only at very specific times is to concentrate the bidding for the liquidity that is being offered, in order to obtain better prices.

Interestingly enough, the preliminary data suggest that although there has been some opportunistic trading in advance of sunshine trades, front running has not occurred with enough frequency or success to undermine the potential of sunshine trading. In addition, the data accumulated so far indicate no systematic overhang as a result of sunshine trading.

DETAILS OF SUNSHINE TRADES DONE TO DATE

For regulatory reasons, the sunshine trades executed to date were not preannounced as widely as the client would have preferred. Generally, the procedure was as follows: On the day of a sunshine trade, Kidder (acting for its expectationless client) started offering (or bidding on) a stated number of contracts beginning at a precise time (e.g., 1:00 P.M.). At that time, the offer was made at or near the prevailing market price for a period of approximately one minute. If no contra-parties were attracted to trade at that time and price, Kidder stopped offering. Fifteen minutes later, Kidder stepped back into the futures pit and reinstated the offer, again for a period of about one minute. This procedure was repeated until all the contracts in the sunshine package were traded. On average, sunshine trades have been executed in five segments, with some being fulfilled entirely on the first try and others requiring as many as nine attempts. Thus, the total of 12 sunshine packages resulted in more than 50 individual trades.[2]

The figures in this chapter attempt to measure the results of 12 sunshine trades that have been completed to date. Each sunshine trade was conducted under the same basic format (subject to the restrictions discussed in note 2). The following section describes the statistics used to evaluate the results of

---

[2] Because of exchange rules interpretations, sunshine trades executed to date were not preannounced in what might be considered an optimal manner. In order to comply with futures market rule interpretations, there was no preannouncement before many of the trades. Instead, the orders were simply sent to the exchange floor for execution, with size fully disclosed, at regular 15-minute intervals. In other cases, where the exchange allowed it, floor personnel followed the client's instructions by announcing the intended trade in advance of its being sent to the pit for execution. In no case did upstairs personnel preannounce trades prior to the orders being sent to the exchange floor. Thus, although the preannouncement process was not as complete as it might have been (for legal reasons), the sunshine transactions were executed with enough of the qualities of open, preannounced trading to make this analysis worthwhile and meaningful.

the sunshine trades.[3] See Table 18.1 for a summary of sunshine trades done to date.

SHORT-TERM TRANSACTION COST MEASURES

The following two statistics are intended to measure the short-term market impact of sunshine trading. They compare the execution price of a sunshine transaction with the price of the futures contract (the *benchmark*) just before and just after the trade. The use of a benchmark that is situated near the time of the sunshine trade is intended to capture only the impact of the trade, and to minimize the effects of extraneous factors such as general market movement. In particular, a short-term measure of market impact may help detect any front running that is suspected of increasing the costs of sunshine trading. In general, it is assumed that any front-running activity would occur over very short time frames.

The use of both pretrade and posttrade benchmarks is meant to detect and measure transaction costs wherever it may be possible to observe them. In this analysis, they are presented essentially as alternative ways to measure transaction costs.

SHORT-TERM MARKET IMPACT, MEASURED FIVE MINUTES BEFORE TRADE. For purchase transactions, this figure is defined as the price of the futures contract five minutes before the trade minus the execution price. For sell transactions, it is defined as the execution price minus the price of the futures contract five minutes before the trade. Thus, positive numbers (i.e., those with a $+$ sign) indicate that the execution price was better than the price five minutes before the trade, and negative $(-)$ numbers indicate that the trade price was worse than the price five minutes prior to execution. If a sunshine trade were creating adverse market impact, then one might expect to see the price of a futures contract rise in the five minutes leading up to a buy transaction and fall in the five minutes prior to a sell execution.

---

[3] The measurement of transaction costs is an important but still emerging discipline. This analysis shares many of the uncertainties regarding methodologies and related issues faced by other studies of transaction costs. In addition, with data from only 12 sunshine trades, more experience needs to be accumulated before inferences may be confidently drawn. Finally, because all the sunshine trades have been executed for a vendor of portfolio insurance, the results shown herein may not be indicative of results obtainable by other types of asset managers.

TABLE 18.1 SUMMARY OF SUNSHINE TRADES COMPLETED TO DATE

Trade	Buy/ Sell	Date	Futures Contract	Symbol	Number of Contracts	Transaction Value (millions of dollars)	Contracts Traded as a Percentage of Total Day's Volume
1	Sell	2/04/86	June S&P 500	SPM	1,112	$ 121.2	29.7
2	Buy	5/23/86	September S&P 500	SPU	620	72.0	15.7
3	Sell	6/10/86	September S&P 500	SPU	1,113	124.3	5.4
4	Buy	6/16/86	September S&P 500	SPU	678	84.1	1.2
5	Sell	7/08/86	September S&P 500	SPU	1,200	134.2	1.3
6	Sell	7/29/86	September NYSE Composite	YXU	254	17.2	2.2
7	Sell	8/07/86	September NYSE Composite	YXU	180	12.3	2.2
8	Sell	8/11/86	December NYSE Composite	YXZ	301	20.8	50.5
9	Buy	8/14/86	September NYSE Composite	YXU	458	32.6	5.4
10	Sell	9/12/86	December S&P 500	SPZ	3,359	389.9	2.9
11	Sell	9/12/86	December NYSE Composite	YXZ	1,096	71.8	4.3
12	Sell	9/12/86	December Value Line	KVZ	163	17.4	5.1
					10,534	$1,097.8	

SHORT-TERM MARKET IMPACT, MEASURED FIVE MINUTES AFTER TRADE. For purchase transactions, this figure is defined as the price of the futures contract five minutes after the trade minus the execution price. For sell transactions, it is defined as the execution price minus the price of the futures contract five minutes after the trade. Again, positive numbers are favorable, and negative numbers indicate unfavorable market impact. With this method, adverse market impact would be indicated by the price of a futures contract falling in the five minutes after a buy execution, and rising in the five-minute period after a sell transaction.

These short-term measures of market impact focus on the changes in the prices of futures contracts, as opposed to the changes in the basis of futures contracts (where the basis equals the difference between the price of the futures contract and the price of the underlying index). Over longer stretches of time, measuring the change in the basis may help eliminate the effect of general market movement on futures prices. Over short time spans and relatively narrow price ranges, however, futures prices can move very independently from the underlying indexes. In addition, the reported prices of the underlying stock indexes are based, at any given time, on the collection of last-sale prices for each of the stocks in the indexes. These last-sale prices can be several minutes (or even hours) old at the time they are reported in the index price. Thus, over short time periods, the index price (and, therefore, the basis) may not provide a sufficiently accurate picture of the market's movement. For these reasons, it was considered appropriate to rely on the changes in futures prices (and not the changes in basis) when attempting to measure short-term market impact.

The short-term market impact of the 12 sunshine trades is summarized in Figure 18.1.

LONGER TERM TRANSACTION COST INDICATORS

Although benchmarks that are situated near the time of the trade can help eliminate extraneous noise, they may not capture the full amount or nature of transaction costs. For example, one could argue reasonably that universal advance knowledge of large supply or demand (one of the features of preannounced trading) could put adverse pressure on the price of a futures contract well before the actual trade. The following statistics are meant to reflect the presence and approximate magnitude of such longer term transaction costs. As indicators, these statistics may not yield precise measures of market impact. Again, both pretrade and posttrade measures are

FIGURE 18.1   SHORT-TERM PERFORMANCE OF ALL
SUNSHINE TRADES

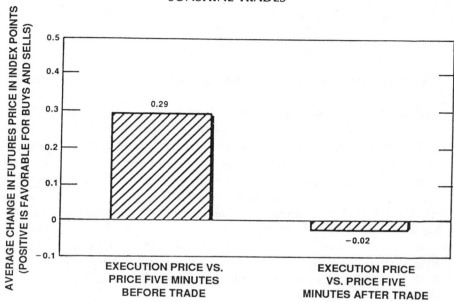

employed in order to capture transaction costs wherever they may be detected.

In contrast to the short-term statistics discussed earlier, these longer term indicators focus on the change in the basis of futures contracts. Over longer time spans, the change in the basis can help remove the effects of general market movement. Thus, it was deemed to be an appropriate measure of the longer term impact of sunshine trading.

BASIS MOVEMENT FROM OPEN

This statistic measures the movement in the basis from the opening of trading on the transaction date to the time of the sunshine trade. For both purchases and sales, a positive number indicates a favorable movement in the basis (from the perspective of the sunshine trader).

The opening basis has been measured at 9:45 A.M. Eastern Time to account for the fact that most equity issues that make up the various stock indexes do not open precisely at 9:30 A.M. Thus, composite index prices at 9:30 A.M. may be more reflective of the previous night's closing prices.

Specifically, this statistic is calculated as follows:

- *For buys:* Basis movement from open = Basis at 9:45 A.M.
  − Basis at time of execution
- *For sells:* Basis movement from open = Basis at time of execution
  − Basis at 9:45 A.M.

BASIS MOVEMENT TO 4:00 P.M. SAME DAY

This after-trade measure is intended to detect any adverse price pressure, or market overhang, on a futures contract that might result from a sunshine trade. If sunshine sell transactions were, for example, exerting downward pressure on futures prices, then one might expect to observe the basis systematically rising after the sunshine trades were completed (or dropping in the wake of sunshine purchases). To maintain consistency, this statistic is defined so that positive numbers are favorable for both purchases and sales; that is, positive numbers do not suggest the presence of market overhang. Although stock index futures trade until 4:15 P.M. (Eastern Time), the primary market for most of the equity issues in the underlying indexes (the New York Stock Exchange) closes at 4:00 P.M. Thus, it was considered appropriate to measure the closing basis as of 4:00 P.M.

- *For buys:* Basis movement to 4:00 P.M. same day =
  Basis at 4:00 P.M. same day − Basis at time of
  execution
- *For sells:* Basis movement to 4:00 P.M. same day =
  Basis at time of execution − Basis at 4:00 P.M.

Figure 18.2 summarizes the basis movement both before and after the sunshine trades. This exhibit also shows the movement in basis from the day before the average sunshine trade, and the basis movement to the day after the average sunshine transaction.

Figure 18.3 shows the results of the sunshine trade that was executed on September 12, 1986, the day on which the Dow Jones industrial average dropped by 34 points (and one day after the Dow fell 86 points). Table 18-2 provides a statistical breakdown of sunshine trades completed to date.

THE STATUS OF SUNSHINE TRADING

In response to the interest shown in sunshine trading, some market officials felt it was appropriate to develop a standard, approved method for executing

FIGURE 18.2   LONGER TERM PERFORMANCE OF ALL SUNSHINE TRADES

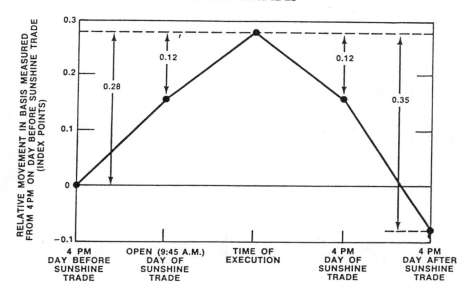

this type of transaction. One concern, for example, was how sunshine trade information could be disseminated thoroughly and fairly to all members of the brokerage and investment communities. As of the time of this writing, the Commodity Futures Trading Commission (CFTC) was deliberating over a formal proposal from the New York Futures Exchange to conduct sunshine trades on its floor. The CFTC had solicited opinions from the public on this proposal and had received comments, both pro and con, from the major exchanges where stock index futures are traded.

LOOKING AHEAD

Some market pundits believe that the real future of sunshine trading lies with the stock market. In the wake of Black Monday, some observers have been calling for "sunshine-like" reforms in equity market-making practices. For instance, it has been argued that the opening and closing of trading on the major stock exchanges would be less volatile if the buy and sell imbalances that tend to occur at those times were broadcast to the investment community. Then the vast coffers of pension funds and money managers could supplement the limited capital of the specialists, making for smoother

FIGURE 18.3   SUNSHINE TRADE: SELL 3359 DECEMBER S&P 500 CONTRACTS, SEPTEMBER 12, 1986

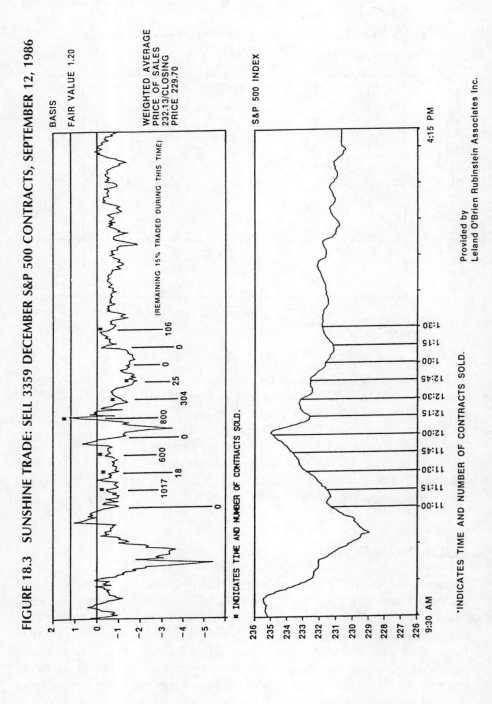

Provided by
Leland O'Brien Rubinstein Associates Inc.

234

TABLE 18.2   STATISTICAL SUMMARY OF SUNSHINE TRADES

	Market Impact Measured 5 Minutes before Trade (Index Points) Positive = Good	Market Impact Measured 5 Minutes after Trade (Index Points) Positive = Good	Basis Movement from Open[a] (Index Points) Positive = Good	Basis Movement to 4:00 P.M. Same Day (Index Points) Positive = Good
Totals	0.29	−0.02	0.12	0.12
Buys	−0.08	0.02	0.00	−0.20
Sells	0.36	−0.02	0.14	0.18
Deferred contracts[b]	−0.04	−0.07	−0.12	0.32
Nearby contracts[b]	0.37	0.00	0.17	0.07
S&P 500's	0.38	0.00	0.33	0.34
NYSE Composite's	0.01	0.08	−0.10	0.01
Value Line's	0.07	−0.13	0.92	0.45

Example: Market impact of 0.10 index points equals two ticks (e.g., the difference between a price of 240.10 and a price of 240.00).

[a] The opening basis has been measured at 9:45 A.M. Eastern Time to account for the fact that most equity issues that make up the various cash market indexes do not trade precisely at 9:30 A.M.. Thus, composite index prices at 9:30 A.M. may be more reflective of the previous night's closing prices.

[b] Any contract with less than 15 weeks to expiration has been classified as a nearby contract.

price adjustments. For its part, the Brady Commission has raised the idea of making the specialist book public when there are serious order imbalances. Such disclosure might attract liquidity providers to the market and help avoid the panic trading that could occur in the face of supply or demand of large but unknown magnitude. Each of these proposals embraces the key principle underlying sunshine trading—that complete, advance disclosure of large order flow information is a good way to attract contra-parties and to obtain better execution prices with lower volatility.

The Editor Asks

Q *Many of the rules and procedures of both the stock exchanges and the futures exchanges are designed to ensure that all investors are treated fairly. The net result is that orders tend to become indistinguishable at the point of execution, regardless of the motivation for trading. This also discourages processes such as sunshine trading, which seeks to differentiate its orders from the throng. Can you suggest any changes to market structures that would simplify trading for* *sunshine traders? Can you see any dangers that would result from these changes?*

A It might be possible for sunshine traders to go off and start their own marketplace, as pension funds and money managers are trying to do with crossing networks and the like. Sunshine traders, however, perhaps more than any other market participant, demand access to anyone and everyone who is a seeker of liquidity. Thus, for sunshine trading to thrive, it must take root with the major stock and futures exchanges. An exchange-sponsored process would assure uniformity in treatment of sunshine trades and would reduce the potential for gaming of sunshine trading. An exchange could, for instance, discourage or even prohibit someone from submitting a large sunshine trade and then pulling it at the last minute in the hope of manipulating the market.

In the futures market, the exchanges would have to build a real-time electronic facility for disseminating bid and offer quote information. Moreover, this system (and vendors who distribute market data) would have to develop a way to transmit and display on quote machines the greater amount of information that accompanies a sunshine trade (e.g., time, size, identity of the sunshine trader, etc.). In addition, sunshine trading would receive a real boost if brokers were not prohibited from disclosing order information outside the futures pit.

In the stock market, the same technological obstacles would have to be surmounted. In addition, sunshine trading would benefit from the opening up of the specialists' book. If buy and sell imbalances were routinely broadcast to the financial community, then sunshine traders would have a means of signaling their intentions. The success of sunshine trading would also depend on the ability of institutions to respond quickly to this order flow information with offsetting orders. Thus, another prerequisite for sunshine trading might be to create more direct institutional access to the exchange floor. Of course, such enhanced access (like the SuperDOT system) has been blamed for creating panic in the stock market.

19

ELECTRONIC TRADING: THE BATTERYMARCH EXPERIENCE

Evan Shulman

Traders who do not have the advantage of company-specific information may wish to differentiate themselves from those who do. Batterymarch accomplished that differentiation by using a time-shared computer to advertise its orders and to execute trades. In so doing, Batterymarch became the first money manager to use computers to trade securities, the first trader to advertise its trading intentions (now known as sunshine trading) and the first to systematically collect trading data, including decision prices, for analysis. Analysis of these data over a large number and dollar volume of trades demonstrates the effectiveness of the system. The analysis also shows the usefulness of price limits and substitute securities in minimizing the observed price effects due to advertising. The question of adverse selection is also raised and partially answered.

Firms that trade in a more conventional manner may wish to replicate this analysis to measure the value of the information they generate, any losses in their shop, and the effectiveness of the brokers who service them.

An individual's view on how to trade is heavily influenced by his view on how to invest. *Information traders* invest on the basis of new and supposedly undiscounted company-specific information. They are single-minded in the pursuit of selected securities and are in a hurry to complete transactions before the rest of the world finds out what they already know. Such investors are not too concerned about paying up another eighth or quarter to get the stock in question. They hide their information trades in

This chapter is based on two case studies at the Harvard Business School. The cases, Batterymarch Financial Management (A) and (B), were written by Professor Andre Perold. We are grateful to Harvard for permission to plagiarize and to Batterymarch for releasing the data to Harvard for analysis.

brokers' ordinary order flow. This makes it difficult for other traders to determine the average value of information this particular investor brings to market. A broker's ordinary business includes not only other information trades (some based on information that has already been impounded in the price of the security), but also the orders of liquidity and value-based traders.

Liquidity and value-based traders have no time-sensitive company specific information. Liquidity traders are simply raising or investing cash or restructuring their portfolios on the basis of life's changing circumstances. Value-based investors stand to buy or sell stock at specific prices. They are, in effect, market-makers operating with very wide bid–ask spreads—buy at $30.00, sell at $40.00.

When market-makers see an order come to market, they must assume that there is some positive probability that the other side is trying to exploit current, and as yet undiscounted, company-specific information. Market-makers will adjust their prices accordingly, and all those who trade with them will pay this adverse selection insurance premium whether or not they do possess information. It is therefore in the interest of liquidity and value traders to differentiate themselves from the information wolves and vultures. Somehow they must demonstrate, with actions, the purity of their intentions. Simply stating that they have no information is unlikely to persuade other traders. What better way to differentiate oneself than to advertise and then wait patiently for the stock to be forthcoming at a specified price?[1]

This was the line of reasoning of Batterymarch Financial Management in 1975. Batterymarch was a value investor, hoping to obtain a significant position in the money management industry. It was further argued at the firm that advertising on a time-shared computer, programed to execute transactions, would allow the firm the benefits of automation. Executed orders would flow directly into its accounting system and would be available to those of its clients' custodian banks. It was noted that delegating to a computer the power to commit the firm's clients to specific trades would be perceived as revolutionary by brokers, competitors, and clients, both existing and potential. Properly handled, this would be viewed as an advantage.

---

[1] Index funds are informationless in our sense of the word and transact for liquidity reasons only. Their managers usually advertise in an attempt to differentiate their trades, but because of the perceived need to track the selected index closely, these investors do not have the luxury of waiting for stock at a specified price. They are passive investors, but active traders in that they do not use limit orders.

In the spring of 1976 Batterymarch first instituted an automated trading system on its own time-shared computer.[2] The firm undertook to do its total stock-trading business with a limited number of brokers, currently 23 in the U.S. market, all of whom agreed to accept greatly discounted commission rates. Although the system changed over time and has changed again since we compiled the data herein, the program worked essentially as follows:

SYSTEM DESCRIPTION

Each of the selected brokers received a password that gave him access to the computer via remote terminal. Once connected, the brokers could print out the firm's "wish list" of purchases and sales. The list included the quantities to be traded for each security, as well as a limit price at which Batterymarch was willing to transact. Because the firm wanted its portfolios to have certain characteristics, it viewed many stocks as substitutes. As a result, the wish lists contained more potential trades than were really wanted: For instance, in the case of purchases, there were more orders than could possibly be bought with the funds on hand.

The purpose of the limit price was to impose price control. For purchases, the limit was the lowest of the last sale price, obtained from the Instinet computer system,[3] last night's close, market adjusted, or the price at which the security first appeared on the Batterymarch wish list, adjusted for market moves. For sales, the limit price was the largest of these three prices (see the appendix to this chapter).

The firm was content to wait for days or even weeks for a security to trade. If a stock had not traded on the system for several days because the limit price was too far out of line with current prices, the stock would be removed from the wish list. If Batterymarch still wanted to trade that stock at current market levels, it would, after not displaying the order for several more days, put the stock back on the system with the limit price reinitialized as though it were appearing for the first time. Removing the stock from the

[2] Batterymarch did the bulk of its trading under this set of rules. Trades not done in this way were small transactions and sets of stocks belonging to new accounts. These latter groups of stocks were to be swapped for securities in which the firm wanted to invest. With such grouped trades the firm solicited bids from brokers to do swap executions, under Batterymarch's guidance, on a best-efforts basis.

[3] See Chapter 21, "Electronic Equity Trading: A Necessity for Efficient Markets," by William A. Lupien.

system for several days was an attempt to cleanse the security of any price impact due to advertising the order.

The implementation of substitute stocks was designed to broaden the list of potential trades, thus speeding up the trading process. Also, substitutes were meant to introduce an element of uncertainty for those who may be, potentially, the other side of the trade. The existence of substitutes would pressure the other side to complete the trade now rather than waiting to see if a better deal came along. If they did not trade now, a better deal for Batterymarch might appear either in the stock in question or in one of its substitutes, in which case the computer would cancel its order, which the other side was considering. Substitutes also made it riskier to front-run the order, a practice whereby traders would go the same way (purchase or sale) that the computer advertised, hoping either that Batterymarch was correct in its judgment or that the presence of its order would drive the price of the stock up, in the case of a purchase, or down in the case of a sale. Traders who engaged in this practice used the known order as a backstop: That is, should the price change not run in their favor, they could always "put" ("call") the stock to fill the Batterymarch buy (sell) order. Brokers were allowed access to the list of potential trades at 7:30 A.M. each day, but they could not transact before trading in that security opened on a recognized market.

When a broker indicated a desire to trade, the computer would check that the order was still good (i.e., that another broker had not executed it or its substitute) and that the price offered met the requirements just listed. If these conditions were met, the computer would acknowledge the trade and print out the delivery instructions for each of the individual client accounts involved.[4] As the trades took place, the computer would update the "wish list" in real time, adjusting the remaining number of shares to be traded in this security and any substitutes. The stock(s) in question would be kept on the list until the full amount traded or the order canceled.

COMMISSION COSTS

Reducing commission costs was one of Batterymarch's goals with this trading system. Although the benefits of automation accrued mostly to the firm (the firm's fees were about in line with those of its competitors), any savings in commissions would go directly to the client.

In its negotiations with brokers, the firm argued that its clients should pay lower commissions, for a variety of reasons:

---

[4] A trade of, say, 100,000 shares could be a collection of smaller trades for several accounts.

1. Batterymarch did not use Wall Street research; its investment decisions were based on commonly available data. Its clients would thus be overpaying if they were charged "standard" rates.

2. The firm was a passive trader; its decisions were not based on new information. Therefore, there was no reason to compensate the other side for the risks undertaken when dealing with informed traders.

3. By letting brokers trade with the system at their own convenience (under the previously described rules), the computer was essentially providing valuable merchandise for the brokers. Indeed, it could be argued that rather than charge Batterymarch clients, brokers should be paying them for their orders.[5]

4. As the firm got bigger and bigger, it felt that its clients should receive volume discounts because of its larger trades.

Initially, brokers agreed to trade on these terms for 10 cents per share when commissions typically ranged from 15 to 25 cents per share. By 1979 the firm had managed to lower this figure to an average of 2 cents per share. The 2-cent rate prevailed through the end of 1987, while standard rates on the street dropped to between 5 and 12 cents. Batterymarch accomplished this by unilaterally lowering the commission paid by its clients. It did this from time to time, each time watching to see if there was any change in trading volume. This lowering of commissions seemed at each stage to have had little effect on the brokers' willingness to trade.

ANALYSIS OF TRADING OPERATIONS

We used two different methodologies for measuring transaction costs. The first of these calculated the execution cost of a purchase as the execution price less the average price of the 10 trades immediately preceding and following the purchase, provided that these neighboring trades were for more than 500 shares and occurred within 30 minutes of the time of the Batterymarch trade. Execution costs for sales were defined analogously, with the sign reversed. The time frame was based on an interval that corresponded to the very short time frames of traders in general. If no other trades had taken place in quantities of at least 500 shares during the 60-minute window around the trade in question, then no such execution cost was calculated.

---

[5] The business was sufficiently attractive, even at these rates, that there have always been a number of brokers waiting to get on the system. This allows Batterymarch to pressure brokers to trade by offering to replace those who trade least with others from the waiting list.

The second methodology, for purchases, used the price of the stock less its closing price on the day traded, adjusted for movements in the market between the time of purchase and the close. Sales were again done in a similar manner, but with the sign reversed. Given many trades, both methods were expected to generate similar results.

We also looked at a variety of statistical data related to each trade—for example, the bid–ask spread at the time of the trade; the market-adjusted performance of the stock up to the time of the trade; and the firm's market capitalization, yield, and beta.

Money management firms that trade in a more conventional way may want to collect and analyze similar data. It is important for managers to know the value of the information they generate. They should also know how much is lost before the firm actually places its orders with brokers, and how much each broker they deal with costs them in terms of slippage and posttransaction costs. That large institutional investors face transaction costs is not surprising but as professionals we should know both the size and the nature of these costs.

DATA

One important by-product of a computerized trading system is that its data are readily available for analysis. We believe this is the first set of data collected that allows the user to look at price differences both pre- and posttrade. We could also look at wished-for transactions and compare stocks traded versus those not traded.[6]

All transactions undertaken over the five months from October 1984 through February 1985 were collected for this analysis. During this period Batterymarch restructured its clients' portfolios, selling $1.7 billion of stock in 86 firms and purchasing another $1.7 billion of equity in 109 different firms. Over this interval the sell list outperformed the market by 0.5%, and the purchase list outperformed the sell list by 4.0%.

INTERPRETATION

The system behaved as intended in that it did not chase prices. In fact, the average stock purchased (sold) underperformed (overperformed) the market

---

[6] All other transaction measurement systems are based on trade data that contain only the elements of stock, price, shares, account, and date of trade. These systems have no way of knowing what happened prior to the trade or to price action in the immediate vicinity of the trade. We believe that these are important aspects of transaction cost analysis that indicate, respectively, the slippage between decision and execution and whether or not the trade really took place at prices different from prices paid by other market participants.

as measured by the Dow Jones Industrial Average, by 0.3% from the previous night's close to execution. Execution costs measured by the first method were less than 0.1%, a small fraction of the bid–ask spread, which averaged 0.8%. Further, the system looked as if it were not getting "bagged" in that measuring from execution to the closing price on the day of the trade, the second method described, generated a transaction cost of some 0.35%, about one-half of the bid–ask spread.

Another way to measure costs was to look at the bid–ask spread at the time of the trade. Assuming the midpoint of this range represents fair value, purchases by the system took place at 55% of the bid–ask spread, sales at 45%. Five percent of the average 0.8% bid–ask spread amounts to 0.04%, a figure consistent with our other measures.

We noted, however, that the restructuring trade took some time to complete. Figure 19.1 gives the quantities wished compared to those executed on each day. On average, 14% of the stock we wanted to sell was executed, and 9% of the stock we wanted to buy was actually purchased. Allowing for substitution at, say, 3 for 1, the 9% figure indicates that the system executed less than one-third of the purchases for which money was available. Were the measuring methodologies or the averages concealing some underlying opportunity cost?

For the restructuring trade we had divided the securities to be traded into two groups, one of which would be advertised on the system while the other, with similar characteristics, would not. As the trade proceeded, these two groups were alternated. The results of this analysis are given in Figure 19.2. Averaged over the period, this analysis indicates that purchases appearing on the system outperformed the market on the day they appeared by an average of 0.21%, while those purchases held off the system underperformed by 0.08%. For sales the results were, respectively, an underperformance of 0.18% and an overperformance of 0.05%. Note that these were averages of all stocks involved in the restructuring effort. Because of the price limit system, the machine would not pay up to effect executions. Rather, it selected those stocks for purchase that had underperformed and those stocks for sale that had overperformed, despite the advertising effect.

This leads to the question of adverse selection: We had found the other side, but was the other side primarily an information trader? Returning to our animal analogy in the introduction, advertising was intended to attract the lambs (the informationless liquidity traders) because the act of advertising implied that we had no time-sensitive information. It was known, however, that advertising would also attract the information wolves. Did we attract a high enough proportion of lambs to wolves?

We decided to look at transaction costs based on our second methodology,

FIGURE 19.1   BATTERYMARCH FINANCIAL MANAGEMENT: BUYS AND SELLS, WISHED VERSUS EXECUTED

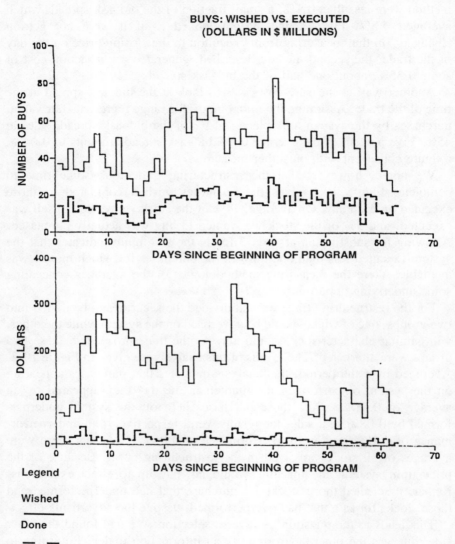

BUYS: WISHED VS. EXECUTED
(DOLLARS IN $ MILLIONS)

Legend

Wished

Done

FIGURE 19.1   (CONTINUED)

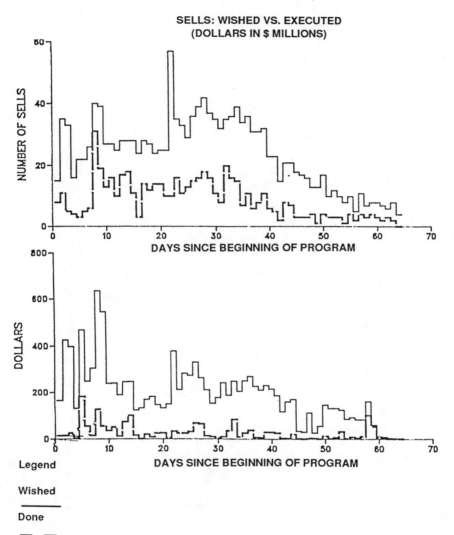

SELLS: WISHED VS. EXECUTED
(DOLLARS IN $ MILLIONS)

Legend

Wished

_____

Done

— —

FIGURE 19.2 BATTERYMARCH FINANCIAL MANAGEMENT: DAILY RETURNS OF WISHED VERSUS NONWISHED STOCKS

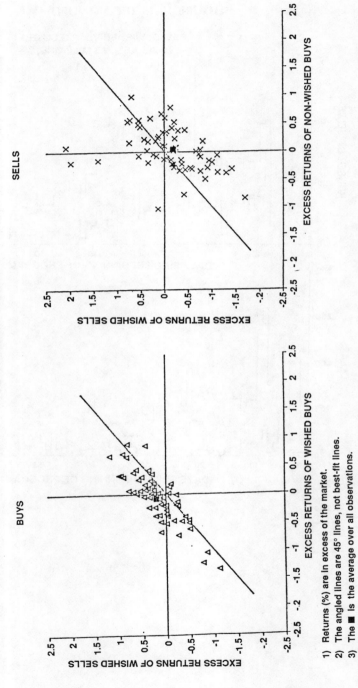

1) Returns (%) are in excess of the market.
2) The angled lines are 45° lines, not best-fit lines.
3) The ■ is the average over all observations.

246

FIGURE 19.2 (CONTINUED)

DIFFERENCE BETWEEN WISHED
& NON-WISHED BUYS

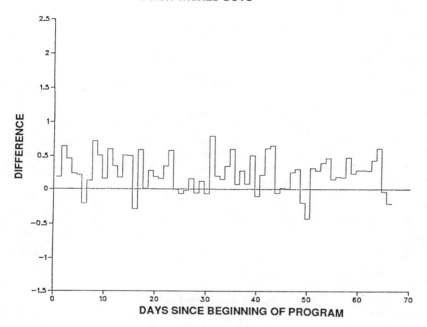

DIFFERENCE BETWEEN WISHED
& NON-WISHED SELLS

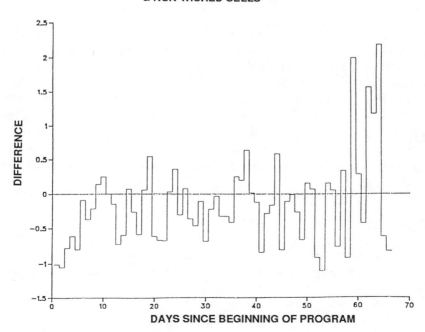

FIGURE 19.3   BATTERYMARCH FINANCIAL MANAGEMENT:
PERFORMANCE OF STOCKS SUBSEQUENT TO TRADING

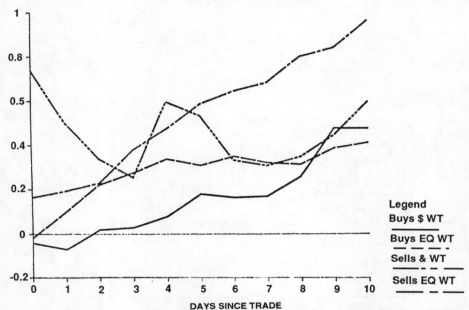

DAYS SINCE TRADE

Note: Cumulative performance (in percentage return) relative to market (S&P 500): that is, market performance = 0. Day 0 performance = Trade-to-close performance relative to market.

but looking out a full 10 days. Figure 19.3 gives those results. There is no question that by the close of trading on the day of execution there was an unfavorable spread, using dollar-weighted figures, of some 0.7%, slightly less than the average bid–ask spread for the stocks traded. We note, however, that for the dollar-weighted calculations, the adverse selection spread between buys and sells narrows to less than 0.2% by day 6 and to zero by the 10th day after the trade. Our collection of data was not complete enough to answer the question of how much of this temporary 5- to 10-day dip or bounce in prices subsequent to our trade it was possible to capture.

SUMMARY

There are different reasons for trading. Traders who do not have the advantage of company-specific information may wish to differentiate themselves from those who do. Batterymarch accomplished that differentiation in a most effective way, using a time-shared computer to advertise its orders and to execute trades. Analysis of the data generated by this system over a large number and dollar volume of trades demonstrates the need for both a price limit system and substitute securities to minimize the observed price effects due to advertising. The question of adverse selection was also raised and partially answered.

Firms that trade in a more conventional manner may wish to replicate this analysis to measure the value of the information they generate, any losses in their shop, and the effectiveness of the brokers who service them.

The Editor Asks

Q *Traders are skeptical of advertising—the sunshine approach to stock trading. They argue that others pick you off when they have information. How would you respond to this criticism?*

A There is no question that active traders with information can take advantage of limit orders, both those on the floor and those residing on computers. All active orders, however (i.e., those that are not advertised), will be treated by other market participants as if there were some positive probability that they have some valuable, as yet undiscounted, company-specific information. As a result, they will pay a small information surcharge or insurance premium on every trade. Those that advertise, on the other hand, will pay only on those occasions where their orders exist as the other side of a trade at the exact moment information comes to market. On these few occasions they will pay close to the full value of the undiscounted information in terms of the postexecution price move. The question then is: On average, who pays more? We will not know the answer to that until those who trade in the normal way release data for analysis as Batterymarch did to Harvard.

APPENDIX: BATTERYMARCH FINANCIAL MANAGEMENT—EXAMPLE OF LIMIT PRICE CALCULATION (FOR FORMULA PREVAILING 1981–1984)

The formula (for purchases) is as follows:
Limit price = Lesser of:

1. Price prevailing when security initially appeared on system, adjusted for subsequent interday moves in the S&P 500.
2. Previous night's closing price, adjusted for subsequent intraday moves in the DJIA.
3. Price of most recent trade.

Suppose security X is placed on the system on day 1 as a purchase, and that its closing price on day 0 was $60.00. The following table shows how to calculate the limit price at, say, 12:00 noon, given the performance of the S&P 500 each day, the performance of the DJIA each morning prior to 12:00 noon, the last trade in X just prior to 12:00 noon, and the closing prices of X each day.

	Day					
	0	1	2	3	4	5
Closing price of X	60	61	63	57	55	
Last trade in X prior to noon (3)		60-7/8	64	59	56	56
Performance of S&P 500 during day		+0.5%	+0.5%	−1	+1	
Performance of DJIA in morning		+1%	−1	−1	+2	−1
S&P 500-adjusted initial price (1)		60.0	60.3	60.6	60.0	60.6
Previous close, DJIA-adjusted (2)		60.6	60.4	62.4	58.1	54.5
12:00 noon limit price (lesser of 1, 2, 3)		60	60.3	59	56	54.5

In this example, X was trading above its limit price (12:00 noon) only on days 3 and 4.

20

INTERNATIONAL TRADING

Thomas Burnett

The decade of the 1980s has witnessed significant growth of international investing by U.S. institutional investors. In 1975, U.S. investors' purchases and sales of foreign securities totaled $14.4 billion.[1] By 1986, the corresponding total of purchases and sales had grown to $438.5 billion.[2] Focusing on foreign equities alone, U.S. investors' purchases and sales were $3.3 billion in 1975 and $10.2 billion in 1986.[3] Private-sector pension funds, for example, increased foreign assets from $3.3 billion in 1980 (1% of total assets) to $45 billion in 1986 (4% of total assets).[4] Similarly, U.S. investors reached out to foreign securities markets through mutual funds and investment companies. Global mutual funds increased from 21 in 1983 and 59 at the end of 1986.[5] Assets managed by these funds grew from $3.5 billion to $15.9 billion over the period.[6] Gross sales of shares in this category of mutual funds increased from less than $1 billion in 1983 to $7.6 billion during 1986.[7] In addition, there are currently more than 25 listed closed-end funds with assets under management exceeding $3 billion.

This increased interest in global investing is also evidenced by the dramatic growth of American Depository Receipts (ADRs), whose shares are traded in the United States and in London. Over 800 foreign-based

[1] *Internationalization of the Securities Markets,* Report of the Staff of the U.S. Securities and Exchange Commission to the Senate Committee on Banking, Housing and Urban Affairs and the House Committee on Energy and Commerce, July 27, 1987, p. II-99 (hereinafter referred to as *SEC Report on Internationalization*).

[2] *SEC Report on Internationalization,* p. II-99.

[3] *SEC Report on Internationalization,* p. II-101.

[4] *SEC Report on Internationalization,* Table II-17.

[5] *SEC Report on Internationalization,* Table II-18.

[6] *SEC Report on Internationalization,* Table II-18.

[7] *SEC Report on Internationalization,* p. II-18.

companies have shares represented in ADR form. The number of ADR shares outstanding has risen 16-fold, from 150 million in 1976 to over 2.4 billion at the end of 1986.[8]

The strong relative performance of the foreign equity markets over the past decade has caused a material decline in the U.S. share of world equity capitalization. At the end of 1976, the U.S. equity market accounted for approximately two-thirds of the world's total equity capitalization. By June 1987, the U.S. market's total had declined to less than 40%. The poor relative performance of the U.S. dollar from early 1985 through 1987 also reduced the U.S. market's share of world equity value. By late 1987, the market valuation of the Japanese stock market had surpassed that of the U.S. market, and the U.S. market dropped from its top rank for the first time since the end of World War II.

Clearly, the U.S. investor can no longer avoid looking abroad for attractive opportunities. An investor who focuses solely on the U.S. equity market would ignore almost two-thirds of the world's equity and would not be able to benefit from the improved performance that well-managed diversification can provide.

The excellent performance of global equity investment is well documented. From the end of 1976 to the end of 1987, the U.S. market (S&P 500) increased 12.5% per year. The non-U.S. EAFE[9] (Europe, Australia, Far East) Index increased 22.7% per year. An investment of $10,000 in the S&P 500 at the end of 1976 would have grown to $36,502 by the end of 1987; a similar $10,000 investment in EAFE Index would have become $92,051.

The dramatic decline of the U.S. dollar beginning in early 1985 accelerated the greater performance trend in foreign equity markets. Even in the August 1982–October 1987 bull market, the U.S. market performance trailed all the major markets in dollar-converted terms. Its year-end 1987 value of 230.4, compared to a dollar-converted 405.9 for the EAFE World Index.[10] Over the 10-year period ending February 23, 1988, the United States ranked 13th among the world equity markets, both in terms of local currencies and in U.S. dollars.[11] The U.S. market was the top performer in only one year (1982) during the seven years from 1981 through 1987.

Apart from the risk–reward advantages of global investing, several nonfinancial factors have contributed to the dramatic increase in U.S.

---

[8] *SEC Report on Internationalization*, p. II-80.
[9] *Morgan Stanley Capital International Perspective*, January 1988, Geneva, Switzerland.
[10] *Morgan Stanley Capital International Perspective*, January 1988, Geneva, Switzerland.
[11] *Barron's*, February 29, 1988, p. 73.

investor participation in foreign equity markets. One key factor is the marked improvement in technology. Investors have developed systems for automatic execution, multicurrency inventory control, and global risk management. A trader in New York can now sit at his workstation and look at the foreign bond and equity markets, the currency markets, and the commodity markets. Simultaneously, he interfaces with an internal trading system that can execute trades and monitor his inventory on a real-time, interactive basis. In addition to these system capabilities, the U.S. investor relies on telex, telecommunications, and facsimile equipment for speedier, more reliable execution and confirmation of any non-U.S. trade.

Reduced government regulatory intervention has also encouraged the trend toward increased internationalization. Local stock exchange membership has been expanded to include foreign controlling parties in Japan, the United Kingdom, Hong Kong, Australia, Canada, and France. Currency repatriation and extensive local currency borrowing are now permitted in the major equity market countries. Many countries have encouraged the development of new investment vehicles such as warrants, listed options, and cash settlement futures. These have attracted capital from other markets to the local Bourses.

The trend to privatization has added noteworthy, high-quality, well-financed companies to the universe of investment opportunities. These new high-quality companies have attracted foreign investors to France, Spain, and the United Kingdom, which have emphasized privatization the most. These new securities have attracted funds from around the world. As a result, international investors are more aware of the opportunities offered in markets outside their local arena.

EQUITY TRADING MANAGEMENT

This chapter is directed to the trading function of large buy-side U.S.-based investment managers rather than the trading function at a sell-side brokerage firm. Buy-side traders primarily execute on behalf of research directors or portfolio managers. They are not asked to make two-sided markets or to carry large risk positions on the short side. Equity trading usually operates as a separate discipline, not co-mingled with research, portfolio management, or marketing.

There are currently more than 100 different ADRs, Canadian, and other non-U.S. equity securities listed on major U.S. stock exchanges. These stocks and equity equivalents (e.g., listed warrants on the ADRs of Hanson Trust and British Petroleum on the NYSE) trade in the same specialist-based fashion as U.S. stocks. These trades execute in U.S. dollars and settle in five business days. Stocks that trade, clear, and settle as listed U.S. stocks should be traded by traders experienced in the specialist-based, listed market. This trading function can be managed separately and does not require separate traders by country or currency.

By contrast, traders responsible for trading foreign stocks with home-country brokers should organize along separate country or currency bloc groupings. Traders can then develop a better working knowledge of each market's special trading characteristics. Currency movements, transaction costs, market information, liquidity, and settlement differ in each market. Each major market requires specific handling and control. Only by specialization can the trading function maximize its contribution to overall performance.

Each trading group then becomes familiar with the specific characteristics of the market. A knowledge of each market and contact with its key players develop. Specific knowledge of each market's currency volatility and of the factors that materially influence that volatility are examined, learned, and factored into the equity trading decisions. The need to learn the operating mechanics of a specific market (auction, open-outcry, specialist, computer input–NASDAQ system) requires that the trading function be specialized by country.

This knowledge is also essential for U.S.-based traders trading the ADR or foreign share in the U.S. market because the underlying share's home trading influences trades in the U.S. market. The international equity traders located in the United States primarily trade when the relevant foreign markets are closed. In the case of the United Kingdom, home markets are open for a short part of the U.S. market's trading day. These traders must be aware of how the stocks they follow traded in their local market overnight. Reports of transactions in these markets must fit the parameters of each market's actual performance.

Traders will study the volume and the open, high, low, and closing prices of each stock to determine whether the execution reports (or "nothing-done" reports) are consistent with local market performance. The trader should question a broker/dealer's execution reports if they appear to conflict with the aggregate local market data. These data are supplied by various independent vendors, such as Datastream, Telekurs, Reuters, and Bridge Data. To facilitate this comparison report process, all large overnight orders should be directed to broker/dealers who have a U.S. presence. The trader can then use his working day with his support staff, office files, and equipment nearby to receive and analyze the reports of overnight orders in local markets.

The U.S.-based international equity trader can also conduct net dealer trades and agency broker trades during U.S. market hours. These trades pose no special problems for exchange-listed shares or shares included on the NASDAQ national market system.

Most ADRs and almost all foreign shares, however, are not listed on an exchange or with NASDAQ. These shares are traded net by dealers in the over-the-counter's "pink sheets" market. Prices are based on the most recent closing price in the local market or the latest quote in London's Stock Exchange Automated Quotation (SEAQ) International system. SEAQ International is a screen-based, NASDAQ-like format that allows dealers in London to make screen markets in non-U.K. equities. Traders in New York should be aware of these London dealer prices when they trade during the 9:30 A.M. to 4:00 P.M. period. The U.S.-based trader who wants a "live" execution in a foreign stock should solicit competing bids and offers from several dealers. This competitive solicitation method provides an opportunity to get the best available price since there is no visible live market in these unlisted, non-NASDAQ issues after noon Eastern Standard Time (SEAQ International closes at 3:30 P.M. in London).

TRADING COSTS

An additional function of equity trading management involves educating the traders as to the true cost of a trade. This education includes the visible costs of commissions, stamp duties, and local transaction taxes. Additionally, it includes hidden costs, late settlements charges, stock loans fees, bank credit line costs, withholding taxes (on interest, dividends, and capital gains), custodian and agent bank fees, and communications expenses required to settle the trades. Traders who fail to understand the full impact of these costs will understate the investor's expenses and inventory and overstate expected performance. Traders aware of these special cost factors can control costs and generate a more accurate picture of risk-adjusted returns.

INTERNATIONAL DERIVATIVE SECURITIES

Alternative vehicles are available in each major equity market. In many cases, an equity derivative product or a synthetic substitute provides more liquidity, cheaper transaction costs, and less complex settlement terms. The use of American Depository Receipts (ADRs) is an obvious example whose convenience applies to all the world's major equity markets.

U.S. commercial banks have now issued over 800 separate ADR programs, each attached to non-U.S. equity or equity derivative (e.g., warrants listed on the NYSE to purchase ADRs of Hanson Trust, P.L.C., and British Petroleum, P.L.C.). Many ADR equities are listed on a U.S. exchange or traded on the NASDAQ National Market System (NMS). These securities are traded on a five-business-day settlement basis and are eligible for Depository Trust Company (DTC) clearing. Dividends on ADR securities are paid in dollars. Companies whose shares underline the ADR must supply reports and financial information to the ADR agent banks for ultimate distribution to the U.S. shareholders.

The experienced trader knows the relative expense associated with an ADR trade compared with a trade in the underlying foreign equity. This expense analysis often leads to the choice of an ADR that is not burdened with local market fees and charges. In addition, there is no need for a costly foreign exchange transaction to purchase or sell the foreign equity.

Conversely, certain markets impose an ADR "tax," such as the 1% issuance fee imposed by the United Kingdom. Once created, these ADRs carry a 1% premium price to the value of the underlying stock. When trading these ADRs, the trader must balance easier settlement, more convenient trading hours, and greater liquidity against the premium that must be paid over home market price.

The international equity trader also needs to be aware of other investment vehicles or equity substitutes that are available in the foreign markets. Exchange traded put and call options are available in Sydney, London, and Amsterdam, and these vehicles can often provide a liquid, leveraged entry into these markets. In addition, listed options trade in the U.S. market on some of the more actively traded ADRs (British Petroleum, Glaxo, Sony, Hitachi, Honda, etc.). Several of the most prominent Australian and British stocks are covered by listed put and call options whose liquidity not only permits speedy access to the underlying equity market, but also provides excellent hedging opportunities. Using bull spreads or long positions in listed options on U.K. stocks, for example, provides a legal avenue for avoiding the stamp duty tax that would otherwise be due on the purchase of a U.K. ordinary share.

The trader should be aware of the cash index futures that now exist in many equity markets. Such listed futures products are traded in Toronto, Hong Kong, London, Sydney, and Singapore (for the Nikkei 225 Index in Japan). The skilled trader understands how these futures contracts influence the trading of the underlying stocks. He also understands how to use these derivative products to gain quick, easy access to the underlying equity market and to hedge existing equity positions. The special risks associated with these markets (liquidity, margin requirements, contra-party failure) should be well understood by the trader even if he elects not to trade directly in the futures market. The movements and gyrations of the trading and expiration of futures contracts will influence the cash market of underlying shares.

Finally, the experienced trader will analyze convertible bonds and warrants as suitable equity substitutes. These securities are prevalent in London and Zurich (especially for Japanese issuers) as active secondary market centers for a vast array of Euromarket issues underwritten over the past two decades. By 1988, over 100 major Japanese companies had issued Eurobonds with yen equity warrants. The professional yen equity trader is able to price these warrants to determine if they should be purchased as Japanese equity substitutes. In Tokyo, a similar number of Japanese companies have issued yen convertible bonds, which are actively traded on the Tokyo Exchange. These also provide a highly liquid alternative entry into the yen equity market. The trader needs to weigh the lower commission costs and higher current income from the convertible against the premium over conversion value that must be paid to invest in the bond. The trader also needs to understand the impact of leverage on a warrant investment that will cost premium and forego dividend income in exchange for a greater capital gain on a significant upward movement in the underlying stock. Similar analysis must be applied to the British, German, Hong Kong, and Australian markets, where an active warrant-trading market exists. Again, the alert trader attempts to understand the players and the mechanics of the derivative product markets in order to better understand underlying equity market movements.

TRADING MANAGEMENT RELATIONSHIPS

Trading management must establish a series of formal procedures to integrate the trading, operations, portfolio management, and control functions. This formal structure encourages a daily dialogue among the separate functional areas which reduces trading costs and prevents costly errors. Once a particular company or market is targeted for investment, the portfolio manager should discuss the various avenues with his trading and operations counterparts. This discussion should lead to the determination of the correct vehicle (foreign ordinary share, ADR, option, warrant, convertible security, or future) in the selected company or market. In addition, this discussion will lead to a focus on the true costs of trading in the selected market and to a method of controlling or minimizing those costs. Constant dialogue between trading, operations, and portfolio management is essential if transaction costs are to be controlled and costly errors avoided.

The trading desk must make the portfolio manager aware of the liquidity constraints and transaction cost structure evident in each local market. In Japan and Germany, for example, fixed commission structures must be anticipated. Similarly, local stock exchange fees or stamp duties in Australia, Hong Kong, Japan (sell-side only), or the United Kingdom (buy-side only) must be factored into any rate-of-return analysis involving investment in those markets. The creation and cancellation of ADRs from and back into foreign shares will involve a charge (usually three to five cents per ADR share) that are part of the investment analysis matrix. Currently, a 1% tax on the creation of ADRs based on United Kingdom stock results in those ADRs being priced at a premium to the underlying equity.

Trading management must constantly guard against errors from executed trades that are not confirmed or correctly booked. Because of the significant volatility in the international marketplace (arising from volatile stock prices and currency movements), undetected errors can cause material losses. These errors result from the investor or its contra-party improperly booking a trade so that ultimate settlement is delayed or not completed, causing errors that can lead to lengthy fails and expensive interest claims.

The errors result from mistakes at the trade execution date. These mistakes are caused by such errors as an improper security title, an inaccurate execution price or amount of shares, an incorrect calculation of local taxes and commissions, or the failure by one side of the trade to book the transaction. In many cases, one of the two participants books an incorrect counterparty to his side of the trade (e.g., broker A books the trade for the account of customer X instead of customer Z, the correct client). Depending on how long they go undetected, these errors can lead to the loss of cash or stock dividends or rights issues entitlements. These must then be claimed against the correct party once the mistake is discovered. Late settlements arising from these errors can also lead to loss of interest by failing to promptly obtain the cash proceeds from securities sales. Significant time, money, and effort can be expended by the institutional investor's operations staff to correct any errors and book trades properly. Only then can claims for lost interest be made against the contra-party or the custodian bank responsible for the settlement delay.

Formal procedures for trading management will prevent potential problems from arising. Portfolio managers must be sure to identify correctly the exact corporate title of an equity security. The traders can then develop formal procedures that identify whether the security is a bearer or registered share, a participation certificate, an ADR, or a foreign ordinary share. In many cases, European companies issue stock under different titles and often issue stock of subsidiaries whose corporate name is similar to that of the parent or another affiliate. Correctly identifying the security at Trade Date avoids costly errors. Buying or selling the wrong security results in a long and short position in two different stocks. Two costly transactions are then required to restore the portfolio to its correct position. These costs are then charged against the portfolio's performance.

A trading function fully integrated with operations and cash control minimizes settlement difficulties. When an order is given to the trading desk, the trader must determine that enough currency is available to buy the requested stock. If a stock is to be sold, the operations unit must be instructed about what to do with the incoming currency. Loans or credit lines may be paid down or expanded. Foreign currency must be made available for purchases when the trading desk is instructed to obtain a dollar denominated execution from the transacting broker. The trading function should also provide automated average pricing (in dollars or foreign currency) and account allocation procedures. The modern trading desk gives its traders a printout of the previous 24 hours' trading activity so that the traders can confirm the details (security title, price, number of shares, contra-party) of each trade. Discovering errors quickly prevents large losses from market and currency movements that increase over time. The trading system should also be able to recall and display all trades over the most recent 30 or 60 trading days to correct quickly any errors that are discovered. These presentations must display currency trades as well as security trades in order to provide an accurate picture of the investor's inventory and position risk.

COST CONTROL

The costs of inadequate systems and procedures for control and coordination are obvious. Poor communications among the trading, operations, and portfolio management functions will lead to a loss of inventory control and account risk management. If costs of delayed settlement, interest claims, and foregone dividends are ignored, then estimated performance will be overstated. Overlooking these costs leads to inaccurate reporting of performance to senior management. Clients will be in for a rude awakening when the understatement of true costs is eventually discovered and the rate of return performance is adjusted downward. Similarly, the failure to monitor accurately ADR exchanges and stock loan requirements can lead to material charges for fails-to-deliver and buy-ins, especially in the tight settlement markets of Japan, Hong Kong, and Singapore.

Unreported or inaccurately booked trades will often lead to significant losses as the stock price and foreign currency change sharply away from their values on the trade date. These errors will eventually be discovered and their losses or costs charged against portfolio performance. In some cases, these costs can be attributed to errors by the executing broker or to the investor's custodian or agent bank. Even if the costs are paid by these outside parties, there will be a cost for the management time spent discovering the error and then negotiating to rectify the inaccuracies. It is clearly preferable to establish procedures that prevent errors from arising and that discover them as quickly as possible after the trade to keep costs to a minimum.

CONTRA-PARTY CREDIT RISK

International equity-trading management must be actively involved in the analysis of contra-party credit risk of both currency trading and securities-derivative trading. The investing institution must rely on its custodian and commercial bank relationships to guide it through the risky path of foreign currency trading. The investor should rely on these banks for definitive advice as to the creditworthiness of dealers in foreign exchange. In addition, the investor should avail itself of the foreign currency trading capabilities of its agent and lending banks for execution and comparative pricing.

The system for executing, booking, and clearing currency transactions needs to be as sophisticated and sensitive to detail as the security-trading system. Traders should coordinate all currency transactions in the same way that equity products are processed and settled. The trading system should display a trade history of currency trades to ease the correction process when errors are discovered. The system should mark inventory positions to market on a real-time basis as the relevant currencies move relative to one another.

Good trading management limits the number of contra-parties involved in foreign exchange transactions. Only the strongest and most experienced, creditworthy institutions should be used when dealing in such a dynamic, volatile market. It is easy to become distracted from the central purpose of trading equities when the risks of foreign currency trading start to weigh on the traders' minds. Foreign exchange transactions should be executed only to support the desired equity transactions. Traders should attempt to "even out the book" each trading day. Foreign currencies are made available "just in time" to purchase securities and sales proceeds, dividends, rights, and so on are converted back into the base currency immediately upon receipt. The investor must conduct a thorough analysis of the credit risk before the traders are permitted to conduct foreign exchange transactions with a new outside party. Trading management can rely on its settlements department for feedback as to which contra-parties are confirming trades accurately and settling transactions correctly and on time. Persistent offenders must be removed from the list of acceptable contra-parties with whom the investor will trade foreign exchange. Fails-to-receive or deliver foreign exchange lead directly to costly and disrupting fails of securities transactions.

Trading management must also analyze counterparty credit risk when selecting broker/dealers for securities trading. The investor often pays for research and investment ideas as well as execution. The benefits of one service must be carefully weighed against the drawbacks of another. From the credit risk viewpoint, large, diversified, global banks and securities firms (or broker/dealers affiliated with or guaranteed by large commercial banks) are the wisest choice. Investors who use local brokers for their insight into a distant equity market need to analyze the credit risk involved. Limits on the maximum amount of outstanding trades or credit balances need to be established. Obviously, the investor should rely on its custodian or agent banks for advice as to the creditworthiness of particular local broker dealers. The investor must insist on DAC-RAP ("delivery versus cash and receive against payment") procedures for settling equity transactions. Custodian banks should implement and enforce these settlement procedures.

Trading management should be wary of "free delivery" risks when selling a foreign equity product in exchange for U.S. dollars. That settlement requires giving up the stock to the buyer's custodian in the local market with payment afterwards (usually on the next business day) into the investor's dollar account at a U.S. bank. Foreign broker dealers that insist on free delivery settlement should not be used by the investor to *sell* foreign shares for payment in U.S. dollars. This procedure involves possible loss of control over the securities prior to being paid. Such broker/dealers can be used to buy foreign shares with U.S. dollars: The investor pays out dollars only after his foreign-based custodian bank notifies him that the desired shares have been cleanly received.

Constant communication between the settlement and trading departments is essential to the process of monitoring contra-party credit risk. The trading managers must be advised at least weekly as to the status of open, unsettled equity trades. Open items are broken down into open receives and open deliveries and grouped by country; by currency; and, most important, by broker/dealer. A thorough analysis will highlight areas or markets or brokers that represent the greatest potential credit risk. Habitual fails or late settlements by any one broker would be the impetus to cut off order flow or commission payments to that broker. The costs of settlement delays often outweigh the benefits of a good research idea or an excellent execution.

Consider the sale of an Australian stock for $12(A) that has not settled several days (or weeks) past settlement date. If the stock drops to $8(A), the investor faces a loss of at least $4(A) per share if the trade were to remain unsettled. The traders need this information on a regular basis so they can pressure the contra-party broker to settle open trades. Trading management should not hesitate to eliminate future dealings with broker/dealers who consistently fail to settle trades on a timely basis.

An additional element of counterparty credit risk relates to the financial size and strength of the broker/dealer. Each broker/dealer must be analyzed independently on the basis of its own financial structure. Affiliates whose transactions are guaranteed or linked to larger, financially stronger entities offer a much more positive credit risk profile than that offered by a smaller, independent firm. Independent dealers located in distant markets represent substantially greater credit risk, and transactions with such firms should be scrutinized carefully. Outstanding transaction balances must be held subject to strict credit limits.

The goal of efficient trading management is to shorten the time between the actual trade execution and the discovery of an error so that corrective action can be taken with the least amount of elapsed time. Shortening this time period between execution and discovery is the best way to keep the economic damage from errors and trade disputes to a minimum.

COMPLIANCE AND REGULATORY ISSUES

The trading desk must be aware of the regulatory implications of any upcoming financings or rights offerings by foreign issuers whose securities are already held in the portfolio. If these issuers do not intend to register the newly issued securities with the Securities and Exchange Commission (SEC), then U.S. investors cannot purchase the new securities for 120 days. This "seasoning" or waiting period is required before the U.S. investor can trade or purchase the new securities. A rights offering not registered in the United States can create additional problems. Absent an SEC no-action letter, a U.S. investor must sell his rights and cannot purchase the new shares through exercise of the rights if the offering is not SEC-registered. It is the trader's task to ensure that the legal advisors and portfolio managers are made aware of any financings or rights offerings that raise the question of seasoning and SEC registration.

A thorough knowledge of foreign market costs and regulations allows traders to check execution costs charged by the transacting broker/dealers. Confirmations and local billings should be checked to prevent the charging of unnecessary costs to the investor. Net trade executions are examined for accurate local market commissions, taxes, and stamp duty fees. The traders also understand how local market costs affect transaction costs of trades done away from the local market (e.g., Australian stamp duty fees on trades executed in Frankfurt, London, New York, or Tokyo).

The international equity trader must be able to help the settlements and processing departments chase down dividends, stock rights, and accrued interest on portfolio securities. The ex-dividend date for an ADR is often not the same date used in the local market. Significant cash flows must be monitored and claimed whenever a cash dividend, right, option, or stock dividend is declared on the foreign share. If such a distribution occurs during the time that an investing institution has put an ADR or foreign share in for exchange or cancellation, then special care must be taken to ensure that valuable rights or cash dividends are not forfeited. The traders can also help the processing department to understand the impact of the local withholding taxes on any interest or dividend payments arising from ownership of the foreign share. In general, it is the responsibility of the trading desk to monitor unusual transactions that may be covered by U.S. or state securities laws. These regulatory schemes directly influence the U.S. investor market for non-U.S. equities. Traders who have a thorough understanding of regulatory influences can contribute maximum value to the investing institution.

SUMMARY

The international equity-trading function is based on communication and coordination with the investing institution's research, portfolio management, systems, settlements, and compliance departments. The well-positioned equity trader is the investor's eyes and ears on the foreign markets, acting to communicate immediately the pulse of those markets. The trading desk quickly funnels news and information from distant overseas markets to portfolio managers, research analysts, and settlements experts to encourage prompt reaction to important events. Currency expertise and execution capability occupy a crucial role in the international equity arena, thus raising the sophistication level of the trading desk beyond that required domestically. Settlement difficulties and foreign broker/dealer credit risk analysis also add to pressures on the non-U.S. equity-trading desk. Trading management should be sensitive to these demands and to the complex needs of the investing institution as it expands to encompass the obvious opportunities offered by international equity markets.

The Editor Asks

Q *It seems that the desire for international trading has outstripped the capacity of the existing structure. I am reminded of the byzantine procedures used in the United States before the DTC froze the movement of the certificate. What factors will have to be brought forth to standardize and simplify international trading and clearing?*

A In order to improve the settlement procedure for international equity trading, the participants (investors, broker/dealers, money managers, etc.) must continue to pressure the authorities in the less mature markets to develop book entry, paperless systems. These systems can work very efficiently, as epitomized by DTC in the United States and the Tokyo Stock Exchange and its affiliates in Japan. Several important markets (London, Sydney, Hong Kong, Paris) remain too dependent on physical movement and outside-party registration to ensure the rapid, efficient settlement offered by a DTC facility. Only continuing pressure from investors, dealers, and institutional managers on the local stock exchanges, commercial banks, and registration facilities will bring about the necessary changes.

Concomitant with changes inside the clearing systems of the overly traditional markets is the development of a supranational institution that will assume the role of central clearing agent. This clearing agent should be structured along the lines of Euroclear and Cedel (Central de Livraison de Valeurs Mobiliers, or Securities Clearing Center), whose success in the settlement of Eurobond trades is an excellent example of how a central facility can tie together several separate markets. Euroclear and Cedel have also achieved marked success in clearing yen equity warrant trades, thereby demonstrating that the concept of a central clearing mechanism can be adapted to the equity market settlement process.

PART SIX

Future Directions in Trading

21

ELECTRONIC EQUITY TRADING: A NECESSITY FOR EFFICIENT MARKETS

William A. Lupien

A decade ago, securities trading via electronic networks and worldwide communications links was still a futuristic vision. Today, it is a reality. The technology is here; it will be a competitive advantage for those who are ready to make use of it, a disadvantage for those who are not.

For those of us who seek that competitive edge, how do we survive in this electronic market environment? First, we must understand what market factors underlie the development of this technology, and identify the kinds of systems created in response to these factors. Only then can we see the shape of today's marketplace, and plan a competitive strategy.

MARKET FACTORS

Several key forces have demanded innovation and adaptation of computer technology in the securities industry worldwide:

- Increased competitiveness in a deregulated environment.
- Changes in market participation, nationally and internationally.
- Dramatic increases in trading volume.
- An increasingly global marketplace.

COMPETITIVENESS. Elimination of fixed commission rates in the United States in 1975 changed a market practice that had existed since the Buttonwood Agreement of 1792. In 1975, commissions were half of the industry's total revenues. By 1986, they were less than one-quarter of the industry's total revenues. Thus, brokerage firms are forced to increase their efficiency and to earn more from principal trading. Automation is the key to such a strategy. This new environment requires greater commitments of capital to support multimillion-dollar trading and back-office systems, and to cover the risks of increased trading exposure.

MARKET PARTICIPATION.   Institutional investors now dominate many world markets, replacing the individual investors' once prominent position. Typically in the United States, institutions buy and sell larger numbers of shares, most often in blocks of 10,000 shares or more. Brokers match much of this business and then send it to the exchange floors to be crossed. Today, more than half of the New York Stock Exchange's volume is in large blocks.

With more and more money under management, institutional investors are searching for ways to diversify their portfolios. Almost one-third of all U.S. investment pension plans now invest some of their funds abroad. In 1986, U.S. pension funds had $45.2 billion invested in international securities.

Dealings in foreign stocks by U.S. investors in the first quarter of 1987 set a record of nearly $40 billion. Foreign dealing in U.S. stocks totaled $113 billion in the first quarter. One expert at Citicorp Investment Bank estimates that about 16% of stock exchange volume worldwide involves counterparties from different countries.

TRADING VOLUME.   The size of today's trading volume demands automated efficiencies in providing the stream of market information necessary in executing and settling trades. Average daily volume on the New York Stock Exchange in 1975 was fewer than 18 million shares. A decade later, average daily volume was 140 million shares. Automation in the securities industry has moved from simply replacing paper processing to computer-driven searches for investment opportunities.

In 1986, U.S. corporations placed more than $1.6 billion of equities with international investors, 20 times the 1985 total. This trend continued in 1987, pushing total overseas equity offerings by U.S. corporations to over $2 billion. In pursuit of international funds, U.S. corporations are listing on multiple exchanges. Chase Manhattan Bank, for example, trades on exchanges in New York, Dusseldorf, Frankfurt, Paris, London, and Tokyo.

Similarly, international companies—and international investors—are coming to the U.S. market. In 1983, Bell Canada became the first North

American company to offer a simultaneous equity issue in Toronto, in New York, and across Europe. British Telecom did the same in 1984 with a syndicated offering in New York, Tokyo, Toronto, and London.

GLOBAL MARKET. The modern trading environment offers multiple markets for a particular stock. Real-time market information is available from a dizzying array of sources and in endless formats and delivery vehicles. Electronic links between exchanges and market participants not only feed market information, but also route orders and execute trades.

Reuters, just one source of market information, collects market data from more than 115 exchanges and over-the-counter markets in over 70 countries. It provides real-time quotations on more than 55,000 stocks, bonds, and options, and distributes market and business information to more than 135,000 video terminals, teleprinters, and mainframe computers.

AUTOMATED SYSTEMS

In this myriad of new market elements, three aspects remain fundamental to securities trading. When we trade, we want (1) the best price for the stock, (2) the most effective execution, and (3) assurance of reliable settlement. How do the various types of automated systems help us achieve these goals?

QUOTATION SYSTEMS. Getting the best price depends first on having current market information. More than a century ago, Baron Reuter stopped using carrier pigeons to carry stock quotes between England and the continent. Instead, he pioneered the use of the telegraph. Although communications hardware is more sophisticated than in 1851, the goal remains the same: to provide information on stock prices and stock activity as rapidly as possible.

Thus, the earliest and now most pervasive automated systems are quotation systems. Reuters, Quotron, Telerate, NASDAQ, TOPIC, ADP, Telekurs, Quick, and other quotation services send us the latest market information. One reason for the tremendous growth in the over-the-counter (OTC) market in the United States has been the development of NASDAQ, the National Association of Security Dealers Automated Quotations system. NASDAQ has given OTC dealers a more efficient pricing mechanism. Dealers have the stock information they need to trade—and trade they have. NASDAQ volume has grown from 1.7 billion shares in 1976 to 28.7 billion 10 years later.

ORDER-ROUTING SYSTEMS.   Still, the market quote is only one of many steps in the trading process. With market information spurring market activity, processing of the growing volume needed a further technological innovation and response. A variety of order-routing systems increase the efficiency of trading activity. On the New York Stock Exchange, first Designated Order Turnaround (DOT) and now SuperDOT speeds the processing of an estimated 70% of orders and 30% of volume. SCOREX, on the Pacific Stock Exchange, is another example of an order-routing system used to route the flow of orders to specialists' posts.

Most order-routing systems, however, only channel the flow of orders to the market-maker. They replicate the order slip. Keystrokes and touch-screens replace the pencil and the time stamp. Order-routing systems lack the technological sophistication to handle the two-way flow of quotations and orders. Negotiation cannot occur.

AUCTION-ORIENTED SYSTEMS.   A more advanced system is Toronto's Computer Assisted Trading System, better known as CATS. In 1985, Toronto became the first exchange to initiate a two-way trading link with an exchange in another country—the American Stock Exchange. Two-thirds of the foreign firms listed on the AMEX are Canadian, so the electronic link was a logical one. Links with the Midwest Exchange have also been established, making it possible to receive quotes and send orders directly to a post at the Toronto Stock Exchange, or to the small-order execution system. CATS is an auction-oriented trading system, which directs order flow into the exchange community.

DEALER-ORIENTED SYSTEMS.   Whereas the auction market drives stock activity through a single or limited number of suppliers creating the necessary liquidity for the inventor. The heart of a dealer market, by contrast, is the multiplicity of market-makers. Thus, dealer-oriented quotation systems, such as the International Stock Exchange's SEAQ or the NASD's NASDAQ, serve as an information link among the various market-makers. The core of this type of market is the trader on the telephone.

The dealer market carries stock activity to any number of participants. In the case of NASDAQ, the stocks are over-the-counter, and a number of dealers may make a market in the stock. An automated system designed for this type of market must gather information from a wide number of sources, and then compile and redistribute it.

Most orders on OTC stocks, however, must be executed through nonautomated channels. Although quotes are broadcast on NASDAQ, most orders are still placed by telephone. Only orders up to 1,000 shares are executed through its Small Order Execution System (SOES). The International Stock Exchange's SEAQ system functions as an automated quotation system much like NASDAQ, with multiple market-makers.

ISE operates SEAQ for international as well as U.K. equities. According to ISE's own update, much of the trading in foreign equities is institutional, based on the size of trades in foreign equities. At ISE, as in other markets, international trading occurs in approximately 2,000 of the global equities that make up over 70% of market capitalization. Automated trading systems will no doubt have to change to reflect this new interest and activity in international equity trading.

Like London, Zurich is also looking to the international marketplace. SOFFEX, the Swiss Options and Financial Futures Exchange, will debut in early 1988 for Swiss exchange members. Throughout Switzerland, member firms will place their orders and quotes for options and futures directly to SOFFEX.

GLOBAL SYSTEMS. A truly global trading network will have to provide not only the dual flow of information and order routing worldwide, but also the capability to emulate a trading crowd. It must permit full negotiation between parties to occur easily. The heart of trading is the interaction between market-makers and market participants. It is an exchange of information that is more than a flow of quotes and a return of orders. A trader must be able to express an interest in a stock, and then encourage the other side to trade at his price and to give him the size he wants. The next level of trading systems, then, is one that not only delivers information and orders, but allows for negotiation as well. Instinet is such a system.

Unlike those automated trading systems that are specific to a particular marketplace or market-maker, or limited by the type or size of an order, Instinet links both buy-side and sell-side traders to a variety of markets and market-makers. It extends automated capabilities—combining delivery of market information and execution with an interactive capability to negotiate—and extends market access to the whole world.

Through Instinet, equity traders can monitor market activity in more than 8,000 U.S. equity securities. They receive last-sale and quote information from the major U.S. stock exchanges and the over-the-counter market. With this information, traders can make decisions about the size and price of the order they want to execute. Then they enter orders or respond to an order that has already been entered for that stock. The contra-parties can negotiate the size and price of a transaction by sending electronic messages. Because of the speed of the network, transactions can occur in seconds.

Trading through an electronic market access network like Instinet enables all players to see and evaluate quotes by market-makers and specialists and to seek the best price. Instinet provides real-time market access on a global basis. Instinet is already linking international traders 14 hours daily, from 8:00 A.M. London time to 5:00 P.M. New York time.

Having developed in the United States, Instinet was a U.S.-dollar-based system primarily linked to the U.S. markets until 1988. Instinet links subscribers to these markets from anywhere a terminal can be installed— virtually anywhere in the world. Equities from other markets are being added to the system, beginning with U.K. equities. This is the beginning of a truly global trading network.

SHAPE OF THE MARKETPLACE

Increasingly, the modern context is a global dealer market, the "crowd" is no longer only in front of the specialist's post, and the "open outcry" of the auction market has become an electronic display of competitive bids and offers from around the world. This increases the number of players in the market-making function.

As this global trading environment evolves, stock exchanges continue to play a major role, making continuous markets and expressing the prices at which securities can be traded. They compete to provide the best trading forum. Order flow will go to the markets with the best prices, the fewest restrictions on participation, and the most reliable methods for clearing and settlement. The markets that offer true liquidity and fair market access will compete successfully. Doing this on a global basis requires electronic trading systems.

Critics of automated systems or electronic trading contend that such systems cannot supplant existing exchanges. Critics, though perfectly correct in this regard, mistake the technology for the market process. Such computer-based systems do not replace the established markets but increase the efficiency with which these markets operate. The market-making function hinges not on any particular processing technology but on the market-maker's ability to manage an inventory of stock to meet market demands.

MARKET ACCESS.   Egress and ingress should be the foremost consideration for the competitive global marketplace. Sufficient order flow can replace some of the need for capital reserves—reserves stretched nearly to the breaking point in October 1987. Most market-makers in the United

States simply do not have the capital available to stop an onslaught the size and scale of October's crash. Specialist firms are fighting their market battles with BB guns when what they need is laser technology.

Over the past 10 years the size of the game has increased, but the capital base of market-makers has not kept pace. Total purchasing power of specialists' firms is estimated to be between $2 and $3 billion for a U.S. market valued between $2 and $3 trillion. The system has worked in the past because the exchanges have maintained the illusion of liquidity. Because exchanges announce they provide liquidity—defined as the ability to deal with minimal price movements—enough orders are sent to the exchange specialist to create liquidity. The specialist can rely on the order flow rather than his own capital to support trading activity and thus can continue the illusion of liquidity.

Today, investors are paying the price for the structural weakness of the market. In an era of microchips, "smart cards," and international data networks, trading mechanisms interrupted by manual paper processing on the exchange floor are hopelessly out of date. In most marketplaces, however, available technology has not been integrated well enough with the market-making process. Traders cannot act on market information as efficiently as they receive it. Computerized systems broadcast market information in seconds, but few trade execution systems can match that speed, because few are fully automated. There is a high-tech outflow of general market information, but a low-tech ingress and egress for traders and investors not located on the exchange floor.

To use DOT as an example, a trader hands an order slip to a clerk, who inputs the order to a device similar to a teletype. The order is routed electronically to a printer behind the specialist's post, where another clerk rips off the order and delivers it to the specialist, who may then fill the order. The process can take minutes—not seconds—to complete, and several more minutes to confirm. In the valuable time that is lost, the market may move significantly. Investors pay for this market inefficiency in higher transaction costs and lost trading opportunities.

Using DOT or similar order-routing systems also eliminates any chance to negotiate with the contra-party to the trade. The specialist receiving the order via DOT may act not only as agent, but also as principal. The best interests of the customer may conflict with the specialist's own interests in the trade; it is a difficult position always to manage fairly.

TRADING ALTERNATIVES.   Innovative institutional investors are developing electronic links that broaden their access to market-makers and trading opportunities. For example, the California Public Employees' Retirement

System (CALPERS) is among several institutional investors interested in direct electronic links to other buyers/sellers. CALPERS goes far beyond a simple broadcast of order interest; it is an integrated system that includes record keeper, reporting, performance, trade and order control, equity and fixed-income research, real-time price feed, execution cost measurement, and electronic settlement.

The pressure on the institutional investor to lower his cost of execution, and especially the price of finding adequate liquidity, has led to the development of a number of alternatives to traditional order execution. Systems like Instinet's Crossing Network or Jefferies' POSIT match orders of buyers and sellers with little or no market impact. Fund managers, such as Trinity Investment Management Corporation, have reported significant savings from lower commissions and reduced market impact when they use the matching systems.[1]

Batterymarch Financial Management is also among the most technologically innovative fund managers. This fund's computer-driven stock selections are constantly updated during the trading day. As certain stocks are bought or sold, the portfolio is reevaluated. Market data are constantly scanned for opportunities to add to or delete from the quantitative fund. Batterymarch advertises a number of orders at any one time, searching for the best buys. Not all will be executed. The strategy is to beat the average market performance.

TRADING STRATEGIES. Yet, all of the electronic systems providing information to investors fall short. All are still relatively shallow systems that spit out information or feed it in—stock by stock, sale by sale. This sequential information flow does not meet the needs of today's marketplace.

An investor rarely thinks in terms of a single stock. Most—whether individual or institutional holders—have a portfolio of stocks and other financial instruments. Yet, the systems allow only sequential, event-driven access to the market, not the dynamic systems required for portfolio management.

Thus, the pipeline in and out of the market is narrow and easily clogged. Trading techniques that depend on execution of a basket of stocks or financial instruments, such as program trading or the hedging technique of portfolio insurance, are too easily derailed by heavy market demand. The flood of orders on October 19, 1987, nearly burst the plumbing of the entire marketplace.

---

[1] William Fallon, "Beyond the Fourth Market," *Intermarket*, September 1987, p. 45. See also Chapter 19, "Electronic Trading: The Batterymarch Experience," by Evan Shulman.

To funnel true liquidity into the system, more players need to be able to get to the playing field more quickly. Institutional investors dominate the market but are restricted in their access to the U.S. marketplace. Market regulations bar them from making markets or from direct access to the specialists on the exchange floor.

Engaging institutions more actively in the marketplace brings a tremendous reservoir of liquidity to the market system. Trading halts, special capital reserves, and other responses to market illiquidity will not work. These approaches do not supply liquidity but merely attempt to keep an illiquid system working.

COMPETITIVE STRATEGIES

Exchanges can no longer control the game by enforcing a cartel of member firms. Trading continues to move away from the exchange floor through upstairs trading of institutional orders and trading with nonmember, third-market firms. The cartel members evade the rules of the cartel, eroding its control of the market. The competitive threat, however, comes not only from off-floor trading but from more efficient international markets as well.

London, Tokyo, Toronto, and Zurich are among the world's major financial centers that have developed the electronic trading systems described earlier. Each is vying for international business, seeking to be the dominant player in the growing international equities market. Their success will be determined by their ability to bring the necessary liquidity to the international market.

INTERNATIONAL SETTLEMENT.   How effective will the international marketplace be? The answer is, as effective as the ability of global investors to obtain delivery of their equities. Although transactions can be completed in seconds, the settlement process can take days, weeks, or even months, depending on local market regulations and capabilities. Whether as delivery of the actual security or via a book entry, there is as yet no single international clearing and settlement system.

Signs of progress, however, are abundant. CDS, the clearinghouse for the Toronto and Montreal exchanges, is linked with the National Securities Clearing Corporation (NSCC) in New York. Japan Securities Clearing Corporation has established relations with the French Depository and Clearing Agency and is also linked to NAME in Holland. London's Talisman system is being linked to the United States through International Securities Clearing Corporation (ISCC), which in turn will be linked to the

NSCC. Automated trading systems can assist this process of global clearing by providing locked-in trade reports without the hindrance of human error or language differences.

Despite the disruption and near collapse of the securities markets in October 1987, the trend toward global equity trading is likely to continue. Competition among major financial centers for this international business will increase, based on liquidity, efficient pricing mechanisms, and the reliability of trade and settlement practices.

INTERNATIONAL REGULATION. Competitive market pressures will force both regulators and practitioners to resolve issues of market access and control, and to set acceptable international standards for trade and settlement practices. Many of today's rules and regulations governing securities transactions, both in the United States and abroad, were designed for yesterday's marketplace. They will no longer serve as they once did.

The United Kingdom, for example, has a two-week account period for trade settlement, making it possible to trade stock for a profit without committing any capital, without breaking any laws. If a stock is bought early in the two-week account period and the same position is closed later in the same period for a profit, no cash is required to cover the trades.

Without a margin requirement, this is a trading environment very much like the U.S. securities markets of the 1920s. The result then was a market almost out of control, which ended with the crash of 1929. Regulations in the 1930s restructured the market. Federal Reserve regulations T and U established margin requirements. Tightening of these requirements reduces speculation and the volatility of the market. Clearly, they are a mechanism for controlling risk.

Margin requirements, trading limits, even market participation and settlement practices all vary country by country, market by market. Yet arbitrageurs look for the same discrepancies, and thereby the same types of trading opportunities, among international markets as they do between stocks and futures. Prudence would call for better methods of managing the risks and ensuring a fair game internationally, as well as domestically.

SUMMARY

Our capital markets depend on investor confidence. The market crash in October 1987 upset that confidence and challenged our basic assumptions about market access and market controls. Clearly, the scope of the securities industry has changed more rapidly than our ability to respond effectively.

We can no longer afford yesterday's antiquated trading methods for today's global marketplace, nor can we ignore the serious economic threat of an international market without appropriate standards and controls. We must face the challenges of this market environment or risk repetition of the market meltdown of October 1987.

Only international communications networks, on-line trading, and automated clearing processes can really serve this global marketplace efficiently. Electronic systems give us the machinery to trade, to settle, and to monitor global financial markets—to make the markets more efficient.

Our effective use of electronic trading systems will depend on the willingness of market professionals to accept the challenges of a global marketplace. We must recognize that this is no longer a competitive choice but a strategic imperative for the economic efficiency of our financial markets.

The Editor Asks

Q *One of the most firmly held beliefs on the floor of the New York Stock Exchange is the need for eyeball-to-eyeball contact among a restricted membership. What is implied by this belief, and do you think that this is a flaw of electronic trading mechanisms?*

A No doubt those on the floor of major stock exchanges have a vested interest in preserving the rules by which they play. They have managed to operate profitably by controlling market information and market access. They function as a cartel, limiting membership to protect their advantage.

The securities market has changed too much in the past 10 years for the market system to continue with the same structure, limited by the same rules and regulations. The New York Stock Exchange has seen its dominant position erode. Members of stock exchanges can no longer afford to resist the adaptation of electronic trading systems that expand the trading arena beyond the stock exchange floor.

Without significant changes in the mechanisms that are used for trading, the financial markets risk a repeat of the free fall of the market in October 1987. The evidence points clearly to systems that were overpowered with sell orders, telephones that weren't answered, resources that were stretched nearly to the breaking point.

Stock exchanges need a technological overhaul. A state-of-the-art system would provide true trading capability and true market access, and would funnel true liquidity into the market. Most exchanges have yet to develop and install such a system. Once they do, the world will be their trading arena; they will have an electronic crowd. They will make their markets accessible worldwide.

22

THE SINGLE-PRICE AUCTION

Steven Wunsch

Although our market-making systems are nearly as strong as they can be, relying solely on market-making for the provision of liquidity is unnecessary and, as October 19, 1987, proved, dangerous. Direct competition between buyers and sellers is the only reliable means of maintaining stability at efficient clearing prices. Single-price auctions are the best means of restoring that competition. An electronic single-price auction system like the one described here, which is being developed by Intex, could easily be integrated into our current market-making structure.

Studies of past market breaks, which analyzed days like September 11–12, 1986, or January 23, 1987, usually concluded that the movements were fundamental adjustments to new information. Even the speed of the adjustments, which may have been aided by program trading, could be thought of as a sign of efficiency.

If we extend that line of reasoning to October 19, we must conclude that we now have really efficient markets. Today's markets are so sensitive to new information that they can drop 23% on October 19 (18 standard deviations), and no one can even agree on what the bad news was. This was followed by a 17% jump by 10:00 A.M. the next morning—responding, we must guess, to good news, again unidentified. The market then "efficiently adjusted" to another wave of bad news by falling 25% in the next two hours (a 40 standard deviation event).

If that was efficiency, then the most impressive display of efficiency we have seen in this country must have been the subsequent 32% rise in the Major Market Index (MMI) contract in 32 minutes (a 101 standard deviation event), once again caused by phenomenal, but unidentified, good news.

Summarized from a talk given at the Investment Management Institute's Conference on Market Liquidity—Strategies for the Next Decade, New York, February 8, 1988.

Those who keep an eye on competition from more efficient markets abroad may be awed at the efficiency of the Simex, where the Nikkei 225 contract declined 80% in one hour, only to rise 364% by the end of the day (179 and 308 standard deviation events, respectively).

The point is obvious: Those could not possibly have been efficient prices or efficiently operating markets. To the contrary, I believe they resulted from a lack of competition in our markets that led to an inability to find efficient prices.

Although our market-making systems are efficient and competitive, relying completely on market-making for liquidity is neither efficient nor safe, no matter how good they are. Markets don't always have to be made; they exist naturally unless something is done to inhibit their formation. Unfortunately, the direct competition between buyers and sellers that produces natural markets is inhibited now by a structure that grants market-makers a virtual monopoly on the provision of liquidity. That's why we went several scary days in October without being able to find a clearing price. I'll conclude by describing a market clearing facility called a single-price auction. This procedure could easily be integrated into our current market-making systems without requiring significant changes.

Let me first explain why I believe our current market-making systems are nearly as good as they can be. What keeps market-making costs low and spreads narrow is competition among market-makers. All of our market-making systems are very competitive and well capitalized. There is a great deal of market-making competition in stocks between well-capitalized upstairs broker/dealers competing against each other in over-the-counter stocks. For listed stocks, they compete against each other and against the specialists on the floors. Although all market-making competition in futures is on the floor, there are no barriers to entering that competition.

If our marketing systems are so good, why did they melt down on October 19? Meltdown is inevitable if you get enough positive feedback—reactive strategies like portfolio insurance—demanding immediate liquidity from a system that relies solely on market-makers. Once you've blown through the book of public orders that defines the rough parameters within which a current clearing price can be found, market-makers are at sea, with no effective means to find a clearing price. The lower they bid, the more there is for sale; the more there is for sale, the lower they bid, and so on. Given the lack of direct competition between buyers and sellers, we should not be surprised that the market-making systems can run amok, frantically seeking a clearing price with multihundred point swings.

Unfortunately, we are asking market-makers to do two things they can't do, one of which would not be beneficial, even if they could:

1. Market-makers cannot by themselves find a clearing price.
2. They cannot stabilize the market at some other price, no matter how competitive or well capitalized they are.

Restoring direct competition between buyers and sellers requires first recognizing that market-makers have a monopoly on the provision of liquidity in today's markets. The monopoly is enforced by rules and practices giving market-makers first shot at all order flow information. Good examples of monopoly practices would be (1) futures market rules barring upstairs discussion of trades and (2) stock market rules keeping the public from seeing the specialist's book.

The best means of leveling the playing field with respect to order flow information is to clear the market periodically with an electronic single-price auction, which promotes direct competition between buyers and sellers. Everyone will get the same view of the order flow and the same opportunity to be part of the price that they and everyone else will get.

Imagine what the opening of the New York Stock Exchange would be like if the specialist's view of the opening order flow were made public. A good step in that direction has already been taken at futures expirations, which has successfully reduced expiration volatility.

Interestingly, the Brady report recommended further consideration of opening the specialist's book as a means of attracting other sides to order imbalances. The report also cited the public exposure of order imbalances as one of the main purposes of circuit breakers. Since the report's release, most of the discussion of circuit breakers has focused on what criteria to use to shut the markets. The much more important issue is what needs to be done to allow them to reopen again at a fair price. They were closed, after all, from Friday's close to Monday, October 19th's open, and from Monday's close to Tuesday's open, with no visible benefit in terms of finding a fair reopening clearing price.

Obviously, the existing facilities are inadequate both at making imbalances visible and at auctioning them off. I believe that the single-price auction can accomplish both goals so well that shutdowns will probably never occur. Even if the market did run through price limits in response to a sudden change in the fundamentals, the single-price auction would be the best way to reopen quickly at a fair price.

SINGLE-PRICE AUCTION

In the future, markets might hold simultaneous single-price auctions every eight hours. For some lucky time zone, this would coincide with the open, the close, and midnight. It's my guess that over half of the total demand for liquidity could be met without market-makers in those three seconds per day that single-price auctions would allow the market to clear. The other 86,397 seconds would not be much different than they are now, with demands for liquidity between clearings being met by market-makers taking risk and earning a spread.

Here's how it would work: Again, it is helpful to note the similarities to how opening prices are set now at the NYSE. Members will place orders for opening price settlement either for themselves or for their customers on terminals. Orders will be sent to a central computer, which adds up all the orders placed and sends the aggregate picture back to the members' terminals and to the general public.

This aggregate picture shows both limit orders in the specialist's book and the direction and size of the imbalance of market orders. Currently, the limit order book is never made public and the imbalance of market orders is made public only at futures expiration. It should not be difficult to send this information back out to exchange members electronically, so that they could see what the specialist sees.

It is a little difficult to read the current output seen by the specialist, so I have worked out a more readily understandable means of display. What is shown here pictorially would be broadcast on a colored computer screen in a live system.

Figure 22.1 shows that the first order to arrive is a market buy order of 5,000 shares. (It could be several market buy orders adding up to 5,000 shares.) This order is represented by the column on the left side of the figure.

FIGURE 22.1

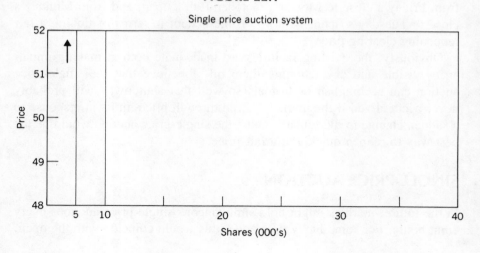

Single price auction system

Price is measured on the vertical axis, size on the horizontal. The *upward*-pointing arrow at the top indicates a willingness to pay whatever it takes to get the order filled, which is the essence of a market order.

Figure 22.2 adds a market order to sell 10,000 shares, 5,000 of which can be paired off with the market buy order, leaving an imbalance of 5,000 to sell. The imbalance is represented now by the *downward*-pointing arrow at the bottom of the screen in the column to the right of the paired orders. The background of the paired orders column has now changed to indicate that we have a trade, and the number 5,000 appears inside the column to show how many market orders are paired. Although we know we have a trade at this point, we don't yet have a price.

Next is another market buy order, this time for 3,000 shares (Figure 22.3). This means that we now have a total of 8,000 shares worth of paired market orders represented by cross hatched background. Note, however, that the actual width of the paired column is not any larger than it was when it was only 5,000 paired. This is so we don't need to take up any more of the screen space than necessary to represent paired market orders. Now, with a total of 10,000 to sell and 8,000 to buy, we have a market order imbalance of only 2,000 to sell, represented by the now narrower column with the arrow pointing down at the bottom of the screen. This paired market orders situation with an imbalance leftover is equivalent to what the specialist now sees on OARS (Opening Automated Report Service). We have not yet seen any limit orders, such as those that would be in the specialist's limit order book, nor do we yet have any indication of the price

FIGURE 22.2

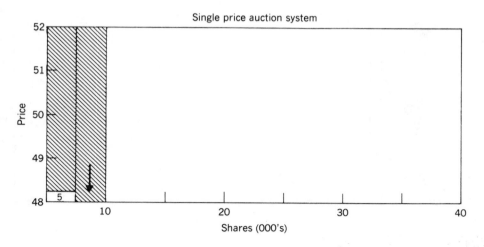

FIGURE 22.3

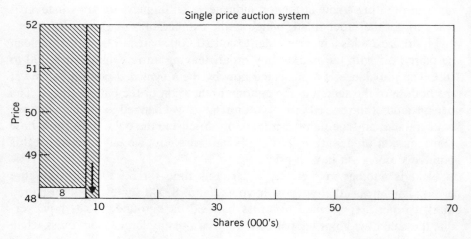

Single price auction system

at which the paired orders will trade, which will be determined by where the imbalance is offset by limit orders on the book.

Figure 22.4 adds a limit order to buy 5,000 shares at 49½, representing by a column rising to that price, to the right of the paired market orders. If no more orders arrived by auction time, this would result in a trade price of 49½, pointed to by the extension of the line coming from the top of the 49½ bid. This price would now clear all the market orders in the system, including the 2,000-share sell imbalance and 2,000 of the 49½ bid. Three

FIGURE 22.4

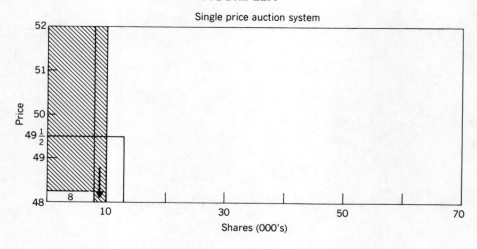

Single price auction system

thousand shares of that bid are left unfilled. The most important numbers to watch are the price that will trade, now 49½, and the total size that will trade, now 10,000 shares, appearing as the cross-hatched area at the bottom of the column.

Figure 22.5 adds several limit sell orders: 3,000 at 50, 5,000 at 50⅛, and 10,000 at 50¼. Since all of these are above the 49½ price that will trade so far, they cause no change in either the price or the size numbers. They would not be executed if the auction took place now. Nevertheless, they represent available size at those prices, which may be tempting to potential buyers.

In Figure 22.6, 100,000 shares of market buy orders and 100,000 shares of market sell orders are added. These show that the shape of the picture doesn't change with increases in the number of offsetting market orders, but the number of shares that will now trade jumps from 10,000 to 110,000. Paired market orders jump from 8,000 to 108,000.

Figure 22.7 adds three limit sell orders and 3 limit buy orders

Sells	Buys
3,000 at 49½	5,000 at 50
2,000 at 49¾	5,000 at 49¾
5,000 at 49⅞	5,000 at 49⅝

Some of the limit buy orders are now above the limit sell orders. If the auction took place right now, more than just offsetting market orders would trade. Total size that would now trade is 115,000 shares, and the clearing price would move to 49¾.

FIGURE 22.5

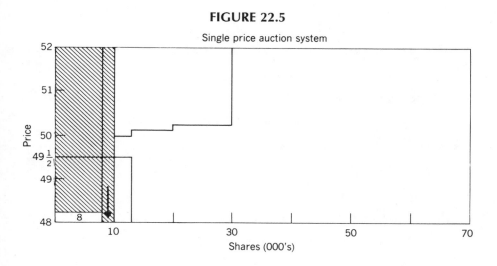

Single price auction system

FIGURE 22.6

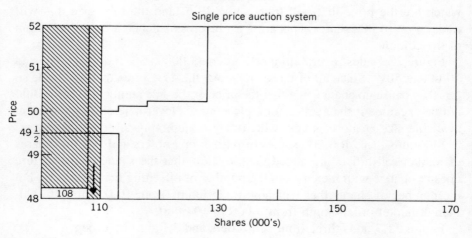

In addition to settling all market orders at 49¾, limit orders more aggressive than that price are also filled in Dutch auction style—namely, the limit order to buy at 50 is filled at 49¾, as is the limit order to sell at 49½. Also, 2,000 of the 5,000 to buy at 49¾ would execute.

Figure 22.8 adds limit orders to buy 5,000 at 51 and 20,000 at 50½, pushing the settlement price up to 50¼ and filling those last two buy orders while leaving the less aggressive buyers unfilled. A total of 133,000 shares trades, filling all the sell orders at lower limits than 50¼, and 5,000 of the

FIGURE 22.7

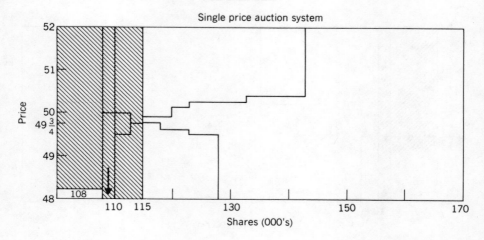

FIGURE 22.8

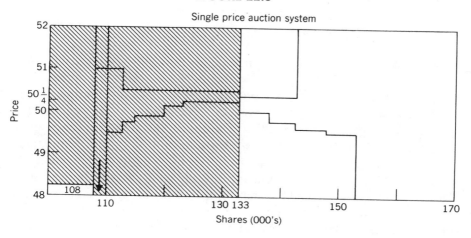

10,000 for sale at 50¼. The other 5,000 shares in the sell order do not execute.

Once the auction takes place, confirmations are immediately sent to the users' terminals. For most traders this is redundant because seeing the settlement price will tell everyone who placed a market order that he completed at that price. Similarly, all limit orders more aggressive than that price were also filled at that price. The only question would be if the settlement price were equal to the user's limit order price: Only half of the limit offer at the 50¼ settlement price is filled.

Note that the central feature of this double Dutch auction is that everyone who bought did so at a price equal to or lower than the price at which he was willing to trade. Similarly, everyone who sold received at least as much as the price he specified.

What would happen if auction time arrived and the market order imbalance were not then offset by limit orders? Under the current system, the specialist would do a little bit of quasi-advertising by broadcasting opening indications of potential prices that he believes might attract offsetting orders. He would not, however, disclose the complete picture.

Under this single-price auction system, everyone would see the complete picture, which would improve the chances of offsetting the imbalance quickly. The system would simply be left open for another minute or so, and someone would step up to take the imbalance at an attractive price. A clearing price would have been found, and the imbalance would be offset.

What if a trader didn't want anyone to know his intentions in the auction? He could put his order in at the last second so no one would have time to react to that order's presence. On the other hand, traders who believed in advertising their orders and the sunshine concept could put orders in as early as possible in order to attract those on the other side who are looking for size.

Some additional points are worth noting. Users should be warned not to use market orders unless they are truly willing to pay or receive any price. This situation now exists with a stock order placed to offset an expiring futures position. Limits should be set at worst-acceptable-case levels, because this maximizes the chances of being filled. The double Dutch auction character of the system will, in all likelihood, result in a much better price. Expiration-related stock orders should be required to be placed early, as they are now. On this system, any resulting imbalances would be disclosed automatically. This, of course, mirrors and expands on the early placement and exposure rules currently in effect for stock orders at futures expiration, which have certainly mitigated expiration volatility. Finally, to make sure the picture being shown is an accurate one, orders, once placed, cannot be cancelled or offset. This shouldn't hamper anyone's style because, as mentioned earlier, no one has to place orders until the last second if he doesn't want to.

The example used to explain how this single-price auction could work has referenced the opening system now used on the NYSE. A nearly identical system could be adopted by any futures exchange, options exchange, or OTC network. As suggested earlier, the NYSE clearly has a lead. The specialist now sees the orders; members could be authorized to see the opening orders as the specialist now sees them. Not far behind, however, could be the Chicago Mercantile Exchange. They could put such a system on the PMT machines they are jointly developing with Reuters. Instinet could perform the same function for any OTC market. Intex, which designs and builds electronic exchange facilities, is interested in further developing the demonstration model presented here into a full-blown system.

SUMMARY

The strength of a continuous market is that anyone can trade at any time he wants to—almost. Under normal conditions, market-makers supply plenty liquidity to satisfy normal trading needs. In times of excessive demands on markets, however, the liquidity provided by specialists and market-makers is outstripped, and stock prices are left floating without moorings. The single-price auction reanchors the market, whether market-makers choose to participate in it or not.

Knowing where to go to trade simplifies the trading process. Knowing *when* to go to trade simplifies it even further. Today, the strict reliance on continuous markets means that buyers and sellers must search for each other *in a time dimension*. They often encounter excessive search costs or wind up paying a market-maker to provide liquidity because no opposite party can be easily found. The specialist post draws traders to a central place to trade. The single-price auction works better: It gathers all buyers and sellers who wish to trade to a centralized time as well as place.

Most investment decisions are part of a systemic process and are frequently decided at regularly scheduled intervals. The decision of when to trade could be calibrated to the time in which a substantial number of buyers and sellers regularly meet. Improving the probability of meeting the other side and reducing the cost of trading will create even greater liquidity than we now experience.

The Editor Asks

Q *You argue that the primary reason that the order book is opened only to the specialist is that it is very profitable to him, and the specialist is in a position to resist change to the procedures. If nothing else, the Stock Exchange is a balancing act of interests and fair compensation. If we take this source of profit away from the market-maker, can we expect to make compensation elsewhere? Where? What are the ramifications?*

A A closed book is indeed profitable to specialists, who are in a position to resist changes to the procedures. It is a mistake, however, to assume what your question implies, namely, that there is some "balancing act of interests and fair compensation" requiring the specialist to return to the marketplace something equal in value to his order flow information monopoly. The affirmative obligation to maintain fair and orderly markets, which is often cited in this context, is, first of all, impossible to maintain when it really counts, such as on October 19. Second, it is bound to retard the discovery of true clearing prices and is, therefore, uneconomic, anyway. Imagine a law allowing auctioneers to buy any of your goods they cannot auction off, and also allowing them to select those who attend the auction. Although they may spend some of the money unfairly made in this situation lobbying the auction rulemakers to keep them in it, it would not be correct to call this "fair compensation."

Market organizers should not feel obligated to provide compensating benefits for the removal of unfair advantages. If we take this source of profit away from market-makers by changing the rules to require a fair, well-attended, public auction, the users of the market will see a reduction in per trade costs, while market-makers will see a reduction in per trade compensation. Market-makers would be wise to focus their future efforts on filling the auction house (perhaps charging a fee for attendance), rather than defending a personal financial interest in the auction prices. Opening the specialist's book at the open of the market is the most important step that could now be taken in this direction. In the modern electronic age, markets that fail to develop efficient auction facilities can easily be replaced by others that do.

23

TRADING TACTICS IN AN INEFFICIENT MARKET

Bruce I. Jacobs and Kenneth N. Levy

If the efficient market hypothesis (EMH) truly described reality, trading would be a rather uninteresting function. Prices would instantaneously and fully reflect all relevant information, and outperforming the market would not be possible. Investors would hold well-diversified passive portfolios, and transactions would be solely rebalancing or liquidity-motivated. Informationless, cross-sectional slices of the market would be common trades.

The preponderance of recent evidence suggests, however, that the marketplace is price-inefficient. A series of articles by Jacobs and Levy have provided substantial evidence contravening market efficiency.[1] The stock market is rife with return regularities, or anomalies. Although passive strategies have become increasingly popular, substantial resources continue to be devoted to active management, which stands to profit from anomaly exploitation. The implications of an inefficient market for trading tactics will be explored in this chapter.

STOCK MARKET ANOMALIES

We classify stock market anomalies into two broad groups—cross-sectional effects and time-related or calendar effects. The tendency for smaller firms and those having lower price/earnings (P/E) ratios to outperform in the longer run are classic examples of cross-sectional effects. Returns often

[1] B. Jacobs and K. Levy, "Disentangling Equity Return Regularities: New Insights and Investment Opportunities," *Financial Analysts Journal,* May–June 1988; "On the Value of 'Value,' " *Financial Analysts Journal,* July–August 1988, pp. 18–38; "Calendar Anomalies," *Financial Analysts Journal,* November–December 1988, pp. 28–37.

differ across firms based on such characteristics. Calendar anomalies have long been part of market folklore, and have recently withstood close scrutiny. These intertemporal return patterns include the January and day-of-the-week effects.

Jacobs and Levy find that some cross-sectional effects, such as small size and low P/E, tend to be associated with unstable return patterns.[2] While these attributes have provided extra rewards over the longer run, there have been periods of perverse performance. We find these return effects are not regular at all to the naked eye, but are often regular in a broader macroeconomic context. Such "empirical return regularities" are driven by macroeconomic forces, and dynamic processes are required to exploit them fully.

Other cross-sectional return effects, such as earnings surprise, are more persistent. We refer to such effects as anomalous pockets of stock market inefficiency. While these anomalies may persist for up to several months, their footprints are evident in weekly or even daily returns. Their effect on returns is substantial enough to give pause to traders.

"Disentangling" interrelated return effects is essential to unravel the cross-currents in the marketplace. For instance, the longer-run outperformance of smaller capitalization stocks is often ascribed to their lower price/earnings ratios. Some maintain that the size effect is a proxy for the neglected firm anomaly. Others have found the size effect to be associated with calendar effects, including January and day-of-the-week effects.

Naive return attributions result from studying one return effect at a time, in isolation from others, under the assumption that anomalies are independent of one another. Only by fully disentangling interrelationships are return attributions "purified." Such pure returns provide useful insights in portfolio management and trading. For instance, some return effects appear stronger in pure form, whereas others dissipate as they are revealed to be mere proxies.

The analysis of cross-sectional effects requires fundamental databases—a relatively recent innovation. On the other hand, time-dated records of market indices often suffice for the study of calendar anomalies. Hence, calendar anomalies can be tracked historically for much longer periods than effects requiring fundamental data.

The availability of a century of data brings enormous statistical power for testing calendar effects but also increases the likelihood of data-mining. If enough patterns are tested, some will appear significant merely by chance. In exploring calendar anomalies, Lakonishok and Smidt caution that

---

[2] Jacobs and Levy, "Disentangling Equity Return Regularities."

significance levels must be properly adjusted for the number of hypotheses examined, out-of-sample tests should be encouraged, and only plausible hypotheses should be tested.[3]

Calendar anomalies often have significant economic impact. For instance, during the Great Depression the Blue Monday effect was so strong that the entire market crash took place over weekends, from Saturday's close to Monday's close. The stock market actually rose, on average, every other day of the week.

Calendar regularities are even more aberrant than cross-sectional return effects. For instance, a skeptic might assert that low-P/E stocks provide outperformance simply because of their greater riskiness. This argument can be deflected but requires potentially controversial assumptions about risk modeling. Others claim that the low P/E characteristic is merely a proxy for value. Although this proposition has some intuitive appeal, Jacobs and Levy find it to be specious.[4] In any case, risk or value considerations appear insufficient to explain calendar anomalies such as the day-of-the-week effect.

Calendar anomalies appear relatively easy to exploit, rendering their continued existence more inexplicable. To arbitrage the P/E effect, investors would have to increase their demand for low-P/E stocks. But there may be psychological considerations inhibiting investors from owning such stocks. On the other hand, to arbitrage the time-of-day effect, investors merely need to schedule discretionary trades to a more advantageous time of day.

Jacobs and Levy suggest that calendar anomalies may also have psychological underpinnings.[5] They generally occur at cusps in time, such as the turn of the year, turn of the month, turn of the week, and turn of the day. Investors apparently behave differently at these artificial turning points, and economic fundamentals do not fully account for these patterns.

Cross-sectional effects are primarily of interest to portfolio managers in selecting stocks, whereas calendar return patterns should be of greater interest to traders. Calendar anomalies are difficult to exploit as stand-alone strategies because of transaction cost considerations. For instance, 100% turnover per week is necessary to capture fully the day-of-the-week effect. Calendar return patterns can, however, be of benefit in timing a preconceived trade.

Before examining calendar anomalies, we turn to those cross-sectional effects with short enough duration to have trading implications.

[3] J. Lakonishok and S. Smidt, "Are Seasonal Anomalies Real? A Ninety-Year Perspective," Johnson Working Paper No. 87-07, Cornell University, May 1987.
[4] Jacobs and Levy, "On the Value of 'Value.' "
[5] Jacobs and Levy, "Calendar Anomalies."

CROSS-SECTIONAL EFFECTS

We will consider three pockets of inefficiency that represent opportunity for traders: return reversal, trend in analysts' earnings estimates, and earnings surprise. Jacobs and Levy disentangle these and other return effects.[6]

Measured in pure form, the return reversal effect becomes quite strong and reliable. Because of short-term fluctuations around fair value, blips in stock prices tend to reverse. But if a jump in price was due to an analyst earnings estimate upgrade or a positive earnings surprise, the outperformance will likely persist and not reverse. Thus, disentangling is vital.

Profits can be generated by exploiting the return reversal effect. Figure 23.1, from Jacobs and Levy,[7] plots monthly cumulative pure returns to a one cross-sectional standard deviation bet on return reversal. This is roughly equivalent to a 16th percentile ranking, so these returns represent a payoff to a very substantial exposure to this attribute. Return reversal is measured in the residual, or beta-adjusted, return of the previous month.

As depicted, a strategy of betting on last month's worst performers would

FIGURE 23.1   CUMULATIVE PURE PAYOFF TO RETURN REVERSAL

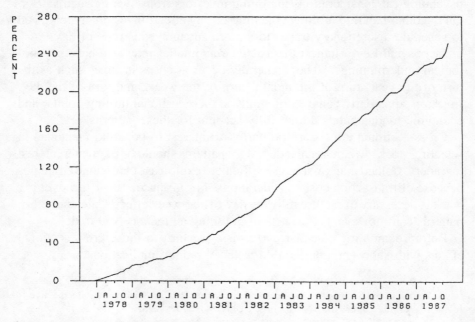

[6] Jacobs and Levy, "Disentangling Equity Return Regularities."
[7] Ibid.

result in consistent and substantial gains. Conversely, last month's winners underperform. This effect has also been documented with weekly returns.

Return reversal may arise from temporary investor overreaction to company announcements or other news events. Jacobs and Levy find that such overreactions underlie several stock market anomalies.[8]

An investment strategy based solely on the return reversal effect would incur substantial turnover. However, a trading overlay might be appropriate when one is planning to transact in any event. Traders having discretion should balance the potential rewards against the market impact cost and market timing risk of adjusting trading speed.

The trend in analysts' earnings estimate effect represents the tendency of stocks to react predictably to revisions in consensus Wall Street earnings expectations. Upgrades generally precede strong returns, and downgrades weak returns. These subsequent returns were first attributed to inefficient information propagation—that is, to the speed of information dissemination. Later, it was demonstrated that revisions in consensus estimates tend to recur, consistent with some psychological explanations. These include the so-called herd instinct among Wall Street analysts and their aversion to forecast reversals. Rather than cutting earnings estimates abruptly, analysts often shave off a nickel at a time and hope no one notices.

Accordingly, trading tactics might accelerate purchases and defer sales of stocks experiencing positive revisions, and vice versa. Closely related to trends in estimates is the earnings surprise anomaly, where an *earnings surprise* is defined as a difference between reported earnings and consensus expectations. Jacobs and Levy find that earnings surprises tend to repeat quarter after quarter in the same direction, and document strong returns subsequent to surprises.[9] These returns may arise in part as a result of the anticipation of repeat surprises. Prices also adjust in response to analyst estimate revisions made in light of a surprise. Indeed, we find an interplay between analyst estimates and earnings announcements, with analysts both partially anticipating and subsequently reacting to announcements.

Brown, as well as Jones, Rendleman, and Latané, presents evidence from daily security returns.[10] The latter study reports that the top decile of stocks ranked by earnings surprise experienced market-adjusted excess returns of 1.3% on the announcement day, 1.7% by the following day, 2.0% after one

[8] Jacobs and Levy, "On the Value of 'Value.' "

[9] Jacobs and Levy, "Disentangling Equity Return Regularities"; "On the Value of 'Value.' "

[10] S. Brown, "Earnings Changes, Stock Prices, and Market Efficiency," *Journal of Finance,* March 1978, pp. 17–28; C. Jones, R. Rendleman, and H. Latane, "Stock Returns and SUEs During the 1970's," *Journal of Portfolio Management,* Winter 1984, pp. 18–22.

week, and 2.8% after one month. Also, the earnings surprise effect appears stronger for smaller stocks.

Kormendi and Lipe have demonstrated the long-term price adjustment to be consistent with the valuation change implied by the earnings release.[11] Nonetheless, the price adjustment is sufficiently slow to have trading implications. Later, we will revisit this return effect in the context of intraday anomalies. We now turn to a review of calendar effects and their trading implications. For a more theoretical treatment of calendar anomalies, see Jacobs and Levy.[12] We will first discuss the January effect.

THE JANUARY EFFECT

A special time for the stock market is the turn of the year. Most individuals have calendar tax years, and many firms close their books at this time. Also, the turn of the year represents a clean slate for government, business, and consumer budgeting, as well as for other purposes such as investment manager performance evaluation. Additionally, investors' cash flows are jolted by bonuses, pension contributions, and holiday liquidity needs.

Stocks exhibit both higher returns and risk premiums in January. These results have been corroborated in many foreign markets. The higher returns, however, stem primarily from the outperformance of smaller stocks. January does not appear to be an exceptional month for large capitalization issues.

The most commonly cited reason for the January return seasonal effect is tax-loss selling rebound. Taxable investors dump losers in December for tax purposes, and the subsequent abatement of selling pressure in January might explain the higher returns.

Another rationale for the January effect is year-end window dressing. In this view, some portfolio managers dump embarrassing stocks at year end to avoid their appearance on the annual report. Similar stocks are repurchased in the new year, resulting in the January effect.

January seasonals have also been noted in returns to a variety of stock characteristics, such as size, yield, and neglect. In the case of small size, the returns occur at the turn of the year—specifically, on the last trading day in December and the first few trading days in January.

[11] R. Kormendi and R. Lipe, "Earnings Innovations, Earnings Persistence, and Stock Returns," *Journal of Business*, July 1987, pp. 323–345.
[12] Jacobs and Levy, "Calendar Anomalies."

Jacobs and Levy report that after fully disentangling, two effects emerge strongest in January.[13] One is a return rebound for stocks with embedded tax losses, especially those with long-term losses. The other is an abnormal return to the yield characteristic, with both zero-yielding and high-yielding stocks experiencing the largest returns. Most other January seasonals, such as those for small size, appear to be mere proxies for these two effects. In fact, pure returns to smaller size exhibit no January seasonal at all, after controlling for other factors. There is also evidence of January selling pressure for stocks with long-term gains, apparently resulting from the deferral of gain recognition until the new year.

Tax-loss selling pressure might be stronger in down-market years, when losses are more prevalent. Also, higher taxable incomes or higher tax rates may strengthen tax-loss taking, although current evidence of such relationships is rather weak.

A January risk seasonal might explain the higher returns at the turn of the year. Traditional measures of risk such as beta, however, are insufficient to justify the January return seasonal. Alternatively, the January return seasonal may be compensation for bearing informational risk. The seasonal may stem from the reduction of uncertainty associated with the dissemination of information after the close of the fiscal year, especially for small, neglected firms. But informational risk also appears to be an inadequate explanation of the January seasonal.

Cash flow patterns at the turn-of-the-year may produce the return seasonal. Annual bonuses and holiday gifts might be invested in the stock market, along with year-end pension plan contributions. Also, savings spent on holiday consumption may in part be replenished. In Japan, where bonuses are paid semiannually, equities exhibit seasonals in January and June.

Conventional theory holds that predictable patterns like the January effect should be anticipated and, in time, arbitraged away. Yet, this and other calendar effects have persisted over the full century for which data are available. Novel cognitive-psychological approaches offer substantial insight into such anomalous market behavior. For instance, Shefrin and Statman have articulated a theory consistent with the observed January effect.[14] Their behavioral model incorporates elements such as the human predilection to use year-end tax planning as a justification for admitting mistakes, and the tendency to ride losers too long.

[13] Jacobs and Levy, "Disentangling Equity Return Regularities."

[14] H. Shefrin and M. Statman, "The Disposition to Sell Winners Too Early and Ride Losers Too Long: Theory and Evidence," *Journal of Finance*, July 1985, pp. 777–792.

The January effect has important implications for stock selection and for trading around year end. Much of the January effect seems to transpire on the last trading day in December and the first few days in January. Prior to the turn of the year, purchases of stocks subject to tax-loss selling should be made quickly, and sales delayed. Conversely, stocks with gains tend to be subject to selling pressure early in the new year, so sales should be accelerated and purchases deferred.

THE TURN-OF-THE-MONTH EFFECT

Recent studies demonstrate anomalous returns at the turn of each month. Though not as dramatic as the January effect, this anomaly is quite substantial. In fact, the stock market's positive returns are fully accounted for by the turn-of-the-month effect.

Figure 23.2 plots average returns to the Dow Jones Industrial Average for trading days near month end for the period 1897 to 1986, using data

FIGURE 23.2   THE TURN-OF-THE-MONTH EFFECT ON AVERAGE DAILY RETURNS

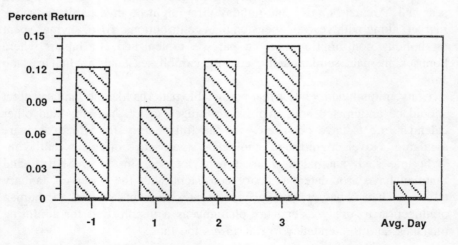

Days are Relative to Month-End:
-1 is last Trading Day of Previous Month
+1 is First Trading Day of Month, Etc.

from Lakonishok and Smidt.[15] Returns are high for each trading day from the last day in the previous month (denoted as day −1) to the third trading day in the current month. These four trading days averaged 0.118%, compared to 0.015% for all trading days. Although this anomaly has existed for at least a century, it has weakened somewhat in the most recent decade.

Month-end portfolio rebalancing is a possible explanation, because some investors might reinvest accumulated cash dividends at this time. A more convincing rationale is based on higher month-end cash flows, such as salaries. Increased demand for equities at month end might produce the observed return regularity. Alternatively, some suggest that the positive returns early in each month are caused by a clustering of positive earnings announcements, but the evidence on this theory is mixed. In any case, by anticipating the turn-of-the-month seasonal, traders can time transactions accordingly.

THE DAY-OF-THE-WEEK EFFECT

As mentioned earlier, stock returns are intimately tied to the day of the week. The market has a tendency to end each week on a strong note and to decline on Mondays. This pattern, which is deeply ingrained in folk wisdom, is often referred to as the weekend or Blue Monday effect.

Figure 23.3 illustrates average daily returns of the S&P Index for each day of the week from 1928 to 1982, using data from Keim and Stambaugh.[16] Monday is the only down day, and is significantly different statistically from all other days. The last trading day of the week—Friday in five-day weeks and Saturday in six-day weeks—has a substantial positive average return. The day-of-the-week effect also exists in other markets. For example, it has been documented for some foreign equity markets, stock index futures, and even orange juice futures.

Measurement error is often suggested as a cause of the observed pattern, especially since the effect appears stronger for smaller capitalization stocks. But this possibility has been rejected by many researchers. Explanations involving specialists, such as the frequency of closing at bid versus ask prices, have also been dismissed by studies utilizing only over-the-counter bids, and other markets with different structural characteristics. Lakonishok

[15] Lakonishok and Smidt, "Are Seasonal Anomalies Real?"
[16] D. Keim and R. Stambaugh, "A Further Investigation of the Weekend Effect in Stock Returns," *Journal of Finance,* July 1984, pp. 819–837.

FIGURE 23.3 THE DAY-OF-THE-WEEK EFFECT ON AVERAGE DAILY RETURNS

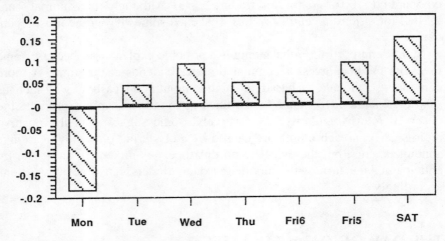

Fri6 = Friday in a Siz-Day Trading Week
Fri5 = Friday in a Five-Day Trading Week

and Levi have proposed trade settlement rules as a partial explanation.[17] But the day-of-the-week effect predates the 1968 advent of current settlement procedures, and the anomaly exists in foreign countries where settlement procedures alone would predict different patterns.

The day-of-the-week effect is related to other anomalies. The weekly pattern is stronger for smaller capitalization stocks. In fact, Keim reports that 63% of the small-size effect occurs on Fridays.[18] There are conflicting findings on the day-of-the-week effect in January. Later, we discuss the interaction of the day-of-the-week effect with holiday and time-of-day regularities.

One class of explanations is based on inventory adjustments. Short sellers might cover positions prior to the weekend for peace of mind and short again on Monday mornings. Specialists might close trading on Fridays at ask prices. Investors might be more inclined to throw in the towel after a

[17] J. Lakonishok and M. Levi, "Weekend Effects on Stock Returns: A Note," *Journal of Finance*, June 1982, pp. 883–889.
[18] D. Keim, "Daily Returns and Size-Related Premiums: One More Time," *Journal of Portfolio Management*, Winter 1987, pp. 41–47.

weekend of introspection. One problem with such rationales is that they may be insufficient to account for the ubiquitous nature of the anomaly. Day-of-the-week effects are evident over the entire century for which we have data, in spite of changing trading mechanics, short-sale regulations, methods of investment management, and even modes of communication.The anomaly is also present in foreign equity markets and in other asset classes.

Explanations rooted in human nature show promise. For example, in experimental market games conducted by psychologists, an effect similar to the day-of-the-week effect has been observed around trading halts. Recently, the day-of-the-week effect has also been related to the human tendency to announce good news quickly and defer bad news. Penman claims that the pattern of earnings and other announcements over the week may actually drive the observed return effect.[19] We indicated earlier that the entire market decline of the Great Depression occurred, on average, over weekends. Not coincidentally, most bad news, such as bank closings, was released after the Saturday close to allow the market to "absorb the shock" over the weekends. As a more recent example, the 1987 string of insider-trading indictments were generally announced after the market close on Fridays.

Thus, to the extent possible, purchases should be made after Monday's decline, and sales deferred to the end of the week. The economic potential of this effect is not trivial. For instance, Harris notes that if one must generate a cash flow of $100,000 per week from an equity portfolio, switching the sale day from Monday to the previous Friday might earn an additional $14,700 per annum.[20]

THE HOLIDAY EFFECT

The unusually good performance of stocks prior to market holidays has long been an article of faith among many practitioners. Recent studies confirm the existence of the holiday effect.

Figure 23.4 plots the average return on the day before each of the eight market holidays for the period 1963 to 1982, using Ariel's results.[21] The average preholiday return of 0.365% dwarfs the average regular-day return

[19] S. Penman, "The Distribution of Earnings News over Time and Seasonalities in Aggregate Stock Returns," *Journal of Financial Economics* 18 (1987), pp. 199–228.

[20] L. Harris, "How to Profit from Intradaily Stock Returns," *Journal of Portfolio Management,* Winter 1986, pp. 61–64.

[21] R. Ariel, "High Stock Returns before Holidays," Sloan Working Paper, Massachusetts Institute of Technology, 1984.

FIGURE 23.4   THE HOLIDAY EFFECT: AVERAGE
PREHOLIDAY RETURNS

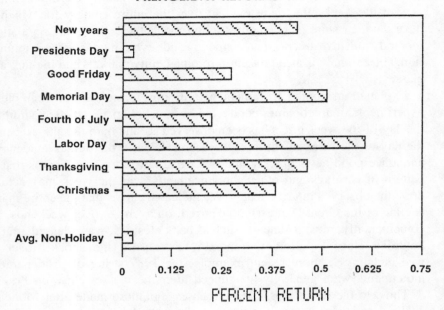

of 0.026%. In fact, 35% of the entire market advance over this period occurred on just the eight preholiday trading days each year.

Lakonishok and Smidt identify another holiday-related phenomenon occurring from December 24 to 31 each year.[22] This period includes not only Christmas and New Year's Day, but also the days between the holidays, which exhibit exceptional returns as well. In fact, the average cumulative return for just these eight calendar days is a remarkable 1.6%. This year-end rally was identified in the Dow and may relate to window dressing in blue chip issues toward year end. In any case, the dollar magnitude of this year-end large-capitalization stock rally is several times the magnitude of the better-known January small-size effect.

The holiday anomaly appears fairly stable over time. In the most recent decade, however, preholiday returns have not been exceptional. The effect does not appear to be a statistical artifact. For instance, it is not driven by outliers, since 75% of preholiday days are up, versus only 54% of all trading days. It appears unrelated to settlement procedures, risk, or any other simple explanation.

---

[22] Lakonishok and Smidt, "Are Seasonal Anomalies Real?"

Another perspective is available by examining holidays not associated with market closings, like St. Patrick's Day or Rosh Hashanah. Such days do not experience abnormal returns. This absence of anomalous returns may be due to the lack of a trading break, or to a lower level of festivity than that associated with the major market holidays. In a class by itself—almost considered the antithesis of a holiday by the superstitious—is Friday the 13th. Studies have examined this day, with conflicting results.

Holiday effects interact with other anomalies. For instance, the holiday effect is stronger for smaller stocks. The holiday effect also swamps the day-of-the-week effect. Monday returns preceding a Tuesday holiday are, on average, positive. Also, after controlling for the holiday effect, the best day of the week shifts from Friday to Wednesday. This is due to the high frequency of holidays falling on Saturday, Sunday, or Monday, which benefits the previous Friday's return.

One potential hypothesis is that preholiday returns represent another manifestation of return abnormalities around trading halts, such as weekends. However, there are important differences. Whereas Mondays are down, on average, the day after a holiday does not exhibit unusual returns. Also, the holiday effect is two to five times the strength of the last-trading-day-of-the-week effect, which indicates that more than simply a trading halt is the cause.

Another possibility is that holiday euphoria leads to short covering and general buying pressure. But there is little evidence of a market correction as the lift in spirits subsequently fades. Although no fully satisfactory explanation of the holiday effect has yet surfaced, psychological reasons appear the most promising. In any case, traders should be aware of this powerful preholiday return regularity.

THE TIME-OF-DAY EFFECT

Just as stock returns do not accrue evenly over the days of the week, so intraday patterns also exist. Although such effects have long been claimed by practitioners, fewer academic studies of intraday anomalies exist because of the recent advent of real-time pricing databases.

Figure 23.5, using data from Harris,[23] plots cumulative returns, at 15-minute intervals throughout each trading day of the week, for a recent 14-month period on the NYSE. Tuesday through Friday exhibit quite similar

[23] L. Harris, "A Transaction Data Study of Weekly and Intradaily Patterns in Stock Returns," *Journal of Financial Economics* 16 (1986), pp. 99–117.

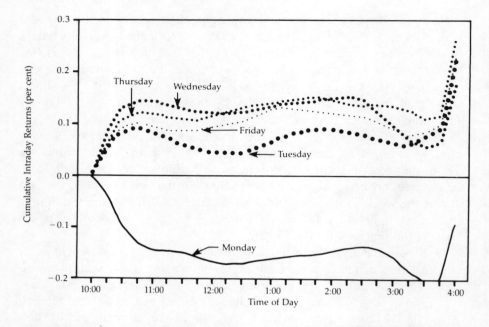

Data from L. Harris, "A Transaction Data Study of Weekly and Intradaily Patterns in Stock Returns," *Journal of Financial Economics*, 16, 1986, pp. 99–117.

patterns: Prices rise for approximately the first 45 minutes, the bulk of the trading day is flat, and another rally takes place the last 15 minutes of the day. The strong opening is roughly attributable to the first three trades of the day in each stock, and the strong close is due primarily to the last trade. In contrast, on Monday, prices during the first 45 minutes of trading are down sharply, whereas the rest of the day resembles the other days of the week.

Harris has also analyzed the close-of-day anomaly in great detail.[24] He finds the average return of the last trade to equal 0.05%, or 0.6 cents per share. The closer the final trade to the close of business, however, the higher the return. Final trades occurring after 3:55 P.M. average a 0.12% return, or 1.75 cents per share.

Intraday studies have rejected a variety of explanations. For instance, the closing price anomaly is unrelated to whether a stock has listed options or trades on a regional exchange beyond the NYSE closing time. Results are not due to data errors because there is little evidence of return reversals at the following open.

[24] L. Harris, "A Day-End Transaction Price Anomaly," University of Southern California Working Paper, October 1986.

Might fundamental values rise at the open and close, causing the observed intraday return pattern? Unanticipated good news toward the close might not be fully reflected in prices until the next morning, particularly if specialists dampen the rise in order to maintain orderly markets. Of course, this would not explain Monday mornings' negative returns. Also, what might account for a rush of good news just before the close? Although stocks that trade right at the close experience the largest day-end effect, those that do not trade near the close do not catch up by morning. This seems to rule out the possibility that marketwide good news accounts for the day-end return anomaly.

There is a relationship between risk and intraday returns. The unusually high opening and closing returns are more variable than returns during the rest of the day. If investors are averse to volatility, they would require higher expected returns at the open and close. But the risk increase is insufficient to explain the magnitude of the observed return effect. Furthermore, Monday mornings' negative returns run counter to this hypothesis.

The open differs from the balance of the day in some important respects. Opening prices are determined by a market call, unlike the continuous market-making process the rest of the day. Also, orders at the open are heavily influenced by foreign investors. Although Amihud and Mendelson find that opening returns exhibit greater dispersion, are less normally distributed, and are more negatively autocorrelated than other returns, it remains unclear why any of these differences would result in the morning return anomaly.[25]

Closing prices are also special. They are used for valuing portfolios, for performance evaluation, as strike prices for program trades, and for settling options and futures contracts at expiration. They are the prices reported in the press and stored in databases. For all these reasons, closing prices might be likely candidates for manipulation, possibly causing the day-end return anomaly. Volume for day-end trades is not abnormally small, however, as would be the case if someone were painting the tape.

Those who must purchase a stock on a given day might conceivable rush to beat the closing bell, thus placing upward pressure on prices. But the converse should hold for sellers. Since the day-end price effect is stronger at the turn of the month, window dressing might play a role. Also, about half of the effect is attributable to changes in the frequency of trades at bid versus ask prices near the close, but the cause of this distributional shift remains unknown.

[25] Y. Amihud and H. Mendelson, ''Trading Mechanisms and Stock Returns: An Empirical Investigation,'' *Journal of Finance,* July 1987, pp. 533–555.

As with the holiday and day-of-the-week effects, the day-end return anomaly may relate to the impending trading halt. As psychological experiments have demonstrated, there may be a behavioral predisposition to bid up prices before the close.

Harris spells out a variety of suggestions for traders seeking to capitalize on this anomaly:

1. Avoid buying early Monday, but on other days buy as early as possible.

2. Sell late on Fridays. On other days, except perhaps on Mondays, selling late is also preferable.

3. On all days, consider submitting a limit sell order priced just above the market right before the close.[26]

Since only the last trade of the day appears abnormal for each stock, only one seller may benefit from the day-end anomaly.

INTRADAY EFFECTS

Recent research has examined the market's speed of adjustment to a variety of events. For example, Dann, Mayers, and Raab find that it takes about 5 to 15 minutes for the price pressure of a large block trade to dissipate.[27] Because such studies require time-stamped transaction records, they have only become feasible in recent years.

Hasbrouch and Ho examine price changes, without attempting to link them to any fundamental news.[28] They find that price adjustments on the NYSE are noninstantaneous, with a half-life of approximately 40 minutes. Also, smaller capitalization stocks display longer adjustment lags.

Kawaller, Koch, and Koch report that price discovery seems to occur in the stock index futures market.[29] Stocks trading less frequently respond with about a 20- to 45-minute lag to changes in the futures price. The futures–spot spread may be useful for timing a preconceived trade.

---

[26] Harris, "How to Profit from Intradaily Stock Returns"; "Study of Weekly and Intradaily Patterns in Stock Returns"; "Day-End Transaction Price Anomaly."

[27] L. Dann, D. Mayers, and R. Raab, "Trading Rules, Large Blocks and the Speed of Price Adjustment," *Journal of Financial Economics* 4 (1977), pp. 3–22.

[28] J. Hasbrouch and T. Ho, "Intraday Stock Returns: Empirical Evidence of Lagged Adjustment," Salomon Brothers Center/New York University Working Paper No. 376, May 1986.

[29] I. Kawaller, P. Koch, and T. Koch, "The Temporal Price Relationship between S&P 500 Futures and the S&P 500 Index," *Journal of Finance,* December 1987, pp. 1309–1329.

Patell and Wolfson analyzed the effect of broad tape earnings and dividend announcements on stock prices.[30] Although regular dividend announcements appear to have no effect, dividend changes and earnings surprises do have an impact on returns. Interestingly, the market reaction to the news occurs in two waves. The first effect happens almost immediately, whereas the second transpires overnight, once nonintraday traders act on the news.

Most of the immediate price adjustment takes place in the first half-hour following the news, with an average reaction of 23 basis points. Prices then react overnight by another 9 basis points, and an additional 13 during the first half-hour of trading the next morning. The reaction appears larger for bigger surprises.

Although adjustment lags might be longer for neglected stocks, there is less liquidity to exploit. Also, a security's risk increases following announcements, and the heightened variability continues into the next day.

CONCLUSION

Mispricings of an ephemeral nature are widespread in the marketplace. Although anomalies are an enigma to efficient market adherents, they represent opportunities to astute traders. Once these short-lived price patterns are identified, trading tactics can be designed to exploit them.

The Editor Asks

Q *Your findings can be reduced to the best times to buy and the best times to sell. When are these times? Can a trader really use these to improve portfolio return?*

A The best time to buy stock is before holidays, and at the turn of the month and the turn of the year. The best day of the week to buy is Monday, around midday.

The best time to buy a particular name is when it has been recently depressed for no fundamental reason, or as soon as possible after a positive news event, like a surprisingly good earnings announcement.

[30] J. Patell and M. Wolfson, "The Intraday Speed of Adjustment of Stock Prices to Earnings and Dividend Announcements," *Journal of Financial Economics,* June 1984, pp. 223–252.

The best time to sell stock is after holidays and at midmonth. The best day of the week to sell is Friday, late in the day.

Trading tactics can improve portfolio return by optimally timing preconceived trades. These tactics can be implemented only when there is some trading discretion. As these mispricings evolve, so will the best rules to follow.

24

INTELLIGENT TRADING SYSTEMS

David Leinweber

A remarkable pair of photographs shows the floor of the London Stock Exchange (LSE) one day before and after the Big Bang of October 27, 1986. The day before, the floor was packed with traders, elbowing each other, shouting, flashing signals, and generally acting like the unruly mob everyone expects. The day after, just about everyone was gone. A tumbleweed could have rolled through the place and no one would have been around to notice. The venerable old LSE was now a venerable new computer network, and the financial world was profoundly changed.

Markets are evolving into electronic entities. Traders are inundated with an ever-larger stream of data on financial instruments interrelated in increasingly complex ways and traded 24 hours a day throughout the world.

The information overload on traders extends beyond simply the rising number of instruments and markets they must consider. The rise of sophisticated quantitative analysis brings a second wave of information that traders must incorporate into their decision-making processes. Intelligent trading systems are the best, and perhaps the only, means to cope with this information explosion. This chapter describes this technology and how it is applied in securities trading.

THE NEW WAVE IN TRADING-ROOM TECHNOLOGY

Market data feeds delivered as video signals are being supplanted by digital feeds, a transformation that will bring profound changes to the operations of

The author wishes to thank Dale Prouty, Mike McFall, and Rich Plevin of Integrated Analytics for their cogent ideas and advice; Don Putnam for his general enthusiasm; and Marguerite C. Moreno and Lucille D. Moreno for their tolerance of odd working hours.

securities firms.[1] Video feeds delivered "pictures of data," designed to be gazed upon by human eyes only—to be "seen but not touched" electronically. Any analysis of data incoming as video required manual transfer of the data to the analytical system, be it as simple as a calculator or as complex as the most esoteric mortgage-backed security futures valuation model ever conceived at midnight by teams of econometricians and former nuclear physicists.

Digital data change everything. Analytics are no longer printouts to be pored over at the end of the day. They are dynamic, volatile information resources providing a competitive advantage for traders and risk managers.

The last generation of trading systems succeeded in delivering video information to traders without requiring a separate screen for each source. The technology may have looked like computers, but it had the soul of cable television. The next generation will do far more than deliver data. It will integrate, analyze, interpret, prioritize, and *add value* to data. Even if all the traders became physicists and the physicists became traders, they could not cope with the onslaught of information. There is a mandate to build more into the trading systems, to make them sufficiently intelligent to apply the tools of financial technology in an increasingly complex and competitive market.

WHAT MAKES A TRADING SYSTEM INTELLIGENT?

What makes anything intelligent? In *The Society of Mind,* Marvin Minsky makes the case that what we call intelligent behavior emerges from the interaction between richly interconnected agents, each of which would not be regarded as especially intelligent in isolation.[2]

Modern trading systems consist of hundreds of these agents: current market data, historical information, financial reports, bond analytics, quantitative models, technical indicators, order entry, and execution. Each of these is certainly useful, but not what anyone who had ever seen a video game would call intelligent. Each of these agents serves only one purpose, and an abundance of single-purpose agents alone won't behave intelligently. They must be able to communicate with and initiate action by others. The human trader currently is called on to provide far too much of the coordination and communication for these agents.

---

[1] P. Sahgal and I. Schmerken, "The New Wave in Trading Room Technology," *Wall Street Computer Review* 5(4) (January 1988), p. 28.

[2] M. Minsky, *The Society of Mind* (New York: Simon and Schuster, 1986).

Intelligent trading systems are the result of the intelligent application of modern information-processing techniques to this coordination task. These techniques include, but are not limited to, elements of the art and science known collectively as *artificial intelligence* (AI).

At this juncture, a mild warning is appropriate. Hyperbolic press coverage of artificial intelligence has contributed to unreasonable expectations for AI applications.[3] We should not expect computer programs to emulate the great thinkers, display common sense, or fully understand natural language. We can, however, expect them to act as beneficial, productive assistants for traders and financial professionals.

KNOWLEDGE-BASED SYSTEMS

The convergence of a number of technological developments has brought the ability to connect everything in a trading system. This doesn't necessarily imply that anything useful or supportive of the trader will emerge from the connection itself. Some means is necessary to integrate diverse information sources to serve useful purposes, with flexibility and without forcing their users to master all the intricacies of each component. Knowledge-based systems provide this means.[4]

The term *knowledge-based systems* (KBS) encompasses, but is not restricted to, conventional AI techniques. KBS include the rule-based paradigms used in expert systems, but are tightly integrated with conventional analytic tools.

Purely mathematical approaches to problems often suffer when the real world declines to conform to rigid assumptions. There are other AI techniques, including variable precision logic, parameter learning, and pattern recognition, that are valuable in building knowledge-based systems that can intelligently apply analytical tools in dealing with the complexities of the financial world.

How do the "new" elements of knowledge-based systems differ from conventional programs? What does the new technology contribute to solving traders' problems?

Strictly speaking, any computable function, including all financial applications, can be implemented with a sufficiently large quantity of

[3] B. Sheil, "Thinking about Artificial Intelligence," *Harvard Business Review,* Fall 1987.
[4] New Science, "Expert Systems: New Opportunities for Financial Services," Conference Report, New Science Associates, Stamford, Conn., March 1987; D. Leinweber, "Financial Applications of Knowledge Based Systems," *IEEE Expert Magazine,* Summer 1988.

312 INTELLIGENT TRADING SYSTEMS

NAND ("not and") gates, or interchange operators, or a Turing machine (the theoretical analogues of machine language programming). At the most microscopic level, all the wonders of the information age come down to manipulations of a profusion of ones and zeroes.

The complexity of doing anything useful on a large scale using only these fundamental approaches is overwhelming. The sheer volume of connections or transition tables required would be enormous, and the match between the "language" constructs and the application so remote that incremental changes would become impossibly demanding. Standard machine architectures, higher level languages, and database technology have reduced practical tasks to a manageable scale. Systems analysis, structured design, and algorithmic implementation are powerful techniques. The success of this approach has been so astounding that the computer industry, which barely existed 40 years ago, is now widely viewed as central to the economic future of the developed world. Computer programs, written in traditional languages, have transformed nearly every facet of business and industry.

Given this enormous success, it is reasonable to ask why anything else is needed. Why should the architects of new trading systems go through the effort of learning and applying knowledge-based technology when existing programming techniques are so powerful?

Here is the reason: Just as the fundamental approaches are far too cumbersome for anyone except circuit designers and logic theorists, there are practical upper bounds on the complexity of amorphous and dynamic problems that can be successfully addressed with conventional programs. These bounds can be broken by incorporating knowledge-based techniques in complex applications. Expert systems and artificial intelligence do not necessarily replace conventional approaches, but they do extend them and make them useful where they were not useful before. To paraphrase Von Clausewitz, the application of knowledge-based systems technology is the continuation of programming by other means.

INTELLIGENT TRADING SYSTEMS AND INFORMATION INTEGRATION

Many of the prototype "advanced trader's workstations" being shown today exacerbate the information overload problem. A screen showing six or eight windows simultaneously, with dozens more available with a single keystroke, further complicates the traders' task of integrating the available information and making timely decisions.

The highest level requirement for a trader's workstation is to integrate market data with analytical tools to support trader strategies and efficient trade executions.

MARKET DATA FEED INTEGRATION.   Before incorporating analytics and high-level support applications, any trading system must deal with the incontrovertible fact that real-time trading requires real-time data. The front end of any trading system must accept multiple sources of data, from dozens of different suppliers. Rich and Micrognosis (together representing an installed base of over 600 major trading organizations) list over 110 distinct data sources they can accommodate. It is now the user's responsibility to select manually the most accurate and timely source for each item of market information required. This increasingly complex task gives rise to a requirement for an automated technique to provide a *best virtual feed*—the most accurate and timely synthesis of current market data.

A combination of conventional and rule-based techniques can be used to synthesize a timely and accurate price feed for use by both human traders and computerized trading systems. The essential advantage realized by these systems is the creation of the best virtual feed, which has minimal delay for each instrument and incorporates predictive pricing techniques to make use of known strong correlations between related instruments (such as near- and far-term options in a stock).

TIMELINESS AND ACCURACY.   All data feeds are subject to errors and delays. When these arise at the primary feed provided by the exchanges or NASD, they will generally be passed on without correction by providers of secondary feeds. Other errors and delays can arise from causes internal to the secondary feed distributor, such as line problems, radio interference, and queueing delays in processing. Published reports cite instances of one feed lagging another by up to a minute. In the absence of accurate time stamping at the point of origin, the feed integration system must take responsibility for selecting the most timely data. Obvious transmission errors need to be detected and corrected. Human users will spot these errors, but it is inefficient to require each and every analytic tool in the trader's arsenal to verify the same data repeatedly.

Application of conventional techniques is valuable in this context. Selection of the most timely feed can be accomplished by tracking the cumulative volume of trading in a security and selecting the source with the highest total volume. During periods of very heavy trading, when the tape lags the market by five minutes or more, the flash prices, intermittently reported by the exchanges, will be more current than the last prices, and can be automatically substituted for the last prices in all cases.

PREDICTIVE PRICING. These issues of timeliness and accuracy are fairly straightforward. A more complex consideration arises from the fact that all feeds provide the *last* price at which a trade occurred. For thinly traded securities, however, the *next* price paid or received for the security may differ significantly from the last price. In many cases, part of the difference can be predicted on the basis of price changes in related, more actively traded instruments, for which more recent prices are available. This is the case for longer term options relative to their underlying common stock and near-term options in the same series. Similar behavior is observed in the case of stocks and convertibles when the stock is close to the conversion price. The reaction of fixed-income security prices to interest rate movements can, to a large extent, be forecast with duration-based models (which are themselves prime candidates for knowledge-based systems).

The idea of the best virtual feed can be extended to include determination of the "true" closing price, exclusive of "noise" transactions.[5] These true closing prices are used extensively for accounting and overnight analytics.

To summarize, the *best virtual feed* consists of an increasingly sophisticated set of processes to ensure the timeliness of current prices and the incorporation of the best available predictive models in providing data to traders and the computer systems that support them.

BEYOND FEED INTEGRATION. Creation of the best virtual feed is just the beginning of intelligent information integration for trading systems. Feeds alone do not make a trading system. Subsequent evolutionary steps are (1) the creation of composite windows incorporating information from all sources in both textual and graphic displays in standard formats and as specified by the user; (2) the activation of composite windows to include active computation and data archiving, facilitating the development of applications that can make use of all real-time and historical information accessible over the network, providing real-time analytic support; and (3) the creation of pseudointelligent automatic assistants to:

1. Follow simple instructions to watch for patterns of interest in monitored and computed data streams, inform the trader, and adaptively tune themselves in response to user feedback.

2. Apply analytic tools in real time and communicate the results to the trader in straightforward operational terms.

[5] J. Cox and M. Rubenstein, *Options Markets* (Englewood Cliffs, N.J.: Prentice-Hall, 1985), pp. 87–92.

Higher level applications, such as hedging for both equities and fixed-income securities and securities evaluation assistants, are accommodated in this environment.

THE LOOK AND FEEL OF INTELLIGENT TRADING SYSTEMS

Consider the look and feel of the integrated trader workstation as it becomes more "intelligent": What will these things be like from the trader's viewpoint?

NO LOSS OF EXISTING CAPABILITIES. Familiar territory stays familiar. No one will lose any functionality he has now. The workstation will allow those who want to stay in "first gear" to operate in their accustomed manner. This level of integration is simply a step away from the disparate "pictures of data" illustrated in Figure 24.1, to the equivalent, but more compact, situation of Figure 24.2. The benefits are ease of access to multiple services on a single screen and fewer terminals on their desks.

FIGURE 24.1 NO INTEGRATION—"PICTURES OF DATA"

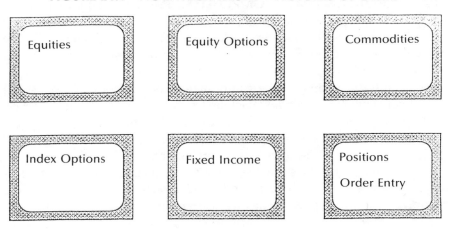

Multiple Disparate Data Sources
and Services

FIGURE 24.2 SIMPLE INTEGRATION USING WINDOWS

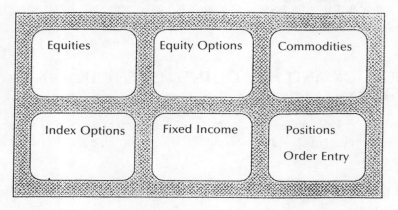

Reduced CRT Population
More Efficient "Pictures of Data"

MULTIPLE DATA SOURCE COMPOSITES. More ambitious users would have a field day. A trader operating in "second gear" could set up multiple specialized windows to help him track all the information from any service on the network, choosing the textual or graphic format he prefers, as illustrated in Figure 24.3. At this level, the best virtual feed takes on the responsibility for finding the best information source. For example, an oil stock trader could use a window tracking the major oils on all world markets while simultaneously presenting prices of spot oil and futures from commodity markets, and watching for energy-related news. The window could also include related stock and commodity price information, real-time and historical, on highly correlated instruments such as coal and transportation securities. As more information is incorporated into the window, the cognitive load on the trader heads for the red line.

ACTIVE COMPOSITES. Shifting up into "third gear," the active composites, the trader brings the power of his own firm's custom analytics to bear on his activities, illustrated in Figure 24.4. Proprietary methods can help reduce the torrent of data to a more meaningful flow of information. Valuation models, measures of volatility, and indications of the firm's

FIGURE 24.3 MULTISOURCE GRAPHIC COMPOSITES

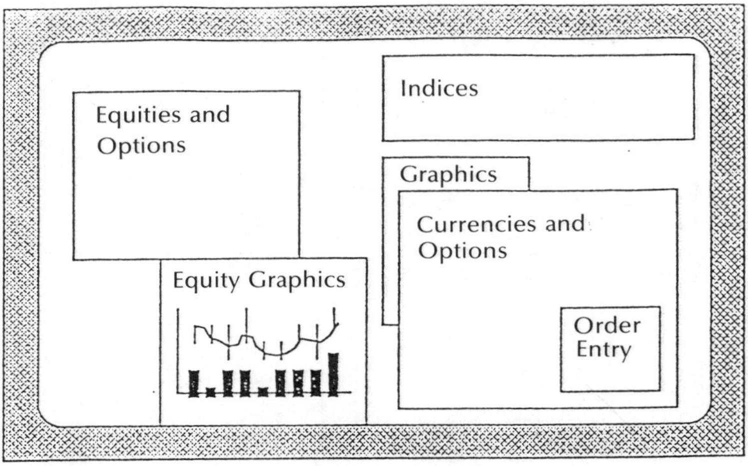

Customized User Graphics
Cross Service Compositing
High Cognitive Loading

overall position in the markets would all be included. Activation of the composites solves the widespread problem of integrating proprietary quantitative methods into daily trading activity. As more analytically based information is incorporated into the composites, the cognitive red line is approached again. The trader is watching for sequences and patterns of events in both direct and derived information. It's time to upshift one last time.

PSEUDOINTELLIGENT AGENTS. In "fourth gear," we revisit the question: If you had everything, where would you put it? Pseudointelligent agents relieve the trader of the responsibility of actually watching everything that needs to be watched and continuously correlating the multiple indicators contributing to a trading decision. Structured natural-language instructions specify the rules for these agents to combine the evidence from diverse data-tracking and analytical tools, detect patterns of interest, and explain

FIGURE 24.4   ACTIVE HIGH-LEVEL APPLICATIONS

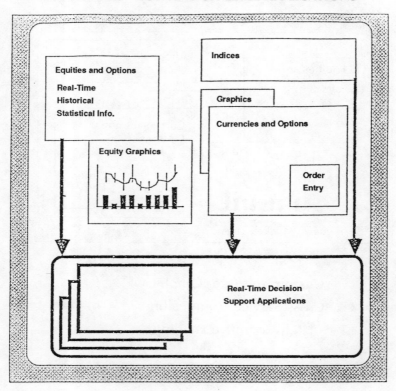

High Level Applications Utilizing
Multiple Services

concisely what was detected to the trader. This is the "society of mind" making an intelligent trading system, as illustrated in Figure 24.5.

In the context of the automotive analogy, the trader has really gone beyond the range of functions available to a single driver in any one vehicle. He now has at his disposal a fleet of Ferraris, with intelligent, diligent, observant drivers who will travel the highways watching out for the boss's interests and calling in on the car phone with clear, concise reports. Whenever warranted, the boss can instantly take over the driver's seat on any of these semiautonomous agents.

The real revolution lies in allowing the users to create pseudointelligent agents that will watch for information across many screens, all unseen by the

FIGURE 24.5   PSEUDOINTELLIGENT AGENTS

All previous levels require active
  initiation/query by trader.

Pseudo-intelligent agents can "watch"
  multiple screens of all levels at all times.

Rules for "watchers" actively combine
  all available services per trader specific
  criteria, expressed in near natural language.

Window, analytics, and composites don't
  have to be on-screen to be monitored.

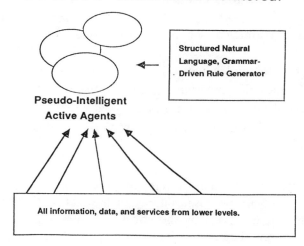

Structured Natural
Language, Grammar-
Driven Rule Generator

Pseudo-Intelligent
Active Agents

All information, data, and services from lower levels.

trader until his criteria for an event of interest are met. At that point, the
agent can bring the event to the trader's attention with a message structured
to present the salient facts in the manner requested, either graphically or as
text. (The text mode of informing traders of events detected by automated
assistants provides a smooth path for users of existing large trading-room
systems to make use of the technology without a total overhaul.)

MULTIPLE-FACTOR ADAPTIVE ALARMS

Today's quote systems allow traders to set price limit alarms. These simple
alarms tend to go off in two ways: too often and too late. Setting a narrow

range of prices results in an alarm that is nearly always on. Setting wide ranges results in a tendency to overlook events of interest until it is too late to take profitable action.

Observation of traders at work reveals a consistent behavior: When an alarm goes off, they quickly check other factors to determine its significance. These other factors include:

- Volumes associated with the price move and their relation to historical volumes in the security.
- Block volume trading.
- Measures of market forces, such as money flows, volumes per point price change, and momentum.
- Trading in related instruments such as options, convertibles, warrants, correlated securities, and issues related by takeover actions.
- Motion in known leading or lagging indicators for the security.
- Changes in option premiums relative to theoretical values.
- Relation of bid, ask, and last prices.
- News on the security, earnings reports, or financial announcements.

Today, traders must manually retrieve information from market data sources to form judgments based on any of the factors listed here. These efforts are limited, however, by the effort and time required to retrieve, analyze, and interpret the relevant information and, in many cases, the lack of recorded historical information that *was* available in the past but was not recorded for future use.

ARCHITECTURE OF INTELLIGENT ALARMING SYSTEMS. The Market Mind™ is an intelligent multiple-factor alarm that can perform the actions that the trader would take if sufficient time were available. The general structure of the system is illustrated in Figure 24.6. It consists of a set of interfaces to the various data sources, an intelligent archiving agent that saves all data required to compute the factors contributing to an alarm at the proper granularity in time, a computational agent that can perform calculations such as moving averages, other statistical operations, and more complex analyses using external programs. An integrating element, based on variable-precision logic and the Dempster-Shafer rules for the combination of evidence, combines the evidence for and against an alarm to produce

FIGURE 24.6   INTELLIGENT BEHAVIOR RESULTS FROM THE INTERACTION OF A MULTIPLICITY OF SIMPLE AGENTS

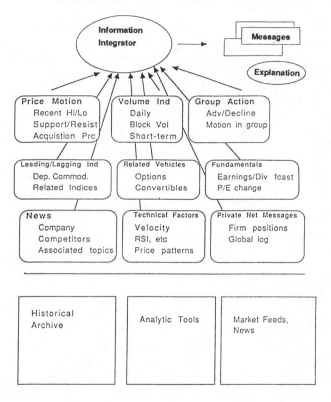

a message indicating the type of alarm (generally up or down) and the total weight of the evidence supporting it.[6]

SUBMERSION OF DETAIL.   This sounds complex, but the details are buried in the system. What the trader sees is a simple window reporting the alarm status on virtually any number of securities, as shown in Figure 24.7. In keeping with the design principles for integrating intelligent applications, it coexists peacefully with the standard market data terminal. The trader's view of the system can stop here, but there is a more sophisticated level of

[6] R. Michalski and P. Winston, "Variable Precision Logic," *Artificial Intelligence* 29(2) (1986), pp. 121–146; P. Haddaway, "Implementation of and Experiments with a Variable Precision Logic Inference System," *Proceedings of the American Association for Artificial Intelligence Conference*, 1986, pp. 238–242.

FIGURE 24.7   GENERAL STRUCTURE OF INTELLIGENT TRADING SYSTEMS

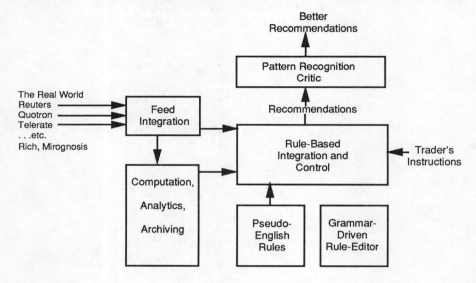

interaction that allow the system to *explain* its conclusions and to be trained to assign greater or lesser weights to the individual indications contributing to them.

Pressing the Explain key shows the factors considered, the comparison criteria, and their relative importance, stated in a simple ''language'' as shown in Figure 24.8. These explanations are essentially identical in form to the instructions given to the MarketMind™ to create the particular set of indicators that generate these alarms. They are listed in the order of the strength of their contribution to the alarm.

One further level of detail is available in the explanation: the data themselves. As shown in Figure 24.9, the indicators themselves can be quickly displayed.

Intelligent alarms are much more than alarms. They function as tireless assistants for many types of trading: fundamental, technical, arbitrage, and quantitative.

SUMMARY

This chapter has briefly described the technology that can be used to support the construction of intelligent trading systems. Intelligent trading systems must support the analytical tools and data streams used in conventional

FIGURE 24.8 THE MARKETMIND™ INTELLIGENT MONITOR ALERTS WINDOW

SQB	65	↓↓↓↓↓	PHH	34⅜	↑↑↑↑↑	CDA	17¾	↓↓↓↓↓	DOV	27¾	↓↓↓↓↓	NII	14½	↑↑↑↑↑
S	41¾	↑↑↑↑↑	ASN	23½	↓↓↓↓↓	FBO	18¾	↑↑↑↑↑	SYY	33⅞	↓↓↓↓↓	CAG	29¼	↓↓↓↓↓
WMB	31¾	↑↑↑↑↑	KB	18⅞	↓↓↓↓↓	AGC	38⅜	↓↓↓↓↓	TIN	46⅞	↓↓↓↓↓	DI	26¼	↓↓↓↓↓
MOB	42⅞	↓↓↓↓↓	FLR	19⅞	↑↑↑↑↑	ACK	33¾	↓↓↓↓↓	DPC	11¾	↓↓↓↓↓	ZY	25⅞	↓↓↓↓↓
HB	29⅝	↑↑↑↑↑	MX	24¾	↓↓↓↓↓	SPW	34½	↓↓↓↓↓	SVU	22⅞	↓↓↓↓↓	DNB	53⅞	↑↑↑↑↑
LZ	34⅞	↓↓↓↓↓	CIW	12⅞	↑↑↑↑↑	SLH	28¼	↓↓↓↓↓	CLX	31½	↑↑↑↑↑	HCA	47⅞	↑↑↑↑↑
ADD	14⅜	↓↓↓↓↓	BG	31¾	↑↑↑↑↑	AZA	23⅞	↑↑↑↑↑	FLE	22¼	↓↓↓↓↓	SCR	28⅞	↑↑↑↑↑
BBN	12¾	↑↑↑↑↑	MRN	36⅞	↓↓↓↓↓	ROR	48	↑↑↑↑↑	RHR	25¾	↓↓↓↓↓	NPK	31½	↑↑↑↑↑
DSN	25⅞	↑↑↑↑↑	CCE	14½	↑↑↑↑↑	ALK	19¾	↑↑↑↑↑	DLS	13½	↑↑↑↑↑	BFI	25⅞	↑↑↑↑
CPC	48⅝	↓↓↓↓	UTX	38⅞	↑↑↑↑	UCL	37	↑↑↑↑	KRI	44⅝	↑↑↑↑	AIG	64	↑↑↑↑
DAL	48⅞	↓↓↓↓	HP	19⅞	↑↑↑↑	MYG	28⅞	↓↓↓↓	GRN	53¾	↑↑↑↑	SLB	33⅞	↑↑↑↑
GH	8⅞	↑↑↑↑	BAC	17¾	↑↑↑↑	CYR	54¼	↓↓↓↓	Z	51⅜	↑↑↑↑	KO	42¼	↑↑↑↑
PHL	17½	↑↑↑↑	HLT	48	↑↑↑↑	JCP	53	↑↑↑↑	JR	26¼	↓↓↓↓	LOC	31⅞	↑↑↑↑
LPX	26⅝	↑↑↑↑	CBT	36	↓↓↓↓	HD	28¼	↑↑↑↑	AMX	23⅞	↑↑↑↑	AOC	27½	↓↓↓↓
LLX	31⅞	↑↑↑↑	CF	15¼	↑↑↑↑	CC	48¼	↑↑↑↑	CTX	26¼	↓↓↓↓	SRR	38½	↓↓↓↓
SNG	55	↑↑↑↑	KR	17⅜	↑↑↑↑	IFF	46½	↑↑↑↑	WHR	24¾	↓↓↓↓	AVY	28⅞	↓↓↓↓
RYL	18¾	↑↑↑↑	GT	48⅞	↓↓↓↓	UJB	22	↓↓↓↓	MCA	45	↓↓↓↓	GLW	64⅞	↓↓↓↓
FQA	29⅞	↑↑↑↑	GNG	14⅞	↓↓↓	SDW	18⅞	↓↓↓	LNC	47⅞	↑↑↑	BIR	24½	↑↑↑
GWF	15⅞	↓↓	TRN	28⅞	↑↑	UAL	97⅞	↓↓	PST	16⅞	↑↑	AAL	24⅞	↑↑
NCB	26¾	↓↓	PRM	17¾	↓↓	ISS	65¼	↓↓	HMY	19⅞	↓↓	BCR	28½	↓↓
TTC	19⅝	↑↑	CUM	48½	↓	ODR	14⅝	↑	AL	29¾	↑	HF	16⅝	↓
MES	69⅞	↑	WX	58		CPH	38¾		DEX	22		ALS	34⅞	
GPS	36⅝		BCC	41		WPM	43⅜		TXN	36⅜		AFP	29¼	
BUD	38⅝		MHP	68⅝		APS	32⅞		PPG	38⅞		BLY	21⅝	
PRD	36		LCE	38¾		DCN	35⅞		OKE	18⅜		AA	51¼	
CA	27⅞		KSF	17⅜		SGP	53¼		GS	34		SFA	11⅞	

Explain Alarm:

This window summarizes the real-time status of mutiple factor alerts for hundreds of securities, baskets, or combinations of instruments. Alerts are positive, shown with upward-pointing arrows, or negative, using down arrows. The number of arrows indicates the strength of the alert, based on quantitative or technical criteria specified by the user. One or more of these criteria must be met for the alert to be shown in the window. An explanation of which criteria caused a particular alert is obtained by typing the name of the alert at the bottom of the screen (see Figure 24.9).

FIGURE 24.9 THE MARKETMIND™ EXPLANATION WINDOW

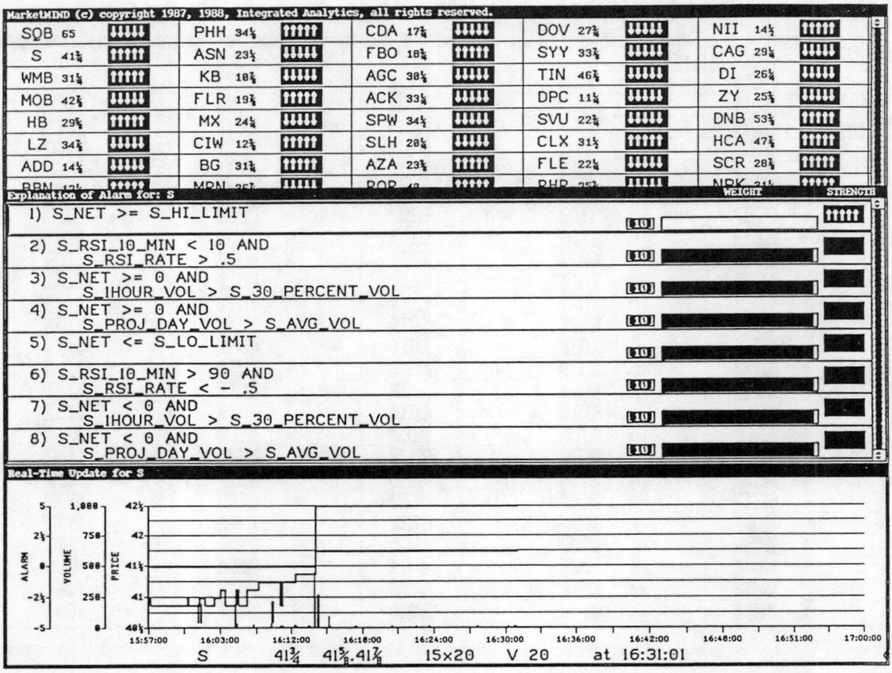

SQB 65	PHH 34½	CDA 17½	DOV 27½	NII 14½	
S 41½	ASN 23½	FBO 18½	SYY 33½	CAG 29½	
WMB 31½	KB 18½	AGC 38½	TIN 46½	DI 26½	
MOB 42½	FLR 19½	ACK 33½	DPC 11½	ZY 25½	
HB 29½	MX 24½	SPW 34½	SVU 22½	DNB 53½	
LZ 34½	CIW 12½	SLH 28½	CLX 31½	HCA 47½	
ADD 14½	BG 31½	AZA 23½	FLE 22½	SCR 28½	
RBN 14½	MRN 25½	POR 48	RHR 25½	NRK 31½	

Explanation of Alarm for: S   WEIGHT   STRENGTH

1) S_NET >= S_HI_LIMIT   [10]
2) S_RSI_10_MIN < 10 AND
   S_RSI_RATE > .5   [10]
3) S_NET >= 0 AND
   S_IHOUR_VOL > S_30_PERCENT_VOL   [10]
4) S_NET >= 0 AND
   S_PROJ_DAY_VOL > S_AVG_VOL   [10]
5) S_NET <= S_LO_LIMIT   [10]
6) S_RSI_10_MIN > 90 AND
   S_RSI_RATE < - .5   [10]
7) S_NET < 0 AND
   S_IHOUR_VOL > S_30_PERCENT_VOL   [10]
8) S_NET < 0 AND
   S_PROJ_DAY_VOL > S_AVG_VOL   [10]

Real-Time Update for S

S   41¾   41⅜·41⅞   15×20   V 20   at 16:31:01

When an explanation is requested, a new window appears. The top of the Alerts Window remains visible. The center portion of the explanation window lists the criteria that can contribute to the alert and the current strength of their contribution. The upward voting criteria in this example are: (1) an adaptive hi-limit that continually adjusts itself based on the absolute level of the stock price and the expected move calculated from the stock's beta, (2) a relative strength indicator and a rate of change in the indicator, (3) a rolling one-hour volume total to detect large blocks, and (4) a projected daily volume to use the observed time–volume to predict when a stock will have an unusually high closing volume. Criteria 5 through 8 are the downward voting counterparts. At the time this explanation was requested, only criterion 1 contributed to the alert. A graph of the alarm status, stock price, and volume is shown at bottom. Graphs of the indicators referenced in each criterion can be brought up on demand.

designs. Moreover, they must provide additional value in allowing traders to integrate indications from a variety of information sources. Provision of a means to learn adaptively from mistakes distinguishes these approaches.

With the rise of 24-hour global trading and the increasing interrelations among securities, the tasks facing traders and trading organizations will become increasingly complex. Intelligent trading systems will follow the chalkboard, ticker tape, video feed, and Fortran as the next step in the evolution of financial systems.

The Editor Asks

Q *The field of artificial intelligence has a notorious reputation for failing to deliver, after great effort and cost, on its promises and expectations. What is different about the approach you suggest that makes it more likely to succeed?*

A AI's bad reputation is only partially deserved. Part of the problem comes from a tendency in the AI research community to disown their successes. These include pattern recognition technology used in optical character recognition, voice response, and military electronics. The original "friendly" interfaces, now central to Lotus and Macintosh products, had their origins in AI labs. This kind of behavior leaves the AI crowd with only unsolved problems.

In financial applications, the notorious reputation comes largely from a misapplication of the technology. People have run off attempting to solve the grand macro- and microeconomic problems of the world. Trying to replace centuries of quantitative economic thought with a collection of if–then rules that can tell you where soybeans are headed, and when, is a futile exercise.

The basic problem is that the "knowledge" people sought to engineer into these systems was conceptual, much too high-level. The approach described here aims lower, at the quantitative tools and computer systems that already exist to support traders. These tools would see far greater profitable use by traders if they were easier to deal with—and we are making them easier to deal with.

25

BOND TRANSACTIONS AND BOND TRANSACTION COSTS

Greta E. Marshall and Wayne H. Wagner

The Department of Labor (DOL) has indicated that it views transaction costs of pension funds to be expenditures of trust assets. As such, the DOL believes, transaction costs should be subject to trust standards; that is, it should be assured that the expenditures are made for the exclusive benefit of trust beneficiaries.

From the standpoint of fiduciary duty, the DOL in its recent release on Section 28(e) made its views clear:

> The fiduciary who appoints the investment manager is not relieved of his ongoing duty to monitor the investment manager to assure that the manager has *secured best execution* of the plan's transactions and to assure that *the commissions paid on such transactions are reasonable* in relation to the value of the brokerage and research services provided to the plan [emphasis added].

The DOL is equally clear that best execution includes more than just the commission:

> An investment manager's responsibility to seek best execution under the circumstances requires the manager to consider not only the commissions for the transaction but *the quality and reliability of the execution* [emphasis added].

This ruling dovetails with the sentiments of plan sponsors that transaction costs are penalizing investment performance.[1] Over the five years ended December 31, 1986, the TUCS median *equity* manager underperformed the

---

[1] See Chapter 2, "A Sponsor Looks at Trading Costs," by Robert E. Shultz.

S&P 500 by 96 basis points per year, whereas the average *bond* manager underperformed the Salomon Broad Index by 60 basis points.

All underperformance results from inferior investment decisions and/or the costs of implementing those decisions. Just as with equities, the bond performance shortfall can be partially explained by management decisions such as quality or duration differences and timing decisions. Yet most sponsors suspect that the major drag on performance is most likely to be transaction cost.

All the attention to transaction costs to date—including this book—have focused on equity transaction costs and totally ignored bond transaction costs. Given that nonequity assets are roughly half of pension assets, it is curious indeed that the subject of bond transacting and bond transaction costs evokes only shoulder shrugs among sponsors, managers, traders—all those who are concerned about transaction costs. This is especially surprising since bond turnover is typically greater than equities. In fact, a major bond management technique for adding value, "swapping," involves many transactions for modest "pickups" in yield or quality.

In preparation for writing this chapter, we conducted a literature search on bond transaction costs. This literature search turned up *not a single published article that addressed bond transaction costs*. We found no transaction cost estimates beyond the usual rule-of-thumb benchmarks—"a quarter to a half on corporates, $\frac{4}{32}$ on governments, more for municipals, junk and thin traders." Few, if any, analyses have been written concerning such questions as:

1. What are bond transaction costs? How can they be measured?
2. Has bond transaction cost affected performance?
3. Do certain bond trades cost more than others? Which ones? Why?
4. What services are bundled into bond transaction costs? Are these services provided at a justifiable price?
5. Are there alternative means of trading bonds, useful under certain circumstances and situations, that may be less costly?

The reason for this is quickly apparent: Bond transaction decisions are devilishly difficult to analyze. It is not that bond transactions are inherently more difficult to analyze; rather, the data necessary to analyze them are simply unavailable. This is in marked contrast to the wealth of data available on equity markets.

It is useful to contrast the operations of the equity markets against those of the bond markets. From that perspective, we can propose some changes that we believe are in the best interests of bond dealers as well as bond investors.

STOCK MARKET FEATURES

Investors who take trades to the NYSE floor or to any of the off-floor "meet" markets stand a good chance of completing their trade without the services of a dealer. On the floor of the Exchange, for example, a floor broker representing a public order can—and frequently does—compete with the specialist to fill the order. Any buyer who offers a better price has standing over the specialist (or any other buyer, for that matter). By the rules of the exchange, any public order has precedence over a specialist order at the same price.

The net effect is that investors compete with dealers to fill the order. The result is a sequence of events that leads to substantial changes in the market:

1. Spreads are narrowed by the competition between investors and dealers. This squeezes dealer profit *per inventory turn*.

2. More capital—investor capital—is available to support the market mechanism. This capital helps dealers lay off risk, which reduces their cost of doing business. (As we learned in October 1987, this second implication can become crucial at times.)

3. Narrow spreads and deeper markets mean more liquidity. Investors are able to trade on finer distinctions between the asset to be bought and the one to be sold. They are more likely to fine-tune their strategies and increase turnover rates. Liquidity leads to more active markets, which means more turns and more frequent opportunities for dealers to earn a spread.

4. The higher velocity of the market more than compensates for the thinning of the spread. The net result is increased profits for the dealers and brokers. In 1975 the New York Stock Exchange, under pressure from institutional investors, abandoned its cherished fixed-commission schedule. The net result, despite dire predictions, was an explosion in volume and far larger commission and dealer income than ever before.

STOCK MARKET INNOVATIONS

There are two innovations created by the New York Stock Exchange that have had tremendous effects on opening the markets and easing market participation:

1. The widespread broadcasting of the current best bid/best offer.
2. The rapid public dissemination of information on completed trades on the transaction tape.

Both of these information streams have the effect of keeping investors better informed about the immediate value of their current holdings or potential purchases. With this information, they are better able to form investment judgments and trading strategies.

The important lesson is that *dissemination of information liquifies markets*. Investors gain comfort, they transact more frequently and with greater confidence, and all market participants gain.

In the process of creating a public record, a historical database is created. University business professors and quantitative managers love databases: They will use them to develop additional investment insights and strategies. As a result, more players with different viewpoints will be drawn to the markets, with more transacting and more liquidity as the result.

Also, the historical database provides the background contextual data for transaction effectiveness measurement. Sponsors are better able to fulfill their fiduciary responsibilities, and more new trading and investment strategies will be devised.

Transaction costs are estimated by comparison to (presumably) neutral prices. The ability to form expectationally neutral prices requires a transaction tape and a record of bid/asked quotes, facilities that no stock trader would dream of living without. In contrast, bond traders operate in near darkness with respect to previous trades and competitive dealer quotes.

A bond transaction tape and a bond quote montage are not difficult to create: A quite similar process occurs constantly for third-market trades. The problem is not technological; rather, it is a problem of perception and willingness to change.

BOND MARKET FEATURES

The bond market is a dealer market: Whenever an investor wishes to transact, he must, with rare exception, do so through a dealer. The dealer buys and sells out of his own inventory, and takes his profits in the difference between the prices at which he buys versus the prices at which he sells.

The bond market is not the only dealer market around; Treasury securities, foreign stocks, and OTC issues are also dealer-based markets.

Clearly, there is something highly *workable* in the nature of a dealer market.

Dealer markets are a historical necessity: When buyer and seller have difficulty finding each other in time and location, the dealer represents the glue that holds the market together. Dealers provide liquidity, give traders the anonymity they desire, and provide the essential financial guarantees that the trade will clear and settle.

Bonds differ from equities in that (1) they have a maturity date and (2) there is a constant need for underwriting new issues. Dealers need an active market in which to sell bonds they may have been required to buy from customers taking down positions in a new underwriting.

Dealer markets are thus a natural adjunct to underwriting: The underwriter commits to both the issuer and the buyers that he stands ready to buy and sell the securities, thus assuring buyers that they can liquidate when they so desire. Buyers are more willing to make commitments, and this reduces interest rates to the bond issuer and greatly enhances the proceeds from the issued securities.

In addition, there is a growing trend for managers and pension sponsors to use bond executions, particularly concessions to dealers for new bond underwritings, as a source of additional soft dollar payments for research services. Those research services may or may not be related to bond portfolio management.

The dealers' need for liquidity has encouraged the explosion of "swapping" activities. Bond dealers invest huge sums in research departments and computer models to present these swaps to their customers. Each swap leaves the dealer with inventory to generate a follow-up swap with another customer. It is difficult to envision an endless chain of swaps, each of them beneficial to all the clients along the chain. Yet it is easy to envisage spread profits to the dealers from each transaction.

BEYOND DEALER MARKETS

The shortcomings of dealer markets stem from the fact that, as the markets grow and become more liquid, the dealers' services become less essential. This is not good news to the dealers. Having worked and put themselves at risk, they expect a continuing lucrative payoff for their efforts. Movement away from strictly dealer-based markets jeopardizes the advantages they have worked so hard to secure.

The major protections for a dealer monopoly are (1) the lack of supply and demand information on the part of buyers and sellers and (2) a reliable method of verifying market prices. Investors now must rely on a dealer's "market sense" or—even worse—a matrix-derived bond price to determine fair market prices for individual bonds. Bond prices are thus estimates of appraised value set by the very dealers who sell to a less than perfectly informed public out of the firm's own inventory. Dealer market sense is effectively little more than an ability to create a dependency surrounding the trading information that is vital to buyers and sellers.

The advantage conferred to the dealers is this: *They, and only they, know where the supply and demands lie.* This is valuable information indeed, and dealers are not likely to give it up willingly in the interest of creating more transparent markets. This attitude, however, may be shortsighted: As we have identified, there are many advantages to more open and transparent markets, and some of those advantages accrue to the dealers themselves.

This is not to suggest that dealer markets are grossly inefficient—as long as sufficient competition among dealers exists. But this competition exists in a particular context, the context as defined by the bond dealer. The question is whether it is *necessary* for a dealer to be imposed in the middle of every transaction. Might there be at least some trades that could be handled less expensively if no dealer were involved? Within any long-standing market structure, some frozen, traditional cost structures that have been developed in well-established and seasoned dealer markets may be taken for granted. Some of these may result in higher transaction costs to bond investors, leading to poorer investment performance.

Still, it is hazardous to get from here to there, and dealers are not likely to undertake that dangerous voyage unless compelled to do so. Herein lies a role for the institutional investors, who have the power to hasten the process of changes that are in their aggregate best interests.

SUMMARY

Equity traders operate in a world dominated by scrutiny, alternative methods of trading, and public disclosure of information. In contrast, the bond market trader operates in an almost medieval atmosphere of secrets and undisclosed deal-making. The evolution of the bond market will pick up speed when sponsors question the frictional costs of trading bonds in the same manner as they have for equities.

The Editor Asks

Q *What specific suggestions would you make to encourage a more efficient and fair bond market?*

A Several innovations (or restorations of certain rules) would ensure a more efficient and fair market. They should apply equally to all stocks and all bonds:

1. All transactions should be reported in a timely fashion on a composite tape available to all investors.
2. Order books should be exposed to everyone, and no trades should be executed that are not exposed on the books.
3. Both buying and selling brokers should be required to identify themselves on every trade.
4. Analysis of transaction costs should be performed for all ERISA stock and bond accounts.

PART SEVEN

Market Structures and Market Efficiency

26

ETHICAL ISSUES IN TRADING

John J. Morton

Ethics is an interesting topic in the investment industry. A practice may initially be considered unethical; but after experimentation, then occasional use, then common use, it often becomes an accepted part of doing business. We currently employ methods of trading that most of us would have dismissed as unacceptable not so long ago. I am not here to accuse anyone or condemn the system. I am someone who, for the past 30 years, has been actively trading in a system that means a great deal to me. I admire the auction process of the New York Stock Exchange; I support it; and I think it is worth saving.

In early 1987, there was an article in *Institutional Investor* that maintained that the client comes second—that "as principle [*sic*] activities grow, an atmosphere of mistrust is enveloping Wall Street's traditional relationships."[1] We must begin to pay attention to what other people say about us. It is satisfying to be respected, and I believe we should all work toward earning that respect.

My presentation is based on a survey that was recently completed by TraderForum, a division of the Institutional Investor Group. It is entitled *"The Buyside Sellside Relationship: Assessments and Predictions."* The TraderForum allows buy-side traders the opportunity to analyze, discuss, and debate issues of interest and subjects of concern. A questionnaire was sent out to both buy-side and sell-side traders. Five hundred forty-five questionnaires were sent out and the response rate was 26%. The results are

Reprinted with permission from "Ethical Issues in Trading" by John J. Morton, 1988, a chapter in *Trading Strategies and Execution Costs*, Charlottesville, Va.: Institute of Chartered Financial Analysts.
[1] H. Sender, "The Client Comes Second," *Institutional Investor*, March 1987.

eye-opening. Let me quote directly from the survey some of the most revealing statements:[2]

> The overwhelming majority of the survey respondents on both the buyside and the sellside agreed that the relationship between the two sides has changed. And a substantial number on both sides believed that these changes have not been for the better. . . . Approximately seven out of every ten traders on both sides agreed partially or fully that the relationship of the sellside to the buyside has become "intrinsically adversarial" since brokerage firms began taking principal positions in the market.

Who is responsible? Each side blames the other:

> Over half the respondents on both sides agreed on one sellside factor as a major contributor to the strained relations: the decline in brokerage commissions. . . . Declining sellside ethical standards were viewed as a problem by almost 40 percent of the buyside respondents, but only 24 percent of the sellside agreed that this was a problem. . . . Both sides concurred in naming large mainstream brokerage firms as most likely to cause problems for the buyside or most apt to be guilty of abuses. Almost a third of the sellside respondents but only 16 percent of those on the buy side identified third-party research firms as most guilty of abuses. . . .
>
> Boutiques were perceived by both sides as being less likely to engage in abusive practices, and regional brokers fared the best of all. . . . More than half of the buyside traders said that they had personally encountered instances of privileged clients receiving first calls before a broker publicly issued a recommendation on a security. Over 40 percent of the sellside agreed that this was a problem. Moreover, almost half of the buyside experienced "frontrunning" (information beating orders to the floor). Again, just over 40 percent of the sellside also saw this as a problem. . . . The two sides agreed that information about orders being fed to middlemen is a substantial problem. More than a third of the buyside traders said that they encountered brokers exchanging information about customers' orders—and beating those orders to the floor.

It is rather disheartening. But there is more:

> Sixty-three percent of the sellside traders said they believed that the buyside push for lower commission rates is becoming more widespread. Over half also predicted that the buyside's expectations of a high level of service will remain,

---

[2] *Buyside-Sellside Relationship: Assessments and Predictions.* Survey conducted by *Institutional Investor* for its TraderForum Research Service, July 1987.

despite lower rates. A similar number believe that the buyside running ahead of the sellside is a problem that will intensify.

What did the *Institutional Investor* say? A growing mistrust is enveloping Wall Street's traditional relationships?

> Several . . . buysiders pointed to the damage that the flow of information can do to the buyside/sellside relationship, with "more and more information flowing to the hedge funds and 'fast money' people instead of the sellside and the buyside working closely together."

That statement cries for attention. Can reasonable people no longer sit down to discuss the problem intelligently and constructively, in the open, or must we continue to self-destruct? Many of us have spent years building and maintaining relationships of trust, and are not ready to abandon them without at least trying to re-create some of the ethics of the past. We have a handshake business. I sell, you buy—a solid contract. We are only as good as our word. One final statement from the survey:

> Almost one-fourth of the traders on both sides . . . agreed that problems have resulted because the sellside firms have become larger and more impersonal. . . . Individual buysiders also cited . . . other factors, including . . . the "large increase in the number of fast money players" . . . and the proliferation of small trading accounts which "are making money off the information they receive from the exchange floors and block trading desks—in direct conflict with their institutional orders."

I think I have made my point. It appears that the industry has some problems.

ADVERSARIAL AND PROPRIETARY TRADING

There are two trading roles identified by the survey that are important— adversarial and proprietary trading. Adversarial trading—also known as frontrunning—is a big problem for both sides according to the survey. This game involves many players; I will discuss two of them. The first player is the middle man, or, as they prefer to be called, flow traders. If one is sufficiently clever to trade flow or momentum successfully, then there is no problem. These middle men, however, trade with privileged information that allows them to take prices that rightfully belong to the initiating customer. Flow traders are considered by most of the major brokers as bona fide customers.

The following is an example of adversarial trading. An institution calls its broker to enter an order to buy 100,000 shares of XYZ. The sales traders assigned to cover these fast-money accounts relay this information on to the middleman as they would to any other customer, hoping to find the other side of the trade. The middleman is not really expected to have the other side. He simply calls another broker and attempts to pick up what is available in the marketplace before the customer's order hits the floor. If the customer appears to be aggressive, the flow trader competes with him for his order for stock flow, and then sells it back to the end customer at a higher price. This is a great business for everyone but the customer. The broker makes money from a good, commission-producing customer, and the middleman makes money without question. The only one who loses is the end customer—and often the customer does not know what has happened. Let me stress that in many cases, the middleman pays the broker more commissions than the institutional accounts. As a result, they are very valuable customers.

The second group that does front running is the brokers themselves. Many brokers have proprietary—or risk-assuming—trading desks staffed by traders who supposedly are willing to commit capital to facilitate customers' demands. To many of us, a good risk trader is a beneficial partner, a person that may add value to a transaction. But some firms have too many of them. They have risk traders assigned to groups or subgroups of industries—one for chemicals, one for retailers, one for oils, one for papers, and so forth. There are so many of them that some may go for days without getting a call from a customer. But they are a profit center, and they must make money.

In terms of front-running, the only difference between the middle men and the brokers is the source of information. The floor of the New York Stock Exchange is the brokers' domain. Their partners are the floor brokers that work for them, and the independent brokers that are employed by them. Most floor brokers today are zoned: Instead of traveling all over the exchange floor to execute orders, they remain in certain small areas. Some cover two or three different posts, some just one specialist firm, and others just one very active stock. Many of the independents used to be referred to as two-dollar brokers because they got a $2 fee for every 100 shares they executed. Since May Day, they have negotiated rates. Many of these two-dollar brokers provide service to the upstairs firms—the risk traders— for a fixed amount each month. Depending on demand, they could receive $2,000 to $3,000 per month for execution and information. These brokers are now referred to as contractual brokers. Many have contracts with more than one firm. The information side of the contract is to monitor orders that are introduced into their zone. Information on significant orders in their area is transmitted to their upstairs partners. If it looks like a rewarding situation, then the risk trader will employ the broker to buy some for their own account along with the end customer.

There we have it—one customer, a middleman or two, and a couple of risk traders or proprietary brokers, all competing for stock. How did this happen? My estimation is that some time ago, Wall Street decided that it would forgo long-term relationships for short-term profits. Many of the young professionals today actually think that this is the way the business should be conducted. They were trained to go for the dollar instead of providing services. We allowed it to happen. Many firms employ traders that are not properly trained. There is no entrance fee for becoming a trader, no qualifying examination. The buy side, at certain times, even makes it easy for the adversaries. One common practice in the execution process is to enter orders in what is commonly referred to as a go-along—a participate-but-do-not-initiate form of execution. They, too, go with the flow. This type of order is very easy to execute. Both the customer and the broker are relieved of any burden to make decisions. The order is simply left with the specialist, who executes it. That is how the middleman and the proprietary trader may take advantage of the order. Can you blame them? After all, nobody is minding the store.

A broker will not run ahead of an order that he or she is responsible for executing. When a broker receives an order from a customer to execute as agent, he then assumes the role of the fiduciary. I believe that no broker will break the trust. At the same time, most brokers and traders in this business do a fine job, are truly dedicated, and work very hard at getting best execution. But one must know the games people play and how to beat them.

BEATING THE PROFESSIONAL TRADING DESK

Trading is an all-day job that takes a great deal of work, study, and principle. Institutions must work at creating truly professional trading desks. Brokers will have to settle for longer term profitable relationships. We all must remember the word "trust." Unfortunately, we now have less trust in the system than we had a few years ago. According to the TraderForum survey, the trust is quickly disappearing. This is not a good situation. One major complaint is the Exchange itself: Does it protect the customer's order? Should it protect the customer's order? I feel very strongly that the Exchange is an agency auction market that charges the customer a commission to execute, and thus has a responsibility to protect that agent from the adversarial forces that prey on the system.

I have been a strong supporter of the auction market for many years. I want to see that process succeed. But if it does not protect the customer then the customer will have to protect himself by whatever avenues are open to him. We can continue to do business the way we are doing it today and probably destroy a good market in the process, or we can work together by returning the ethics and integrity to the trading arenas, and returning the market to the customer. One thing we must never forget is that we all work for the customer. The customer pays us a fee to protect his interest. We had better start earning that fee.

Let me comment on one other subject: In the survey, brokers claimed that they had to resort to this adversarial type of trading because the institutions had driven the commissions so low that they could not make an economic living. My question is: What is "economic"? I honestly do not know whether commissions are too high or too low; but I do know that the buy side did not drive them down. Competition drove them down—competition from the industry itself. Some brokers are willing to work for less and pass that savings on to their customers, which is certainly appreciated—and that is competition from within the industry. A handful of smaller firms may execute well and profitably for themselves at something less than what the majors need to break even—and that is competition from within. Third-party firms, many of whom are the major firms themselves, can charge a rate and then rebate a portion of that fee to pay for additional services provided—and that is certainly competition from within.

COMMISSIONS

There are a few other facts that merit discussion. According to the Greenwich study on commissions by Charles Ellis, actual dollars that have been paid out by institutions have increased by almost 400% since May Day, 1975. In part, the increase is a function of volume. At the same time, we have introduced many efficiencies into this system: The Depository Trust Company has grown to such a level of efficiency that it now can clear most of the domestic trades; and with affirmation between customers, those trades will clear on settlement date without problems. This results in a lower cost of settlement to the broker and a decline in the cost of carry, the interest cost, to the broker. There is automation in the form of DOT (Designated Order Turnaround) and SuperDOT systems. This reduces floor costs for brokers. Over the same period, ticket size has tripled, so there is more production on each ticket. We are probably costing our tickets incorrectly. Perhaps commissions should be figured by tickets rather than in cents per share. That is how Wall Street figures their commissions—$20, $30, $40 per ticket. Everything else is profit. But they charge us on a cents-per-share basis.

I wish that I had solutions to all of these problems, but I do not. Brokers claim that customers have to pay for liquidity, and that is one reason for higher commissions. But is it? If some institutions use the broker for liquidity, should those that do not subsidize that activity? Or if an institution uses liquidity for one account, should the other accounts in that institution subsidize that activity? Similarly, perhaps we should negotiate a separate rate on trades that use the broker's capital. Brokers claim that we must provide research, and that that cost is part of the commissions. But if we use one or two of their analysts, or one or two of their stories, must we subsidize all of the other analysts and stories? If we use none of their analysts, should we subsidize activities that add no value to our process? These other activities should be segregated from the agency business, and they should pay their own way.

There is plenty of room in this business to provide a comfortable living for most of the participants, but we must get rid of the excesses. The money belongs to the customer, and the customer must be represented. The damage is not beyond repair; there are too many good people in this industry. Perhaps if we work together, we can smooth out the process and return the market to the ultimate owners of securities.

The Editor Asks

Q *You've laid your finger on some issues of deep concern. In search of some answers to these problems, could you list three positive steps that an institutional trader can take to protect his customers' interests, either short-term or long-term?*

A Customers will have to learn to insulate their inquiries from front-runners. Customers should force brokers to decide whether they will protect the customer's best interest or their own. They should declare their primary interest as either proprietor or agent, but they should not tolerate brokers posing as agents and acting as proprietors.

Best execution should be the responsibility of the executing institution, and not transferred to a broker. The broker should be the tool, but the institution should possess the mind.

Alternative markets must be explored to minimize transaction costs.

27

THE ECONOMICS OF THE DEALER FUNCTION

Jack L. Treynor

The bulk of securities trading is motivated by the investor's desire to improve his performance, at the expense of the investor on the other side of the trade: We cannot buy an underpriced security unless the seller sells it too cheap. We cannot sell to avoid the price consequences of bad news without imposing these consequences on the buyer.

This sort of trading—adversarial trading—has the two fundamentally different motives illustrated in the previous paragraph: *value* and *information*. When done by financial institutions, it begins with two different kinds of research—analysis (à la the CFA program, Graham and Dodd, etc.) and investigation, respectively—conducted by two fundamentally different types of investment organization (top down and bottom up, respectively)—and ends in two fundamentally different kinds of trading (the selling of time and the buying of time, respectively).

The information trader is eager to trade before his information gets into the consensus: In order to trade at a time of his choosing, he willingly pays someone else's price. The value trader is willing to wait until he finds substantial discrepancy between price and value: In order to trade at a price of his choosing, he trades at a time chosen by someone else. This is why we say the former is buying time, while the latter is selling time, with the price of the time bought and sold being the discrepancy between the trade price of the security and its value.

It is probably obvious that, although both would prefer their trading counterparts to be innocent—what we have called *liquidity-motivated*—rather than adversarial, information and value traders are destined to do most of their trading with each other. In practice, however, this fundamental truth about securities markets is obscured by the intermediation of dealers—

exchange specialists, OTC dealers, and block positioners. On one hand, the dealer has no information that can damage the value investor who trades with him. On the other, the dealer's spread is typically so small that it represents a negligible cost to the information investor. Thus, dealers' motives are remarkably innocent.

How does the dealer survive doing business this way? What does it really cost to do business with the dealer? These are important questions for the investor, which can be resolved only by understanding the economics of dealing.

A dealer facilitates market liquidity by intermediating between transactors to whom time is important in exchange for charging buyers a higher price than he pays sellers. A value-based investor may also fulfill this function, but at a larger bid–asked spread than that imposed by the dealer. Relative to the value-based investor, the dealer has limited capital, hence limited ability to absorb risk; he will thus limit the position—long or short—he is willing to take.

When the dealer's position reaches a maximum, he will lay off to the only other transactor motivated by price—the value-based investor. The dealer's price is tied to the value-based investor's price at these layoff points. As the value-based investor shifts his prices in response to new information, the dealer's interior prices shift along with his layoff prices.

An investor should realize that, when he trades with the crowd, he is trading at the value-based investor's spread, which may be many times the size of the explicit dealer's spread. More generally, the actions of the crowd—whether it is buying or selling, and in what volume—will determine whether the price of trading quickly is high or low, hence whether the value of his information justifies trading.

MARKET-MAKERS

A market-maker may be defined as someone who accommodates transactors to whom time is important in return for the privilege of charging buyers a higher price than he pays sellers. By this definition, both dealers and value-based investors (VBTs) are market-makers. Yet their roles differ in several important respects:

- In amount of capital, hence ability to absorb losses.
- In length of holding, hence exposure to getting bagged.
- In the spreads (i.e., the difference in bid and asked price imposed on simultaneous purchases and sales).

In particular, the VBT's spread is larger than the dealer's spread; we call them, respectively, the "outside" and "inside" spread. In the absence of dealers, transactors in a hurry would buy and sell at prices that differ by the full outside, or VBT, spread—even if purchase and sale took place only seconds apart. By intermediating between hurried buyers and hurried sellers, a dealer enables them to benefit from each other's trading, even if the trades aren't simultaneous.

Dealers are thus valuable to transactors in a hurry, because they greatly reduce the spreads encountered by those transactors. By doing so, they also greatly improve the liquidity of the markets in which they deal. Alas for the dealer and for market liquidity, a seller is not always followed by a buyer. Indeed, even if the arrival of buyers and sellers is random, a seller may be followed by a long run of sellers (or a buyer by a long run of buyers), with the result that the dealer builds up a large position.

Compared with the VBT, the dealer has very limited capital with which to absorb an adverse move in the value of the asset. Furthermore, the dealer's spread is too modest to compensate him for getting bagged. The dealer consequently sets limits on the position—long or short—he is willing to take. When his position reaches a limit, he lays off to the only other transactor in the market who is motivated by price—the value-based investor. (Strictly speaking, when his position grows uncomfortably short, he "buys in"; to avoid circumlocution, we shall use the term "lay off" algebraically.) In effect, the value-based investor is the market-maker of last resort. Figure 27.1 combines these elements in a diagram.

In the problem we address, the value-based investor's bid and asked price and the standard size of orders coming to the dealer for accommodation are givens. We also take as given the maximum position—long or short—the dealer is willing to assume. We ask two questions:

- How will the dealer's mean price—the mean of his bid and asked—vary with his position?
- How big will the dealer's spread be? What determines it?

We shall assume that VBTs get new information as soon as the dealer's customers. Otherwise, of course, accumulations in the dealer's position will not be unaffected by the arrival of new information.

When information reaches the VBT, his bid and asked prices shift to reflect it. Because the dealer's price is tied to the VBT bid and ask at his layoff points, his prices move along with the VBT prices. In general, therefore, dealer prices are responding to two different forces—changes in the VBT's estimate of value and changes in the dealer's position.

FIGURE 27.1 DEALER'S SPREAD AND MAXIMUM POSITION

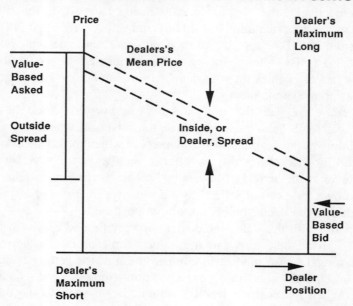

DETERMINING THE DEALER'S SPREAD

Dealers have salaries, telephone bills, and other costs, just like any businessman. Unless these costs have a significant variable component, however, a dealer's dominant variable cost will be the cost of laying off. If, in dealing, price is related to variable cost, then the price the dealer exacts for his services—the dealer's spread—will be related to the cost of laying off—the outside spread.

In the limiting case of perfect competition among dealers, the revenues the dealer receives from his accommodations will equal the costs of laying off. Because the outside spread will typically be many times the dealer's spread, however, revenues will equal costs only if layoffs are far less frequent than accommodations. More precisely, the ratio of the two spreads must equal the inverse ratio of the respective transaction frequencies. To obtain this ratio, we need to know the frequency of transactions.

THE FREQUENCY OF LAYOFFS

Perhaps the simplest way to think about this problem is in terms of accommodation trades of a fixed size. Such trades cause the dealer's position to jump from one inventory position to an adjacent position. The continuum of dealer positions is thus reduced to a number of discrete positions, like beads spaced evenly along a string. Purchases and sales arrive in random order (but equal frequency), so moves up or down the string occur in random order. This is illustrated in Figure 27.2.

At the ends of the string are beads corresponding to the dealer's maximum tolerable positions. We call them the "layoff positions." (We assume the dealer is willing to adjust his layoff positions so they are separated by a whole number of standard accommodations.) When the dealer's position reaches either extreme, the next transaction may move it back toward a neutral position or forward beyond the dealer's maximum. In the latter case the dealer either buys in (paying an asking price above his own asking price) or lays off (realizing a bid price below his own bid). Thus every share (every unit) laid off represents a loss to the dealer.

If there are no fixed costs of laying off that can be spread over the units laid off, it behooves the dealer to lay off only the units (long or short) acquired in accommodating the current trade. After such a layoff, his position is restored to the layoff position, from which subsequent accommodations will sometimes move him back toward the neutral position at no additional layoff cost.

To define this process algebraically, let X be the dealer's position, X^* the dealer's maximum position, S the standard accommodation and $G(X)$ the frequency with which the dealer finds himself in that position in the steady state. Then, for interior positions, we can write:

$$G(X) = 0.5\ G\ (X - S) + 0.5\ G(X + S),$$

reflecting the fact that buy and sell accommodations are equally likely. In other words, the frequency with which the position X occurs depends on the frequency with which the adjacent positions occur, times the probability (0.5 in each case) of moves from those positions toward the X position, rather than away from it.

FIGURE 27.2   DEALER'S STRING OF TRANSACTIONS

Intermediate Positions

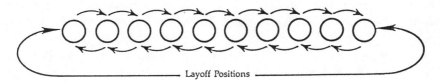

Layoff Positions

We can rewrite this relation as follows:

$$0.5\ G(X) - 0.5G\ (X - S) = 0.5G(X + S) - 0.5G(X).$$

Now its meaning is clearer: The rate of change of $G(X)$ is everywhere the same. Only a straight-line function of X satisfies this condition. Furthermore, the symmetry between buy and sell orders dictates that this function be symmetric with respect to positive and negative values of X. The only straight-line function that satisfies this condition is a horizontal line: $G(X)$ is a constant; the probability of each position is the same.

If layoffs are the same size as a standard accommodation then, when a dealer reaches his layoff position, his next accommodating transaction is equally likely to (1) move him one position closer to neutrality or (2) force him to lay off, in which case the net effect is to return him to the layoff position. If X^* is the upper layoff position, then in the steady state we have:

$$G(X^*) = 0.5G(X^*) + 0.5G(X^* - S),$$
$$G(X^*) = G(X^* - S) = G(X).$$

A similar result holds for the lower layoff position.

If all possible positions, including layoff positions, occur with the same frequency, then layoff positions occur with a frequency equal to the standard accommodation divided by twice the dealer's layoff position, times two, because there are two layoff positions. But layoff positions actually lead to layoffs only half the time. Thus layoffs occur with a frequency equal to the standard accommodation divided by twice the dealer's layoff position:

$$\text{Layoff Frequency} = S/2X^*.$$

The spread, $p_a - p_b$, that enables the dealer to break even is:

$$p_a - p_b = S/2X^*\ (P_a - P_b),$$

where $P_a - P_b$ is the outside, or VBT's spread. If the dealer charges more than this, he's covering at least some of his other costs. Not surprisingly, the competitive inside spread is proportional to the outside spread. But it also increases with the size of the standard accommodation and varies inversely with the maximum position the dealer is willing to take.

DETERMINING THE DEALER'S MEAN PRICE

Now, what about *price*—i.e., the mean of the dealer's bid and asked? The dealer's current price should relate in a rational way to what the price is expected to be in the future. Otherwise, his current price will create profit opportunities across time for those who trade with him.

At positions between his layoff positions, the dealer should set price according to the price he expects to be setting one trade later. The next trade will, of course, move his position up or down with equal probability. If the price the dealer would set in those positions is known, then the price he sets in his current position must be the probability-weighted average of those two prices; otherwise he will create easy profits for those trading against him.

Let the prices for the three positions $X - S$, X and $X + S$ be $p(X - S)$, $p(X)$ and $p(X + S)$, respectively. Because the adjacent positions are equally likely, we have:

$$2p(X) = p(X - S) + p(X + S).$$

This is clearly another straight-line function of position:

$$p(X) - p(X - S) = p(X + S) - p(X).$$

The positions immediately beyond the respective layoff positions have known prices corresponding to the prices at which value-based investors will accommodate the dealer. The straight-line price function must satisfy those prices. If we let S be the standard transaction quantity, then we have:

$$p(X^* + S) = P_{\text{BID}} = P_b,$$
$$p(-X^* - S) = P_{\text{ASK}} = P_a$$

and

$$p(X) = \frac{P_a + P_b}{2} - \left(\frac{P_a - P_b}{X^* + S}\right)\frac{X}{2}.$$

The ratio $(P_a - P_b)/(X^* + S)$ measures the sensitivity of the dealer's mean price to changes in his position. It depends on both (1) the outside spread, reflecting the risk character of the asset, and (2) the dealer's willingness to take a position.

What these results show is that it is expensive to buy when everyone else is in a hurry to buy and expensive to sell when everyone else is in a hurry to sell.

We have begged the question of how big a position the dealer should tolerate. The answer probably has something to do with whether value-based investors, who help determine the dealer's mean price, get new information as quickly as information-based investors. It probably also has something to do with the risk character of the dealer's other assets, and with the size of his capital. Rich people make the best dealers.

PRICING LARGE BLOCKS

In the real world, of course, the individual accommodation trades brought to the dealer will vary in size. This raises the question: How should the dealer price trades larger than the standard trade? In particular, should he price the trade on the basis of the average position incurred in accommodating a trade, or the final position? If the average, then the cost of large trades is the same as the cost of small trades. If the final, the effective cost is much higher.

If large trades are frequent, then they will affect the probabilities we have assumed for transitions from one dealer position to another. If such trades are sufficiently infrequent that we can safely ignore their effects on the probabilities, then we can treat the occasional large trade as a string of standard trades.

Consider, for example, the cost of a large round trip as depicted in Figure 27.3. If the dealer's purchase and sale prices are based on his average position, then the cost of the round trip is the shaded area in the figure. This implies a cost per share equal to the area divided by the number of shares traded or the inside spread. If, however, the dealer's prices are based on his final positions (i.e., after the customer's purchase is completed and after the customer's sale is completed), then the round-trip cost of trading is depicted by the shaded area in Figure 27.4.

Unfortunately for the customer, the key to rational pricing behavior on the part of the dealer in this situation is our earlier comment that "the dealer should set price according to the price he expects to be setting one trade later." *This* price is determined by the dealer's final position when the trade is completed—not his average position during the trade. Although the *next* trade is equally likely to be in the same direction or the opposite direction, he knows that the *current* trade is equivalent to an unbroken run of standard-sized trades in the same direction.

A dealer will price a large block on the basis of his final position (rather

FIGURE 27.3   COST OF LARGE ROUND TRIP, BASED ON DEALER'S AVERAGE POSITION

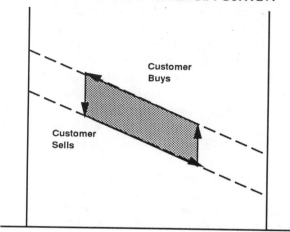

than an average of his intermediate positions) because, in contrast to the assumptions underlying the standard accommodation model, he knows that his position will not fluctuate randomly around the intermediate positions. Instead, it will fluctuate randomly around the final position. The prices corresponding to that position should thus apply to the whole block. This, of course, implies that the size effects in prices are not reversible: The

FIGURE 27.4   COST OF LARGE ROUND TRIP, BASED ON DEALER'S FINAL POSITIONS

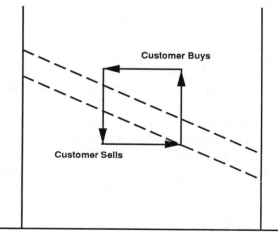

customer doesn't get back when he sells the block what he paid when he bought it.

What about the cost of trading a series of smaller blocks—i.e., of trading so the dealer doesn't know how big the whole series is until the last trade? In this case, the customer can get intermediate prices for intermediate trades, paying the final price only for the final trade. Of course, if the smaller blocks are big enough to push the dealer to his maximum, then nothing has been gained, because the outside spread price would have governed if the entire block had been handled as a single trade. In the meantime, too, the customer runs the risk that the information motivating his trade will get impounded in the price (i.e., the mean of the VBT's bid and ask) before he completes his trade.

In sum, (1) a large block will move the dealer's position, hence his price, in a direction that will increase the price of the trade, unless (2) the dealer's position is already at the maximum limit to which the block would otherwise move him, in which case (3) the size of the block has no effect on the dealer's price.

VALUATION ERRORS IN VBTS' ESTIMATES

So far we have assumed that VBTs estimate the value of the asset in question correctly. This implies that they agree, in which case the cumulative probability distribution of their assessments is the Z-shaped distribution given in Figure 27.5. Actual bid and asked prices, set one-half the outside spread below and above the assessment, will have their own cumulative probability distributions, which will also be Z-shaped, echoing the shape of the assessment distribution.

If the assessments of value-based traders are in error, however, they will be dispersed around a central assessment, and their cumulative probability distribution will no longer be Z-shaped. It will instead be S-shaped, as in Figure 27.6, with gradually rounded corners and long, tapering tails. As before, the distributions of value-based traders' bid and asked prices will echo the assessment distribution. They too will now be S-shaped rather than Z-shaped, with rounded corners and long, tapering tails.

The bid and asked distributions will still be set one-half the outside spread to the left and right, respectively, of the distribution of value assessments. But something curious has happened: The distance between the upper tail of the bid distribution and the lower tail of the asked distribution has narrowed. Error in value-based traders' assessments has reduced the dealer's cost of laying off.

**FIGURE 27.5   CUMULATIVE DISTRIBUTION OF VALUE-BASED
ESTIMATES OF VALUE, WHEN ESTIMATES ARE CORRECT**

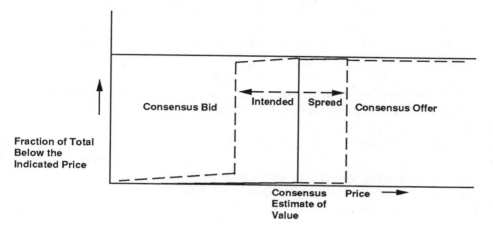

**FIGURE 27.6   CUMULATIVE DISTRIBUTION OF VALUE-BASED
ESTIMATES OF VALUE, WHEN ESTIMATES ARE IN ERROR**

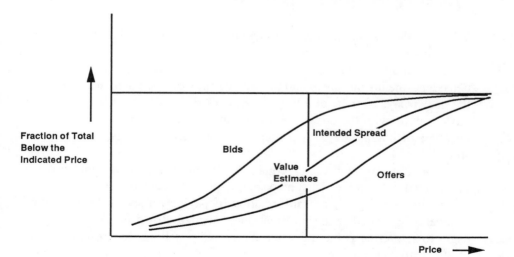

Strictly speaking, if the error distributions have infinitely long tails, the dealer's cost of laying off has been eliminated. What really matters to the dealer are the prices that elicit the necessary volume of bids and offers from the tails. It should be clear that, as the average (e.g., standard) error in value-based traders' assessments increases, the cost of laying off in the required volume declines.

Many investment professionals assert that their work in assessing security values not only serves their clients, but also makes security markets more efficient. It is certainly true that, without value-based investors, dealers would have no one to lay off to. But now we see that, if competition among dealers is sufficiently brisk, any reduction of outside spread resulting from value-based investors' errors will be passed along to the inside spread, thereby improving market efficiency. In this case, of course, dealers will be indifferent between less error on average in value-based investors' assessments and more; it is their customers who are the ultimate beneficiaries of larger assessment errors.

If, on the other hand, dealers are not subject to the pressures of competition, then the savings they realize from an increase in the average size of value-based traders' assessment errors will not be passed on to their customers in the form of smaller inside spreads. Markets will not be more efficient. And dealers will no longer be indifferent between less error and more—which is to say, between higher standards of investment analysis and lower ones.

THE ECONOMICS OF INVESTING

What are the lessons for the reader who wants to be a successful investor, rather than a successful dealer?

First, in reckoning the cost of any trade, there are two spreads to consider—the inside spread and the outside spread. The latter, which is what the dealer pays to trade at a time of his choosing, is also what the investor pays to trade with the crowd. Normally invisible to the investor, it is often an order of magnitude or two bigger than the more readily visible inside spread.

Second, when an investor comes to the market with insights not yet impounded in the price, what he pays for speed depends on what the crowd, often motivated by different information, is paying for speed. In particular, it depends on whether the information-motivated crowd is eager to buy or eager to sell. If he is buying when the crowd is selling, for example, he is in effect market-making to the crowd. He is receiving, rather than paying, some or all of the outside spread. And if it turns out that the information motivating the crowd was not yet in the price, he will get bagged along with those other investors who make it their business to accommodate information-motivated investors—namely, value-based investors.

Third, and more generally, what the information-motivated crowd is doing—whether it is buying or selling, and in what volume—determines the current price of trading fast. The investor needs to know this price in order to judge whether the time value of his own insight is high enough to make the price worth paying. If it is, he trades. If it isn't, he doesn't trade.

Fourth, because orders motivated by liquidity tend to arrive as a random mixture of buys and sells, whereas orders motivated by information don't, the latter are much more likely to push the dealer to the extreme of laying off to or buying in from the value-based investor. These considerations are important for the value-based investor attempting to set his spread so that gains from liquidity trading will be large enough to offset losses on information trading.

Fifth, because liquidity-motivated trading is by definition uncorrelated with information-motivated trading, hence with trading by the crowd, its expected cost is the inside spread. But the cost of "pseudo" information-motivated trading is the outside spread. The volume of "pseudo" trading is critical to the viability of the value-based investor.

Finally, the functions of a trading desk should be to

(a) estimate the inside spread on all securities of interest to investors;

(b) estimate the outside spread;

(c) maintain running estimates of outside bid and ask on all securities of current trading interest: the price of trading quickly is the difference between the price of the trade and the mean of the outside bid and ask;

(d) obtain from research estimates of the time value of current recommendations and

(e) match (c) and (d).

APPENDIX

Our argument for each position occurring with the same frequency is highly heuristic, to say the least. When the dealer's possible positions are reduced to a limited number of discrete states, the basic structure of the problem is that of a Markov process. It is well known that the steady-state probabilities of such a process are related to the transition probabilities by the requirement that the product of the vector of steady-state probabilities and the matrix of transition probabilities be the same vector of steady-state probabilities.

We can thus test our heuristic conclusion that the dealer's position frequencies are all equal by testing the truth of the following matrix equation given in Inspection confirms that the equation is satisfied.

$$
\begin{pmatrix} 1 \\ 1 \\ 1 \\ 1 \\ 1 \end{pmatrix}
\begin{pmatrix}
0.5 & 0.5 & & & \\
0.5 & 0 & 0.5 & & \\
 & 0.5 & 0 & 0.5 & \\
 & & 0.5 & 0 & 0.5 \\
 & & & 0.5 & 0.5
\end{pmatrix}
=
\begin{pmatrix} 1 \\ 1 \\ 1 \\ 1 \\ 1 \end{pmatrix}
$$

The Editor Asks

Q *The slope of the line in Figure 27.1 represents the change in price for a given change in inventory. This can be thought of as a measure of the efficiency of that market. What factors would have the effect of decreasing that slope and increasing market efficiency?*

A An increase in dealer equity will enable him to take more position risk. More position risk means the dealer can accumulate bigger position changes before he lays off or bring in points anchoring the line in Figure 27.1 increases (which, of course, is why rich people make the best dealers).

Unfortunately for the value-based investor, most liquidity-motivated trading will never reach him. Because of its random nature, it will result in dealer layoffs and buy-ins only occasionally. Instead, value-based investors must rely on pseudoinformation trades. Stampeded by new stories and sentiments of greed or fear, they will drive the dealer to buy in or lay off, respectively—thereby generating profitable trades for the value-based investor. Valid information, on the other hand, will also tend to drive the dealer to layoffs or buy-ins, transferring the cost of getting bagged from the dealer to the value-based investor. To survive, the value-based investor must make up on harmless information what he loses to damaging information. The greater the volume of the former relative to the volume of the latter, the smaller he can set his spread and still survive. But his spread is the vertical distance between the end points anchoring the line in Figure 27.1.

28

BUTTONWOOD II: CONSIDERING ALTERNATIVE MARKET STRUCTURES

Wayne H. Wagner

In 1792, the founders of the New York Stock Exchange began to meet under the buttonwood tree at what is now 68 Wall Street in lower Manhattan for the purpose of exchanging securities. We can presume that it was awkward and expensive to express trading interests in the eighteenth century. How could a captain from New Bedford hope to find the Virginia farmer who was looking for the security he had to sell? It was a necessity to hire someone to act as agent.

Obviously, the system worked—and worked well. The commission was reasonable, and the system got the job done: People were able to trade securities, and entrepreneurs got access to capital to build their ventures and to collect their rewards. Over time, the system became even more convenient, as the agents became middlemen, taking positions between the times buyers and sellers arrived. Because order arrival was sporadic, the capital provided by this "specialist" function was a tremendous advance.

In order to trade, however, the investor had to divulge his identity and the nature of his trade *before* he could trade: The broker was privilege to *who* was about to trade, and the exchange in turn knew *what* was about to trade. In other words, a trader had to enfranchise the exchange community with a gift of enormous value—the knowledge of who was willing to trade and under what terms. Over time, a tradition developed whereby this knowledge was (and is) regularly and systematically divulged to individuals and organizations to whom this information is the stock-in-trade of their highly profitable business.

Today, nearly 200 years later, the system retains the same basic form, and it still works well. Traders worldwide continue to send most of their orders to trade under the spreading branches of the NYSE. And the franchise is probably more valuable than ever: Consider what an advantage it is to know the ideas and intentions of large, aggressive institutional investors.

CHANGING THE EXCHANGE

How many other systems of commerce can boast two centuries of solid tradition in the face of constant change, change, change? This one has survived and prospered because we all accept that it gets the job done in a satisfactory way.

The NYSE, along with peripheral markets, has evolved to provide the facilities that traders as a group want and demand. Similarly, it has minimized the things traders want to avoid. It has taken its "degrees of freedom" in areas the users consider irrelevant; its costs are assessed in areas traders consider least important.

Why are market orders used? Because traders want them! Why do program trades exit? Because they satisfy a need! Why isn't it cheaper to trade? Because traders have been satisfied with the present costs. Given the intensity of competition, and the robust capacity for change evident in the current structures, it seems likely that the desired facilities are available at the lowest cost possible. To argue otherwise is to embrace a "conspiracy" theory, one that would be difficult to justify on theoretical or practical economic grounds.

We have the market we deserve: It exists in its current form because it is the best solution to the trading problem as presented. Yet it is not the only possible solution. Other markets operate differently, and still others could be created by the institution of new processes. If a broad enough spectrum of users believed that these new processes offered worthwhile advantages, a constituency for new trading solutions would be created.

Now consider the following facts:

- In this age of specialization, most trades now occur between a few hundred fiduciaries. One can count either the owners of the assets or their hired managers, and still come up with a few hundred entities.

They could easily all fit on the floor of the exchange and act for their own interests.

- These fiduciaries command far more capital than the whole specialist system, or even the whole of Wall Street. They really don't need the capital of the exchange community they are accustomed to relying upon to finance their trading.

- These fiduciaries are so large they can, and in many cases do, make their own markets. The largest equity managers boast that they can handle as much as 60% of their trading within their own client base, in-house.

- Communication of information is efficient, cheap and instantaneous, with computers handling most accounting of funds and most transfers, often without benefit of human hands. Most "money" exists in the form of electrical impulses spinning around on disks.

- The Department of Labor is pressing ERISA plan fiduciaries to recognize trading costs as an expense of the plan.

Fiduciaries are becoming increasingly suspicious of the tendency of their managers in aggregate to underperform the market by substantial amounts. According to the data of the Trust Universe Comparison Service, only 38% of professional managers measured beat the S&P 500 over the five-year period ending December 31, 1986.[1] The average shortfall was approximately 1%. According to the performance data gathered by SEI Corporation, eight of 10 managers underperformed the market index over a 15-year period.[2]

Where does the performance go? Could the exchange process be something other than a zero-sum game as far as the beneficial owners are concerned? Is secrecy and liquidity something used partially *against* as well as *for* the interests of the owners?

The 1986 NYSE *Fact Book* reports that members earned commission income of $8.249 billion and "trading and investment profits" of $10.987 billion.[3] These figures (especially the trading and investment profits) include elements besides equity profits, but when added together and divided by the total value of dollars traded, they imply a 1.98% transaction cost. This,

[1] The Trust Universe Comparison Service is a cooperative performance comparison service operated by Wilshire Associates, Santa Monica.

[2] *Funds Evaluation Report* (New York: SEI Corporation, 1987).

[3] New York Stock Exchange, 1986.

when allocated to the two sides of the trade, comes close to the size of the manager shortfall.

The message increasingly heard from plan fiduciaries is that trading costs are too high.[4] This implies that certain market participants may be willing to forgo some currently supplied trading benefits in favor of developing a market mechanism that stresses other benefits—namely, lower cost.

If the demand exists, can the market mechanism be altered in such a way as to reduce the cost of trading? The place to start is with a determination of where the costs lie in trading. We hypothesize the critical cost factors in the current market to be the following, listed in order of increasing importance:

- Labor costs
- Indirect (bundled) costs
- Risk-assumption costs and
- Information loss

The only effective way to reduce costs is for sponsors and their managers to (1) attempt to minimize information loss and (2) bear directly more of the labor, indirect, and risk-assumption costs. The challenge is to design an exchange mechanism that accomplishes these cost-saving goals.

LABOR COSTS

Labor costs are high because key elements of the trading process are currently delegated to highly compensated Wall Street traders using expensive facilities in the traditional manner. A portfolio manager's decision to buy or sell a security triggers a labor-intensive sequence of telephone calls, trade tickets, market intelligence gathering, price negotiations, confirmations and settling trades.

There is little doubt that Wall Street has traditionally attracted talented and highly motivated individuals. They are highly compensated, both in direct compensation and in privileged access to vital information. To do their job, they are supported by an extensive array of facilities. Upstairs trading rooms, for example, are supported by some of the largest communication and data systems available.

---

[4] Trading costs include commissions, market impact, market-maker spreads, clearing costs—the total (but untraceable) difference between what the buyer pays and what the seller receives.

Once an order gets to the floor, however, securities still trade as though the fastest message was still sent by horse! In an age when messages travel at 186,000 miles per second, orders (other than DOT orders) are still walked from the place where the client is contacted to the stump where the trade occurs. Just when a trader most wants to provide control, guidance and instructions, his agent is physically out of touch. We trust that the agent is acting in the client's best interests, but it is unsettling to have no control over last-second decisions and adjustments. We seem to pay dearly for the traditional shoe leather on the floor of the Exchange.

One key to lowering labor costs is to replace expensive person-to-person communications with less costly electronic access. At the same time, direct electronic access avoids expensive miscommunications that lead to costly trading mistakes and clearing failures.[5]

INDIRECT COSTS

Transaction costs buy more than just execution. By "paying up" for transacting, investment managers also receive research and other "soft dollar" benefits at no extra charge. The superb security and economic research available through the brokerage industry would be very expensive for the managers to create or acquire by themselves. Indeed, it is critical to most active managers. Even quantitative managers access analytic power and data from the brokerage community.

Managers may well be reluctant to sacrifice these benefits in exchange for reduced commissions, even though transaction costs may represent a substantial handicap to investment performance. In fact, pressure from these managers modified ERISA to permit continuation of soft dollar practices.

The Department of Labor, however, looks askance at the practice, insisting that transaction cost dollars represent an expenditure of fiduciary trust assets.[6] The DOL is pressing for an accounting of where these trust assets are spent, and some justification that they are being spent wisely in the interests of beneficiaries.

From the sponsor's view, this part of the cost of professional investment management is invisible and frequently confused with transaction costs. If transaction costs are to be lowered, this bundling of research services must

---

[5] Labor costs are also high because of errors and complications in the clearing process, but that is not the subject of this chapter.

[6] Remarks by Morton Klevan, deputy administrator, Office of Pension and Welfare Benefits, Department of Labor, at the Institutional Investor Conference, January 1987, New York.

be brought *above*-board. Investment management fees may have to rise to cover the additional cost of research paid for in cash by the investment managers. If past experience with unbundling in other industries is any indication, the sum of the payments for the parts will be less than the bundled payment for the whole.

RISK-ASSUMPTION COST

Risk-assumption costs occur when managers demand that a broker assume the risk as buyer-of-last-resort in order to complete a trade. As the advertisement of a major block house proudly and appropriately proclaims, they "Take Risks and Commit Capital." Risks here include individual company risk, market risk, and trading supply/demand risk—factors that move stock prices before the broker can relieve himself of the position. In effect, the broker sells the manager an option on the stock, as the broker guarantees execution at a specific time and price. As is true of any option, the risk is proportional to the time of exposure and represents the cost of "liquidity."

Liquidity is commonly thought of as the willingness of the broker to assume the position—for a price—until the natural other side arrives. In the final analysis, however, the only *real* source of liquidity is the natural investor ultimately on the other side of the trade. Without the contra side of the trade, the broker's limited capital would quickly be tied up, and his ability to provide bridge liquidity would disappear.

Risk-assumption costs arise from a desire to trade immediately, without waiting for natural liquidity on the other side. To the extent that this demand for liquidity arises from unawareness or lethargy, it can be avoided. If risk is proportional to time of exposure, however, costs can be reduced by increasing simultaneity. How that might work is illustrated by the following analogy.

Suppose a person insisted on instant liquidity every time he traveled by air: At whatever movement he decided to travel, the necessary equipment and crew would be ready to respond instantly. This would clearly be expensive, not only because of the high cost of transporting one person alone, but also because of the expenses incurred to keep equipment and personnel on "standby." That is the effect of instant liquidity: Substantial resources must be available on standby for whenever they are called upon, and they must be paid for while idle, as well as when in use.

Most of us don't demand instant liquidity in air transport; we go to Kennedy Airport at 6:00 P.M. to catch American Airlines #21 to Los Angeles. In air transportation, liquidity is *gathered together* by establishing a specific departure time; travelers agree to wait for the scheduled opportunity to travel, because it is significantly cheaper than demanding instant service.

Securities markets could work similarly, by gathering liquidity in a "call-to-market" trading environment. The expensive facilities required to provide instant liquidity would not be chosen unless absolutely needed. Perhaps it would not be quite as convenient as the current system, but those willing to bear the inconvenience could economize on the cost.

A call-to-market system is in common use even now. Any auction, such as the Treasury bill auction, is a call-to-market. Secondary distributions represent an explicit call-to-market. Many foreign exchanges operate at least partially on a call-to-market basis. Even the establishment of the opening price on the floor of the NYSE is a call-to-market.

While a call-to-market environment would seem to pose little inconvenience to passive and quantitative managers, some active managers might worry that they would be unable to execute their decisions instantly. Doesn't information arrive in real time, they would argue, and doesn't the price series reveal costly information as it is acted upon?

To a certain extent, most institutional investment decisions result from a contemplative processing of gathered information, rather than from instant reaction to news items. Perhaps a call-to-market system would create problems for managers who apply technical intraday timing methods or use close-to-the-source information, but these managers are atypical of institutional investors.

Is it possible that the value of instant liquidity is overestimated?

If a broker knows where the natural other side can be found, he may give the appearance of bearing risk, when little or no risk truly exists. (Remember, true liquidity exists only when the broker can quickly lay off his positions.) Suppose a manager receives a "hot tip" and uses a principal trade to unload stock. The broker will assuredly discount his bid to reflect his assessment of the manager's information. (In all probability, the broker is already a better informed adversary and knows as much or more than the manager; at minimum, he knows more than the manager about the desires of other traders.) He will also intuitively factor the probable holding time into his bid.

If the tip is true, the manager "wins" at the expense of the supplier of natural liquidity, whoever ends up on the other side of the trade. Yet few traders think of themselves as suffering an information disadvantage in most trading situations. The broker wants both sides of the trade to believe they were treated fairly. If the other side is another institution with whom the broker maintains an ongoing relationship, he is unlikely to "bag" this other valued customer (at least not too frequently). Nor is a passive trader a sitting duck; we know that index funds track the indexes, as promised, which means that they cannot be systematic losers in the trading game. It is doubtful, based on the performance records, that institutional investors systematically win at the expense of the investing public.

So is the value of instant liquidity real or illusionary? If instant liquidity is not as valuable as commonly perceived, it is little more than a mere convenience, masquerading as a substantive benefit and achieved at a higher-than-justifiable price.

But consider the environment of an institutional trader: The portfolio manager's investment decisions are obviated if the trader fails to execute. Failing to complete the trade is a no-win proposition for the trader: He can use his skills to do the best he can, but the thought pattern within which he operates places the highest value on completion—i.e., liquidity. In this process, the brokerage community is his strongest ally, and the exchange community has cleverly laid strong foundations by building up and reinforcing the perceived need for its services. The interests of the sponsor (who has been told that he is not competent to interfere with the professional managers' investment decisions) may be considered at best only peripherally in this self-reinforcing trading process.

INFORMATION LOSS

Information loss occurs when the fact that someone wishes to trade is revealed without compensation in the process of trying to find liquidity on the other side, either through principal or agency trading.

Other than accepting a risk-assumption cost, as outlined above, there are only two ways to find the other side of a trade—advertising or responding to the advertising of another. The advertising may be done directly or through a broker. This is true for almost all current trading mechanisms.

Market orders, secondary offerings, and sunshine trades initiate advertising. Participate orders respond to advertising. Best-efforts trades, fourth-market trades, limit orders and third-market orders either initiate advertising or respond to advertising. Market-on-close orders, principal trades and program trades advertise or go through a facilitator. A few types of trades—such as inventory fund trades and in-house, informationless "perfect" crosses—can be executed without involving advertising. All other trading techniques involve some exposure of trading willingness prior to execution. The amount of exposure may vary, but the majority of trades are not executable until after at least one side has revealed intent. If the trade goes through a broker, both sides may telegraph their intentions, possibly to the detriment of both.

There are no effective prohibitions against the broker or the exchange using this information for its own account, acting in its own interest. In fact, the use of this information is *sanctioned;* by implicit agreement, this privileged information compensates the broker/specialist for conducting markets in the preferred manner.

The bottom line is that, as markets currently operate, traders must perform destructive testing to assess the market for a potential trade. After the test has been performed, the advantage of exclusive knowledge of intention is lost. The traders have tipped their hands to some part of the exchange community. How strange it would seem to a manufacturer to give his competition advance notice of his product intentions!

Why do traders accept this? In truth, they have little choice. Current markets work this way because that's the way traders have decreed they want them to work. Few have seen any need for a system that operates in true and complete secrecy. Liquidity is the revealed preference.

Who wants it to work this way? The exchange community is privy to valuable information concerning who is willing to trade what, when and at what price. The investment manager passes off much of the expense of running an investment operation to the brokers. These costs are then passed without direct accountability to the beneficial owners and sponsors through commission costs and trading impact.

Who is going to ring the bell on this triumph of hope over experience? Only the sponsor or the beneficial owner, whose money it is anyway. Only sponsors can create a market of new priorities, a market that stresses low execution cost and holds managers accountable for the effects of transaction costs.

Many sponsors are reluctant to interfere with the decision/execution process of their managers. Indirectly, however, the pressure for incentive fees is designed to encourage managers to consider how productively they utilize client assets.[7] The experience to date is that managers, left to their own devices, are often either unconcerned or defensive about transaction costs. Perhaps managers have become overly dependent on the brokerage community for services that improve the economics of the investment management business.

Below, we illustrate a market that is organized to emphasize low cost, yet provides sufficient liquidity without players having to reveal their intention to trade.

---

[7] R. Grinold and A. Rudd, "Incentive Fees: Who Wins? Who Loses?" *Financial Analysts Journal*, January–February 1987.

A CALL-TO-MARKET EXCHANGE:
FEATURES AND BENEFITS

A "call-to-market" exchange centralizes liquidity by specifying a time that trades will take place. All parties wishing to trade under the terms of the call meet in one place at one time to trade whatever volume crosses under mutually acceptable terms.

This suggests a direct electronic call market for stocks that applies the cheap and accurate system we have for communication of information right to the point of exchange. Sponsors and their fiduciaries could represent their own interests, without the intervention of facilitators. It might require waiting the few minutes or hours or days for natural liquidity to occur, but after all, aren't sponsors usually trading among themselves anyway? If sponsors as a group benefit, any given sponsor must expect to benefit.

A call-to-market exchange accepts *good orders* up until the time of the match; those securities that pair off become executions; those that do not are canceled and can trade at the next call or through other means.

A call-to-market exchange requires that the participants (the sponsors and their fiduciaries) bear (*make* instead of *buy*) more of the direct labor costs of securities exchange. It requires that they pay their managers fees adequate to cover cash payment for the required research services. It also requires that they wait for liquidity (for departure time), and thus bear risk to avoid paying a facilitator to assume the risk. Finally, they avoid information leakage; it is not necessary to divulge the nature of intended trades, except to a totally neutral and totally secret "black box."

PRICE DISCOVERY IN CALL-TO-MARKET
EXCHANGES

But wait . . . aren't we forgetting something important? Isn't the key function of the market to *set* prices? How does a call-to-market exchange provide that function with revealing the side/size of the imbalance?

Before we address the issue of price discovery, it is important to realize that most orders do not affect price in any market, including the current one. Consider the actions of a specialist as he opens the book in the morning. If the volume of buy orders approximates the volume of sell orders, the market should open unchanged. In any market, a small amount of trading sets the price; most of the rest is merely ticking off. A cross, a natural meeting of liquidity, does not change the price.

Like any market, a call market needs a price discovery mechanism, a means of determining the price at which supply and demand are balanced. That function is provided by a market-maker and/or the use of limit orders.

Who is a market-maker? Basically, anyone who is willing to buy at one price and sell at a higher price. It doesn't have to be someone who is anointed to perform the function. It could, for example, be any of the very large index funds, with an inventory of billions of dollars in literally thousands of stocks. Wouldn't their clients be pleased to put that passive inventory into auction to pick up a little liquidity-provision profit? Or consider the massive pension funds: They could offer to buy and sell securities from their vast holdings. Like stock lending, it's a more productive use of the assets that lie there anyway; it represents *latent earning power*.

The point is, anyone can be a market-maker. In economic terms, anyone who stands ready to trade, for whatever motivation, *is* a market-maker while trading that stock.

The easiest way to make a market is with a pyramid of limit orders. The more anxious the other party is to trade, the more stock the accommodator is willing to accept, provided the price is right. By printing the executions, all parties would know that the price has moved, driven by an excess of supply or demand. The print, however, does not reveal information about what has not yet traded; there is no predictive information in a done trade.

What if the liquidity is not there? What happens to a trader with a massive position to trade? Does he have to wait interminably to complete his trade?

Not necessarily. He could conduct a sale, announcing his willingness to trade, like a secondary distribution or a so-called "sunshine" trade. This would encourage the other side of the trade to meet him at his time schedule at a mutually acceptable price. The interesting feature of a totally revealed, announced trade is surprisingly similar to that of a totally secret trading mechanism: There is no information advantage granted to any party. Only selective information divulgence leads to information leakage.

SUMMARY

We have created the market we deserve. Those exchange functions that traders want are provided at a cost considered fair—or at the least at a cost that has become more or less traditional—and create a need for facilitators who are handsomely rewarded for their efforts. The single most important function demanded is liquidity, and investors are historically willing to pay what it takes to get it. In order to make this type of market function, however, trading intent must be revealed; unfortunately, the current market does not and cannot remain neutral once trading interest has been revealed.

The term "market-*maker*" could hardly be more appropriate: When liquidity is demanded as the primary focus, markets must be *made*, the time gaps between arrival of traders bridged by either the liquidity provided by the market-maker or the ability of the market-maker to ferret out the other side of the trade. This service does not come free.

But liquidity is not the only possible goal of an exchange system. Low-cost trading could be the focal point. Changing the focal point implies changing the system, and changing the system can result only from changes in motivation. Current market participants show little interest in changing the system; only the sponsors, the beneficial owners, can induce change. This will occur only if sponsors (a) want a change and (b) demand a change.

One alternative to a continuous market that emphasizes liquidity and requires a well-compensated exchange community to provide it is an *automated, secret, neutral call-to-market exchange.* Such a market will allow lower trading costs because of higher efficiency, centralization of supply/demand in time as well as in location, and reduction of information leakage concerning trading intentions. Table 28.1 summarizes the differences between the two systems.

Many developments suggest that sponsors desire changes in the current system. These developments include:

- The resounding acceptance of low-cost passive management;
- Pressure for lower commission costs and interest in trade monitoring;
- Pressure for accountability of managers in the form of incentive fees; and
- Legal pressure to account for transaction dollars as fiducial assets.

TABLE 28.1 CURRENT EXCHANGE VERSUS CALL-TO-MARKET EXCHANGE

Liquidity-Oriented Exchange	Cost-Oriented Exchange
Liquidity supplied by broker/exchange	Liquidity supplied by sponsor/manager
On demand	Time-centralized
Trading information leakage	Trading information neutrality
Labor intensive	Electronic
Bundled costs	Direct assessment of costs
Provides features demanded by managers	Provides features demanded by sponsors/owners

If corporate sponsors addressed transaction costs and other pension issues in the same manner they approach direct-line business issues, what questions would they be likely to ask?

- Shall the sponsor *make* or *buy* investment strategies?
- How can the desired investment result be produced at less cost?
- What is desired from managers and brokers as they operate as suppliers of services to the pension plan?
- How can managers and brokers be motivated to provide the nature and quality of services demanded at a fair price?
- Without compromising the duty to beneficiaries, how can the cost of providing desired pension benefits be reduced?
- Without compromising the duty to beneficiaries, how can the risk to the corporation from this line of business be reduced?
- How can pension activities be subjected to the same discipline as the other demands on corporate cash flow?

If a low-transaction-cost system is demanded, it will be created. The flexibility, the spirit of service and accommodation that started at the buttonwood tree, will provide the new facilities that market participants demand—and at the lowest cost.[8]

The Editor Asks

Q *Go a little bit further and lay out the key characteristics you would build into your version of a less costly market.*

A I see three.
  The first is electronic access, complete including the limit book and open to all. This will relieve the physical pressure on the floor and open the possibility for the second recommendation:
  The second is to allow institutions to act for their own interests if they

[8] The author wishes to thank Edward Story of Plexus Group and William Lupien and Tibor Fabian of Instinet Corporation for their many helpful comments and suggestions.

choose. We would need accreditation: knowledge testing, creditworthiness, bonding, and all the other factors needed to ensure that the institution will make good on the trade.

Finally, organize a periodic call-to-market, the details of which I have just explained, and probably run along lines similar to those proposed by Steven Wunsch.

INDEX

Abel, Stanley S., 63
Active trading, passive trading *vs.*,
  186–187. *See also* Information
  traders.
ADP, 269
Adversarial trading, 339–341, 345
Affirmative obligations, 113–114
  defined, 81
All or none (AON), defined, 67
American Depository Receipts (ADRs), 92
  growth in, 251–252
  and international derivative securities,
  255–256
  and international trading, 253–255, 258,
  263
American Stock Exchange (AMEX), 4, 31,
  108, 212, 214, 216
  and broker-dealer trade flow, 94–95
  and CATS, 270
  PER of, 161
American Telephone and Telegraph
  (AT&T), 33, 34
Amihud, Y., 305–306
Arbitrageurs, 165
Ariel, R., 301
Artificial intelligence (AI), 168, 311, 324
Association of Stock Exchange Firms, 4
Auction, single-price. *See* Single-price
  auction.
Auction market (systems), 126, 270
  crossing compared with, 199–200
Automated systems, in electronic equity
  trading, 269
  auction-oriented systems, 270
  dealer-oriented systems, 270–271

global systems, 271–272
order-routing systems, 270
quotation systems, 269
Avon Products, 6

Basket trades, 119, 175
Batterymarch Financial Management,
  electronic trading at, 237–239,
  248–249, 274
  analysis of trading operations at,
  241–242
  commission costs at, 240–241
  data at, 242
  interpretation of, 242–248
  system description of, 239–240
Bear, Stearns and Company, 6, 7, 154,
  155
Becker, A. G., 8
Beebower, Gilbert L., 59, 137, 144
Bell Canada, 268–269
Bell System Pension Funds, 6
Berkowitz, Stephen A., 31
Best-efforts order, 119–120
  defined, 117
Best virtual feed, 313, 314
Block traders:
  functions of, 156–159
  vs. package trading, 171, 172–173
  vs. specialists, 153–156, 159
  vs. sunshine trading, 225
Bodurtha, Steven, 223
Bond transactions/transaction costs,
  327–329, 332–333
  and bond market features, 330–331
  and dealer markets, 331–332

Bond transactions/transaction costs (*cont.*)
  and stock market features, 329
  and stock market innovations, 329–330
Book, defined, 67
Brady commission, 235
Bridge Data, 254
Bridge liquidity, 112–113
Bridge Trading Company, 212
British Petroleum, 253, 256
British Telecom, 269
Broker(s):
  credit considerations of, 98–99
  -dealer trade flow, 94–96
  floor, 82–87
  functions of, 97
  proprietary, 340–341
  roles of, in transaction settlement,
    96–99
  selecting, 73–74
  settlement efficiency of, 97–98
Brokerage commission, as component of
  trading costs, 127, 128–129, 131
Brown, S., 295
Burnett, Thomas, 251
Buttonwood Agreement (1792), 267
Buy-in, defined, 106

California Public Employees' Retirement
  System (CALPERS), 273–274
Call markets, 120
Call-to-market exchange
  features and benefits of, 368
  price discovery in, 368–369
Cap order, defined, 67
CATS. *See* Computer-Assisted Trading
  System.
CDS, 275
Cedel, 264
CFA program, 345
Chase Manhattan Bank, 268
Chicago Board Options Exchange, 157
Chicago Mercantile Exchange, 87, 156,
  157, 176, 288
Citicorp Investment Bank, 268
Clean or do nothing, defined, 67
Clearing, defined, 75
Cohen, Kalman J., 120
Commission costs:
  at Batterymarch Financial Management,
    240–241
  evaluating and measuring, 148–149
Commission rate, obtaining best execution
  at best, 75–77

Commissions:
  as component of transaction costs, 48–49
  ethical issues related to, 342–343
Commodity Futures Trading Commission
  (CFTC), 233
Competitive strategies, in electronic equity
  trading, 275
  international regulation of, 276
  international settlement of, 275–276
Computer-Assisted Trading System
  (CATS), 205, 270
  crossing compared with, 205–207
Consolidated Tape, 88
Continuity, defined, 80–81
Continuous Net Settlement (CNS) system,
  96
"Costs are not significant" trading
  technique, 119
Cross, crossing, electronic, 118, 120–121,
  197–199, 207–208
  attractiveness of, 200–202
  compared with auction systems, 199–200
  compared with other computer-assisted
    systems, 205–207
  criticisms of, 208–209
  defined, 67, 197
  external, 198
  internal, 198
  limitations, to, 202–203
  and passive trading, 188
  private or arranged, 198
  sources, 204–205
Cross-clean. *See* Clean or do nothing.
Crossing Network, The. *See* Instinet
  Corporation.
Cross-sectional effects, 294–296
Cross-trading, defined, 187–188
Cuneo, Larry J., 144
Custodian(s):
  functions of, 100–101
  relationship with investment manager,
    102
  roles of, 100–102

Dann, L., 306–307
Datastream, 254
Day-of-the-week effect, 299–301
Day order, defined, 67
Dealer, 51
  -broker trade flow, 94–96
  market, 160
  -oriented systems, 270–271
  role of, 51

Dealer function, economics of, 345–346, 357–358
 determining dealer's mean price, 351–352
 determining dealer's spread, 348
 frequency of layoffs, 348–350
 market-makers, 346–347
 pricing large blocks, 352–354
 valuation errors in VBTs' estimates, 354–356
Depository Trust Company (DTC), 11, 31, 101, 103, 108, 342
 -eligible securities, processing of trades in, 91–96, 106
 Institutional Delivery System (DTC-ID) of, 92, 93–94, 104
 and international trading, 256, 264
Depth of market, defined, 79
Derivative securities, international, 255–257
Designated Order Turnaround (DOT) system, 153, 161, 165, 175–176, 273, 343
 description of, 33, 82, 83
 introduction of, 165
 and order-routing systems, 270
 and package trading, 178, 179
 and Scorex system, 88
Direct crosses, 118
Disney, 6
Do it away, defined, 67
Dollars, soft, 22–25
Dow Jones Industrial Average, 9, 183, 232, 243, 298
Downstairs traders. See Specialists.
Dunn, Patricia C., 171

EAFE Index, 252
Earle, Dexter D., 3
Edwards, Mark, 45
Electronic crossing networks. See Cross, crossing, electronic.
Electronic equity trading, 267, 276–278
 automated systems in, 269–272
 competitive strategies in, 275–276
 market factors in, 267–269
 shape of marketplace in, 272–275
Electronic trading, 161, 166. See also Batterymarch Financial Management, electronic trading at.
 impact of, 166–167
 vs. manual trading, 168–169
Ellis, Charles D., 18, 27, 186, 342

Employee Retirement Income Security Act (ERISA, 1974), 8–9, 65, 149, 333, 361, 363
 results of, 185
Equity trading management, 253–255
Ethical issues in trading, 337–339
 and adversarial and proprietary trading, 339–341
 and commissions, 342–343
 and professional trading desk, 341–342
Euroclear, 264
Execution cost:
 after-trade measures of, 144–147
 high-low midpoint measure of, 141–143
 previous price used as benchmark for measure of, 144
 trade-weighted average price of day measure of, 143

Federal Reserve, 276
Fill or kill (FOK), defined, 68
Financial Analysts Journal, 23
Floor, 79–80
 brokers, 82–87
 change on, 87–88
 governor, 86
 players on, 80–82
Ford, 84–85
Fortune, 66
Fourth-market trades (orders), 118, 120–121
Fouse, Bill, 162
Franklin, Benjamin, 77
French Depository and Clearing Agency, 275
Front running, 66, 67, 339–340
Funston, G. Keith, 5

General Motors Corporation, 4, 80
Give up, defined, 68
Glaxo, 256
Global systems, 10, 11, 271–272
Go along, defined, 68
Goldman, Sachs & Company, 6, 7, 154
Good 'til canceled order (GTC), defined, 68
Graham and Dodd, 345
"Gravitational pull" trading technique, 120
Great Depression, 293, 301
Greenberg, Alan, 155
Greenwich Research Associates, 18, 73, 342

Grossman, Sanford, 211–212

Hanson Trust, 253, 256
Harris, L., 301, 303–305, 306
Hasbrouck, Joel, 36, 307
Heeger, Mike, 87
Held order, defined, 68
Hitachi, 256
Hit the bid, defined, 68
Ho, Thomas S., 36, 307
Holding period:
  defined, 54
  importance of, 55
  and liquidity concession, 54–55
Holiday effect, 301–303
Honda, 256
Hyperinflation, 8, 9

IBM, 25, 204, 215, 224
Illiquid stocks, 211, 214, 220
  controlling trading time and dollars in,
    216–218
  trading flexibility in, 218–220
  trading strategies for, 215–220
Immediate or cancel (IOC), defined, 68
Index arbitrage, 167, 181–183
  introduction of stock, 165
  and program trading, 175
  risk in, 178
Index funds, 173, 174–175, 186
  growth of, 176, 179–180
  need for, as investment alternative,
    172
  passive management of, 186, 187
  passive trading by, 190–192
  turning active portfolios into, 192–193
Indirect costs, 363–364
Inefficient market, trading tactics in, 291,
    307–308
  cross-sectional effects, 294–296
  day-of-the-week effect, 299–301
  holiday effect, 301–303
  intraday effects, 306–307
  January effect, 296–298
  stock market anomalies, 291–293
  time-of-day effect, 303
  turn-of-the-month effect, 298–299
Information-based investor, 50, 51, 52
Information integration, intelligent trading
    systems and, 312–313
  beyond feed integration, 314–315
  market data feed integration, 313

predictive pricing, 314
timeliness and accuracy, 313
Information loss, 366–367
Information traders, 116–117, 237–238,
    345
In line/in here, defined, 68
In line or work, defined, 68
Instinet Corporation, 271–272
  The Crossing Network of, 204–206,
    207, 274
Instinet Trading System, 104
  Clearing Interface System (CIS) of,
    104
Institutional Investor, 66, 337, 339
Institutional Investor Group, TraderForum
    of, 337, 341
Intelligent trading systems, 309–310,
    322–324
  defined, 310–311
  and information integration, 312–315
  and knowledge-based systems (KBS),
    311–312
  look and feel of, 315–319
  and multiple-factor adaptive alarms,
    319–322
Interactive Data Corporation (IDC), 212
Intermarket Trading System (ITS), 88
International Securities Clearing
    Corporation (ISCC), 275
International Stock Exchange Automated
    Quotation (SEAQ), 255, 270, 271
International trading, 251–253, 263–264
  compliance and regulatory issues in,
    262–263
  and contra-party credit risk, 260
  and cost control, 259–260
  and equity trading management,
    253–255
  and international derivative securities,
    255–257
  and trading costs, 255
  and trading management relationships,
    257–259
Intex, 279, 288
In touch with (ITW), defined, 68
Intraday effects, 306–307
Investing, economics of, 356–357
Investment performance, and transaction
    costs, 17–19

Jacobs, Bruce I., 291, 292, 294, 295
  and calendar anomalies, 293, 296, 297
January effect, 296–298

Japan Securities Clearing Corporation, 275
Jones, C., 295

Kawaller, I., 307
Keim, D., 299, 300
Knowledge-based systems (KBS), 311–312
Koch, P., 307
Koch, T., 307
Kodak, 25
Kormendi, R., 296

Labor, Department of (DOL), 17, 19, 22, 65, 115, 361
    and broker selection, 73–74
    and indirect costs, 363
    technical release number 86-1 of, 20–21
    on transaction costs, 327
Labor costs, 362–363
Lakonishok, J., 292–293, 299–300, 302
Latane, H., 295
Leaves, defined, 68
Leinweber, David, 309
Levi, M., 300
Levy, Gus, 154
Levy, Kenneth N., 291, 292, 294, 295
    and calendar anomalies, 293, 296, 297
Lewis, Cy, 154
Limited order, limited price order. See Limit orders.
Limit orders, 83, 117, 120–121
    defined, 68
Lipe, R., 296
Liquidity:
    bridge, 112–113
    defined, 68, 213
    market, 111–113
    measuring, 211–214
    and trading costs, 27–29
Liquidity-based investor, 50, 51
Liquidity concession, defined, 54–55
Liquidity traders, 116–117, 238
"Liquidity whatever-the-fair-price" trading technique, 118–119, 123
Loeb, Thomas F., 48, 125, 162
Logue, Dennis E., 31
London Stock Exchange (LSE), 309
Lose stock, defined, 69
"Low cost, whatever-the-liquidity" trading technique, 120–121
Lupien, William A., 267
Luskin, Donald L., 153

McInish, Thomas H., 145
Maier, Steven F., 120
Major Market Index (MMI), 279
Malkiel, Burton, A Random Walk Down Wall Street, 162
Manager:
    and growth, 56–57
    impact of, 52–53
    style of, 53–54, 55–56
    -trader relationship, 45–46, 60–61
    and value, 57–58
Managing trading process, 39–41
Manipulation, defined, 69
Manus, Stephen P., 183, 185
Market, existing, 113–115
(Market) coming in, defined, 69
(Market) coming on, defined, 69
Market factors, in electronic equity trading, 267
    competitiveness, 267–268
    global market, 269
    market participation, 268
    trading volume, 268–269
Market impact, as component of transaction costs, 49–50
Market liquidity, 111–113
Market-makers, 186, 346–347, 370
Market-maker's spread, 186–187
    as component of trading costs, 126–127, 128, 131
Market mechanism, 126
Market Mind multiple-factor alarm, 320–322
Market not held order, 119–120
    defined, 84, 117
Market-on-close (MOC) orders, 118, 119
    defined, 69, 117
Market-on-open orders, 117, 119
Market order, 83, 119
    defined, 69, 117
Market patterns, and favorite trading syndrome, 36–39
Marketplace, shape of, in electronic equity trading, 272
    market access, 272–273
    trading alternatives, 273–274
    trading strategies, 274–275
Market price, defined, 69
Market structures, alternative, 115–116, 359–360, 369–372
    call-to-market exchange, 368–369
    changing Exchange, 360–362
    indirect costs, 363–364

Market structures, alternative (*cont.*)
  information loss, 366–367
  labor costs, 362–363
  risk-assumption costs, 364–366
Marshall, Greta, 327
Match, defined, 69
Mayers, D., 306–307
Mendelson, H., 305–306
Merrill Lynch, 5, 85
Middlemen, 339–340, 341, 359
Midwest Exchange, 270
Miller, Merton, 211–212
Minimum lots, defined, 69
Minsky, Marvin, *The Society of Mind,* 310
Mnuchin, Bob, 154
Morton, John J., 337

NAME (Holland), 275
National Association of Securities Dealers
  (NASD), 94, 270, 313
National Association of Securities Dealers
  Automated Quota (NASDAQ), 108,
  128, 269, 270–271
  and broker-dealer trade flow, 94–96
  and international trading, 254, 255
  /National Market System
  (NASDAQ/NMS), 32, 88, 212, 214,
  256
  SOES (Small Order Executive System)
  at, 161, 271
National Investment Sponsor Federation,
  21–22
National Market System. *See* National
  Association of Securities Dealers
  Automated Quota (NASDAQ).
National Plan Sponsor Federation, 203
National Securities Clearing Corporation
  (NSCC), 106, 108, 275–276
  and broker-dealer trade flow, 94–96
Natural buyer/seller, defined, 69
Negotiated market, 126
New York Futures Exchange, 233
New York Stock Exchange (NYSE), 4, 31,
  34, 89–90, 108, 212, 214, 216
  and affirmative obligations, 80–81,
  113–114
  auction process of, 337, 342
  and broker-dealer trade flow, 94–95
  changing, 360–362
  dominance of, 153
  DOT and SuperDOT of, 161, 165,
  175–176, 178–179, 183, 270
  fixed-commission schedule of, 329

  floor of, 79–88, *passim,* 111, 156
  innovations created by, 329–330
  and membership contact, 277
  Rule 387 of, 92
  and single-price auction, 282, 288
  specialist system of, 21
  strength and solidity of, 88–89
  trading data on, 64–66, 74
  upstairs trading at, 157, 158, 160
  volume on (1960s), 6–7, 162
  volume on (1970s), 8, 268
  volume on (1980s), 9, 162, 268
New York Stock Exchange Fact Book, 66,
  67, 361
Noser, Eugene A., Jr., 63
Not held, defined, 69, 84, 117

OARS (Opening Automated Report
  Service), 283
Odd lot, defined, 70
Off-board, defined, 70
Offer, defined, 70
On print only, defined, 70
Opening only, defined, 70
Open order. *See* Good 'til canceled order.
Oppenheimer & Company, 154
Ord, J. Keith, 145
Order(s):
  defined, 63
  entry, time of, 63–64
  number of shares placed at one time,
  64–67
  -routing systems, 270
  time frame in which to execute, 74–75
  types of, 67–73, 117–118
  working, 83–86
Over-the-counter, defined, 70

Pacific Coast Stock Exchange, 34, 88,
  270
Package trading, 171, 181, 183–184
  background of, 171–172
  defined, 171, 191
  growth and development of, 173–175
  and growth of indexing, 179–180
  in 1980s, 175–180
  vs. passive trading, 183–184
  rationale for, 172–173
  stock index futures and, 176–178
  SuperDOT and, 178–179
  usefulness of, 180–181
Participate (do not initiate) orders, 119–120
  defined, 70, 117

Passive management, 167
  advent of, 162–163
Passive traders. *See* Liquidity traders.
Passive trading, 185, 195–196
  for active managers, 194–195
  vs. active trading, 186–187
  discussion of, 187–190
  historical perspective on, 185–186
  by index funds, 190–192
  vs. package trading, 183–184
  of small stocks, 193–194
  turning active portfolios into index
    funds, 192–193
Patell, J., 307
Penman, S., 301
Pension and Investment Age, 66
Pension fund regulation, 19–25
Perold, Andre, 138
Perry, Jay, 154
Plexus Group, 204, 205
Plus tick. *See* Up tick.
Polaroid, 6
POSIT (Portfolio System for Institutional
    Trading), 204–205, 206, 207,
    274
Positioning, defined, 70
"Possibly hazardous, need agent" trading
    technique, 119–120
Post, George B., 153
Price concession, as component of trading
    costs, 127, 128, 131
Priest, William W., Jr., 144
Primary. *See* Primary distribution.
Primary distribution, defined, 70
Principal trades, 117, 118
Program trades, 118–119, 176
  advent of, 163–165
  defined, 117, 191
  and index arbitrage, 175
Proprietary trading, 339–341
Pseudo-information-based investor,
    50–51
Public offering. *See* Primary distribution.
Pull back, defined, 70

Quick, 269
Quotation systems, 269
Quote, defined, 70
Quotron, 269

Raab, R., 306–307
Reagan, Ronald, 67
Regional Interface Operation (RIO), 96

Regulation:
  electronic equity trading and
    international, 276
  and international trading, 262–263
  pension fund, 19–25
Rendleman, R., 295
Reporter, 85–86
Reuters, 254, 269, 288
Rich and Micrognosis, 313
Risk-assumption costs, 364–366
Round lot, defined, 71

Sagan, Carl, *The Dragons of Eden*, 123
Salomon Broad Index, 328
Salomon Brothers, 6, 7, 154
S&P 500 Index, 45, 63, 134–135, 328,
    361
  and package trading, 176–178
  and passive trading, 192
  and sunshine trading, 225
Scale, defined, 71
Scale order, defined, 71
Scattered, defined, 71
Scholes, Myron, 144
Schwartz, Robert A., 120
SCOREX system, 88, 270
Seat, defined, 71
Secondary offerings, 118, 120
Securities Act Amendment (1975), 19
Securities and Exchange Act (1934), 87,
    149
Securities and Exchange Commission
    (SEC), 17, 19, 31, 32, 127
  and international trading, 262
  Section 28(e) of, 19, 20, 23, 38
  and specialists, 154, 155
SEI Corporation, 219–220, 361
Selling short against the box, defined,
    71
Settlement, transaction, 91, 106
  avoiding problems in, 102–106
  broker's roles in, 96–99
  custodian's roles in, 100–102
  for DTC-eligible securities, 91–96
  period, reducing five-day, 107–108
Severoglu, Cem, 211, 219
Shefrin, H., 297
Short covering, defined, 71
Short position, defined, 71
Short sale, defined, 71
Shulman, Evan, 237
Shultz, Robert E., 15, 90
Simex, 280

Single-price auction, 279, 280, 281, 288–289
  description of, 281–288
Sinquefield, Jeanne Cairns, 211
Small stocks, passive trading of, 193–194
Smidt, S., 292–293, 299, 302
Soft dollars, 22–25
Sony, 256
Southern New England Telephone Company, 6
Specialist market, defined, 72
Specialists:
  vs. block traders, 153–156, 159
  defined, 72
  functions of, 72, 80–82
  skills acquired by, 86
Spehar, George M., 161
Spread, as component of transaction costs, 49
Stambaugh, R., 299
State Street Bank and Trust Company, 36, 39
Statman, M., 297
Stay on the bid side, defined, 72
Stay on the offer side, defined, 72
Stock ahead, defined, 72
Stock index futures (SIFs):
  introduction of, 175
  and package trading, 176–178
  and sunshine trading, 223
Stock market:
  anomalies, 291–293
  crash (October 19, 1987), 3, 9, 11, 20, 89, 90
  institutionalization of, 8–10
  return of individual investor to, 5
Stocks, Bonds, Bills and Inflation (Ibbotson and Sinquefield), 211
Stop limit order, defined, 72
Stop order, defined, 72
Story, Edward C., 197
Strict scale, defined, 72
Sunshine trades, 118, 120, 160, 223–224, 235–236
  basis movement from open of, 231–232
  basis movement to 4:00 P.M. same day of, 232
  vs. block trading, 225
  criticisms of, 225–227, 249
  defined, 200
  done to date, details of, 227–228
  future of, 233
  logic of, 224–225

longer term transaction cost indicators of, 230–231
  short-term transaction cost measures of, 228–230
  status of, 232–233
SuperDOT, 161, 175–176, 183, 236, 343
  and order-routing systems, 270
  package trading and, 178–179
Swiss Options and Financial Futures Exchange (SOFFEX), 271

Talisman system (London), 275
Telekurs, 254, 269
Telerate, 269
Third market:
  defined, 72
  trades (orders), 118, 120–121
Ticker tape, 87, 90
Time-of-day effect, 303
To come, defined, 72
To go, defined, 72
Tokyo Stock Exchange, 88, 205, 257, 264
TOPIC, 269
Top or low limit, defined, 73
Toronto Stock Exchange (TSE), 38, 67, 205, 207, 270
Tracking error, 163, 165
Trade flow:
  broker-dealer, 94–96
  institutional, 92–94
Trade-processing problems, avoiding, 102
  communication of breakdown information, 103
  posttrade follow-up, 104–106
  processing broker trade input, 103–104
  setup and maintenance of subaccount information, 102–103
Trader(s):
  information (active), 116–117, 237–238, 345
  liquidity (passive), 116–117, 238
  -manager relationship, 45–46, 60–61
  rational, 50–52
Trades:
  measuring cost of executed, 141
  types of, 117–118
Trading motivations, 116–117, 118
Trading post, defined, 73
Trading strategies:
  in electronic equity trading, 274–275
  for illiquid stocks, 215–220
  types of, 50
Trading System Technology, 67

Trading techniques:
    evaluating, 131–132
    taxonomy of, 111, 118–121
Trading (transaction) costs, 15, 47–48, 59
    appraisal of, 125–126
    bond, 327–333
    components of, 48–50, 126–127, 137, 138
    defined, 31
    early focus on, 15–17
    estimating, 127–129
    evaluating vs. measuring, 139–148, 149–150
    implications of study of, 129–131
    importance of, 31–32, 41
    investment performance and, 17–19
    liquidity and, 27–29
    managing trading process, 39–41
    and market mechanism, 126
    market patterns and favorite trading syndrome, 36–39
    nonmanager influences on, 58–59
    and pension fund regulation, 19–25
    in perspective, keeping, 139
    total, 138–139
    transacting in listed stocks, 32–35
Transaction settlement. See Settlement, transaction.
Treynor, Jack L., 50, 138, 345
Trinity Investment Management Corporation, 274

Trust Universe Comparison Service (TUCS), 45, 46, 327–328, 361
Try to lift, defined, 73
Turn-of-the-month effect, 298–299

Unlisted stock, defined, 73
Upstairs traders. See Block traders.
Up tick, defined, 73

Value-based investor (VBI), 50, 51, 346–347, 350
    valuation errors in estimates of, 354–356
Value-based traders (VBT), 238

Wagner, Wayne H., 79, 111, 144, 218, 327, 359
Wall Street Journal, 141
Walsh, Vincent, 91
Weinstein, Will, 154
Whitcomb, David K., 120
Wilshire Associates, Trust Universe Comparison Service (TUCS) of, 45, 46, 327–328, 361
Wilshire 5000 Index Stock Universe, 127, 129, 218
Wolfson, M., 307
Wood, Robert A., 145
Wunsch, Steven, 279, 372

Zero plus tick, defined, 73
Zoning, defined, 83